Born of Water and the Spirit

The Mercersburg Theology Study Series
Volume 6

The Mercersburg Theology Study Series is an attempt to make available for the first time, in attractive, readable, and scholarly modern editions, the key writings of the 19th-century movement known as the Mercersburg Theology. We believe this will be an important contribution to the scholarly community and to the broader reading public, who can at last be properly introduced to this unique blend of American and European, Reformed and catholic theology.

Published Volumes
1. *The Mystical Presence and the Doctrine of the Reformed Church on the Lord's Supper*
Edited by Linden J. DeBie
2. *Coena Mystica: Debating Reformed Eucharistic Theology*
Edited by Linden J. DeBie
4. *The Incarnate Word: Selected Writings on Christology*
Edited by William B. Evans

Volumes in Progress
3. *The Church in History: Selected Writings of Philip Schaff*
Edited by David Bains and Theodore L. Trost
5. *"One, Holy, Catholic, and Apostolic": Nevin's Writings on Ecclesiology*
Edited by Sam Hamstra
7. *Selected Writings of Emanuel V. Gerhart*
Edited by Annette Aubert
8. *The Early Creeds*
Edited by Charles Yrigoyen

**Volumes Planned
(Details Subject to Change)**
9. *Essays in Church History*
Edited by Nick Needham
10. *The Heidelberg Catechism*
Edited by Lee Barrett
11. *The Mercersburg Liturgy*
Edited by Michael Farley
12. *Schaff's America and Related Writings*
Edited by Stephen Graham
13. *Philosophy and the Contemporary World*
Edited by Adam S. Borneman
14. *Mercersburg and Its Critics*
Edited by Darryl G. Hart

Born of Water and the Spirit

Essays on the Sacraments and Christian Formation

By
JOHN WILLIAMSON NEVIN,
PHILIP SCHAFF, and EMANUEL V. GERHART

Edited by
David W. Layman

General Editor
W. Bradford Littlejohn

Foreword by
Peter J. Leithart

WIPF & STOCK · Eugene, Oregon

BORN OF WATER AND THE SPIRIT
Miscellaneous Writings on the Sacraments

The Mercersburg Theology Study Series 6

Copyright © 2016 David W. Layman and W. Bradford Littlejohn. All rights reserved. Except for brief quotations in critical publications or reviews, no part of this book may be reproduced in any manner without prior written permission from the publisher. Write: Permissions, Wipf and Stock Publishers, 199 W. 8th Ave., Suite 3, Eugene, OR 97401.

Wipf & Stock
An Imprint of Wipf and Stock Publishers
199 W. 8th Ave., Suite 3
Eugene, OR 97401

www.wipfandstock.com

PAPERBACK ISBN: 978-1-4982-3548-8
HARDCOVER ISBN: 978-1-4982-3550-1

Manufactured in the U.S.A.

Contents

Foreword (by Peter J. Leithart) | vii
Editorial Approach and Acknowledgments | xi
General Introduction (by David W. Layman) | 1

ARTICLE 1
Nevin and Bushnell: Christian Nurture and Baptism (1847) | 34
    Editor's Introduction
    "Educational Religion," by John W. Nevin
    "Educational Religion:
        Review of Dr. Bushnell's Tract Continued [Part 2]," by John W. Nevin
    "Educational Religion:
        Review of Dr. Bushnell's Tract Continued [Part 3]," by John W. Nevin
    "Educational Religion:
        Review of Dr. Bushnell's Tract, Concluded [Part 4]," by John W. Nevin
    "Baptismal Grace":
        A Conversation between Nevin and "Inquirer" for the Weekly Messenger
    "Dr. Bushnell and Puritanism," by John W. Nevin

ARTICLE 2
"Noel on Baptism" (1850) | 78
    Editor's Introduction
    Article, by John W. Nevin

ARTICLE 3
"The Apostolical Origin of Infant Baptism" (1852) | 116
    Editor's Introduction
    Article, by Philip Schaff

ARTICLE 4
"Wilberforce on the Eucharist" (1854) | 129
    Editor's Introduction
    Article, by John W. Nevin

ARTICLE 5
"The Efficacy of Baptism" (1857) | 156
    Editor's Introduction
    Article, by Emanuel V. Gerhart

ARTICLE 6
"The Old Doctrine of Christian Baptism" (1860) | 192
    Editor's Introduction
    Article, by John W. Nevin

ARTICLE 7
"The Bread of Life: A Communion Sermon" (1879) | 214
    Editor's Introduction
    Article, by John W. Nevin
    Appendix

    Bibliography | 245
    Subject and Author Index | 259
    Scripture Index | 264

Foreword
by Peter J. Leithart

Debates about infant baptism were inconclusive during the Reformation and they still are. Texts are batted here and batted there, Greco-Roman households are speculated upon, covenantal paradigms clash by night. When a theological debate has gone on inconclusively for half a millennium, one gets suspicious: Suspicious that the opponents are talking *past* each other, suspicious that they are talking past one another because they are not talking *to* each other very much, suspicious that no one feels much pressure to resolve the issue. If one is cynical as well as suspicious, he might wonder whether the debate is infected by turf protection and grandstanding, by budgets and institutional commitments.

These are worthy suspicions, but the more fruitful suspicion is that the two sides do not share too little but too *much*. They are too much of the same mind to reach a point of genuine disagreement.

Nevin sensed this more than anyone else. Some American Christians baptized infants, others did not, but they shared a religious ethos and fundamental theology. Presbyterian or Baptist, American Christians shared what Nevin (somewhat unfairly) described as Puritan piety.

Nevin described the foundational issue in various ways. At times, he called attention to the inherently corporate, churchly character of Christianity, rooted in the "whole constitution of the world" and expressive of a humanity that is "an organic whole, manifold and one at the same time." Any baptismal theology that treated humanity as "a vast living sand-heap" was going to end badly.

Elsewhere, Nevin insisted that Christianity is both natural and supernatural. In his view, Bushnell and Baptists both failed to maintain this unity. The former naturalized the supernatural, reducing Christian nurture to parental care and failing to build "educational Christianity" on an objective churchly foundation. For their part, Baptists attempted to make faith clear and reasonable and "mechanical." At the extremes, American Christianity exhibited a "fanaticism" that dislodged the supernatural from any connection with created things.

Foreword

Positively, Nevin recognizes that we can get to the real debate only if we look behind the narrow question of infant baptism to the issue of sacramental grace. Baptist theology has no room for the "old church" notion of sacrament, a union of an outer and inner element, a visible sign joined in a "real mystical or sacramental union" with the invisible "celestial grace." Only the old church view ensures that baptism is a divine act, rather than a human confession. Only on this basis can we have a genuine Christian nurture, since nurture depends on a supernatural grafting of the child into the church. Only on this basis can we affirm what the New Testament says about baptism – that it saves, that it is the washing of regeneration, that it is for the remission of sins. So long as Presbyterians rejected the old church notion, they we incapable of justifying infant baptism.

In my view, Nevin gets very close to the heart of the issue, but that raises a further suspicion. Baptist and paedobaptist cannot resolve their disagreement because they are too much in agreement on fundamental questions about natural and supernatural, about corporate and individual, about the legitimacy of the old church doctrine of sacramental grace: If these are the reasons for the interminable debate, why wasn't Nevin more successful in pushing through to a clearer disagreement and perhaps even resolution? Why did his incisive work make so little apparent headway?

There are obvious historical reasons for this failure. Nevin was not widely read, and was soon forgotten. In his time, he was an eccentric outsider, and his advocacy of sacramental grace had little resonance in American Protestantism. He was part of a growing wave of interest in liturgical theology, but the liturgical movement was at the time largely confined to Roman Catholicism and the high church party of the Church of England. Princeton was in no mood to reconsider its sacramental assumptions; nor was Dabney, not to mention Thornwell. Even within his own denomination, Nevin's efforts to promote liturgical renewal threatened to break into schism. Nevin's sacramental theology was stillborn.

One suspects that there is a theological reason as well. Bold as his proposals are, Nevin does not fully escape the assumptions he challenges. The problems are most evident in Nevin's sermon on the bread of life. He arranges nature and spirit in a hierarchy, insisting that "the spiritual [is] first, inmost, primordially substantial and real; the natural secondary, outmost, phenomenally transient, and universally dependent on the spiritual every moment for any shadow of existence it may seem to have in its own right." He even speaks, weirdly, of celestial food being offered "under cover" of material food. We see a similar problem in his flexibility regarding the mode of baptism. If the specific form of the sign is as indifferent as Nevin suggests, why should the baptism of *infants* be crucial? We seem to be slipping a step back toward the fanaticism that he elsewhere renounces.

Clarity about infant baptism is possible only when *every* vestige of rationalism and fanaticism is expelled, and that can only be done with a sacramental theology thoroughly grounded in a theology of creation. Sacraments are not esoteric deviations from the mechanics of a world without magic. We live in a world pre-loaded for sacramental use. Bushnell was wrong to naturalize the supernatural. But we must supernaturalize the natural.

Baptism is not, of course, a natural use of water, nor the Lord's Supper a normal meal. But the difference is not in the degree of miraculousness. The "natural" use of water is miraculous; even at our *daily* meals we do not live by bread alone. Lunch helps me *think* more clearly, and a cold drink refreshes my *soul*. Water washes away dirt – how weird is *that*?

What makes baptism baptism is Jesus' command and promise, His authorization. What makes the Lord's table the Lord's table is Jesus' command "Do this" and His promise to feed us through bread and wine. There is no need for covers, veils, or hierarchies of spirit and matter. In the sacramental, there is only God the Creator, Jesus the Lord of His church present by His Spirit, the materials of creation, and the people to whom he gives them.

Though Mercersburg falls short, the work of Nevin and his colleagues deserves careful study. If the seeds he planted died as soon as they fell into the ground, that is no surprise. It is the miracle of seeds that they must die to bear fruit. The times have ripened. We see a sprout is breaking through hardened soil.

Editorial Approach and Acknowledgments

The purpose of this series is to reprint the key writings of the Mercersburg theologians in a way that is both fully faithful to the original and yet easily accessible to non-specialist modern readers. These twin goals, often in conflict, have determined our editorial approach throughout. We have sought to do justice to both by being very hesitant to make any alterations to the original, but being very free with additions to the original in the form of annotations.

We have decided to leave spelling, capitalization, and emphasis exactly as in the original, except in cases of clear typographical errors, which have been silently corrected. We have, however, taken a few liberties in altering punctuation—primarily comma usage, which is occasionally quite idiosyncratic and awkward in the original texts, but also other punctuation conventions which are nonstandard and potentially confusion today. In several articles the volume editor has added quotation marks to the original author's quotes as required by modern conventions. We have also adopted standard modern conventions such as the italicization of book titles and foreign-language words. The entirety of the text has been re-typeset and re-formatted to render it as clear and accessible as possible; pagination, of course, has accordingly been changed. Original section headings have been retained; in articles which lacked any section headings in the original, we have added headings of our own in brackets.

Original footnotes are retained, though for ease of typesetting, they have been subsumed within the series of numbered footnotes which includes the annotations we have added to this edition. Our own annotations and additions, which comprise the majority of the footnotes, are wholly enclosed in brackets, whether that be within a footnote that was original, or around an entire footnote when it is one that we have added.

Source citations in the original have been retained in their original form, but where necessary, we have provided expanded citation information in brackets or numerated footnotes, and have sought to direct the reader toward modern editions of these works, where they exist. Where citations are lacking in the original, we have tried as much as possible to provide them in our footnotes.

In the annotations we have added (generally in the footnotes, though very occasionally in the form of brackets in the body text), we have attempted to be comprehensive without becoming cumbersome. In addition to offering citations for works referenced in the original, these additions fall under three further headings:

1. Translation
2. Unfamiliar terms and historical figures
3. Additional source material
4. Commentary

We have attempted to be comprehensive in providing translations of any untranslated foreign-language quotations in these works, and have wherever possible made use of existing translations in standard modern editions, to which the reader is referred.

Additional annotations serve to elucidate any unfamiliar words, concepts, or (especially) historical figures to which the authors refer, and where applicable, to provide references to sources where the reader may pursue further information (for these additional sources, only abbreviated citations are provided in the footnotes; for full bibliographical information, see the bibliography).

Accordingly, we have sought shed to light on the issues under discussion. Although most commentary on the texts has been reserved for the General Introduction and the Editor's Introductions to each article, further brief commentary on specific points of importance has occasionally been provided in footnotes to facilitate understanding of the significance of the arguments.

We hope that our practice throughout will help bring these remarkable texts to life again for a new century, while also allowing the authors to be heard in their own authentic voices.

Acknowledgments

As volume editor, it is usual at this point to recognize all the libraries that provided resources for one's research. The first place of honor in the present project must go to Google Books—a research library available from the comfort of one's easy chair. The editor cannot begin to calculate the miles and time saved by this resource. There were of course a small number of texts that required more traditional methods of access: the editor is grateful for the librarians and staff at Philip Schaff Library at Lancaster (Pennsylvania) Theological Seminary, the Archives of the Evangelical and Reformed Historical Society at the same location, and the Beinecke Rare Book & Manuscript Library, and the Sterling Memorial Library, both of Yale University. (Lancaster Theological Seminary also hosts an important resource in digitized versions of *The New Mercersburg Review*; the numbers from years 1985–2009 can be accessed, as of October 31, 2015, at http://archive.lancasterseminary.edu/items/show/130.)

Editorial Approach and Acknowledgments

The General Editor, Brad Littlejohn, has been a model of motivating energy and insight into how best to shape my editorial contribution. I learned to implicitly trust his judgments and criticisms. It is therefore a matter of regret, that (as he notes in the next paragraph) over the next several volumes he anticipates setting aside the present enterprise to pursue other projects. I have only been willing accept his request that I take up the task, grateful for his astonishing accomplishment in bringing (with this volume) four volumes to press, knowing that we have the models and resources he has developed, and trusting to divine providence to be faithful to both his past accomplishment and his vision.

As the General Editor, I would like to extend my profound thanks to David for the enormous work he has put into this volume, leaving relatively little work to do on my end. His thoroughness and dedication to tracking down every detail that needed to be annotated was a model of historical scholarship. I am particularly grateful to him for being willing to step into my editorial shoes for future volumes in the Mercersburg Theology Study Series, as I transition out of my role as General Editor to focus on other projects and commitments. I would also like to thank once more Christian Amondson and the whole team at Wipf and Stock for their dedication to this project, and to the Mercersburg Society (especially Deborah Rahn Clemens, John Miller, Thomas Lush, Linden DeBie, and Carol Lytch) for their ongoing support of it.

General Introduction

In the summer of 1847, John Williamson Nevin, a German Reformed theologian, was discussing a tract out of New England, *Discourses on Christian Nurture*,[1] by a New Haven Congregationalist pastor, Horace Bushnell. At stake in the discussion was the question of the status of infants and children in the church. Congregationalists (the descendants of the Puritans and Pilgrims), the Dutch and German Reformed, and the Presbyterians all practiced infant baptism. This inherited practice, however, was under attack, especially by the Baptists. Many Congregationalists who had been "converted," whether in the revivals led by English preacher George Whitefield, or his indigenous imitators, left their "dead" ministers for "Separate Baptist" churches.[2] As we shall see throughout this volume, "baptistical" would become a synonym in Nevin's polemics for the allegedly common features of the revivalist-conversionist movement in antebellum America. The central act of this movement was "conversion," a change in a person's spiritual state, generated out of a psychological crisis. These crises were experienced in the "revival meeting," which sought to generate the change, and thereby give large groups of people a felt awareness of spiritual renewal and wholeness, a "new birth." This volume can be viewed as the literary remains of American Protestant leaders who, in different ways, were not persuaded by, and attempted to resist, the emerging evangelical consensus.

However, the pressure on the nonrevivalists was not wholly external. All branches of the Reformed tradition were under pressure from the "revived" in their own denominations. Paedobaptists were under a great deal of stress to defend their inherited praxis. As will be shown in articles 2 and 5, it seemed to Nevin and his younger colleague Emanuel Gerhart that most paedobaptists had abandoned the spiritual principle while unsuccessfully struggling to keep the ritual form; indeed, in

---

1. Bushnell, *Discourses on Christian Nurture*. Nevin's discussion, which began in the *Weekly Messenger of the German Reformed Church*, started on Wednesday, June 23, 1847, and continued for three more numbers. His essays, "Educational Religion," and the ensuing discussion, including the questions by and responses to "Inquirer," are the substance of art. 1 in this volume.

2. Ahlstrom, *Religious History of the American People*, 1:350–60. Ahlstrom quoted Whitefield: "I am verily persuaded, the Generality of Preachers talk of an unknown, unfelt Christ. And the Reason why Congregations have been so dead, is because dead Men preach to them" (351).

their minds, they were struggling to keep the form precisely *because* they had already lost the principle.

Nevin's anxiety must be at least part of the explanation for his reaction in a minor exchange in 1847 in the *Weekly Messenger*, the periodical of the German Reformed Church. Nevin had completed his four-essay response to Bushnell's *Discourses on Christian Nurture*. He had agreed with Bushnell that a child's Christian experience arose out of some "organic" connection to the nurture provided by Christian parents, and thus "the child is to grow up Christian,"[3] but was concerned that this organic connection, as interpreted by Bushnell, was a purely natural one of ordinary human nurture and education, such as any parent should provide for a child. To the contrary, Nevin thought the organic unity of infant and churchly life was created by "baptism as a divine sacrament," in which there was "a divine power objectively present" in "the Church as a new supernatural constitution."[4] Three weeks later, an alien voice, known to us only as "Inquirer," intruded in the conversation. "Does the Professor understand by 'baptismal grace' the same as is commonly denoted by the phrase 'baptismal regeneration'?"[5] Nevin demurred: he generally did not use such language because of its imprecision. He did, however, say this much: he rejected baptismal *regeneration*, as he assumed it was understood both by his readers and the "Inquirer." There was no "such change of the subject as is commonly understood." He did, however, affirm "baptismal *grace*," by which he meant that baptism made a person part of the spiritual life of the church, and it was through that corporate life that a person experienced salvation.[6] That did not satisfy "Inquirer." Two weeks later, he presented Nevin with a series of questions: Was this grace "*saving* grace"; if so, was the grace based on the faith of the parent, or on the "'objective force' of the sacrament itself"; if the grace was "short of saving grace," then what was the nature of Nevin's disagreement with "those from whom he dissents"?[7] In response, Nevin wanted to distinguish between a "grace that is able through faith to save him" (*yes*) and a "grace that actually saves" (*no*). Most certainly the power of baptism was an "objective force," not a "mere human act." At this point, Nevin lost his temper. Indeed, it is fair to say that he became downright hostile. He sniffed at the ordeal of "submitting publicly to such anonymous catechization." He wondered if "Inquirer" had a "standpoint" from which to raise intelligible questions or was "a mere bundle of theological negations." He accused his interlocutor of "plump, barefaced rationalism" and concluded that "in the church of the Heidelberg

---

3. Quoted in *Weekly Messenger* 12, no. 41 (June 23, 1847) 2450; original in Bushnell, *Discourses on Christian Nurture*, 6.

4. *Weekly Messenger*, July 14, 1847, 2461.

5. "Inquirer," *Weekly Messenger*, August 4, 1847, 2475. Full texts are to be found in art. 1.

6. Ibid.

7. *Weekly Messenger*, August 25, 1847, 2486.

catechism," they should not need to hash out whether there was a "sacramental force of *some* kind in the ordinance of holy baptism."[8]

This reaction was uncalled for. The questions of "Inquirer" were valid. What exactly was salvation? What role did baptism play in bringing it about? If Nevin rejected baptismal *regeneration*, then what exactly did baptism *do*, and why was paedobaptism essential to what it *did*? Even the editor of the Weekly Messenger was concerned lest the reader think that "the participation of the sacraments necessarily confers grace upon the recipient, independent of the state of his mind at the time."[9] Observe that there are at least three terms—"regeneration," "grace," "salvation"—that overlap in the matrix of Christian experience, but are not necessarily identical. ("Conversion" would also be part of this matrix.) Nevin seemed unwilling to engage in the work necessary to define and distinguish those terms.

The puzzle remains *why* Nevin was unwilling. At the same time, he was studying the Heidelberg Catechism; one of his illustrations for the "Church Spirit of the Catechism" was that "baptism is not only a symbol of the washing of regeneration, (Qu. 73), but a solemn authentication of the fact itself—the proper body of its inward soul—in all cases where the requisite conditions of its presence are at."[10] Titus 3:5 was cited in support of Question 71: "According to his mercy he saved us, by the washing of regeneration, and renewing of the Holy Ghost."[11]

"Regeneration" has done a great deal of heavy lifting in theology since at least the Great Awakening.[12] Nevin's own reaction shows that some important contrast in theology and praxis was at stake. But what? In the Authorized Version that everyone used in the English-speaking world, the Titus text was the only biblical use of

---

8. *Weekly Messenger*, September 1, 1847, 2490.

9. *Weekly Messenger*, August 4, 1847, 2475. These comments directly allude to a column on p. 2476; however, they were part of the editor's explanation of his decision to print the question by "Inquirer," and certainly expressed concerns that the editor had about Nevin's essays on "Educational Religion."

10. Nevin, *History and Genius of the Heidelberg Catechism*, 152. *History and Genius* is scheduled to appear in volume 10 of MTSS.

11. Heidelberg Catechism (1849), 165. This version presented itself as a "faithful and exact" English translation of the "*Signat.* Heidelberg, Sept. 1, 1684" edition, which had been reprinted in Philadelphia in 1777 and Easton 1829 (pp. iv, v). The editor presumes Nevin was using one of those editions. The Heidelberg Catechism was compiled in 1562 by Zacharias Ursinus and Kaspar Olevian for the Elector Frederick III, and became the confessional document of the Palatinate. See Bierma, Gunnoe, and Maag, *Introduction to the Heidelberg Catechism*. The Catechism seems to have been important in Nevin's transition to "evangelical catholicism": Nichols, *Romanticism in American Theology*, 48–49; he began his study of it almost as soon as he arrived at Mercersburg as part of a centennial celebration of the German Reformed Church (see Appel, *Life and Work of John Williamson Nevin*, 145–56). The results took two distinct forms, a series of essays in the *Weekly Messenger of the German Reformed Church*, and the aforementioned *History and Genius*.

12. Perry Miller noted: "On the definition of 'regeneration' Protestants expended their greatest ingenuity and differed among themselves most furiously" (*The New England Mind in the Seventeenth Century*, 9).

"regeneration," as applied to Christian experience.[13] The plain sense of the text is that "regeneration" takes place through the "washing" that occurs in baptism. That is certainly how it was interpreted by the church fathers.[14] John Calvin had also connected regeneration with baptism: both circumcision and baptism represent regeneration.[15] Regeneration was a process, brought about "through continual and sometimes slow advances." For Christians, it was a "race of repentance, which they are to run throughout their lives."[16] Nevin had the scriptural, theological, and confessional resources to say that regeneration happened at baptism, even while affirming that it was a lifelong process, not an instantaneous event. Indeed, it seems that he was saying exactly that in the contemporaneous *History and Genius of the Heidelberg Catechism*. So what kept him from saying so in response to "Inquirer"?

Baptism, the Unitary Covenant, and Federalism

When Ulrich Zwingli began the Swiss Reformation, he probably shared the hermeneutical premises later stated by the radical splinter group the Swiss Brethren: all rituals and practices had to be based upon explicit scriptural warrant.[17] This led logically to the rejection of infant baptism, an opinion Zwingli acknowledged he had initially shared.[18] Certainly such a radical interpretation was consistent with Zwingli's antisacramentalism in both baptism and Eucharist.[19] By 1524, however, Zwingli was defending infant baptism. His primary argument was that the ritual of baptism was equivalent to "circumcision among the ancients"; since Israelite infants were circumcised, so likewise infant children of Christian parents were to be baptized.[20] A more

---

13. In Titus 3:5, "regeneration" has disappeared from some contemporary translations (NRSV, NIV, NAB, NJB, REB)—and thus is not used in the Bible; the ESV, RSV, NASB, and Holman Bible still use it.

14. See Gorday, *Ancient Christian Commentary on Scripture*, 9:304, 305.

15. Calvin, *Institutes*, 2:1327.

16. *Institutes* 1:601–2. On the topic of regeneration as interpreted throughout the Christian tradition, see Hewitt, *Regeneration and Morality*, 3–14. He referenced the Calvin text on p. 5.

17. González, *Story of Christianity*, 2:50, ascribed the view "that all [uses] that had no explicit scriptural support must be rejected" to Zwingli. Edward Peters described Zwingli's "growing dissatisfaction with practices and institutions for which he could find no Scriptural precedent or justification" (Introduction to Samuel Macauley Jackson, ed., *Ulrich Zwingli, 1484–1531: Selected Works* [repr. ed., 1972], xix).

18. Bromiley, *Zwingli and Bullinger*, 119, 139; Jackson, *Ulrich Zwingli*, 123–24 note.

19. Zwingli himself said: "Baptism . . . does not justify the one who is baptized, nor does it confirm his faith, for it is not possible for an external thing to confirm faith" (Bromiley, *Zwingli and Bullinger*, 138). A later interpreter said: "Baptism had no sacramental efficacy," but was "a public promise of a Christian upbringing" (Peters, Introduction to Jackson, *Ulrich Zwingli*, xxiii). Zwingli summarized his sacramental doctrine in "An Account of the Faith of Huldreich Zwingli Submitted to the Roman Emperor Charles": "sacraments are given as a public testimony of that grace which is previously present to every individual" (47).

20. Zwingli, *Refutation of the Tricks of the Baptists*, in Jackson, *Ulrich Zwingli*, 139.

detailed supporting argument was made from the nature of the covenant. God had made a covenant with Adam when he created him. This covenant was confirmed with Noah and then Abraham, who received circumcision as the covenant's "sign."[21] Just as circumcision did not require understanding or assent to be effective, so baptism did not require the conscious faith of the recipient. Infants *were* in the covenant; *because* they were in the covenant, *therefore* they received the sign.[22] Since this was true of circumcision, it was likewise true of baptism. The covenant God made with Adam and confirmed with Abraham in the sign of circumcision was identical to the covenant God has made with the church.[23] An infant born to a Christian parent was properly baptized, since by birth the child was *already* part of the people of God.

Calvin deepened and systematized Zwingli's doctrine of the unitary covenant. He was aware of arguments that the old covenant was a purely worldly one, for the sake of earthly well-being. He had nothing but contempt for the idea: this made Jews to be "more like beasts than men," "satiated for a time with God's benefits . . . only to perish in eternal destruction."[24] The spiritual goal of the two covenants was identical, since the Jews as well as the Christians "had and knew Christ as Mediator."[25] Just as the denial of the unity of the covenant debased God's covenant with the Jews, denying baptism to infants "lessened" God's grace to Christians and made it "more obscure" than it had been for the Jews.[26]

At the beginning of the Reformed dogma of baptism, then, the claim was made that the promise to children under the "old" covenant equally applied to children under the "new" covenant. Both were "in" the covenant by virtue of birth;[27] for Jews the sign of covenantal membership was circumcision, for Christians it was baptism. Even while this motif was being developed, another Reformed tradition was gestating.[28] Heinrich Bullinger was a colleague of Zwingli at Zürich, and was generally viewed as his successor. He seems to have been the source of a complex matrix of ideas and practices, in which he expanded the unitary covenant to integrate theological claims about God's relationship with humanity with political and social insights about the proper ordering of human community. Since what that relationship and that ordering have in common is *covenant*, Bullinger's insights came to be known as "federalism" (from the Latin *foedus*, "covenant"). "Federalism understands the relationships between God and the world and among humans as based on covenants among the members,

---

21. Ibid., 219–21.
22. Ibid., 223.
23. Ibid., 227–36.
24. Calvin, *Institutes*, 2:1333.
25. Ibid., 1:429–30. The entirety of ch. 10 (1:428–49) is devoted to this theme.
26. Ibid., 2:1328–29.
27. Ibid., 2:1329; Cf. Zwingli, "An Account of the Faith," 42–43.
28. Thus the subtitle of one of the important studies of this tradition: Baker, *Heinrich Bullinger and the Covenant: The Other Reformed Tradition*.

some tacit and inherited from the past, others explicit and made or renewed in the present."[29] Theologically, federalism said that "God is the faithful One, who makes covenant and keeps covenant." Sociologically, "the inner nature of social groups and the relationships among them are understood as covenantal."[30] Although J. Wayne Baker gave credit to Zwingli for the origin of "covenant theology,"[31] he concluded that "Bullinger had a firmer and more fully developed hermeneutical basis for his covenant idea" and he more "strongly affirmed the bilateral nature of the covenant, mutual responsibilities of God and man in this contract."[32] This idea of "mutual responsibilities" included humanity's responsibilities for proper social order.

Covenant and Conversion: The Puritans

Reformed thought and polity made its way to England as Marian exiles returned from Geneva and other centers of Protestant piety on the Continent. They brought with them a mature covenant theology. The unitary covenant had been split into a covenant of grace and covenant of works.[33] The covenant of works was "'made [with Adam] with the condition of perfect obedience, and is expressed in the moral law.' The covenant of grace 'is that whereby God freely promising Christ, and his benefits, exacts again of man that he would by faith receive Christ, and repent of his sins.'"[34] This bifurcated covenant enabled the Puritans to simultaneously insist that a Christian needed to evoke the awareness of being in the covenant of grace as an act of divine election, even while impelling human acts of *covenanting*. They were to experience themselves as being in a state of grace that had been freely given; at the same time, their election was to motivate them "to promote the general moral and spiritual reformation of the realm."[35] The two sides of the covenant came across the Atlantic, in the sermon John Winthrop preached to the Puritans on the *Arbella*. Like the Israelites leaving Egypt and entering the Promised Land, the Puritans had "entered into covenant" with God. If God brought them safely to America/Israel, he would "expect a strict performance" of its "articles."[36] Obedience would lead to blessing; but if they only pursued their

---

29. McCoy and Baker, *Fountainhead of Federalism*, 12.
30. Ibid., 13.
31. As did Lillback: *Binding of God*, 311.
32. Baker, *Heinrich Bullinger and the Covenant*, 15.
33. There is considerable debate over whether the "split" occurred, and if so, when it was done. The claim was introduced by McGiffert, "Grace and Works," 464, 467; "split" occurs on 485. See also Holifield, *Theology in America*, 39: he dated the split to 1562, to Ursinus, coauthor of the Heidelberg Catechism. For a contrary position, see Lillback, *Binding of God*, 287–91.
34. McCoy and Baker, *Fountainhead of Federalism*, 40–41, quoting William Perkins, *Werkes*, 1:70. The use of Perkins would seem to corroborate McGiffert in contrast to Lillback.
35. McGiffert, "Covenant, Crown and Commons in Elizabethan Puritanism," 44.
36. Winthrop, "Model of Christian Charity," 90.

"pleasures and profits," then they would "surely perish out of the good land."[37] His peroration summoned the Puritans/Israelites to "choose life."[38] In keeping this covenant, they were to be guided by a "double law . . . : the law of nature and the law of grace, or the moral law or the law of the gospel."[39] The moral law commanded mutual aid, rooted in the golden rule, while the law of the gospel enabled this obedience because, against the natural desire of "every man" to "seek himself only," Christ enters the "soul and infuseth another principle, love to God and our brother."[40]

Winthrop's formulation was full of paradoxes. They were Christians, living in accordance with the gospel, "the law of grace," who identified with ancient Israel. They *were* Israel.[41] The covenant had bilateral conditions—they did not need to keep the covenant if their journey ended in failure; but the covenant was a covenant of grace, a covenant they could only own if they had been owned. Predestination was not merely a dogma, but lived experience. The Word of God convicted and converted them. They *experienced* justification by grace and faith alone. Their salvation was wholly rooted in God's sovereign election and therefore was not merited.[42] At the same time (there was always an *at the same time* with the Puritans), they knew that having been elected, they had moral and spiritual responsibilities. The first of these responsibilities was to put oneself in a spiritual position to *experience election*, to gain "assurance" that one was among the elect. The would-be Christian had to struggle to experience grace and *know* God's forgiveness as an experiential reality. To know that one was in covenant with God was to have *covenanted* with God, to depend on his grace, and to follow his commands in all of life. Puritans voluntaristically covenanted with God to appropriate for themselves the absolute covenant of God to save those who so covenanted with him.[43]

This paradoxical spirituality helped give rise to the practice of the conversion narrative (or, "conversion relations"). Although all children of Puritan "saints" had been baptized as infants, by 1635[44] an American Puritan had to give a narrative of how God had converted him or her. An "unconverted" Puritan could not participate in the Lord's Supper or have one's children baptized. Prior to this time, "conversion" was fundamentally a moral and ecclesial act: the "convert" shifted allegiance from the accepted participation in the religious and political establishment to the new commu-

---

37. Winthrop, "Model of Christian Charity," 92.

38. Ibid.; see also Deut 30:19–20.

39. Winthrop, "Model of Christian Charity," 83.

40. Ibid., 84, 87.

41. See Bozeman, *To Live Ancient Lives*, 11, and Foster, *Genetic History of the New England Theology*, 34.

42. On predestination as an *experienced reality*, see Dewey Wallace, *Puritans and Predestination*, esp. 6–8, 50–52, 101, 196, and Haller, *Rise of Puritanism*, 89, 93–96.

43. Von Rohr, *Covenant of Grace in Puritan Thought*, 80, 188–90; Holifield, *Theology in America*, 40–42.

44. The date comes from Ahlstrom, *Religious History of the American People*, 1:194.

nity of the "saints."[45] But in the New World, there was no *other* community to convert *to*. "Conversion" needed a new focus: the "subjective mood"—heretofore simply the affective pole of the experience—became its content.[46] The would-be member had to "relate" how God had revealed his sinfulness, and then describe how, through the "means of grace," he had come to experience "saving faith."[47]

However, the next generation of children grew up in the emerging comforts of New England. They lacked a sense of tension between what the community was and what the community ought to be. An entire cohort of young adults had been baptized, but had not experienced conversion. Since they could not have their own children baptized, the spiritual leaders looked forward to the future of New England with anxiety.[48] In 1662, they promulgated the "Half-Way Covenant," which said that baptized but unconverted members of the church could have their own children baptized.[49] This meant the next generation of children were brought under the authority and nurture of the church, and could likewise have *their* children baptized. Although it may have temporarily settled the nerves of New England's patriarchs, the solution did not endure. Anticipation was pitched too high; too many people believed that conversion was still necessary, even if they themselves had not experienced it. A century of conversionist doctrine fostered unsatisfied desires;[50] the resolution of those passions had dimensions only hinted at in this astonished—and astonishing—description by a later historian: "For six provocative years, New England's emotions and interest had been aroused by these religious pulsations. Eager with anticipation and overready for the climax, New England on September 14, 1740, received George Whitefield."[51] Later

45. Morgan, *Visible Saints*, 36–47, 76–77. See further Coolidge, *Pauline Renaissance*, 64–67, 147, and Brauer, "Conversion," 231–35.

46. Perry Miller discussed this mood at length in *The New England Mind in the Seventeenth Century*, which he called "The Augustinian Strain of Piety": 3–34. Thus an unidentified Puritan described his or her journey to and in America: "I thought I should find feelings" (quoted in Heimert and Delbanco, *Puritans in America*, 15).

47. Morgan, *Visible Saints*, 68–71, outlined the "morphology." For explanations of the emergence of the narrative requirement, see Morgan, 62–63, 80–88, and Brauer, "Conversion," 236. Descriptions of these narratives can be found in Hall, *Worlds of Wonder*, 119ff.

48. The problems of the Puritan doctrine of baptism and conversion are summarized in Holifield, *Theology in America*, 53–54. Cotton Mather described the concern for children who wanted to "renew their baptismal-covenant" but "could not come to an experimental account of their own conversion" (*Magnalia*, II, 277ff.; quoted in Foster, *Genetic History of the New England Theology*, 28).

49. Morgan, *Visible Saints*, 113–38; Holifield explained the difficulties the Half-Way Covenant generated for Puritan baptismal doctrine (*Theology in America*, 54–55). It should be noted that not all New England congregations implemented the Half-Way Covenant.

50. On the failure to "endure," see Foster, *Genetic History of the New England Theology*, 35–43, and Brauer, "Conversion," 236; on "unsatisfied desires," see Brauer, "Conversion," 238.

51. Gaustad, *Great Awakening in New England*, 24. Note the erotic terms Gaustad used, apparently without any awareness. Whitefield was an English preacher strongly influenced by John and Charles Wesley; unlike the Wesleys, however, he remained a Calvinist. An itinerant, he preached in the fields, thus presenting his message to all who would come and listen. Although he preached without notes, he was an experienced theater actor in his youth, and brought the skills of memorization and dramatic

Christian history and hagiography would describe this as the "Great Awakening."[52] Evangelicals can justifiably point to it with pride as the foundation of the characteristically American expression of Protestantism. The revivals created a religion that was energetic, passionate, mobile—suited to the open fields and dark forests of the new continent. People gained a direct sense of God's presence in their lives. Once the converting event was complete, they *knew* they were "saved." The "assurance" that had, a century earlier, taken a Puritan weeks or even months to gain, was granted them in the relatively short span of days or hours. A complex confidence-in-striving gave way to a boastful certainty of salvation that bordered on antinomianism.[53] What once took a whole lifetime to achieve could now be grasped in a virtual instant. The eschatological promise of salvation descended in the twinkling of an eye, and became immanent.

Another element of the revivals must be acknowledged. Both Whitefield and another notable itinerant preacher, James Davenport, were young bachelors.[54] "Emotional appeal . . . was the very essence of revival."[55] This emotional appeal was a continuation of the "subjective mood" that the Puritans had brought to and developed in New England. But it lost the bond to the community inherent in the Puritan covenant. The structure of federalism was "designed" to hold together grace and works, predestination and human responsibility, the freedom of God's election and obligation of responding to and abiding by the moral law.[56] The Puritans sought for conversion, but understood conversion as a process that took place throughout the whole of a saint's life. In this sense, "salvation" remained eschatological, the final port of call providing final respite at the end of a long and difficult pilgrimage. The revivals that began around 1740 kept the predestinarian framework of conversionism. Conversion was a divine act, a decisive event that gave virtually certain evidence of God's predestinating choice.[57] However, that conversionism was now alienated from the carefully balanced system of covenantal action among God, community, and saint. From now on, the inheritors of the Puritans separated into

---

expression to his preaching. See Noll, *History of Christianity*, 91–95; Lambert, *Inventing the "Great Awakening*," 88ff.; Kidd, *Great Awakening*, 40ff. Although Whitefield claimed that the core of his preaching was the classic Reformation doctrine of "*justification by faith alone* in the imputed righteousness of Jesus Christ," he criticized apparent Christians who lacked "a real experience of a work of regeneration and true conversion," and rather depended on their regular "attendance on public worship and the holy sacrament" ("An Answer to the Second Part of an Anonymous Pamphlet," 4:168; "*Law* Gospelized," 4:395, 401, 400; emphasis original). One can infer that for Whitefield, conversion (not public worship) made justification an *experiential* reality.

52. Noll, *History of Christianity*, 91–113.

53. Lovejoy, *Religious Enthusiasm in the New World*, 182.

54. Expressed another way, revivalists exuded "sex appeal." For a description of Davenport's revivals, see Goen, *Revivalism and Separatism in New England, 1740–1800*, 21, quoting *Diary of Joshua Hempstead of New London, Connecticut*, 379.

55. Lovejoy, *Religious Enthusiasm in the New World*, 184.

56. Ibid., 62; see also Coolidge, *Pauline Renaissance*, 119–20, on how federalism held together different aspects of the covenant.

57. Kidd, *Great Awakening*, 14–16, 277–78.

distinct schools,[58] each of which kept safe some fragment of the Puritan vision, but none of which maintained it as a living whole.

Converting Conversionism: The Trajectory of a Religious Experience

Revivalism and conversionism have defined American evangelicalism for close to three centuries. It created the narrative that a second round of revivals soon after creation of the United States was a "Second Great Awakening." Actually, religious leaders continued to seek and spawn revival movements between 1760 and 1800,[59] so the later periodization is artificial and tendentious. However, the narrative took hold, especially supported by accounts of the dramatic events at Cane Ridge, Kentucky, in August of 1801.[60] After several years of anticipatory prayer and preaching, Christians were summoned to a "camp meeting" in the wilderness. In the wildness of nature, brought together in a "critical mass"—maybe as many as twenty-five thousand—of spiritually and emotionally hungry people, seekers expressed their experience of God's presence in a panoply of astonishing physical and psychological displays: jerking, dancing, ecstatic laughter and barking. Such phenomena can be explained in part as due to the "powerful psychological release" provided to people whose lives were characterized by isolation, "subject to a hard and perilous life" on the American frontier.[61] Traditional history saw camp meetings as an American innovation, and more negatively, "grotesque novelties."[62] However, more thorough scholarship has placed the camp meetings in a long tradition of Scottish Presbyterian piety, specifically of the "sacramental fair."[63]

The sacramental fair was a multiday gathering that drew people for fasting, prayer, preaching, and the sacrament of the Lord's Supper. In Scotland, sacramental fairs can be traced back to 1620, becoming central to Scottish piety between 1688 and 1750.[64]

> The sacramental occasion had come to embody an evangelical synthesis of conversionist preaching and eucharistic practice. In the sacramental occasion

---

58. See Noll, *History of Christianity*, 98, and *Dictionary of Christianity in America*, 8, 10–12, for summaries of the major schools. See further Guelzo, *Edwards on the Will*, 143–49.

59. See Kidd, *Great Awakening*, 268ff. and 312ff.

60. The following description is based on Ahlstrom, *Religious History of the American People*, 1:524–28; Schmidt, *Holy Fairs*, xi–xxv.

61. Noll, *History of Christianity*, 167. Ahlstrom gave an extensive excerpt from Barton Stone, describing the various "exercises": *Religious History of the American People*, 1:526–28.

62. Schmidt, *Holy Fairs*, xi.

63. This reorientation is largely due to Schmidt, *Holy Fairs*, who showed how Cane Ridge is best understood as being in the tradition of Scottish sacramental fairs. Note how Peter Cartwright, while being aware of its origin, redefined it as a "camp meeting" (Schmidt, *Holy Fairs*, xi–xxix). See further Westerkamp, *Triumph of the Laity*, and Long's *Eucharistic Theology of the American Holy Fairs*.

64. Schmidt, *Holy Fairs*, 19–32, 41–49.

> the salvation of sinners was coupled with the confirmation of saints as complementary processes in the revivification of a community.... These sacramental revivals... were for the whole community, churched and unchurched, sinners and saved.... The communion season drew people into the pilgrimage and kept them going once on the journey. For these evangelical Presbyterians salvation and the sacrament were intimately related, even inseparable. Conversion and communion had flowed together in this tradition.[65]

The fairs would generally begin with a fast on Thursday and a service of preparation on Saturday. The sacrament itself would be celebrated on "the Sabbath," followed by a service of thanksgiving on Monday. Those who wanted to take communion would be questioned and counseled as to their spiritual state; if they were deemed prepared, they would receive a "token" that would represent their "ticket" to the Table. Also, psalms were sung in their "old tunes."[66]

The sacramental fairs were periods of enormous energy and emotion, as people came from all over the countryside, or, in the case of frontier America, from isolated hamlets in the forests. Certainly the particular pleasures of the camping experience facilitated a transformation of the sacramental fair into the American camp meeting.[67] However, those camp meetings lost key aspects of the fair. No longer were people brought together to (re)generate the community. While the conversion experiences took place in an ersatz community, they were the conversion of an individual. The convert gained a personal sense of God's presence and power, and no longer needed the sacrament as the capstone of the whole experience.[68] The felt response to the preaching was its own validation.

Besides the loss of Christian community and sacramental experience, there was another widely recognized and fundamental shift in the revivalism that emerged in the nineteenth century: it made the individual responsible for his conversion. The revivals around 1740 spontaneously resolved the urgent problem for the descendants of the Puritans: How could they experience God's sovereign, converting grace? Conversion was therefore a divine action, evidence that God had predestined a person for salvation. But in the early national period, Americans were no longer waiting for God to act. They were resolving their own problems. One did not wait for God to "save one's soul," one acted to save it. By 1830, evangelicalism put the would-be convert in the driver's seat. The exemplar of this "Arminianized Calvinism" was Charles

---

65. Ibid., 49–50. See also Westerkamp, *Triumph of the Laity*, 34.

66. Schmidt, *Holy Fairs*, 58–61, 72–73; Long, *Eucharistic Theology of the American Holy Fairs*, 2–5.

67 The clear connecting link was James McGready, a Presbyterian minister who grew up in western Pennsylvania and ministered in Kentucky. For his role in the Cane Ridge revivals, see Ahlstrom, *Religious History of the American People*, 1:524–25. Yet as Schmidt showed, McGready ministered through the sacramental fairs. Long presents McGready's communion sermons in *Eucharistic Theology of the American Holy Fairs*, 63–81.

68. Schmidt, *Holy Fairs*, 207–8, described how nineteenth-century revivalism broke the bond between revival and participation in the sacrament; see also Brauer, "Conversion," 241.

Grandison Finney.[69] Trained as a lawyer, after a conversion experience he almost immediately began to preach. He told people not to wait for God to act. *"Religion is the work of man."*[70] Revival required a deliberate and conscious strategy, appealing to the individual's power to choose. It "is not a miracle. . . . It is a purely philosophical result of the right use of the constituted means."[71] By "philosophical" Finney meant "psychological": revival made use of human beings' psychological constitution to elicit the desired response. Finney's revivalism was a deliberate effort of religious salesmanship: the product he was selling was *obedience to God.*[72]

Before Mercersburg: Reading Nevin as a High-Church Calvinist

John Williamson Nevin was born in 1803 to an apparently affluent and educated farmer near Shippensburg, Pennsylvania, about forty-five miles southwest of that state's capital. He remembered his childhood Presbyterianism as "staid, systematical, and grave," and expressed in the regular practice of the "means of grace." He recalled the communion seasons, as inherited from the "holy fairs" of Scotland, albeit without a notable revivalistic component.[73] He went to Union College in Schenectady, New York, in 1817, and had his first exposure to revivalism, which he later described as "the genius of New-England Puritanism."[74] After college, he experienced the first in a series of what appears to have been a psychosomatic ailment. He then continued his studies at Princeton Theological Seminary (1823–1826). After another "breakdown," he was called to teach Bible at Western (now Pittsburgh) Theological Seminary, another Presbyterian school, in 1830. He taught there for ten years, until financial problems and tensions in the Presbyterian Church motivated him to accept a call from an equally needy seminary at Mercersburg, Pennsylvania. Thus, in 1840 Nevin became a theological teacher of the German Reformed Church.

---

69. Noll, *History of Christianity*, 170; McLoughlin, introduction to *The American Evangelicals*, 6–10. Nathan O. Hatch described how the camp meetings were an expression of religious democracy (*Democratization of American Christianity*, 49–58, esp. 56). Finney was born in 1792 and converted in 1821. After theological study with his pastor, he was ordained in the Presbyterian Church in 1824, and began preaching that year in upstate New York. He used "new measures," especially the "anxious bench" (a bench at the front of the church house where the "anxious" would come to seek conversion), protracted meetings, and public prayer by women. He attempted to reinterpret Calvinism to make it palatable to the new democratic mood: one could choose to be saved, and become responsible in moral and social reform (abolitionism, temperance, etc.).

70. Finney, *Lectures on Revivals of Religion*, 9; emphasis original.

71. Ibid., 12. See further pp. 17–18.

72. Ibid., 9, 14, 398.

73. Nevin, *My Own Life*, 4–5. D. G. Hart gave reasons for believing that Nevin's childhood congregation was "old side," i.e., nonrevivalistic (*John Williamson Nevin*, 38).

74. Nevin, *My Own Life*, 8.

General Introduction

James Hastings Nichols began his history of Nevin's life with the confident claim that Nevin "grew up in 'Puritanism.'"[75] But the above summary implies an urgent question: *Which* Puritanism? By 1800, the deterioration of Puritanism's spiritual and theological integrity was well advanced.[76] Nichols tied Nevin's "conversion" experience during college to a "*restrained* type of revivalism, set in the context of *high Calvinist teaching* on divine sovereignty" and noted the revivalist never used the "new measures."[77] Nichols's description of the ministerial catechism and visitation a young Nevin experienced looks more churchly than revivalistic. He accurately described the fairs as a basic institution of Presbyterian sacramental experience, but didn't seem to know anything of their history or significance.[78]

However, in that case, how do we explain the astonishingly innovative stance that Nevin and his colleagues at Mercersburg took in the context of American theology? How do we get *from* Nevin's childhood Presbyterianism *to* Mercersburg? Linden DeBie (editor of the first two volumes in this series) has urged interpreters to find the catalyst for the emergence of Mercersburg Theology in Nevin's exposure to "idealism and speculative theology."[79] His formidable scholarship in the MTSS editions of *The Mystical Presence* and *Coena Mystica* has made such a construction seemingly incontrovertible. As a result, when he criticized a number of recent interpreters, specifically including this editor, for departing "from the older, sound view of Nevin as very much influenced by German scholarship," one is inclined to credit his judgment.[80] However, Nevin's work between 1830 and 1840 still has not received sustained attention. It is difficult to accept the judgment that it did not contribute to the distinctive themes of Mercersburg, if it remains unread and unexamined.[81]

Nevin's "restrained revivalism" was already manifested in a 1832 text. A group of ministers in the Pittsburgh area had sponsored the republication of Joseph Lathrop's *Christ's Warning to the Churches*, a polemic against itinerancy from New England, and

---

75. Nichols, *Romanticism in American Theology*, 5.
76. Guelzo, *Edwards on the Will*, 208–39.
77. Nichols, *Romanticism in American Theology*, 12, 13; emphasis added.
78. Ibid., 7.
79. DeBie, editor's introduction to Nevin, *The Mystical Presence*, MTSS edition, xxxv.
80. Ibid., xxxiii, note 46.
81. By way of example, DeBie criticized this editor's use of Nevin's earliest monograph, *Summary of Biblical Antiquities*, to show "an incipient concept of development" (DeBie gave no citation, but was quoting Layman, "Nevin's Holistic Supernaturalism," 198). DeBie responded, "There was nothing original . . . in the work and it was based entirely on Jahn's very popular *Antiquities* whom Nevin would later repudiate" ("Germ, Genesis, and Contemporary Impact of Mercersburg Philosophy," 29–30). To the contrary of DeBie's generalization, there *was* one chapter that appears to be Nevin's own reflection: *Summary of Biblical Antiquities*, vol. 2, ch. 1 (2:7–31; 2nd ed., 235–56). It was entitled "General History of Religion" and, based on a textual comparison, was a substitution for Jahn's "Historical View of the Religion of the Bible" (*Biblical Antiquities*, 152ff.). Jahn's chapter was genuinely (for the early nineteenth century) a historical survey of ancient Hebrew and Jewish religion; in contrast, Nevin's chapter was a description of divine revelation in the Old Testament from a *Christian theological* perspective. This is the chapter that will be used in the following argument.

Nevin wrote a new introduction. Nevin complained that a "religion teacher" could "gain authority" simply by being "full of zeal, and noise, and passion." He urged his readers to uphold "the divine institution of the ministerial office, and the binding authority of ecclesiastical order." At the same time, he thought, the very appeal of these false teachers was a result of "lukewarmness, and formality, and inactivity of the churches," and he closed with a prayer that God would "visit all our congregations with the spirit of revival."[82]

So Nevin wanted revival, but wanted it carried out in the regular order of churchly life. What kind of revivalism did he want? What were its psychological presuppositions? In 1833, he preached "Election Not Contrary to a Free Gospel."[83] Nevin was trying to resolve the apparent contradiction between the scriptural and dogmatic truth of divine election, and the freedom to choose the gospel. Nevin said that the contradiction existed only in "speculation," and humans, with their limited knowledge, should not be expected to be able to fully resolve it, since that would assume they could see the world with God's eyes. It was the nature of the will to be free, but the freedom of the will was consistent with divine foreknowledge. Thus the choice was both certain (in God's foreknowledge) and free. Furthermore, Nevin argued freedom *required* the choice to be certain. In an utterly arbitrary world, human freedom would be lawless, and thus meaningless. The will acted in accordance with the "particular constitution of life out of which the actions of men proceed," which was to be free. Yet the operation of that constitution was lawful, and therefore certain according to God's foreknowledge.[84]

In this formulation, Nevin was outside of the world of traditional Puritan experience. The Puritans had always made predestination the existential fulcrum of conversion. Divine election was *felt*; conversion relations became normative because Puritans experienced a need for the would-be member to give a narrative of how that election was manifested in his or her religious experience. However, Nevin had no need for this entire structure, since he did not understand predestination (or election) as a felt reality.

> The sense of guilt—the apprehension of wrath—the desire of salvation—are all independent of this whole subject [of election]. The consciousness of acting freely, in accepting or refusing to accept the grace of Christ, is never disturbed by any speculation to which it may give rise. All the motives to holiness, are just what they would be if there was no difficulty in the case. The difficulty is

---

82. Nevin, introduction to Lathrop, *Christ's Warning to the Churches*, 11–14. Nichols summarized this text in *Romanticism in American Theology*, 25–26.

83. Nevin, "Election Not Contrary to a Free Gospel," 209–24. The editor gratefully acknowledges DeBie's mention in *The Mystical Presence*, MTSS edition, xxxix; it is also cited in Nichols, *Romanticism in American Theology*, 21.

84. Nevin, "Election Not Contrary to a Free Gospel," 223. For this sermon's continuity with Nevin's later position, see Nevin, "Human Freedom," reprinted in *Human Freedom, and A Plea for Philosophy* (scheduled for publication in vol. 13 of MTSS).

not practical; and it should never be allowed to interfere with the soul's action in any case.[85]

Therefore, Nevin's understanding of conversion cannot be assimilated to Puritanism's view. Conversion did not answer the question: "Am I among the elect?"

The nearest we get to an answer to this question is in an 1838 sermon, "The Seal of the Spirit."[86] Nevin interpreted the "seal of the Spirit" as an awareness of an already-present salvation. This seal was communal, not individual, since it designated the recipients as "members of the spiritual family of God, in distinction from the world that lieth in sin," and was "the *common* privilege of christians; not an attainment which a few only might be expected to realize. . . . It is the proper fruit of saving faith."[87] The "seal" was the promise of ultimate salvation, which differed from "present salvation . . . not in kind, but only in degree."[88] Therefore, election appears to have been analogous to assurance in Nevin's mind: a confirmation and realization of the ongoing process of salvation, a process that took place in Christian community. Two observations can be made: firstly, although in theory Nevin still held to the invisible/visible distinction, he didn't share the Puritan attempt to separate out the true saints from those who simply participated in the church's external life; secondly, Nevin already recognized that salvation was a process—in contrast to revivalism, which made the eschatological verdict of "justified" present in the moment of "conversion."

Nevin's concern with the church had already been adumbrated in *Summary of Biblical Antiquities*. The history of the world was directed toward the welfare of the church. In the midst of the seemingly meaningless ebb and flow of worldly power, God was providentially at work to achieve its final triumph. "History is studied correctly and understandingly, only when this relation of God's general providence, in all the changes of earth, to his will concerning the church, is seriously and attentively regarded."[89] Therefore, the church was the focus of God's activity, and the mechanical processes and patterns of a fallen world were only comprehended when they were read in connection with it, when they were perceived to contribute to its eventual consummation. It would be easy to overstate the significance of what Nevin was saying here. He was a long way off from the Mercersburgian concern with historical development.[90] But he was much further from the ahistorical interpretations of Puritans and Baptists, both of whom, in different ways, tied the church's character to a supposedly primitive past.[91] He already knew that, while he affirmed the church

---

85. Nevin, "Election Not Contrary to a Free Gospel," 215.
86. A summary of this important text can be found in Layman, "'Seal of the Spirit' (1838)," 64–68.
87. Nevin, *Seal of the Spirit*, 4; emphasis original.
88. Ibid.
89. Nevin, *Summary of Biblical Antiquities*, 2:11; 2nd ed, 239.
90. A concept explored particularly in the essays to come in vol. 7 of MTSS.
91. The pursuit of an allegedly primitive, and therefore pure, past is a basic theme of American religion. On the Puritans, read Bozeman, *To Live Ancient Lives*; for the later phenomenon, see Hughes

had been one body throughout the ages (beginning immediately after the Fall), "its measure of spiritual advantage, and its outward constitution, have been greatly altered through the process of time. It has had, as it were, an infancy, a childhood, and a full grown manhood."[92]

From *Biblical Antiquities* to "The Seal of the Spirit" (which includes almost all of his time in Pittsburgh), Nevin articulated an embryonic concern with historical change[93] and the processive nature of spiritual experience. This included a prescient awareness of the historicity of *ideas*. He had studied the Old Testament in its original Hebrew. He came to believe that the "kingdom of God," as the whole fabric of God's working in time and space, was constantly manifesting that activity in ever-changing ways. To understand God's revelation in Scripture and the history of redemption, one had to understand the *thoughts* of the biblical writers. Those thoughts had historically specific contexts, and the contexts could and did change. When Nevin opened the 1831 winter session of the Western Theological Seminary (thus at the very beginning of his career) he said: "The costume of the Jewish mind at the time of the Saviour, was not precisely what it had been before the captivity, or in the age of Moses. The power of moral and political circumstances had, as is usual in the history of nations, modified in some respects its ancient form. The progress of this change, the eye of the student should follow." He was saying this to insist on the study of Hebrew: the student could not hope to understand the New Testament without entering into the "mind" of its writers and their "forms of thought"; and those forms were "predominant[ly] Hebraic."[94]

Through all these pre-Mercersburg texts runs the undercurrent of another theme: the need for a spiritually vital Christian experience. "Religion [Is] a Life," Nevin pronounced in a series of four essays in the middle of his Pittsburgh tenure.[95] Religion was an affective state—"sentiment more than mere intellection"—of "the *love of* God" expressed in attitudes of "gratitude, and trust, and hope and admiration, and self-immersion into the divine will." When the sinner heard the gospel, he was in a state

---

and Allen, *Illusions of Innocence* and Hughes, *American Quest for the Primitive Church*.

92. Nevin, *Summary of Biblical Antiquities*, 2:12; 2nd ed, 240. See below, art. 2, for Nevin's use of Irenaeus's idea of believers' growth recapitulating the process of Christ's life, death, and glorification. Mercersburg Christology derived a "Second Adam" motif from Irenaeus, as discussed by William B. Evans in his general introduction to Nevin, Schaff, and Gans, *Incarnate Word*, vol. 4 of MTSS, xxvii–xxviii.

93. DeBie traced Nevin's emerging historical consciousness in his introductions to Nevin, *The Mystical Presence*, MTSS edition, xxiv–xxv, and Nevin and Hodge, *Coena Mystica*, MTSS edition, xxvii–xxviii. DeBie was largely working from Nevin's *My Own Life*, 139–49, anthologized in Appel, *Life and Work of John Williamson Nevin*, 79–88; see also Nichols, *Romanticism in American Theology*, 42–45.

94 Nevin, *"Claims of the Bible,"* 20n.

95. Nevin, "Religion a Life," *Friend* 2, no. 25 (December 25, 1834) 198; no. 28 (January 15, 1835) 222–23; no. 29 (January 22, 1835) 230; no. 30 (January 29, 1835) 238–39. These essays are reprinted in full in the *New Mercersburg Review*, no. 17 (1995) 37–45.

of separation from God. The gospel presented a "vision of unspeakable love . . . in the history of the Lord Jesus Christ," to which the God-starved soul responded by loving surrender to this new "power of an imperishable life." This surrender led to a "process of regenerating and sanctifying grace," which was like the "development of a plant," and "carries in itself the germ of its own most perfect state from the beginning, and grows by unfolding itself from within."[96] Already we see the theme of the Christian life as a *process* and *growth*, and the motif of a plant's "germ" that Nevin would put to use in his discussion with Horace Bushnell.

Nevin spent most of the remainder of these essays criticizing some incomplete conceptions of "religion." It was not "knowledge,"[97] nor an "abstract" "system of theology" like those of "Calvin, Turretin, or Pictet." Theology was to the life of religion what astronomy was to the sensed experience of the heavens. Scientific laws had to refer to "real phenomena"; likewise, speculative laws of theology had to refer to actual spiritual experience. Religious life was a reality "belonging historically to the human soul," and "found historically active in the mind of God and the mind of the human sinner."[98] What did he mean by "historically"? Since he had already used the metaphor of "germ" and "plant," he certainly thought of religious life as a *living, changing* thing. It grew, and gradually expressed the life that was in its "germ" (today we would say "genes," or "DNA"). Even more significantly, "historically" seems to have been the opposite of "artificial," or perhaps more simply, "dead." At the end of the first number of "Religion a Life," he had warned against "the grand error of our nature," which was "to attach itself to the mere forms of sense and time."[99] Nevin attacked these "mere forms" in another essay that immediately followed the conclusion of "Religion a Life." Due to humanity's "naturally carnal" nature, some religious people wanted "the benefit of religion," while remaining attached to the "life of sense," of sensual reality. In order to have their cake and eat it, too, they replaced religion's "living power" with certain external "forms": moral virtue, religious rituals, doctrines, "outward expressions of religious *sentiment*," and the "*forms* of experimental religion." (The last two were probably identical in Nevin's schema.) In each case, what these forms lacked was *life*: mere virtue without "its living principle"; worship without "the sentiments of devotion they assume to express"; doctrines without the spiritual "facts to which they pertain"; *forms* of religious feeling or experience (clearly including the forms of conversionism) without the "living force of evangelical *principles*."[100]

In summary, Nevin wanted a religion that spontaneously arose and sustained itself. It grew (like a plant) through time (like a historical phenomenon). It was "real,"

---

96. Nevin, "Religion a Life," December 25, 1834, 198; repr., *New Mercersburg Review*, no. 17, 38–39, emphasis original.

97. Nevin, "Religion a Life," December 25, 1834, 198; repr., *New Mercersburg Review*, no. 17, 39.

98. Nevin, "Religion a Life," January 15, 1835, 222; repr., *New Mercersburg Review*, no. 17, 40.

99. Nevin, "Religion a Life," December 25, 1834, 198; repr., *New Mercersburg Review*, no. 17, 39.

100. Nevin, "Grand Heresy," all emphases original.

not "fake." It had its own vitality within itself. It sprang up "naturally," as a necessary unpacking and expression of its "germ." In a word, it was *organic*. This conclusion implies that when Nevin began using "organic" in the early 1840s at Mercersburg, he had not undergone any radical religious or theological change. To be sure, Nevin's later interpretation of *organic* almost certainly came from Friedrich Rauch, a German émigré who was Nevin's first colleague at Mercersburg before Rauch's premature death in the spring of 1841.[101] However, if in fact the *elements* of Nevin's later spiritual and theological vision were already present when he was at Pittsburgh, then Rauch's concept of "organical identity" can best be understood as a catalyst, "shocking" the elements of Nevin's thought into an integrated system.

But until that reintegration took place, Nevin remained under the umbrella of evangelical piety. That is not surprising. He wanted a vital, energetic religion, and the evangelical patterns of behavior (including "revival") were generally thought to be the "appointed means" for such a religiosity. However, he tied those procedures to ecclesiastical order. Only later would he realize how out of order (relative to his perception) revivalism had become. On the other hand, Nevin understood those means in two idiosyncratic ways. Against the Puritan tradition, conversion was not a sign of election, which supernaturally snatched the sinner out of an unregenerate state. This mitigated the psychological crises generated by the Puritan process of conversion. Nevin *did* regard "religion" as a supernatural reality, but without the tension that could so easily snap back upon the convert. The supernatural quality lay in a communal realm of moral change and spiritual renewal. This new realm was in explicit contrast to the world, the present realm of sense and self. In short, conversion took place in churchly life. Further, the means were not external forms that could easily be imitated. "Life" was spiritual power for Nevin. It manifested itself, like a plant grew, like the history of an organism or an identifiable social body. Religion was not something that a person "did." It came to a person in embodied, corporate activity. Therefore, there is no reason to doubt Nevin's own judgment, just before he wrote "The Seal of the Spirit":

> I belong theoretically and experimentally to the Old School in theology, as I have belonged to it theoretically at least from my childhood. I am not conscious of having changed materially in my views as touching the points which divide the two schools [of New School and Old School], unless it be in coming to see more clearly and fully the emptiness of our modern divinity.[102]

---

101. Rauch wrote his *Psychology* based on an idealistic platform. For his concept of "organical identity," in which the underlying identity was "life," see *Psychology* (1840), 18–21, 171, 182–83; 4th ed. (1846), 22–25, 182–83, 195. Nichols (*Romanticism in American Theology*, 46–48) and D. G. Hart (*John Williamson Nevin*, 75–77) discuss Rauch and Nevin.

102. *Christian Herald*, October 1837, quoted in Nichols, *Romanticism in American Theology*, 33. What did Nevin mean by "modern divinity"? He might have meant Finneyite revivalism or Nathaniel Taylor's "New Haven theology" (on the latter, see Kuklick, *Churchmen and Philosophers*, 94ff., and Guelzo, *Edwards on the Will*, 240–56). But they were both new movements, and unlikely to have been thought of in formal terms as a school of divinity. Perhaps he was referring to "New Divinity," which

Consequently, this editor agrees with D. G. Hart that "the rest of his life was a search to recover the churchly faith" he had lost in his exposure to revivalism.[103] It would take the move to Mercersburg to continue that search.

"Regeneration": The Problem for Nevin in 1847

Earlier we faced the question, why did Nevin attack "Inquirer," rather than answer him? Baptismal regeneration evoked a visceral reaction among all thinkers within the Reformed tradition. Horace Bushnell regarded the doctrine "as a great error" because "no faith, in the parents, is necessary to the effect of the rite" and "the child is said to be actually regenerated by the priest."[104] He referred to earlier views, apparently in the early church, in which "peculiar sacramental or magical power . . . convey[ed] a grace immediately to the subject."[105] Bushnell's claim that a child could simply grow up a Christian was criticized by Bennet Tyler, an Edwardsean (i.e., revivalist) theologian, but Bushnell and Tyler concurred in attacking baptismal regeneration.[106] They wanted to avoid anything that looked like magic; as we will see, Nevin agreed with them.

Furthermore, Nevin did not like the term "one way or the other, simply because of its very uncertain and precarious sense."[107] One feels this obscurity in modern scholarly work on the subject. One reads scholars saying what Puritans thought about "regeneration," and looks in vain for the textual support of the alleged thoughts. The important 1991 study of Glenn A. Hewitt, *Regeneration and Morality*, is illuminating and frustrating by turns. He often used the word "regeneration" when he was discussing "conversion" or some other category of Christian experience.[108] Precision is of

---

rejected "the use of the means" for conversion (church attendance, prayer, Bible study). It insisted that the sinner had to simply repent; it also rejected the original Puritan notion of the "church-in-society" and wanted to limit the church "to real Christians" (Guelzo, *Edwards on the Will*, 118–19, 124). Since Nevin probably lacked the perspective to interpret the differences among these movements, perhaps "modern divinity" simply designated what Finney, Taylor, and New Divinity had in common: *conversionistic* divinity.

103. *John Williamson Nevin*, 59. The reader should consult the objection of Linden DeBie in the editor's introduction, to Nevin, *The Mystical Presence*, MTSS edition, p. xxxiii, note 44.

104. Bushnell, *Discourses on Christian Nurture* (1847), 50, in Bushnell, *Views of Christian Nurture, and of Subjects Adjacent Thereto* (1848), 36–37.

105. Bushnell, *Argument for "Discourses on Christian Nurture"* (1847), 25; *Views of Christian Nurture*, 88.

106. Tyler, "Baptismal Regeneration," 397–414. His response to Bushnell was *Dr. Tyler's Letter to Dr. Bushnell on Christian Nurture*. The author of "Baptismal Regeneration" is not listed, but Tyler claimed credit for it in *Dr. Tyler's Letter*, 20. Tyler's antagonists in "Baptismal Regeneration" were primarily high-church Anglicans and Episcopalians. Tyler argued that if one construed regeneration as directly tied to the moment of baptism, one was forced into contradicting the biblical picture of the Christian regeneration. Nevin eventually attempted to avoid these contradictions by viewing regeneration as a lifelong process, not as a moment in time, whether as ritual or experience.

107. Nevin, *Weekly Messenger*, August 11, 1847, 2478.

108. E.g., he said that Rom 6:2–4 "associates" regeneration with baptism. Neither the word nor

the essence: revivalism had established "conversion" as the central event of Christian experience. The entire debate among the four theologians he discussed was if and how that neologism was related to other received categories. To assume that regeneration meant conversion, or justification, or the like, in a given theologian is to beg the question.

Given the current difficulty of sorting out the configuration of the various terms, imagine a theologian, immediately immersed in debate and polemics of existential urgency, struggling to unravel the knots. Nevin must have wished for Alexander's sword to solve the riddle. If revivalism had not threaded the knot, it certainly tightened it. George Whitefield responded to an anonymous polemicist who had vilified the various enthusiasms of the Methodists. Among his complaints was that they represented conversion as "sudden and *instantaneous*." Whitefield simply mocked the idea that this was (as the polemicist thought) a "fanatical peculiarity," and immediately shifted the ground of the disagreement to "instantaneous regeneration." If the polemicist accepted baptismal regeneration (presumably as an instantaneous event), then he could not consistently object to instantaneous regeneration tied to a religious *experience*. In other words, Whitefield thought that both the polemicist and the Methodists agreed that regeneration was instantaneous, the only question being whether it took place in baptism or conversion. Whitefield dismissed baptismal regeneration as the "*Diana* of the present age*,*" which can be explained by inferring that for Whitefield, conversion/regeneration, not baptism, was essential to beginning the Christian life. Finally, in spite of Whitefield's fobbing off the claim of "peculiarity," the above summary of Puritanism shows that in fact, somewhere between the Puritan conversion narrative and Whitefield's conversionism, there *was* an innovation that made conversion/regeneration instantaneous, rather than a gradual transformation throughout the life of the Christian.[109]

Finney followed Whitefield in equating conversion and regeneration. For Finney, it followed that regeneration was an instantaneous event, generated by a conscious,

---

the concept is found in that passage (Hewitt, *Regeneration and Morality*, 5). It talks about death to sin and "walk[ing] in newness of life. " To equate that to revivalist regeneration is to beg the question. He had a brief paragraph on Luther. But judging by his references, Luther was talking about conversion, repentance, or justification. He was on much firmer ground with Calvin (5). Calvin equated repentance and regeneration, and viewed both as a lifelong process. His paragraphs on the Puritans (6–7) talked about conversion, but did not show if and how that related to regeneration. He claimed an inversion that placed conversion *after* regeneration, but gave no texts or sources to illustrate it (7). His next footnote referred to sources on changes in the concept of *conversion* . . . which does not tell us what we need to know.

109. Whitefield, "Remarks on a Pamphlet," in *Works* 4:240–41, all emphases original. See also Whitefield, "Regeneration," 53–58, for evidence that Whitefield understood regeneration to be identical to conversion. When Whitefield called baptismal regeneration a "Diana," he was using a common metaphor for "false idol" ("Diana" was the Authorized Version's translation of the Ephesian idol in Acts 19:24ff.) Was Whitefield correct to imply that baptismal regeneration was a peculiar preoccupation of his era? If so, the prima facie explanation is that conversionism had *made* it a preoccupation. Nonconversionists then replaced regeneration in conversion with regeneration in baptism.

willed decision to obey God's law.[110] As already argued, although revivalist conversionism had the *affect* of the Puritan experience, it lacked the careful balance of predestination and voluntarism, election and moral responsibility the Puritans had sustained. Furthermore, Finney's conversion/regeneration was naturalistic: it was simply a human choice, as one might join a political party. The practical results of conversion often seemed to be little more than a decision to live a better life and contribute to worthy causes by giving up an unnecessary vice—say, stop drinking coffee.[111]

Nevin first engaged Finney's naturalist conversion/regeneration praxis in *The Anxious Bench* (1843; second edition, 1844). A conversion happening under the tutelage of a revivalist was thought to be "the gate of paradise," that "it serves *some* purpose in the regeneration of the soul." Indeed, Nevin thought, for some converts, "the ground of regeneration" was much "the same form with a resolution to sign a temperance pledge."[112] So at this point, Nevin's understanding of "regeneration" was a negative reaction to what he viewed as the false praxis of the revivalist. It was not a mere human choice, it was not produced by an emotional response to a manipulative and choreographed religious event, it was not as easy as "saying yes to Jesus," as one might say today. Beyond that, Nevin distinguished between conversion and regeneration. In the body of the text, he had argued that "infant conversion" was "not only possible, but altogether natural . . . under the faithful application of the means of grace."[113] So conversion of an infant meant his or her gradual spiritual transformation through the sacraments and churchly nurture. Then in a note, he further explained that gradual conversion did not imply gradual *regeneration*. "Regeneration is instantaneous, but as such not to be perceived directly in any case by the subject. It can be perceived only in its effects. But these belong to *conversion*, the change that flows from regeneration." Regeneration can happen at any time in life.[114] In sum, regeneration was instantaneous; conversion was a (usually) gradual series of spiritual changes that resulted from regeneration. Conversion was known by its effects; regeneration, being entirely mysterious, could not be "perceived" by the person experiencing it.[115]

---

110. Hewitt, *Regeneration and Morality*, 29. The source was Finney, *Lectures to Professing Christians*, 239–40. (Hewitt cited a later edition.) Whitefield and Finney, however differed on another key point: for Whitefield (and the Puritans), conversion was a divine act, while for Finney, it was a human choice.

111. See Finney, *Lectures on Revivals of Religion*, 386–87; Finney, *Lectures to Professing Christians*, 38, 75. His twofold argument was that coffee diverted monies better given to religious work, and it had no nutritional value.

112. Nevin, *Anxious Bench* in Yrigoyen and Bricker, eds., *Catholic and Reformed*, 67, 68, 98, emphasis original.

113. Nevin, *Anxious Bench* in *Catholic and Reformed*, 111. See Hewitt, *Regeneration and Morality*, 132, on regeneration as instantaneous in Nevin.

114. *Anxious Bench* in *Catholic and Reformed*, 112 note, emphasis original.

115. This reads identically to the position of Samuel Hopkins: *Works*, 3:235ff., quoted in Foster, *Genetic History of the New England Theology*, 135. See Holifield, *Theology in America*, 140–41, for the placement of regeneration before conversion in Hopkins's (and Joseph Bellamy's) theology.

Nevin developed his understanding of "regeneration" in *The Mystical Presence*. At first, he simply referred to the usage of "regeneration" as connected to baptism, which then was employed by analogy to express the same power of the Eucharist. If baptism could spiritually wash, the Eucharist could be spiritual food.[116] When Nevin began to make his own "scientific" case for the doctrine of the mystical presence, a key element was that regeneration "inserted" one into Christ. However, becoming part of this "new order of existence" did not happen "at once. This would be magic." So it was not instantaneous, nor was it tied to a decisive, identifiable moment.[117] Furthermore, it was not a product of human choice; rather, it was brought about when a "new life" entered into "the inmost core of our personality," which then became "the seed of our sanctification." Therefore, Nevin was committed to regeneration as the origin of this new spiritual existence, analogous to human birth. Regeneration was "done to" the Christian, not "done by." It was both the beginning and continuation of a "supernatural" process that, by 1846, he understood as churchly, sacramental, processive, historical, and "living." "*Christ's life as now described . . . constitute[es] the* CHURCH. . . . The process . . . takes place in the way of history, growth and regular living-development."[118]

This formulation suggests an interpretation of Nevin's reaction to "Inquirer." The latter's questions[119] assumed that the central issue was the experimental location of *salvation*. This assumption granted the revivalist premise: that "conversion" brought "regeneration," and thus the whole of the salvific process, *instantaneously*.[120] Nevin couldn't allow revivalists to define the terms, since that would have surrendered the argument from the start. After all of Nevin's work on *The Mystical Presence* and the Heidelberg Catechism,[121] *"Inquirer" had completely missed the point*. No wonder Nevin was indignant.

---

116. Nevin, *Mystical Presence* [MTSS edition], 56–57, 119.

117. Ibid., 149. Was Nevin differing with his formulation in *The Anxious Bench*? *The Mystical Presence* distinguished "inserted into him by our regeneration" and being "set over into this new order of existence." It was the latter that Nevin specifically said was not "wholly at once." It is possible to interpret "regeneration" as the beginning point, and the "new order of existence" as its continuation. It was the latter that was processive. This would be consistent with *The Anxious Bench*. The second option is to argue that as Nevin became more fully aware of the implications of his organismic metaphor in *The Mystical Presence*, he was dispensing with the vestiges of revivalist piety, including the notion that regeneration was an instantaneous event in the spiritual life of the new Christian. After all, if it was not a perceptible event, what was the theological need of determining whether it was instantaneous? The editor prefers the second interpretation. Supporting the suspicion that Nevin's interpretation was malleable is the fact that in *"The Seal of the Spirit,"* he called regeneration a "process" (p. 3).

118. Nevin, *Mystical Presence* [MTSS edition], 149, all emphases original. Also see pp. 153, 157, 198 note.

119. Specifically in his follow-up inquiry, *Weekly Messenger*, September 1, 1847, 2490.

120. *Weekly Messenger*, August 4, 1847, 2475: Nevin responded to what he thought was "Inquirer's" assumption that if baptismal regeneration was the case, then baptism was "*invariably and immediately* accompanied with regeneration" (emphasis added). He rejected this formulation, and in contrast emphasized that what happened in baptism was *grace*, and that baptism was a "divine *act*."

121. Nevin specifically mentioned that "in the church of the Heidelberg catechism," one shouldn't

General Introduction

Mercersburg and Its Adversaries

Anti-Romanism

At the time Nevin wrote the essays on Bushnell, Philip Schaff had been his colleague for three years. After the death of Rauch in 1841, the German Reformed Church had returned to the motherland; its representatives were directed by church leaders and theologians to Philip Schaff. Twenty-four years old, he possessed "scholarship, Christian fervor, and attachment to students," and was credited with a "certain adaptability of his nature" that should ease his adjustment to America.[122] He was ordained in Germany and arrived at New York in July 1844. Schaff brought to America "high-church" beliefs and the view that the church continues to develop through history.[123] In his inaugural lecture, "The Principle of Protestantism," he began with historical illustrations of the principle that the Reformation was neither a "*Revolution*" nor a "simple *Restoration*," but the "*legitimate offspring*" of the medieval Catholic Church.[124] Unfortunately for the young scholar, American Protestantism was steeped in virulent anti-Catholicism. Resistance to the perceived peril of renewed papal authority was a defining trait of Protestant identity.[125] An argument had been made within the German Reformed Church that the true precursors of Protestants were the Waldensians, who maintained the "landmarks" of genuine apostolic Christianity.[126] *Principle of Protestantism* had challenged this account of Christian history, and its advocates attacked it on grounds of "Romanizing." A complaint made its way to the York (Pennsylvania) Synod in October 1845; Schaff and Nevin were exonerated by a vote of thirty-seven to three.[127]

Nevin quickly incorporated Schaff's emphases; in his introduction to the English translation of Schaff's lectures, he said, "Organic . . . implies . . . *development, evolution, progress.*"[128] This was an evolution (!) of Nevin's organicism, which had been a

---

have to respond to such questions: *Weekly Messenger*, September 1, 1847, 2490.

122. David S. Schaff, *Life of Philip Schaff*, 71–72.

123. Penzel, *German Education*, 87–124; Nichols, *Romanticism in American Theology*, 71–74.

124. The lecture was enlarged and translated by Nevin as Schaff, *Principle of Protestantism*. See pp. 36, 49, emphasis original.

125. Billington, *Protestant Crusade*.

126. Thompson and Bricker, editors' preface to *The Principle of Protestantism*, 7–17.

127. David Schaff, *Life of Philip Schaff*, 114–20; Good, *History of the Reformed Church*, 225–30.

128. Schaff, *Principle of Protestantism*, 19; emphasis added. Schaff held a "romantic conception of the church as a social organism" (Nichols, *Romanticism in American Theology*, 67)." The romantic conception in general emphasized "the continuity of life and flow, growth, development"; the German idealism that held this view interpreted reason as the faculty that grasped "the totality of things in their essential interconnectedness" (*Encyclopedia of Philosophy*, 7:206; *Oxford Companion to Philosophy*, 822). Schaff learned from F. H. W. Schelling that history was "ultimately the revelation of God" in which the apparently mundane ebb and flow of history was in truth working toward its necessary goal (Penzel, *German Education*, 117–18). Schelling taught him "that what *Vernunft* [reason], when properly used, perceives is the revelation of God in Christ." "Historical development" therefore results

biological metaphor: the spiritual life of a Christian grew out of Christ's own life, as a plant out of a seed.[129] If we accept the commonplace that Mercersburg Theology began with *Principle of Protestantism*,[130] then it is defined by this synthesis of Nevin's organicism and Schaff's developmentalism. Since Nevin had always attempted to unpack the "germ" of Christian life, it is understandable that under Schaff's influence he then went back to the early church to determine the core "DNA" of Christianity. He commenced with the question, was contemporaneous evangelicalism a repristination of early Christianity?[131] As he went deeper into the texts, continuing with a careful examination of Cyprian's life and writings, the fundamental contradiction became clear: the "ancient church . . . was constitutionally Catholic."[132]

These essays created a firestorm. Nevin and Schaff were again guilty of "Romanizing."[133] Much later, Schaff would attempt to blame Nevin for making a "wrong & reactionary turn with [his] Anglican Crisis & articles on Cyprian, etc."[134] Although Schaff's judgment has been taken at face value, some critical evaluation is needed. Schaff himself acknowledged that Nevin's historical judgments were correct.[135] At the height of the crisis, Emanuel V. Gerhart, president of Heidelberg College (the German Reformed school in Tiffin, Ohio) and professor of theology, confidentially complained that Schaff also—like Nevin—presented "every imaginable difficulty

---

in a "merging of reason with the Christian faith." Penzel observed that this philosophy of history made a "comfortable pillow" for Schaff, from which he felt no need to stir (ibid., 118).

129. The contrast can be seen by comparing Nevin, "Catholic Unity," in Nichols, *The Mercersburg Theology*, 37–38 with "The Church," in ibid., 62. Only in the latter was the organism interpreted in terms of historical development. Nevin's organicism had deep roots in Old School Presbyterianism. In the debate among Nevin, Bushnell, and Hodge on Christian nurture, Hodge said the organismic language used by Bushnell was "as familiar to Presbyterians as household words" (Hodge, "Bushnell on Christian Nurture," 502). This organicism can be traced back to the unity of eucharistic piety and conversionism in the Scottish sacramental fairs (Schmidt, *Holy Fairs*, 49–50; Westerkamp, *Triumph of the Laity*, 29–30, 34). Besides the sermon "Catholic Unity," the mature expression of Nevin's view before he heard Schaff, is the second edition of *Anxious Bench*: "Man *must* be wrought upon by a force, deeper and more comprehensive than his separate self. . . . Religion in this form becomes strictly a life, the life of God in the soul (in *Catholic and Reformed*, 108, 109; repr. Thompson, ed., *The Anxious Bench, Antichrist, and Catholic Unity*, 66, 67). So perhaps his organicism can be best categorized as a religious social psychology, in contrast to a romantic-idealistic view of history. (The presumed conduit of idealism to Nevin was Frederick Rauch's *Psychology*.) "Catholic Unity," *Anxious Bench*, and "The Church" are slated for publication in vol. 5 in MTSS.

130. Good, *History of the Reformed Church*, 423; Appel, *Life and Work*, 250; Schaff, letter to Theodore Appel, February 13, 1889 (The Philip Schaff Papers, Evangelical and Reformed Historical Society, Lancaster, PA [hereafter, "Schaff Papers, ERHS"]).

131. Nevin, "Early Christianity," in *Catholic and Reformed*, 199ff., 207–11.

132. Nevin, "Cyprian"; "Early Christianity," in *Catholic and Reformed*, 309.

133. Standard treatments of the crisis are Good, *History of the Reformed Church*, 271–76, 282–85; Nichols, *Romanticism in American Theology*, 192ff.; Hart, *John Williamson Nevin*, 148–63. See further Payne, "Schaff and Nevin, Colleagues at Mercersburg."

134. Unpublished letter to Theodore Appel, February 13, 1889, Schaff Papers, ERHS. David Schaff located the wrong turn all the way back to *The Mystical Presence* (!) (*Life of Philip Schaff*, 121).

135. Schaff, "German Theology and the Church Question," 140.

against Protestantism," while failing to provide solutions that were "satisfactor[y]" for his readers or students; he *also* was one-sided in describing the "advantages and claims of the R. Cath. Ch."[136] Since Schaff seems to bear at least some of the responsibility, something else was going on when everyone pondered *Nevin's* crisis. It didn't help that Nevin was overworked as president of Marshall College, serving without remuneration, and dealing with a church that failed to provide sufficient support and resources.[137] There is no doubt that he was seriously considering the claims of Rome, but he desperately needed both spiritual and vocational assurance. Since Schaff fingered the "The Anglican Crisis" (of mid-1851), perhaps that is the place to start.[138] In response to the English crown's control of the Church of England, Nevin held that the church's authority was supernatural. A church's claims, rituals, and polity were avowed to be of *divine* origin; and the only way of apprehending them as such was through *faith*. In the case at hand, it was not the state's prerogative to determine the meaning of baptism, since "the measure of the church is its own communion." He was defending the spiritual integrity of a religious community to define itself, its authority, and the meaning of its rites. It would be hard to see this as beginning a move to "Romanizing." But then Nevin went on to point out that here it was the Catholics who were standing up for religious freedom, over against the secularizing claims of the English religious establishment. There was, he mocked, a supreme contradiction of Protestants in Great Britain supporting "royal supremacy in matters of religion against the Catholics, while yet professing to disown it for themselves."[139] Some thought must therefore be given to the possibility that this was Nevin's *real* error in the eyes of the Protestants around him. With a single theological pinprick he had simultaneously punctured two dominating ideas of Protestant piety: that *it* was the bearer of freedom, toleration, and religious independence; and that evangelicals could repudiate *faith* in the *supernatural* signification of the sacraments, and still be *a church*.

What Did Infant Baptism Mean?

Consequently, the debate over baptism was significant to the later period of creativity among the Mercersburg thinkers. Nevin's discussion with Bushnell anticipated an intra-Reformed debate that formed in the middle of the 1850s. In 1857, *Biblical Repertory and Princeton Review* drew attention to "The Neglect of Infant Baptism." The author presented statistics that revealed a catastrophic collapse of infant baptism. At

---

136. Gerhart, unpublished letter to J. H. A. Bomberger, October 14, 1852 (The Emanuel V. Gerhart Papers, Evangelical and Reformed Historical Society, Lancaster, PA [hereafter, "Gerhart Papers, ERHS"]).

137. Hart, *John Williamson Nevin*, 141ff.; Nichols, *Romanticism in American Theology*, 192ff.

138. This essay concerned the "Gorham case," named after an English minister found unsound on baptismal regeneration. He appealed to the Judicial Committee of the Privy Council, a secular body, which found in his favor.

139. Nevin, "The Anglican Crisis," 378, 374, 384; scheduled for vol. 13 of MTSS.

the beginning of the national period (1811), Presbyterians had twenty infant baptisms per one hundred communicants. The year prior to the publication of the essay (1856) that figure was down to 5.1. Dutch Reformed had done marginally better, with a rate of 6.8 in 1856. But among Congregationalists and New School Presbyterians, that year the rate was 1.6 and 2.4 infant baptisms per one hundred communicants, respectively. Paedobaptism appeared to lack the theological will to sustain itself.[140] Could paedobaptism be given a theological justification? Bushnell had already argued for an "educational religion" in which a child simply grew up under the Christian influences of his or her parents (see article 1 in this volume); Nichols described Bushnell as "simply analyzing social psychology"; "baptism was not a sacrament but a rite representing facts and relations which were independently true and effective."[141] Charles Hodge's baptismal theology was "federal": children with at least one Christian parent were already members of the "visible church," and were therefore "within the covenant." Infants were baptized because they were *already* "federally holy," and therefore were to receive the "sign and seal" of that state.[142] As we have seen, federalism was a powerful systematizing principle that linked the elements of human society. It illuminated the social bonds that existed among family, church, and state, and thus revealed the deeper structures of sociality. But that was also its weakness. If an infant was already within the covenant, then why did it need baptism? In that sense, the paedobaptist was theologically no further ahead than the Baptist: in both cases baptism simply ratified a state or relation that already existed. As Emanuel Gerhart argued in his analysis of the Presbyterian arguments in the 1850s, they implied that infants were members of the invisible church through *natural* birth, not through baptism.[143] In other words, federalism seemed to reduce the supernatural state or conditions formed through churchly praxis to natural human relations—which was exactly Nevin's critique of Bushnell a decade earlier.

To be sure, Calvinists attempted to maintain the supernatural ground of Christian piety. A year before Gerhart's essay, Nevin responded to Hodge's *Commentary on the Epistle to the Ephesians*. He began by critiquing "Arminianism" as being unable to account for the church as invested with supernatural power and creating in its participants new spiritual life. But then, he said, Hodge's Calvinistic reading went to the other extreme, by reducing God's action to an absolute decree of election. It was supernatural indeed, but separated from lived religious experience. If Arminian conversionism was simply the natural dynamics of religious experience, Hodge's

---

140. "Neglect of Infant Baptism," 73–101 [no author identified, but presumed to be Charles Hodge]; Emanuel Gerhart responded to it in art. 5, below. The present discussion is based on the summary in Nichols, *Romanticism in American Theology*, 238–39; however, the editor has corrected some of the numbers with data from "Neglect," 82–84, 90, for consistency.

141. Nichols, *Romanticism in American Theology*, 242, 243.

142. Hodge, "Neglect of Infant Baptism," 76–77.

143. "The Efficacy of Baptism," art. 5 below.

Calvinism was "mechanical," that is, it had no *living* power to bring about its end.[144] Christ was not needed in Hodge's system, except in an "external" way, to accomplish the election God had already decreed.[145] Therefore, federalism also found it difficult to explain the power of baptism. The elect were saved through a supernatural process that had already taken place in the mind of God. Baptism didn't "do" anything to further that process along, except that an infant was "federally holy," incorporated by covenant through his presumptively[146] Christian parents into the church. It did nothing to change federal holiness into actual holiness. In contrast, Nevin insisted that there needed to be living (*organic*) reality, in and through which the promises made in divine election were realized.[147] Baptism, then, was a necessary initiation that brought a person (infant or adult) from the world into the new, supernatural body of the church. The grace it claimed as being present in its life was first enacted in its initiatory rite.

Biblicism and Premillennial Adventism

Beneath both questions of ecclesiology and baptism were questions of authority. Protestants of course have always been committed to *sola scriptura*: "Scripture was the sole necessary and sufficient source of Christian theology." However, the Reformers were always careful to bind the Bible to "the context of the historical continuity of the Christian church."[148] Even mid-eighteenth-century revivalists continued to recognize the need for a trained ministry to properly interpret the Bible. Ironically, at first Biblicism emerged among the antirevivalist liberals, who claimed the right to interpret the Bible apart from all theological systems or ecclesiastical authorities. But the "democratization" generated by Arminian revivalism resulted in the adoption of Biblicism by ordinary Christians. One could say the idea "mutated." American evangelicals asserted the "right of private judgment": every man (and woman) had both the power and the right to read and interpret the Bible for him- (her-) self. This Biblicism gave "certainty" in a time of "sectarian confusion," it justified and motivated "common people to open the Bible and think for themselves," and (in so doing) "freed people from staid ecclesiastical establishments."[149]

In retrospect, it is easy to be sympathetic to the democratic masses. They were in a new land, and it was not clear why the traditional establishments and confessions should have held their allegiance. Their Protestant past gave them an inherited

---

144. Nevin, "Hodge on the Ephesians," 59–62.
145. Ibid., 224, 229, 231.
146. See art. 5 below on the issue of "presumptively."
147. Nevin, "Hodge on the Ephesians," 243.
148. McGrath, *Christian Theology*, 66, 188. For a more detailed analysis of the reformers, see Gerrish, "Word of God," 51–68.
149. Hatch, *Democratization of American Christianity*, 179–83.

authoritative text; their Biblicism authorized them to interpret it in accordance with their democratic polity.[150] Furthermore, for the remainder of the century, all the religious vitality would be on their side. Lastly, it is easy to pick at the apparent contradictions of the Reformers: they insisted on the primacy of the "literal" or "historical" meaning of Scripture; yet Luther held the infamous "canon within a canon," and Calvin (as we have seen) read the new covenant back into the old.[151] Calvin might have found grounds for infant baptism in the Abrahamic covenant, but it was equally clear to Baptists —on a *literal* reading—that it simply wasn't there. Against the alleged oppression of Romanism, the Reformers had claimed the right of individual, reasoned interpretation of Scripture. Now that their confessional inheritors had become the putative oppressors, it was inevitable that the two-edged sword would be turned against them.

That did not keep Nevin from savaging the apparent duplicity of appeals to private judgment. Nevin addressed its advocates as "sectarians," who on the basis of "private judgment" claimed the right to set up any new religious community that might have come to an enthusiast's mind. They might have argued most energetically that one needed to have faith in the Bible, but they could not summon up equal faith in "the fact of Christianity itself, as a divine supernatural reality, subsisting in the life of the Church through all ages."[152] There was, Nevin thought, a spiritual living reality traceable through history, one with a concrete, corporate identity. In spite of their ostentatious assertion of spiritual freedom, sectarians gave backhanded acknowledgment of churchly authority, through the assertions of their own rule over the lives of their adherents. But such authority was a "miserable fragment" of true Christianity catholicity, and "while it professes to make men free, it teaches them to become slaves" to its particular hobbyhorses.[153]

Twenty-five years later, Nevin was facing a very different religious world. The democratized revivalism that had smashed the old religious establishments was now itself the establishment. American Protestantism was identified with the kingdom of God, and (what would now be called) parachurch ministries sought to spread this kingdom throughout the world, even as they sought to transform public life by the moral norms of Protestant culture. Nevin's sectarians *were* the church, whose catholicity was manifested in the common American religious life. Its foundation was the Bible, interpreted by the "common sense" available to all, energized by revivalist piety, which had become increasingly domesticated by 1870. The embodiment of this new

---

150. According to "rational choice" sociology, when people convert they attempt to hold on to as much of their religious past as is consistent with their new social ties: Stark, *Triumph of Christianity*, 74–75.

151. Gerrish, "Word of God," esp. 57, 61, 64, on the literal meaning.

152. Nevin, *Antichrist*, repr. in Thompson, ed., *The Anxious Bench, Antichrist, and Catholic Unity*, 45.

153. Ibid., 44 note; Nevin, "The Sect System," 143–44.

revivalism was Dwight L. Moody, who appeared as a modern businessman, carrying out revivalism with businesslike efficiency. His primary appeal was to the new sentimentalities of the middle class, which were the old securities of mother, home, and pious small-town American life.[154] While Moody had a conservative version of American progress, there was a liberal view developing at the same time. In 1886, the very year of Nevin's death, Andover Theological Seminary published *Progressive Orthodoxy*, which endorsed evolutionary and developmental views of Christian history and theology. This "New Theology" came to believe that the supernatural life of Christianity was experienced through natural human progress. Nevin had been outflanked on both left and right: the liberals accepted Mercersburg's affirmation of historical development, but thereby collapsed the supernatural into natural human culture; the revivalists had created their own catholic consensus of biblical literalism and moralizing sentimentalism.[155]

Both the revivalists and the liberals were moralizing and sentimental. But one issue separated them: the future. Liberals were enamored with the new evolutionary model. The kingdom of God was at hand, to be revealed through the upward trajectory of human history and culture. This confidence had evolved out of the dominant eschatological theory of antebellum Protestantism. The majority opinion had been that the American experiment was one of the signs of the impending kingdom. The church-in-America would bring about the "millennium." This belief was therefore known as "postmillennialism," since it held that Christ's return and the consummation would come *after* the millennium.[156]

However, among the theological conservatives, this optimistic reading was supplanted by claims that Christ, not the church, would bring about the millennial transformation. The new interpretation synthesized ancient Christian chiliasm, the Puritan belief that the ancient Hebrew prophecies were being realized in America, the biblical literalism fostered by evangelical "commonsense" hermeneutics, and a more negative perspective on the American future after the Civil War. The new eschatology was dubbed "premillennialism": the advent of Christ would occur *before* the millennium, and his supernatural power would create the one-thousand-year reign.[157] This view will be represented in article 7, where Nevin restates and critiques the hermeneutical assumptions of a Prophetic Conference of 1878 in New York City.[158] Since the rise of Biblicism at the beginning of the century, evangelicals had insisted

---

154. Albanese, *Americans*, 157.

155. Marsden, *Fundamentalism and American Culture*, 11–39. For Moody as businessman, see p. 31; on the rise of "New Theology," see pp. 25–26.

156. Ibid., 48–50.

157. Ibid., 51ff.

158. "The Prophetic Conference: New York, October 30, 31, November 1, 1878: Christ's Second Coming," *New York Tribune*, Extra No. 46.

on the transparency of the meaning of Holy Writ.[159] The speakers at the conference affirmed that the New Testament clearly taught Christ's "appearing" as a "personal and imminent event." It was the common expectation of early Christians based on a literal interpretation of the New Testament, until it was supplanted with allegorical interpretation.[160] Nevin responded that the meaning of the Bible was not natural, but supernatural. It was not known through human reason, but the same Holy Spirit that inspired the original likewise spoke in and through it in the present. Scripture, like baptism and Eucharist, had to be filled with a "mystical presence," a supernatural power known to faith. Christ needed to be "the Inspiration of his own Word," as Nevin entitled his penultimate essay. As he had done his entire theological career, Nevin here dismissed two sides of what he regarded as a false antinomy: "verbalism" (think the evangelical concept of "verbal inerrancy") and "realism," which viewed Scripture as any other text. "At best" these two theories only provide a "natural inspiration," "a providential leading of ordinary human thought and speech." Rather, what was required was "the actual descent of the Divine itself into such human thought and speech."[161] Ironically, the anti-Mercersburg historian James I. Good grasped the continuities within Nevin better than some modern historians: "one thing he clung to in it all [his historical development], and that was the supernatural, both in the Bible and in the sacraments. . . . He was a speculative mystic at first, but later his mysticism overcame his speculativeness and he rested in simple faith in God's Word."[162]

Nevin, Schaff, Gerhart: Beyond Mercersburg

With the essay by Emanuel V. Gerhart (1858), we are beginning to move toward the end of the constructive energy of Mercersburg Theology. Nevin had resigned his presidency of Marshall College in 1853, and moved from the town of Mercersburg in 1854. His final task had been the merger of Marshall with Franklin College in Lancaster, Pennsylvania; the united school was opened in Lancaster in the spring of 1853.[163] At the same time Schaff had taken a long trip to Europe, during which time the seminary closed its doors. He returned in November of 1854, in time to attend the inauguration of Bernard C. Wolff as his colleague at the seminary (still at Mercersburg) while

---

159. For the role of commonsense realism ("Baconianism") in providing the hermeneutical foundation to prophetic literalism, see Marsden, *Fundamentalism and American Culture*, 55ff.

160. "The Prophetic Conference," 3, 7. "Personal" was opposed to a metaphorical reading of the consummation; "imminent" meant it could happen at any time (rather than occurring *after* the millennium).

161. Nevin, "Christ the Inspiration of His Own Word," 38–39. See also Nevin, "Sacred Hermeneutics": "The sense of God's Word must proceed from the Word itself" (7). For a modern interpretation of how such a hermeneutics might have worked, see DiPuccio, *Interior Sense of Scripture*, 87–102.

162. Good, *History of the Reformed Church*, 599.

163. Appel, *Life and Work*, 432–43; Hart, *John Williamson Nevin*, 178–79.

Nevin eventually located in Lancaster City in 1858.¹⁶⁴ The physical and institutional distance between the erstwhile colleagues may have contributed to some estrangement, since Schaff would later say, "I believed he cooled down towards me after I left for New York [in 1864], or *perhaps after his resignation in 1853.*"¹⁶⁵ There are signs that Nevin's allegiance to Schaff's theory of "historical development" was not as firm or close as generally portrayed. At the end of "Early Christianity," he surveyed some theories of historical development, beginning with Schaff's, without committing himself to any of them. Moreover, at the end of "Cyprian," if an interlocutor were to ask "what precise construction *we* propose to apply to subject, we have only to say that we have none to offer whatever.... We have had no theory to assert or uphold."¹⁶⁶ Eighteen months later, at the end of "Wilberforce on the Eucharist," (article 4 below), he defended Calvin's distinct eucharistic theory as the only alternative to the theory of the Roman Catholic Church, leaving open the possibility that the "outward diversity" of the doctrine could "resolve itself fairly into the laws of historical development and growth." "Growth" probably signaled that he was beginning to move back toward his own native organismic metaphor of biological change. Nevin's abandonment of Schaff's theory was complete twenty years after that essay, when he dismissed "development" as a "treacherous amphibological term," and suggested it be replaced with "historical movement."¹⁶⁷ With that, he had returned to his pre-Schaffian concept of history as simply *change.* Schaff meanwhile stayed at Mercersburg until 1863, when he moved to New York City, and beyond the range of the German Reformed Church. (The seminary would finally move to Lancaster, across from the college, in 1871.) Nevin's extended sabbatical had been sufficiently recuperative so that he could return to part-time teaching at Franklin and Marshall in 1861; after more difficulty at the college, he resumed the reins as president in 1866, to finally retire in 1876.¹⁶⁸

That leaves us to examine the return of Emanuel Gerhart to the Mercersburg orbit. Gerhart had been educated at Marshall College and Mercersburg Theological Seminary. Although his studies overlapped Nevin's teaching for a year, it was "Rauch who was his first leading preceptor" and introduced him to "an intimate acquaintance with the best elements of German philosophy and theology."¹⁶⁹ Nevin, who is described as his "friend," presided at his wedding. His first pastorate was in Gettysburg, Pennsylvania, in 1843, until he began mission work in Cincinnati in 1849. Soon after, Gerhart was asked to lead the new Heidelberg College in Tiffin, Ohio.¹⁷⁰ While

---

164. Appel, *Life and Work,* 443–44; Hart, *John Williamson Nevin,* 173–74.
165. Letter to Theodore Appel, February 13, 1889; emphasis added (Schaff Papers, ERHS).
166. Nevin, "Early Christianity," in *Catholic and Reformed,* 291–97 (overview of theories), 305 (three alternatives); "Cyprian," 562–63.
167. Nevin, "Reply to 'An Anglican Catholic,'" 421.
168. Appel, *Life and Work,* 590, 628–33, 741; Hart, *John Williamson Nevin,* 181–84, 225.
169. Apple, "Crown of Dr. Gerhart's Life," 2.
170. Yrigoyen, "Emanuel V. Gerhart: Apologist for the Mercersburg Theology," 485–500.

there, he became convinced that both Schaff and Nevin had abandoned Protestantism.[171] But by 1855, he was back east as president of Franklin and Marshall. In 1868, he moved to Mercersburg to take up the presidency and professorship of systematic theology; he served the seminary until his death in 1904.[172] He went on to write *Institutes of the Christian Religion*, the only systematic theology from a Mercersburgian point of view.[173] Is it correct to say, as one interpreter did, that Gerhart was a "leopard which definitely changed its spots"?[174] At the beginning of Nevin and Schaff's collaboration, this "native son" of the German Reformed Church expressed uncertainty about elements of their theology. Although he thought he agreed with them in broad and general terms, he couldn't accept their "expressions" "precisely." Eighteen months later, he had "difficulties" with the theme of Nevin's (recently published) *The Mystical Presence*, but admitted his view had "materially changed" (presumably in the direction of greater agreement with Nevin).[175] As the crisis developed, he became more and more distressed. He "never did approve of" Nevin's "indefiniteness and obscurity, and his magisterial and denunciatory spirit." Gerhart recognized that Nevin's enemies shared the blame, but Nevin's "*own* reprehensible manner" caused them to respond in a "dog eat dog" fashion.[176]

At the height of the crisis in October 1852, in the midst of his harshest critiques of the two professors, he was still able to affirm that there was "more energy, spirit and life, more hearty and earnest cooperation in our church, [?], than I have ever seen. This argues an actual advance, brought about by the activity and zeal of the ministers educated in our Sem'y, & in great measure by the earlier writings of Dr. N."[177] And what was that work of Nevin that Gerhart was affirming? Most certainly Nevin's studies of the Heidelberg Catechism:[178] "the time has come when *you* & others should take up the pen *against* these Romish innovations, and in favor of the *Ref'd* character of the Ref'd Ch. and of the Heid. Cat."[179] A year later he assured J. H. A. Bomberger that

---

171. Gerhart, unpublished letter to J. H. A. Bomberger, October 14, 1852 (Gerhart Papers, ERHS).

172. *Franklin and Marshall College Obituary Record*, 2:97–102. His election took place in July 1854, and he accepted it on September 30 while still in Tiffin; but he does not seem to have moved until the following year.

173. Apple, "Crown of Dr. Gerhart's Life," 2.

174. Maxwell, *Worship and Reformed Theology*, 153. See further Yrigoyen, "Emanuel V. Gerhart: Apologist," 494–97 on the question of change in Gerhart's theology. Yrigoyen gave more extensive quotations from Gerhart's letters, although this editor's transcription and interpretation has been done independently.

175. Gerhart to J. H. A. Bomberger, December 31, 1845, and May 2, 1847 (Gerhart Papers, ERHS).

176. Gerhart to J. H. A. Bomberger, January 17, 1852 (Gerhart Papers, ERHS); emphasis original.

177. Gerhart to J. H. A. Bomberger, October 14, 1852 (Gerhart Papers, ERHS). The uncertain word is most likely "last" or "least" —perhaps he meant to say "at last," i.e., "finally."

178. Further confirmation of this reading can be found in DeBie, "First Signs of Contention," 13–14: "Gerhart praised the efforts of Mercersburg Theology in aiding the denomination in its renewed interest in the [Heidelberg] Catechism and the benefits that followed from that interest."

179. Gerhart to J. H. A. Bomberger, October 14, 1852 (Gerhart Papers, ERHS); emphases original;

my system of philosophizing and my Theology are more *churchly* than they have been at any time, and I must sympathize heartily with all the general principles of what may properly called Mercersburg Theology, yet I see so much on both sides, that I consider very wrong and unchristian, that I am utterly unwilling to take sides with either party as regards the course of conduct pursued during the last six or eight months.[180]

The editor therefore concludes that Gerhart believed he held to the fundamental "churchly" position of Mercersburg Theology. Through the crisis, he became "more hostile now than ever to what is termed New England Theology and the disorganizing radicalism of the age, and on the other [sic] my attachment increases to the old sound views of the church, its sacraments and its cultus."[181] He opposed the harsh polemicizing and could not justify Schaff's and Nevin's apparent willingness to defend "Romish innovations" with greater zeal and insight than they applied to confessional Protestantism. He was committed to the Heidelberg Catechism, which Nevin had expounded and defended in the 1840s. In other words, Gerhart was indebted to Nevin's work *as it had been presented apart from the influence of Schaff*. The resolution came as Nevin avoided the type of historical research carried out in "Early Christianity" and "Cyprian" and separated himself from Schaff's intellectual influence. Gradually, his psychospiritual crisis passed and he reidentified with Protestantism. The fears of Romanizing eased, and Gerhart saw his way clear to reaffirm the Mercersburg tradition as it had matured in the German Reformed Church.

---

he also urged "firm adherence to the Heid. Cat." (Gerhart to J. H. A. Bomberger, July 20, 1853 [Gerhart Papers, ERHS]). It was Schaff who had introduced the idea that the Roman Church was a source of theological truth. Nevin then misapplied Schaff's analysis. The editor wishes to emphasize that he blames neither Nevin nor Schaff. The problem arose when Nevin attempted to appropriate a method that was not congenial to his theological presuppositions.

180. Gerhart to J. H. A. Bomberger, October 21, 1853 (Gerhart Papers, ERHS); emphasis original.
181. Gerhart to J. H. A. Bomberger, July 20, 1853 (Gerhart Papers, ERHS).

Article 1

"Nevin and Bushnell: Christian Nurture and Baptism"

(By John W. Nevin)

Editor's Introduction

While Nevin was taking the theological journey described in the introduction, Horace Bushnell was attempting to refine his ministry in North Church of Hartford, Connecticut. Bushnell and Nevin were close contemporaries, since the former was born in 1802. Both his parents had inherited enterprises in the textile industry, and Bushnell worked in "the mill" from the age of fourteen onward. His father was Methodist and his mother Episcopalian. When they moved to New Preston in 1805, the only church in town was Congregational; their religion seemed more a matter of respectability than confessional commitment. Bushnell went to Yale in 1823, but seems to have lost his faith.[1]

As a result, after college he tried teaching and journalism, and finally returned to Yale to study law. He was appointed a tutor; his responsibilities included taking turns leading daily prayers in the chapel. Although he did so, his lack of religious certainty made him question his role as a religious leader. When revival came to Yale in 1831, Bushnell and his charges "stood unmoved apparently when all beside were in a glow." Bushnell resolved to meet with his students, acknowledge his spiritual situation, and challenge them to make a choice. According to a fellow tutor, the room became a "Bochim, a place of weeping." This mysterious event simulated the conversion experience conventional in "new measures" revivalism. Bushnell acknowledged that it might be viewed by some as "a conversion by the want of truth more than by the power of truth." He had not resolved his intellectual doubts of God's existence; however, he *could* "tak[e] the principle of right for [his] . . . law." He prayed "to the dim God, dimly felt, confessing the dimness for honesty's sake, and asking for help that he may begin

---

1. Cheney, *Life and Letters*, 32, 53.

a right life." *Bushnell was doing the right thing*—by his childhood religion, in the eyes of his fellow tutors, and by his students.[2]

Now that Bushnell had the requisite religious experience, he was ready to pursue the clerical career his mother had always desired for him. The same year, he entered Yale Divinity School; after graduation, he received a temporary position at the North Church in Hartford. Many of its parishioners had left First Church, where the minister was a revivalist and held to traditional Puritan doctrine.[3] By the time Bushnell arrived, the North Church was caught up in the "Tyler-Taylor controversy"; Bushnell's future depended on finding a language that both sides could recognize.[4] He obviously succeeded. It seems likely that he did so because his own religious psychology was a perfect fit for the congregation: besides the general discomfort with revivalism, Bushnell saw it as "fastidious, wary of religious extravagance, consciously proper. . . . 'Moral, honorable . . . beneficient and habitually reverent . . .'"[5] For both Bushnell and the congregation, religion had more to do with social responsibility and propriety than it did with religious experience.

However, one doctrine encumbered Bushnell's confidence from the beginning: infant baptism. At his ordination examination, the elders were not satisfied with his explanation.[6] Bushnell attempted to rectify this shortcoming with a series of writings on "Christian training"; he was asked to rewrite and publish this material: it first appeared in 1847 as *Discourses on Christian Nurture*.[7] Among the respondents was Nevin; his four-part essay, published in the *Weekly Messenger of the German Reformed Church*, forms a substantial part of this article. However, Bushnell's "educational religion" really did go against the grain of New England orthodoxy. Bennet Tyler (of the Tyler-Taylor controversy) published an open letter to Bushnell. His central concern was that the argument would "lead people to flatter themselves that they are Christians, while they are strangers to genuine piety."[8] If conversion was a gradual trans-

---

2. Ibid., 55–56, 58–59. "Bochim" alludes to Judges 2:1–5, where the Israelites wept at their failure to fully expel the pagan peoples. Bushnell's description comes from a sermon, "The Dissolving of Doubts," which interpreters take as his recollection of this conversion: Edwards, *Of Singular Genius*, 31–33; Dorrien, *Making of American Liberal Theology*, 112–13.

3. Cross, *Horace Bushnell*, 43.

4. Smith, introduction to *Horace Bushnell: Selected Writings*, 11–13. Bennet Tyler's position on original sin was orthodox, while Nathaniel Taylor said that sin was in the act of sinning. Both were conversionists, but while Tyler held the older view that conversion was a direct act of God, Taylor shared the Finneyite belief that conversion was within the power of human choice. See Edwards, *Of Singular Genius*, 44, 47.

5. Cross, *Horace Bushnell*, 46–47.

6. Bushnell, *Argument for "Discourses on Christian Nurture,"* 24; repr. in *Views of Christian Nurture*, 85. Hereafter this particular edition of the text will be cited in the form *Argument for "Discourses,"* x/y. See further Cheney, *Life and Letters*, 283–84, and Edwards, *Of Singular Genius*, 44–45, 85.

7. Bushnell, *Discourses on Christian Nurture*.

8. Tyler, *Dr. Tyler's Letter to Dr. Bushnell on Christian Nurture*, 1; available at http://place.asburyseminary.edu/ecommonsatsdigitalresources/124/# . Tyler held to the traditional Puritan doctrine of human depravity, and the need for spiritual regeneration through the Holy Spirit (4–6).

formation that arose out of the normal patterns of family nurture, then how was one to know if one was truly a Christian? As a result of the controversy, the publisher, the Massachusetts Sabbath School Society, limited sales of *Discourses* to individual buyers; Bushnell responded with *An Argument for "Discourses on Christian Nurture."* This included particular attention to Nevin's essays;[9] Nevin responded with "Dr. Bushnell and Puritanism," the final component of the present article. The reaction of the society was to stop all distribution and return publication rights to Bushnell. So he combined *Discourses on Christian Nurture*, a revised version of *An Argument for "Discourses on Christian Nurture,"* and other material, into a new volume: *Views of Christian Nurture, and of Subjects Adjacent Thereto*.[10]

Bushnell's central thesis was that "the child is to grow up a christian." In contrast to the Puritan belief that the child was a sinner, and thus needed to experience "conversion," the child ought to perceive that he or she had always desired goodness. Nevin couldn't understand how Bushnell would have thought this position consistent with Puritan theology. In Essay 2, Nevin began to analyze the reasons for the confusion. Puritanism recognized that the Christian life required a supernatural transformation, a "new creation." Nevin agreed with Puritanism on this point. However, Puritanism had interpreted this "new creation" individualistically, and therefore magically. A person was "converted" through a sudden event that broke the connection with ordinary life. Here Nevin agreed with Bushnell: authentic religion was not simply a single person's experience or belief; it occurred in a community, and flowed "naturally" out of the life of that community.

Essay 3 began to crack the nut of Nevin's disagreement. Christianity was both supernatural and natural. It was connected to the elements of human experience, yet was also a new reality. He reaffirmed Bushnell's critique of revivalism, but he also (with Puritanism) thought "nature" to be "depraved," and therefore requiring a *supernatural renovation. Bushnell's reinterpretation of the Puritan doctrine of human depravity implied that an infant did not inherit original *sin*, but a flawed spiritual constitution. Thus, as with Nathaniel Taylor, the child was not blamed until he or she sinned. Therefore, Bushnell thought, a child *could* be nurtured in such a way as to do good in the very first moral act. Nevin responded that this made regeneration to be a natural human process of education: the child was gradually shaped to be good, and he further argued that it confused "principle" and "condition." For Nevin, there were two contrasting "principles," or constitutions: fallen humanity, and the new Christian life. The nurture by the Christian parent was merely a "condition"—essential, like rain is to a plant—but not the "principle" of life. The principle of Christianity was found in the church, and not in natural human nurture. It appeared to Nevin that Bushnell based infant baptism on the ordinary connection of parent and child. The parents' faith motivated them to nurture the child in a Christian manner, and baptism

---

9. *Argument for "Discourses,"* 33–38/100–109.
10. The story of the three texts is told in Edwards, *Of Singular Genius*, 87–92.

signified the "presumption" that parental faith would, in the educational process, be communicated to the child. So Nevin turned the argument of the "mechanical" connection between faith and baptism, previously used against Puritanism, on Bushnell. For Bushnell, there was no *organic* connection between baptism and Christian growth. Christian nurture could happen with or without baptism. In contrast, Nevin tied the spiritual growth to the grace present in baptism itself. Thus the church was integral in Nevin's view to an extent lacking in Bushnell, and it was the church that was the embodied expression of the supernatural constitution of new life in Christ.

Nevin's final entry did little to advance the argument; he was rather concerned with the ecclesiastical politics evidenced in the debate. It would contribute more to the analysis to summarize Bushnell's further response to Nevin, as stated in *Argument for "Discourses on Christian Nurture."* He imagined that Nevin and he agreed on the meaning of organic. However, for Bushnell, the antonym of "organic" was "individual"; he thought that the passive/active distinction less fully made the same point: the will of the parents, presumably guided by the Holy Spirit, *acted upon* the child, who received this spiritual influence *passively* (= "organically").[11] In contrast, Nevin meant more by "organic" than "communal"; it also meant "historical," "natural," "spontaneous," and (most importantly) "living." Secondly, Nevin thought that the organic connection came through the church, not the natural family. Bushnell acknowledged that he probably could not accept what Nevin said about the church and the sacramental grace of baptism;[12] but he seemed to have convinced himself that Nevin's supernaturalism could be best understood as communicated through familial nurture. In contrast, Nevin first and last was making an argument from the spiritual priority of the *church*, not of the family. Bushnell and Nevin exaggerated their similarities and (especially Bushnell) obscured their differences.

Bushnell also responded to Nevin's distinction of "principle" and "conditions." He thought that "organic laws . . . are only *occasional conditions* under which depravity and spiritual life are developed," and behind those conditions were *principles*, which could be either evil or good. Assuming this reading, Bushnell answered that the principle was not evil or good, but simply the soul itself.[13] Here he was working out of a commonsense realism that held the soul to be a substance, a concrete thing to which different states of consciousness could adhere. In contrast, Nevin was by now an idealist, and held that organic laws were themselves principles, with power to actualize themselves. Further, Nevin viewed the soul, not as a principle, but a substratum into which the principle—whether the old life of flesh, or the new life of Christ's life—was placed.[14] It is not surprising that Nevin concluded that Bushnell was simply another manifestation of decadent Puritan "rationalistic supernaturalism."

11. Bushnell, *Argument for "Discourses,"* 32/98; see also 36/104: "remedy for individualism."
12. Ibid., 34/101–2.
13. Ibid., 37/106, emphasis original.
14. See, e.g., Nevin, *The Anxious Bench* in *Catholic and Reformed*, 107; "Catholic Unity," in Nichols,

"Educational Religion"[1]: Discourses on Christian Nurture

By Horace Bushnell; Pastor of the North Church, Hartford.[2]

A respected young brother[3] in the ministry has done me the favor lately of placing a copy of this little pamphlet in my hands, with the request that I would give my thoughts upon it in the way at least of a general review.

The pamphlet itself is well entitled to such notice, on various accounts. Its subject is one of the very highest importance; closely related to the central question of the times, the true nature of the Christian Church; and of the radical, vital bearing on all that is practical in the idea of religion. Its author is one of the most distinguished preachers of New England. The tract is written with great originality and force, and has been favorably noticed, so far as I have seen, by the common evangelical press. It carries of course a popular character, and has been published, in fact, by the "Massachusetts Sabbath School Society," for the use particularly of families. It contains much most valuable truth, especially needful to be enforced upon the attention of the Church at this time; and may be regarded as a most respectable and salutary protest against one of the worst forms of error with which our modern Protestant Christianity is called to contend. The tract is at bottom contrary to the whole Puritan theory of religion; and yet, strange to say, the author is himself a Puritan and fails at last to make any real and full escape from the power of his own system. His tract might seem to be in one view, a plea for the Church against the reigning individualism of the age; and yet it is found to be itself radically unchurchly throughout. All the more instructive to a thoughtful mind however, may we not say, on this very account! Altogether, it well deserves attention.

The general object of the tract is presented in its answer to the question, "What is the true idea of christian education?" The answer is embraced in the proposition:

---

ed., *Mercersburg Theology*, 37–38.

1. [*Weekly Messenger of the German Reformed Church*, n.s., 12, no. 41 (June 23, 1847) 2450.]
2. [Bushnell, *Discourses on Christian Nurture*. This edition is available on Google Books.]
3. [According to Nichols, *Romanticism in American Theology*, 240, this was Henry Harbaugh.]

> *That the child is to grow up a christian.* In other words, the aim, effort and expectation should be, not as is commonly assumed, that the child is to grow up in sin to be converted after he comes to a mature age, but that he is to open on the world as one that is spiritually renewed, not remembering the time when he went through a technical experience, but seeming rather to have loved what is good from his earliest years.[4]

This proposition it is attempted to establish by various considerations; drawn partly from what may be called the human side of the subject, and partly from the position in which it is placed by the divine will as expressed, in various ways, through the gospel itself.

The considerations of the first class brought forward are: 1. That there is "no absurdity in supposing that children are to grow up in Christ": but a "very clear, moral incongruity" rather, "in setting up a contrary supposition, to be the aim of a system of Christian education."[5] It is unnatural in the highest degree to think that a christian parent can be at all at liberty to train up his child in the service of the devil; and yet he must propose nothing less than this if he may not seriously believe that it is possible to bring him up as a christian and make it his aim accordingly to do so from the very start.

2. "It is to be expected that christian education will radically differ from that which is not christian."[6] This last, as all know, brings up the child as a sinner only, whose only hope at best is in future conversion. Are christian parents to aim at nothing more? Or does the difference come only to this, that they are to teach their children biblical facts and doctrines, the knowledge of which is hoped may facilitate their conversion at some later day? But if they are left to grow up with the impression that all this cannot be expected to produce any fruit till they are come to a mature age, and that they are in the mean time to have no other character than children have, without such instruction, what purpose can it serve, save to enforce the practical rejection of all the lessons they are taught? Must they be piously brought up, by the very nature of the case, to a state of impenitency, which is only made worse by the many privileges and opportunities they are thus permitted and doomed to abuse?

3. "All Christian parents would like to see their children grow up in piety, and the better Christians they are, the more earnestly they desire it; and the more lovely and constant the christian spirit is, the more likely is it in general, that their children will early display the christian character."[7]

---

4. [Bushnell, *Discourses on Christian Nurture*, 6–7.]

5. [Ibid., 12. Nevin (or the printer) frequently (but not always) failed to supply quotation marks where proper attribution would require them. The editor has supplied the quotation marks where needed.]

6. [Ibid., 15.]

7. [Ibid., 18–19.]

4. "Assuming the corruption of human nature, when should we think it wisest to undertake or expect a remedy?"[8] Growth in years only adds strength to the power of sin and diminishes the susceptibility of the soul to good impressions. Infancy and childhood are the ages most pliant to good, most full of promise for virtue and piety.

5. "It is implied in all our religious philosophy, that if a child does anything in a right spirit, even loves anything because it is good and right, it involves the dawn of new life." "Is it then incredible that some really good feeling should be called into exercise in a child?" Must we hold the counsel absurd: "Children, obey your parents in the Lord, for this is right"?[9]

6. "Children have been so trained as never to remember the time when they began to be religious. Baxter was at one time much troubled, because he could recollect no time when there was a gracious change in his character. But he discovered, at length, that 'education is as properly a means of grace as preaching,'[10] and thus found a sweeter comfort in his love to God, that he had learned to love him so early."[11]

7. "Once more, if we narrowly examine the relation of parent and child, we shall not fail to discover something like a law of organic connection, as regards character, subsisting between them; such a connection in fact, as makes it easy to believe, and natural to expect, that the faith of the one will be propagated in the other."[12]

"Such are some of the considerations," according to the tract, "that offer themselves, viewing our subject on the human side, or as it appears in the light of human evidence all concurring to produce the conviction, that it is the only true idea of christian education, that the child is to grow up in the life of the parent, and be a Christian, in principle, from his earliest years."[13]

A view is next taken of the light in which the subject is placed, by the revelation which God has made of his character and will in the gospel.

---

8. [Ibid., 19.]

9. [Ibid., 23.]

10. [Richard Baxter (1615–1691) was a Puritan divine who was a vigorous defender of paedobaptism; his writings were characterized by "deep unaffected piety and . . . a love of moderation" (*Oxford Dictionary of the Christian Church*, 172). The purported quote by Bushnell of Baxter was probably a paraphrase of Matthew Sylvester, ed., *Reliquiae Baxterianae*:

> My next Doubt [of salvation] was, lest *Education* and *Fear* had done all that ever was done upon my Soul, and *Regeneration* and *Love* were yet to seek; because I had found Convictions from my Childhood, and found more *Fear* than *Love* in all my *Duties* and *Restraints*.

> But I afterwards perceived that *Education* is God's ordinary way for the Conveyance of his Grace, and ought no more to be set in opposition to the Spirit, than the preaching of the Word; and that it was the great Mercy of God to begin with me so soon. (6–7)

Nevin ended *The Anxious Bench* (1844 ed.) with a description of Baxter's work and ministry, presenting it as a model of the "system of the catechism," in opposition to the "system" of the "the anxious bench" (*Anxious Bench*, in *Catholic and Reformed*, 121–26).]

11. [Bushnell, *Discourses*, 24–25.]

12. [Ibid., 26. Where Nevin placed the semicolon, Bushnell had a period.]

13. [Ibid., 33.]

1. "According to all God has taught us concerning his own dispositions, he desires, on his part, that children should grow up in piety, as earnestly as the parent can desire it; nay, as much more earnestly, as he hates sin more intensely and desires good with less mixture of qualification."[14]

2. "If there be any such thing as christian nurture, distinguished from that which is not christian, as is generally admitted, as the scriptures clearly assert, then is it some kind of nurture which God appoints." And can it "accord with the character of God, to appoint a scheme of education, the only proper result of which shall be that children are trained up under it in sin?"[15] Or would it be less absurd, to suppose church education appointed of God to produce, first a harvest of sin, and a harvest of holiness?

3. God "expressly" lays "it upon us to expect that our children will grow up in piety, under the parental nurture, and assumes the possibility that such a result may ordinarily be realized. '*Train up your child*'—how? for future conversion?" Not so, but—"'*in the way he should go*, that when he is old he may not depart from it.'" So in the New Testament: "'Bring them up *in the nurture and admonition of the Lord*.'"[16] A nurture to holiness, not sin.

4. "A time is foretold, as our churches generally believe, when all shall know God, even from the least to the greatest." "Then at least children will grow up in Christ." Can this time "come too soon"?[17] Do we believe that it can come at all?

5. "We discover in the scriptures that the organic law already spoken of, is distinctly recognized, and that character, in children, is often regarded as in some very important sense derivative from their parents."[18] This is a truth established on all sides, both in respect to bad character and to good. "The scriptures have a perpetual habit," we may say, "of associating children with the character and destiny of their parents. In this respect, they maintain a marked contrast with the extreme individualism of our modern philosophy."[19] Our nature is viewed as an organism.

---

14. [Ibid., 34.]

15. [Ibid., 36.]

16. [Ibid., 37.. All emphases Nevin's.]

17. [Ibid., 38. The biblical reference is to Jer 31:34. Antebellum evangelicalism was generally "postmillennial," i.e., the "return of Christ" would take place *after* the millennial period. Consequently, the millennium would not be an act of Christ supernaturally imposing his rule upon the world, but rather the proper and natural end of the progress of the gospel in America specifically, and on the earth generally. In other words, there was a general hope that American Christianity would eventuate in an era when "all shall know God." After the Civil War, evangelicals began a gradual shift to an eschatology of *premillennialism*: Christ comes *before* the millennium, which is thus a supernatural manifestation of his earthly rule. The reader can get some sense of some of the presuppositions of premillennialism in Nevin's sermon "Bread of Life," (art. 7, below) in which he criticized the hermeneutics of the "Prophetic Conference" of 1878. General discussions can be found in *Dictionary of Christianity in America*, 136, 919, 929. More detailed exposition, and reasons for the shift are given in Marsden, *Fundamentalism and American Culture*, 48–55.]

18. [Bushnell, *Discourses*, 39.]

19. [Ibid., 41.]

6. Hence the institution of infant baptism. It supposes "an organic connection of character between the parents and the child; a seal of faith, applied over to the child, on the ground of a presumption that his faith is wrapped up in the parent's faith; so that he is accounted a believer from the beginning."[20]

This in a general way is the argument, by which Dr. Bushnell endeavors to carry out and enforce his proposition, that the child of christian parents should be so educated that he may grow up a christian, without any such process of conversion as is needed to bring an adult sinner into the same state.

The view, as he remarks himself, is certainly different from that which is commonly held in our American churches; but it is rather strange he should add his confident belief, that it is "inconsistent with no scheme of doctrine generally held or accepted." It would be indeed "a somewhat singular phenomenon," as he styles it, if the current view of christian nurture were found to be "no necessary or even proper inference from any current doctrine or opinion."[21] It is not in this way, that the practical is wont to sunder itself from the theoretical,[22] in the sphere of religion. Where a false system of religious life has become thus widely established in the christian world, it is not possible that it should be entirely independent of the ecclesiastical doctrines and opinions that may be current at the same time; and one might suppose, that there should be no particular difficulty in tracing the wrong practice, noticed in the present case, to its proper source in this form.

The current view of christian nurture, as opposed by Dr. Bushnell, has been the product to a great extent undoubtedly of the Puritan theory of religion. It may be said to be in special affinity with the genius of Methodism; as it finds also its fullest home in the system of the Baptists. But it must be acknowledged, that these forms of religion are themselves derived from the Puritan principle. They owe their origin to it historically and constitutionally; and so far as the point before us is concerned, they can only be said to carry out to its last consequences the original tendency of Puritanism itself. It is notorious, that the view of christian nurture which Dr. Bushnell condemns, has come in and gained ground in the Church, only with the introduction and prevalence of this tendency, first in England, and more extensively since in our own country. This in fact is understood, and, affirmed indirectly, by Dr. Bushnell himself. His own doctrine he tells us, as to the substance of it at least, "is not a novelty, now rashly and for the first time propounded, as some might be tempted to suppose.—It is as old as the Christian Church, and prevails extensively at the present day, in other parts of the world."[23] The same acknowledgment is virtually involved, also in what he says, in another place, when he remarks:

---

20. [Ibid., 42–43.]
21. [Ibid., 3 (preliminary "Advertisement").]
22. [The text reads "theatrical," certainly a misprint.]
23. [Bushnell, *Discourses*, 7.]

The European churches generally regard Christian piety more as a habit of life, formed under the training of childhood, and less as a marked spiritual change in experience. In Germany, for example, the Church includes all the people, and it is remarkable that, under a scheme so loose and with so much of pernicious error taught in the pulpit, there is yet so much of deep religious feeling, so much of lovely and simple character, and a savor of Christian piety so generally prevalent in the community. So true is this, that the German people are every day spoken of as a people religious in nature: no other way being observed of accounting for the strange religious bent they manifest. Whereas it is due, beyond any reasonable question, to the fact that children are placed under a form of treatment which expects them to be religious, and are not discouraged by the demand of an experience beyond their years.[24]

If the case be thus represented, the practice of the whole ancient Church, and the practice of the European Church generally still, in favor of what may be denominated educational religion, it ought to be plain that the contrary practice, by which this sort of religion is discredited and in a great measure rejected, is one of the fruits of Puritanism—a result legitimately flowing from it at least, if not expressly comprehended in its life at the first.

The subject will be resumed in another communication.

24. [Ibid., 25.]

"Educational Religion: Review of Dr. Bushnell's Tract Continued [Part 2]"[1]

The theory of religion which Dr. Bushnell opposes proceeds on the assumption, that Christianity is something supernatural—a new, heavenly life, which is derived to man by the power of the Holy Ghost directly from God. And this assumption of course is all right. Christianity is thus supernatural, a new creation in Christ Jesus. Christians are born of God, and are the subjects thus of a higher order of existence, than that which belongs to the unconverted world around them. But is assumed still farther, that this new creation holds no continuous, historical connection with the order of the world in its natural form. It is related to this only in an abrupt, outward way, without coming to any actual organic union with it in the form of life. The supernatural is regarded as something altogether abstract. Grace is a mere influence from the other world, made to reach over to its subject by a sort of divine magic. It becomes identical thus in the end with the idea of religious *experience*. All is subjective; and so the theory runs out practically at last into a system of rank individualism, in which religion comes to be viewed as an original, independent concern, in every instance, between man and his Maker. Each single man, by help of the outward supernatural *apparatus* provided by Christ for the purpose, is expected to get it in full for himself directly from the Bible and God's Spirit.[2]

---

1. [*Weekly Messenger of the German Reformed Church*, n.s.,12, no. 42 (June 30, 1847) 2454.]

2. [With this text, Nevin began to concatenate a number of antinomies—objective and subjective, inward and outward, organic and mechanical, organic and individual, supernatural and magical, catholic and sectarian—into an integrated theology of how and in what sense God supernaturally manifested himself in the world, in short, a theology of revelation. The editor has previously defined this theology as "holistic supernaturalism" (Layman, "Nevin's Holistic Supernaturalism," 193–208). "Holistic supernaturalism" was opposed to a "dualistic" supernaturalism, which he saw manifested in two distinct forms. Princeton theology separated "objective" doctrine and "subjective" Christian experience. While doctrine was inductively derived from a supernaturally inspired and protected Bible, that doctrine had to be subjectively realized in the believer (Loetscher, *Facing the Enlightenment and Pietism*, 26, 76, 170–71, 226, 251; Hoffecker, *Piety and the Princeton Theologians*, 8–9, 12–15, 25–27, 63, 67). In Nevin's judgment, this made Christian experience external to the doctrine that articulated the experience. Therefore, the experience had to be achieved "mechanically." At the other extreme was revivalism. In one sense, the experience of revivalism was "organic." The doctrine *was* the conversion experience. However, as Nevin had already argued, that experience was generated by human excitement (was "subjective") and was therefore finally "Pelagian," a production of human will and effort

Against this prevalent conception Dr. Bushnell protests, with great force. He has the sound feeling that religion, to be real, must be objective and organic, and not simply the product of individual thinking and willing. "The tendency of all our modern speculation[s]," he tells us,

> is to an extreme individualism, and we carry our doctrines of free will so far as to make little or nothing of organic laws; not observing that character may be, to a great extent, only the free development of exercises previously wrought in us, or extended to us, when other wills had us within their sphere. All the Baptist theories of religion are based in this error. They assume as a first truth, that no such thing is possible as an organic connection of character, an assumption which is plainly refuted by what we see with our eyes, and by the declarations of scripture. *We* have much to say also, in common with the Baptists, about the beginning of moral agency, and we seem to fancy that there is some definite moment when a child becomes a moral agent, passing out of a condition where he is a moral nullity, and where no moral agency touches his being. Whereas he is rather to be regarded, at the first, as lying within the moral agency of the parent, and passing out by degrees through a course of mixed agency, to a proper independency and self-possession. The supposition that he becomes, at some moment, a complete moral agent, which he was not before, is clumsy and has no agreement with observation. The separation is gradual. He is never, at any moment after his birth, to be regarded as perfectly beyond the sphere of good and bad exercises; for the parent exercises himself in the child, playing his emotions and sentiments, and working a character in him, by virtue of an organic power. And this is the very idea of christian education, that it begins with nurture or cultivation. And the intention is, that the christian life and spirit of the parents shall flow into the mind of the child, to blend with his incipient and half-formed exercises; that they shall thus beget their own good within him, their thoughts, opinions, faith and love, which are to become a little more, and yet a little more, his own separate exercise, but still the same in character. The contrary assumption, that virtue must be the product of separate and absolutely independent choice, is pure assumption. As regards the measure of personal merit and demerit, it is doubtless

(*The Anxious Bench*, in *Catholic and Reformed*, 57, 81, 93, 99, 109 passim). Although the revivalists *also* affirmed traditional Christian doctrine, *that* doctrine was also external to the experience. Nevin thought that the revivalistic doctrine qua experience was wholly other than what he would come to view as "evangelical catholicism." In the place of these two allegedly inadequate views of divine revelation, he here began to develop a "holistic" (perhaps better *integral*) view in which "the supernatural life of the *Logos*"—manifested in the liturgical praxis of the church as "the mystical presence"—was "experienced in the supernatural transformation of personal existence, history, cosmos, and human community" (Layman, "Nevin's Holistic Supernaturalism," 205). The mutations of this integral supernaturalism would culminate at the end of his life in a series of writings and essays that adumbrated a hermeneutics that will be partially expressed in the final essay of this volume, "The Bread of Life." For summaries of this hermeneutics see Layman, "Nevin's Holistic Supernaturalism," 201–5, and more fully DiPuccio, *Interior Sense of Scripture*, esp. 79–114.]

true that every subject of God is to be responsible only for what is his own. But virtue still is rather a *state* of being than an act or series of acts; and if we look at the causes which induce or prepare such a state, the will of the person himself may have a part among those causes more or less important, and it works no absurdity to suppose that one may be even prepared to such a state, by causes prior to his own will; so that, when he sets off to act for himself, his struggle and duty may be rather to sustain and perfect the state begun, than to produce a new one. Certain it is that we are never, at any age, so wholly independent, as to be wholly out of the reach of organic laws which affect our character. . . . We possess only a mixed individuality all our life long. A pure, separate, individual man, living *wholly* within, and from himself is a mere fiction. No such person ever existed, or ever can. I need not say that this view of an organic connection of character subsisting between parent and child lays a basis for notions of Christian education, far different from those which now prevail under the cover of a merely fictitious and mischievous individualism.[3]

"The scriptures," Dr. Bushnell tells us again,

have a perpetual habit, if I may so speak, of associating children with the character and destiny of their parents. In this respect, they maintain a marked contrast with the extreme individualism of our modern philosophy. They do not always regard the individual as an isolated unit, but they often look upon men as they exist in families and races, and under organic laws. Something has undoubtedly been gained to modern theology, as a human science, by fixing the attention strongly upon the individual man, as a moral agent, immediately related to God, and responsible only for his own actions; at the same time there was a truth, an important truth, underlying the old doctrine of federal headship and original or imputed sin, though strangely misconceived, which we seem, in our one sided speculations, to have quite lost sight of. And how can we ever attain to any right conception of organic duties, until we discover the reality of organic powers, and relations? And how can we hope to set ourselves in harmony with the scriptures, in regard to family nurture, or household baptism, or any other kindred subject, while our theories exclude or overlook precisely that, which is the basis of all their teachings and appointments?[4]

All this, so far as it goes, is sound and important. The whole constitution of the world contradicts the unit or atom theory of religion. Humanity is not an aggregation, but an organic whole, manifold and one at the same time; not a vast living sand-heap merely, as the Pelagian philosophy assumes, but the power of a universal life, revealing itself under endlessly diversified forms, and yet always identical with itself, and always reaching forward as a process to a general or universal end. The whole bears the parts,

---

3. [Bushnell, *Discourses*, 29–32, emphases original.]
4. [Ibid., 41–42.]

not the parts the whole. Every man includes in himself two forms of existence. He exists as an individual in himself and for himself, and he exists also in the race as the medium through which a life more general than his own reveals its presence. And yet his nature is not twofold on this account; as though these two forms of existence were joined together in his person, in a simply mechanical, external way. They condition and include each other, in such way that neither could have place truly at all apart from such connection. They are only two *sides*, we may say, of one and the same life.

Is it not so in fact, throughout all nature? Does not the general reveal itself in the particular, and does not the particular exist only *as* a revelation of the general? Can they be sundered in a single case? Is not every rose a rose, as truly, as it is *this* or *that* rose; a revelation of the universal rose life, as well as the single flower it shows itself for the senses? And why then should we find any special mystery, in the extension of the same law to the higher life of man? The individual is indeed exalted here to the character of a person, self-conscious, exercising reason and will; but for this very reason, the singularity of the life is only more intimately joined with its generality, than before; for reason and will are in their very nature general, and personality is precisely the consciousness of an existence, in this form, more broad than the separate and single life of the subject himself.

The whole man then, soul and body, exists in organic union, with his race. The blood that flows in his veins is *human* blood; the mind that thinks within him, is part and parcel, of the rational *humanity* to which he belongs. He is borne at every point, from the womb to the grave, on the bosom of a life which is the bearer of millions besides continually in the same way. He lives, moves, and has his being, in the social system to which he belongs; not as something that is external to himself; but as the necessary form of his being itself, that is interwoven with its inmost texture, and that cannot be sundered from it without its destruction. Abstract a man from the family, the state, and the race, and you abstract him into a sheer nullity. He cannot be born, cannot live, cannot come to thought or speech, cannot be developed physically, intellectually, or morally, save by the force of a life more general than his own, always surrounding him, always flowing into him, always filling him with its presence.[5]

Such most clearly is the constitution of our humanity, in its common natural form. The Pelagian view of life is extremely shallow, as contrary to all experience as it is to the plain sense of God's word. Most assuredly there was "an important truth," as Dr. Bushnell intimates, "underlying the old doctrine of federal headship and original or imputed sin."[6] Only let the doctrine descend to its proper depth, so that the connection between Adam and the race shall be regarded as a life connection really, like that

---

5. [For earlier statements by Nevin of this "organicism," see *Anxious Bench*, in *Catholic and Reformed*, 106–8; *The Mystical Presence*, MTSS ed., 142–49, 183–85; the response of Charles Hodge is in Nevin and Hodge, *Coena Mystica*, 122–26. Hodge never engaged the substance of the theory, but simply dismissed it as "in all its essential features Schleiermacher's theory" (126); that then was the point to which Nevin responded (126 ff.).]

6. [Bushnell, *Discourses*, 42.]

between root and branches, not simply an outward artificial bond for low purposes, and it will be found the only view of the world in which a sound reason can at all possibly acquiesce. "By one man sin entered into the world, and death by sin, and so death passed upon all men, for that all have sinned."[7] The race sinned in Adam and fell with him, in his first transgressions. He stood in the case their federal head, because he was their true organic head.[8]

But if the natural constitution of the world be thus organic, all life the union of the general and particular in the same subject, it is not possible to avoid the conclusion, that the higher constitution to which it is advanced by Christianity, must be of the same character. Christianity cannot contradict the reigning law of the world's life under other forms. To be real, it must be the completion of humanity itself, in its normal, most deeply native character. It cannot be related to the world, in the way simply of magic. It must enter into the life of it, organically, historically, objectively. Otherwise all becomes a phantom.

The view which Dr. Bushnell opposes, wrongs Christianity in fact, just in this way. It will not allow it to come to a real, organic union, with the actual constitution of the world. No wonder he should have no patience with it, in his heart. Orthodoxy itself, in this form, becomes a gross contradiction. What sense can there be especially in infant baptism? The rite involves, he tells us, in all its grounds and reasons, the same view of christian education, he is seeking to establish. "One cannot be thoroughly understood and received without the other. And it is precisely on this account, that we have so great difficulty in sustaining the rite of infant baptism. It *ought* to be difficult to sustain any rite, after the true sense of it is wholly gone from us."[9] Most true certainly, and worthy of earnest consideration.

The subject will be resumed in a third article.

---

7. [Rom 5:12.]

8. [To describe Adam as the "federal" head of the human race was to say that all humans are "in" Adam (and therefore somehow morally culpable for Adam's sin) by way of a "covenant" (Latin, *foedus*). See the discussion of the origins of federalism in the general introduction. According to the Puritans, God set before Adam a "covenant of works": do this and live. Adam broke the covenant; "and we as his posterity, incurred the just penalty" (Miller, *New England Mind*, 377). Exactly how humanity was included in Adam's fall remained one of the central problems of Puritan theology. Suffice it to say that in the act of creation, and the "covenant of works" implicit in that event, every man was included in Adam *covenantally*. Nevin thought that federal headship was dependent upon and secondary to organic headship, i.e., Adam and every man form a *living* unity, not merely a *federal* unity. He objected that federalism broke apart the doctrinal affirmation (man is "in Adam") and the lived experience of that affirmation (dialectically recognized by being overcome through the unity the believer has "in Christ")—its unity was "mechanical." For a more positive interpretation of the relation between federalism and Nevin's organicism, see Hart, *John Williamson Nevin*, 97.]

9. [Bushnell, *Discourses*, 50.]

"Educational Religion: Review of Dr. Bushnell's Tract Continued [Part 3]"[1]

Christianity, to be at all what it claims to be, the absolute religion, the form in which the life of the world is advanced to its highest possible perfection, must connect itself with the life of the world in a real and historical way. To conceive of it as a supernatural system merely, brought to bear upon the experience of particular persons under a wholly abstract form, is to overthrow its title to credit altogether. To be real, it must be human; supernatural and yet natural also; a new life and yet a continuation strictly of the old life at the same time. In any other view, it becomes fantastic.

But with all this, Christianity can never resolve itself of course into the constitution of life, as found beyond its own sphere. It is after all a new creation, in the fullest sense of the term, and not the product simply of powers and resources, that lay involved in humanity, before it appeared. It will not be enough then to vindicate its historical character, by making it part and parcel of the course of nature, as comprehended in the previous history of the human race. This were only to exchange the error of the Gnostic, for the error of the Ebionite or common Humanitarian Jew. And so any view of religion, that directly or indirectly involves a consequence of this kind, tending to sink the conception of the supernatural Christianity into the sphere of *mere* nature, must be regarded as to the same extent defective and false.

Now it is just here, that I find myself constrained to be dissent earnestly from the general doctrine of Dr. Bushnell's tract, notwithstanding all my respect for the merits by which it is characterized in other respects. As a plea against the particular theory of religion to which it is opposed, it is worthy of general praise. In asserting the organic nature of the life of God in the Christian world, as laying a proper foundation for the idea of educational religion, against the popular Methodistical and modern Puritan way of looking at the subject, Dr. Bushnell has rendered the church undoubtedly good service; and it may be trusted, the testimony he has been bold enough to utter in this form will not fail to be heard and felt, with good practical consequences, far beyond the bounds of his own congregation. I feel thankful, that such a man is made to utter himself in such a style, in the bosom of Puritan New England; and the fact may be hailed, it seems to me, as one among many signs, which serve to indicate at this time

1. [*Weekly Messenger of the German Reformed Church*, n.s., 12, no. 43 (July 7, 1847) 2458.]

helpful tendency at least, in the spirit of the age, towards sound church feeling and true church faith. In the midst of the wretched unchurchy prejudices and rampant, fanatical individualism, that unhappily surround us on all sides, it is truly refreshing to find, here and there, men like Dr. Bushnell standing forward, and challenging the attention of the world to "a more excellent way." May their number be multiplied continually! The publication before us, is good; contains much truth; deserves to be circulated and read, on this account. But still it seems to me seriously defective, in the general view just mentioned. The posture it occupies, is not after all that which the nature of the subject requires.

Dr. Bushnell strongly asserts the organic, historical nature of religion; his whole argument turns on the idea, that it is so connected with the established constitution of our common human life, as to be involved, in this respect, in the operation of its general laws. But is it anything more at last than this established constitution of our common human life itself? No doubt, Dr. Bushnell would say that it is much more than this, a divine life letting itself down into the experience of God's people. And yet, it must be confessed that the tendency of his tract is throughout towards a contrary conclusion. If I have not altogether mistaken its sense, it bases its theory of educational piety on the constitution of nature, in the case of men, rather than upon the constitution of grace, as a strictly supernatural system. In other words, the argument is rationalistic.

This appears, in the first place, in the view which the tract takes of original sin or natural depravity. A great difficulty in the way of this whole idea of organic, educational religion, must be confessed to lie in the doctrine here brought into view. If our nature be radically corrupt, how can it be expected to unfold itself, by simple religious culture to a truly christian form? The case would seem to require at least a supernatural change to begin with; for the development of a christian character and life, there must be at hand in some form a corresponding ground from which such process may grow; if parents are to expect that their children will grow up christians, and to educate them in this view, they require certainly a guaranty somewhere that their children are in fact capable of all that is expected and proposed in their case. Does Christianity then lay any supernatural foundation for such culture, in the depraved nature of children? It does not appear, that Dr. Bushnell rests his theory of educational religion, on such a supposition. Rather his theory excludes every imagination of the sort. And still he holds that children, notwithstanding their depraved nature, may grow up christians, and that it is our duty and privilege to educate them with this expectation. He supposes therefore a real general possibility of christian development, in their case; which must be considered to lie in the force of such training itself, as brought to bear on their natural constitution. The assumption seems to be simply, that although all children come into the world under a law of corruption and guilt, the constitution of the world is still such, if only the conditions of a strictly pious education are present, it may be calculated certainly that this original depravity will be surmounted, so as to admit from the start a regular unfolding of the life under a truly christian form. Christian parents are bound, it is said, to bring up their children *as christians*. The duty is absolute, rests upon all. Are all to believe then, that the necessary basis of the christian life is at hand in the case of their children? For such faith, some objective ground is needed; otherwise it can be no better than blind presumption. Where then is this objective ground? Wholly, it would appear, in what may be called the natural resources of the case itself. Educate your children as *christians*; and they will be such; the process itself will make the thing both possible and actual at the same time.

But is not this in fact to deny the doctrine of original depravity, even while it seems to be admitted? If the process of christian education, applied to the general constitution of our nature, be sufficient to produce christian character, it must be certainly because our nature itself is capable of being expanded, in a direct natural way, into a christian form, as well as into the form of impenitency and sin. It is the old creation after all then, which notwithstanding its corruption, is found sufficient to evolve from itself, by virtue of its own general organic constitution under the presence of the proper conditions, all that is comprehended in the idea of Christianity.

Dr. Bushnell assents fully to the doctrine of our general natural depravity; but it is certainly made to assume, under his hands, a form that robs it at last to a great extent of its proper force. If I have properly apprehended his meaning, he makes it to be a sort of necessary accident nearly to our moral probation, which so far from precluding the possibility of christian development in the case, is to be viewed rather as itself the occasion or medium by which it is to take place. "There are many," he tells us, "who assume the radical goodness of human nature, and the work of christian education is, in their view, only to educate, or educe, the good that is in us."[2] Every such theory he holds to be wrong. "The natural depravity of man," he goes on to say,

> is plainly asserted in the Scriptures, and if it were not, the familiar laws of physiology would require us to believe, what amounts to the same thing. And if neither Scripture nor physiology taught us the doctrine, if the child was born, as clear of natural prejudice or damage, as Adam before his sin, spiritual education, that which trains a being for a stable, intelligent virtue hereafter, would still involve an experiment of evil, *therefore a fall and bondage under the laws of evil*; so that, view the matter as we will, there is no so unreasonable assumption, none so wide of all just philosophy, as that which proposes to form a child to virtue, by simply educing or drawing out what is in him. The growth of christian virtue is no vegetable process, no mere onward development. It involves a struggle with evil, *a fall* and rescue. The soul becomes established in holy virtue, as a free exercise, only as it is *passed round the corner of fall and redemption*, ascending thus to God through a double experience, in which it learns the bitterness of evil and the worth of good, fighting its way out of one and achieving the other as a victory. The child, therefore, may as well

2. [Bushnell, *Discourses*, 21.]

begin life under a law of hereditary damage, as to plunge himself into evil by his own experiment, which he will as naturally do from the simple impulse of curiosity, or the instinct of knowledge, as from any noxious quality in his mold derived by descent. For it is not sin which he derives from his parents; at least not sin in any sense which imports blame, but only some prejudice to the perfect harmony of his mold, some kind of pravity or obliquity which inclines him to evil.³

This sounds very much like a great deal that is to be heard, on the subject of sin, in Germany within the precincts particularly of what may be denominated, in a general way, the Hegelian theology. Sin, according to the school, is a necessary condition of virtue or piety, on the part of created intelligences. Holiness for man is a process, that includes in its very conception, the idea of a free election of good, in opposition to evil; the position or assertion of the one can be accomplished, only by the conscious negation of the other; a state of innocence, in order that it may become a state of positive righteousness, must in the first place show itself transiently at least a state of sin. The *fall* according to *Daub*,⁴ for instance, a mere mythological representation at best, is to be viewed as a happy transition in human history—the passage of the world in fact from the imprisonment of a state of nature, into the sphere of moral freedom. Is this the theory of Dr. Bushnell, Pastor of the North Church in Hartford? Possibly there may be some mistake in the case; but really the language just quoted, cannot easily be taken in any different sense. And yet it is strange doctrine certainly, to be endorsed by an "Association of ministers" in orthodox New England, and published by the *Massachusetts Sabbath School Society*.

Apprehended in this way, the natural pravity of the human race forms to be sure no bar to the idea of educational religion. Hereditary or not hereditary, the fact of our corruption comes at last to the same thing; it is the first stadium only in the process of christian sanctification itself; the only form indeed, under which the constitution of our nature as it exists, could by any possibility evolve itself into a character of righteousness. The whole case is in itself perfectly normal. All that is needed, is the exhibitions of the proper appliances in the way of christian education, and it may be expected confidently to provide for itself. The organic laws of the world's life, as it actually stands, are a sufficient guaranty, that the spiritual development here will be in

3. [Ibid., 21–23; emphases Nevin's.]

4. [Carl Daub, d. 1836, German Protestant theologian of the "speculative school," went through all the major idealistic systems—Kant, Schelling, Hegel—as frameworks for reinterpreting Christian theology. The earliest attempt at an intellectual history of Mercersburg said that the philosophy of Frederick Rauch (Nevin's predecessor at Mercersburg Seminary) was "virtually the same as that of Carl Daub" (Appel, *Life and Work*, 141; see also Ziegler, *Frederick Augustus Rauch*, 36). James I. Good, *History of the Reformed Church in the U. S.*, rejected the theory of theological continuity between Rauch and Nevin, although he acknowledged that Rauch's "philosophical position may have prepared the way for Mercersburg by his emphasis on organism and by his realism" (106). (Good regarded Rauch with approval, but thought Nevin had misappropriated Rauch for a sacramentalist agenda.) Observe that in the text, Nevin's view toward Daub's understanding of the fall was negative.]

the right direction, a steady triumph of virtue over the pravity in the midst of which it is born. "Take any scheme of depravity you please," says our author, "there is yet nothing in it to forbid the possibility that a child would be led, in his first moral act, to cleave unto what is good and right, any more than in the first of his twentieth year. He is, in that case, only a child converted to good, leading a mixed life as all christians do. The good in him goes into combat with the evil, and holds a qualified sovereignty. And why may not this internal conflict of goodness cover the whole life from its dawn, as well as any part of it? And what more appropriate to the doctrine of spiritual influence itself, than to believe that as the Spirit of Jehovah fills all the worlds of matter, and holds a presence of power and government in all objects, so all souls of all ages and capacities have a moral presence of the Divine Love in them, and a nature of the Spirit appropriate to their wants."[5]

With this theory of natural pravity is naturally associated, in the next place, a corresponding theory of regeneration. Dr. Bushnell fully admits, of course, the necessity of such a change. But it seems to resolve itself with him very much into something, that comes after all from the organic action of our human life in its common natural form. Our nature, it would appear, includes in itself, notwithstanding the necessary damage at the fall, the recuperative force that is required to bring it again into right condition; and where the proper advantages are enjoyed in the way of christian education, including of course the *divine* influences that belong to the Gospel—which however compass "all souls of all ages and capacities,"[6] ready to act when needed—it may be expected that the life will actually right itself from the start, and flow forward thus, with true conversion, in the channel of holiness, and not in the channel of sin. Christianity is allowed to require a new heart, in order to a right life. But who has told you, our tract asks, that a child cannot have the new heart thus needed? "Whence do you learn that if you live the life of Christ, before him and with him, the law of the Spirit of Life may not be such as to include and quicken him also? And why should it be thought incredible, that there should be some really good principle awakened in the mind of a child? For this is all that is implied in a christian state."[7] —"Assuming the corruption of human nature," it is said again,

> when should we think it wisest to undertake or expect a remedy? When evil is young and pliant to good, or when it is confirmed by years of sinful habit? And when, in fact, is the human heart found to be so ductile to the motives of religion, as in the simple, ingenuous age of childhood? . . . A right spirit may be virtually exercised in children, when as yet it is not intellectually re-received [sic], or as a form of doctrine. Thus if they are put upon an effort to be good, connecting the fact that God desires it and will help them in the endeavor, that is all which, in a very early age, they can receive, and that includes every

---

5. [Bushnell, *Discourses*, 14–15.]
6. [Ibid., 15.]
7. [Ibid., 14.]

thing—repentance, love, duty, dependence, faith. Nay, the operative truth necessary, to a new life may possibly be communicated through and from the parent, being revealed in his looks, manners and ways of life, before they are of an age to understand the teaching of words; for the christian scheme, the gospel, is really wrapped up in the life of every christian parent, and beams out from him as a living epistle, before it escapes from the lips, or is taught in words. And the Spirit of truth may as well make this living truth effectual, as the preaching of the gospel itself. Never is it too early for good to be communicated. Infancy and childhood are the ages most pliant to good. And who can think it necessary that plastic nature of childhood must first be hardened into stone, and stiffened into enmity towards God and all duty, before it can become a candidate for christian character![8]

All this *seems* to mean, that the capabilities of our common human nature are such, as to warrant the expectation of christian development, where it is subjected from the beginning to proper christian influences. The right development in such case, secured by the help of God's Spirit, is to be taken itself for the regeneration to righteousness, which has become necessary in consequence of the fall. This carries certainly a very rationalistic aspect.

In both cases, that of organic evil and that of organic good, natural pravity and the new life of grace, Dr. Bushnell fails, it seems to me, to distinguish properly, between the idea of principle or ground, and the idea of mere occasion or condition. In every organic development, both of these are necessary, at every point, to the process in which it consists. The life of the plant, for instance, starts from a certain *principle*, in the living seed or germ, out of which it grows. This principle it can never outgrow, or leave behind; its whole life stands in the power and presence of it, to the end; it is the plastic law, that determines its interior form, its character and type, throughout. And yet the principle is not sufficient of itself to produce the plant, or even to uphold it, when produced, for a single day. It can vegetate and grow only under certain *conditions*. It must have soil, moisture, heat, light; to call out, and support the actual life process, in which vegetation consists. These conditions moreover are not something external simply to the life of the plant; they enter into, and become part of its very nature. The life, as an actual process and result, can no more be sundered from its conditions than it can be sundered from its principle. Both enter, with equal necessity, as joint factors, into its constitution. But still, notwithstanding this, condition and principle are never the same thing; nor can we say that the action of the first is, in any sense, a continuation only of the action comprehended in the last. This Dr. Bushnell has not properly kept in mind. His theory of hereditary sin, and hereditary piety, is such as confounds apparently all real distinction, between the principle of life in each case, and the conditional agencies that enter into the process of its actual development.

8. [Ibid., 19, 20–21.]

Educational Religion

The character of the child, he tells us, is actually included in that of the parent, as a seed is formed in the capsule, and matured there by nutriment derived from the stem, till it is gradually prepared for separation. "There has been much speculation," he adds,

> as to whether a child is born in depravity, or whether the depraved character is superinduced afterwards. But like many other great questions, it determines much less than is commonly supposed; for, according to the most proper view of the subject, a child is really not born *till he emerges from the infantile state*, and never before that time can he be said to receive a separate and properly individual nature. The declarations of scripture, and the laws of physiology—compel the belief that a child's nature is somehow depravated by descent from parents, who are under the corrupting effects of sin. But this, taken as a question relating to the mere *punctum temporis*, or precise point of birth, is not a question of any so grave import, as is generally supposed; for the child, *after birth*, is still within the matrix of the parental life, and will be more or less for many years. And the parental life will be flowing into him all that time, just as naturally, and by a law as truly organic, as when the sap of a trunk flows into a limb. . . . Will, in connection with conscience, is the basis of personality, or individuality, and these exist as yet only in their rudimental type, as when the form of a seed is beginning to be unfolded at the root of the flower. At first, the child is held as a mere passive lump in the arms, and he opens into conscious life under the soul of the parent, streaming into his eyes and ears, through the manners and tones of the nursery. A little farther on, it is observed that a smile wakens a smile—any kind of sentiment or passion, playing in the face of the parent, wakens a responsive sentiment or passion. . . . Next the ear is opened to the understanding of words. . . . Farther on, the parents begin to govern him by appeals to will. . . . Their will and character are designed to be the matrix of the child's will and character.[9]

Very beautiful this, and full of most important truth; well worthy of being laid to heart by our liberty pedants, and all worshippers of the great Diana,[10] "Private Judgment," out of the Church or in the Church, the wide world over. But is it a correct and sufficient view of the fact we call original sin? Has this fact no necessity, other than the *conditions* by which life is developed? Is it really a question of no account, whether our depravity be something back of *all* development, or the product of the development itself? The whole doctrine of native depravity, it is to be feared, will be found to stand or fall ultimately with this distinction.

---

9. [Ibid., 27, 28–29; emphasis original.]

10. ["Diana" was a widely used metaphor for any cliché or shibboleth that seemed idolatrous to the critic. This term came from the Authorized Version's translation of the Ephesian goddess in Acts 19:34 (modern translations follow the Greek text in rendering it "Artemis").]

The same confusion of principal and condition is presented to us again, in Dr. Bushnell's view of the new life which we have by the gospel. His language concerning the organic connection of character, that holds between parent and child, is not indeed designed, he ensures us, to assert a power in the parent to renew the child, or to imply that the child can be renewed by any agency of the Spirit less immediate, than that which renews the parent himself. But it comes to something nearly of the same sort, in the end. "When a germ is formed on the stem of any plant," he says,

> the formative instinct of the plant may be said in one view to produce it; but the same solar heat which quickens the plant, must quicken also the germ and sustain the internal action of growth, by a common presence in both. So if there be an organic power or character in the parent, such as that of which I have spoken, it is not a complete power itself, but only such a power as demands the realizing presence of the Spirit of God, both in the parent and in the child, to give it effect.[11]

And in all this it is assumed, that the living gospel enveloped in the light of the parent, may reach over organically, by the solar influence of God's Spirit, (a condition in the case, no principle,) to the natural constitution of the child, so as to make it spiritually alive; an assumption which can hardly be accepted as orthodox.

Dr. Bushnell's system is defective, in making no proper account of the Church. To this we now come.

---

11. [Bushnell, *Discourses*, 33.]

"Educational Religion, No. 4: Review of Dr. Bushnell's Tract, Concluded"[1]

The general defect of Dr. Bushnell's theory becomes particularly apparent, it seems to me, in the view he takes of Christian baptism.

He sees clearly, that the system which he opposes leaves no room properly for the use of this sacrament, in the case of children. It is in fact the very view of religion that is always assumed by the Baptists, and their argument against a practice at the Church with regard to this point; and to be consistent, it ought always to be carried out to the same unchurchly extremity. The practice of infant baptism is indeed out utterly without meaning, if religion be a thing of wholly individual separate experience, and incapable altogether of organic transmission; if the baptized child be incapable of a regular development from the beginning, into the form of a truly christian life. Allow this fundamental assumption, in the case of the Baptists, as it is now too generally done by those who still cling traditionally the ancient church practice, and it becomes at once impossible to withstand their sectarian confidence. The rite of infant baptism involves in all its grounds and reasons, as Dr. Bushnell remarks, the same view of Christian education that is maintained in his tract; which itself also serves to show, as he adds, that this view is not new, but older by far than the one now prevalent, as old in truth as the Christian Church. "It is radically one with the ancient doctrine of baptism and regeneration, advanced by Christ and accepted by the first fathers."[2] "No man ever objected to infant baptism," Dr. Bushnell well observes in another place,

> who had not at the bottom of his objection false views of Christian education; who did not hold a notion of individualism in regard to christian character in childhood, which is justified neither by observation nor by Scripture. It is the prevalence of false views on the subject, which creates so great difficulty in sustaining infant baptism in our Churches. If children are to grow up in sin, to be converted when they come to the age of maturity, if this be the only aim and expectation of nurture, there really is no meaning or dignity whatever in the rite. They are even baptized unto sin, and every propriety of the rite as a seal of faith is violated. . . . And it would certainly be very singular, if Christ

---

1. [*Weekly Messenger of the German Reformed Church*, n.s., 12, no. 44 (July 14, 1847) 2461.]
2. [Bushnell, *Discourses*, 50.]

Jesus, in a scheme of mercy for the world, had found no place for infants and little children; more singular still, if he had given them the place of adults; and worse than singular if he had appointed them to years of sin as the necessary preparation for his mercy. But if you see him counting them one with you, bringing them tenderly into his fold with you, there to grow up in him, you will not doubt that he has given them a place exactly and beautifully suited to them. And is it for you, to withhold them from that place? Is it worthy of your tenderness as a Christian parent to leave them outside of the fold, when the gate is open, only taking care to go in yourself?[3]

The truth is, the Baptist theory of religion is extremely cold and heartless; and it is only strange that any part of the Christian world should be able to acquiesce at all practically in so dreary a system.

But what now after all is the force that belongs to infant baptism, in the theory of Dr. Bushnell? Nothing more, it would seem, than this, that it indicates the fact of such an organic relation between parents and their children in our common human constitution, as is sufficient to authorize a presumption that these last, properly educated, will grow up into the faith and piety which may belong already to the first. The rite is found in this way to have *meaning*, which in any other view it could not be allowed to have; its meaning however lies, in the end, not so much in any virtue it may be supposed to carry in its own constitution, as in the general law of educational, hereditary religion already established in the order of the world, as an independent fact, of which men are simply reminded and assured in this way; as we might easily conceive of some civil ceremony applied to the infant also, putting a ring for instance on one of its fingers, to show it entitled to inherit the estate of its parents, which could have force only on the ground of a general law of inheritance actually established under this form in the state, and without this must be utterly absurd.

Infant baptism, according to Dr. Bushnell, supposes the fact of an organic connection between the parent and the child; and is a seal of faith in the parent, applied over to the child, on the ground of a presumption that his faith is wrapped up in the parent's faith; so that he is accounted a believer from beginning. "We must distinguish here," he tells us,

> between a fact and a presumption of fact. If you look upon a seed of wheat, it contains in itself, presumptively, a thousand generations of wheat, though by reason of some fault in the cultivation, or some speck of diseases matter in itself, it may in fact never reproduce at all. So the Christian parent has in his character a germ, which has power, presumptively, to produce its like in his children, though by reason of some bad fault in himself, or possibly some outward hindrance in the Church, or some providence of death, it may fail to do so. Thus it is that infant baptism becomes an *appropriate* rite. It sees the child in the parent, counts him presumptively a believer and a christian, and with

3. [Ibid., 59, 60.]

the parent baptizes him also. . . . It must be presumed, either that the child will grow up a believer, or that he will not. The Baptist presumes that he will not, and therefore declares the rite to be inappropriate. God presumes that he will, and therefore appoints it. The Baptist tells the child, that nothing but sin can be expected of him; God tells him that for his parents' sakes, whose faith he is to follow, he has written his own name upon him, and expects him to grow up in all duty and piety. . . . We have much to say of baptismal regeneration as a great error; which undoubtedly it is, in the form in which it is held; but it is only a less hurtful error that some of us hold in denying it. The distinction between our doctrine of baptismal regeneration, and the ancient scriptural view, is too broad and palpable to be mistaken. According to the modern church dogma, no faith in the parents is necessary to the effect of the rite. Sponsors too are brought in between all parents and their duty to assume the very office which belongs only to them. And what is worse, the child is said to be actually regenerated by the act of the priest. According to the more ancient view, or that of the Scriptures, nothing depends upon the priest or minister, save that he execute the rite in due form. The regeneration is not actual, but only presumptive,[4] and every thing depends upon the organic law of character pertaining between the parent and the child, the church and the child, thus upon duty, and holy living, and gracious example. The child is too young to choose the rite for himself, but the parent, having him as it were in his own life, is allowed the confidence that his own faith and character will be reproduced in the child, and grow up in his growth, and that thus the propriety of the rite as a seal of faith will not be violated. In this way too is it seen, that the christian economy has a place for all ages; for it would be singular, if after all we say of the universality of God's mercy as a gift to the human race, it could yet not limber itself to man, so as to adapt a place for the age of childhood, but must leave a full fourth part of the race, the part least hardened in evil and tenderest to good, unrecognized and unprovided for—gathering a flock without lambs, or I should rather say, gathering a flock away from the lambs.[5]

In all this, we have no recognition of the true character of baptism as a divine sacrament. Dr. Bushnell has a high opinion of the *rite*, as appointed by Christ to be

---

4. [Bushnell directed his criticisms in several different directions simultaneously. (1) The infant was *presumed* to be a believer, not because of his own faith, or any actual state of spiritual transformation, but because of his *parents'* faith. The power of the "germ" to produce further spiritual growth was not in the infant, but in the parents. (2) However, Bushnell also rejected "baptismal regeneration" *as then held*, since he thought it incorrectly understood that "the child is said to be actually regenerated by the act of the priest." Bushnell thought regeneration was only *presumptive*. Nevin shared Bushnell's rejection of "baptismal regeneration"—see "'Baptismal Grace': A Conversation between Nevin and 'Inquirer'" in this article. However, Nevin could not abide the subjectivity constructed by the *presumption*. He wanted an *objective* grace (not objective regeneration). The concept of "presumption" would become key in the debate between Emanuel Gerhart and Lyman Hotchkiss Atwater of Princeton: see art. 5 in this volume.]

5. [Bushnell, *Discourses*, 43–44, 50–51; emphasis original.]

the sign and seal of faith on the part of his people; and he ably vindicates the practice of the Church in extending it to infants, on the ground that they are in fact organically involved in the religious life of their parents, and so of course fairly comprehensible in the force of such a covenant transaction entered into on their account. But the relation of the sign to the thing represented, remains for him throughout altogether mechanical and external. The fact on which the force of infant baptism rests is fully at hand, whether the ordinance takes place or not, and as it would seem for all alike; the fact namely that the parental character is the natural matrix in which is formed the character of children, so that if the proper conditions be present christian education may be expected to result in a development of piety from early childhood. The case itself includes a *presumption* of this sort, and infant baptism has force as it serves to express and authenticate the presumption thus known to exist. That there should be any force in the baptism itself, more than such outward reference, seems not to have come into Dr. Bushnell's mind. He would probably reject altogether the idea of "sacramental grace," as a divine power objectively present in the ordinance, under any view; making common cause here with the unchurchly system which it is the object of his tract to oppose, and showing himself to be, notwithstanding all his opposition, under the power of the same system still in his own mind. As a protest against individualism his tract is good; but it is not spoken from the right ground. It makes no account of the Church as a new supernatural constitution, added to the constitution of mere nature; and in consequence of this, its theory of religion remains at last rationalistic.

The idea of educational religion meets us every where in the Scriptures. It enters besides into the whole theology and practice of the Church from the beginning. The modern Puritan system so current now in this country, which assumes that children must grow up in a state of alienation from God, to be converted afterwards in an extraordinary way, is an innovation clearly upon the general order of Christianity, as it has come down to us from other times.[6] It throws confusion upon the whole past history of the Church, and makes it difficult to understand her most venerable usages and institutions. It contradicts besides the analogies of nature, and the inmost instincts of the heart; which we often find strong enough accordingly to triumph in some degree over the authority of the system, where it has come to be unhappily established; shaping the practice of christian parents in opposition to their theory, or at least setting one part of their practice in uncomfortable discrepancy and conflict with another. From all sides, the conviction forces itself irresistibly on the earnest believer, that the salvation of Christ is for infants and children as well as adults, and that the law of organic comprehension by which they are included in the life of their parents in the sphere of nature, is made to extend also with full force to the sphere of grace. But then the sphere of nature is not itself the sphere of grace; and the Church accordingly has never thought of resolving the phenomena which belong to this last, into such agen-

---

6. [A clear statement that shows that for Nevin, "the modern Puritan system" meant what the editor has been calling "conversionism."]

cies and powers as belong only to the first. The theory of educational religion that has entered into the practice of the Church from the beginning, may easily be seen to rest upon a far deeper foundation than this. It assumes throughout, that the constitution of nature, as such, is entirely insufficient, by any laws or resources it may be supposed to possess, for the purposes of Christianity; and that these purposes can be reached, only through the medium of a higher constitution, including in itself powers and resources of a strictly supernatural kind. This constitution is held moreover to be actually at hand in the organization of the Christian Church itself; which is the continuation of Christ's life in the world and denominated for this very reason his body, the fullness of Him that filleth all in all.[7] Admit the idea of such a divine constitution, at hand in the Church for the ends of the Christian salvation, and there is room to receive and honor, to the same extent, the old church theory of educational religion, as recognized by the whole Protestant world in the age of the Reformation. But let this idea vanish into thin abstraction, as it has done palpably to a great extent in our modern Puritan system of thinking, and the old church theory will no longer be able to stand. It will either be given openly to the winds, as by the unhappy Quakers and Baptists, (whose name is legion;)[8] or suffered to fall into practical decay, as by other sects that have the baptistic principle, though still traditionally bound by a contrary profession. And when some laudable attempt may be made even to surmount the contradictions in the case of Dr. Bushnell's late tract, it is likely to run out, also, into sheer rationalism, under cover of an orthodox name.

Christianity is in one view, as I have said before, the perfection of nature. Its relations to the world is never, as the sect spirit[9] assumes, abrupt, violent, fantastic, or

---

7. [Eph 1:23.]

8. [Allusion to Mark 5:9; Nevin was suggesting that Baptist piety had demonic overtones.]

9. [Nevin critiqued this "sect spirit" in "The Sect System," and *Antichrist; or, The Spirit of Sect and Schism*. These works are to appear in MTSS vol. 5. Previous editions of "The Sect System" include *Catholic and Reformed*, 128–73; "The Sect System" and *Antichrist* are excerpted in *The Mercersburg Theology*, ed. James Hastings Nichols, 95–119. Nevin argued that sectarians began by asserting the Bible was the only guide to faith, claiming this is the only sure defense against "human dogmas and opinions" (*Mercersburg Theology*, 97). However, since the Bible was interpreted by "private judgment," idiosyncratic opinions about what exactly this Bible meant proliferated. This generated a virtually infinite diversity of religious opinion. Yet the sects continued to insist on the validity of their own private religious vision. Sects attempted to bind their followers to their private concerns, but these "shibboleths and passwords" were only "the fruit of accident or caprice in the history of its founder" (ibid., 103, 102). Their arbitrary origins in some person's private religious experience deprived them of an awareness of being rooted in a spiritual and ecclesial history, a traditioned past that shaped and provided norms for the present. It militated against the development of a rational theology, since any theological science "has to do with the whole of Christianity, and is thus at once both churchly and historical" (ibid., 108). Sects lacked a substantial, churchly reality, developing through space and time, that could be studied, scientifically comprehended, and developed in response to new spiritual situations. Sects were paradoxically both fanatical and rationalistic: fanatical by virtue of their one-sidedness, and rationalistic because religious obligations were conceived as "obedience to certain laws" rather than growing out of a sacramental, churchly life (ibid., 111). A modern scholarly description of the religious situation can be found in Hatch, *Democratization of American Christianity*, 80–81.]

magical. Christ came truly *in the flesh*, and his Church is in the flesh still. But he came, at the same time, as the real revelation of a higher life in the world; a life that was not in it before; a life that has been in it always since, and according to his own promise will be so always to the end of time. Christianity then, is not the mere constitution of nature, as it stood before, but the fact of a divine, supernatural constitution, incorporated with the course of nature, by means of the Church. To question this, is to question the fact of the incarnation itself, and involves the very essence of Rationalism. The Church accordingly is the proper object of *faith* (as in the Creed) no less than the person of the theanthropic Saviour himself. To resolve it into the laws of our common life, is infidelity in disguise. At the same time, its whole constitution is in harmony with the laws of this life. It is the supernatural in human natural form. The higher life of the Church is the life of humanity itself, exalted into its own proper sphere. The new creation then carries out and completes the sense of the old creation. It is the old organism still, with all its original necessary laws; only lifted into a higher order of existence. Such as it is however, its results spring not from the flesh as such, but from the presence of supernatural powers and resources made permanent in the flesh by Jesus Christ; and we might as well pretend to reduce the miracles of healing which Christ once wrought to the general category of animal magnetism, as undertake to resolve the objective grace of the Church into the action of laws that begin and end with the constitution of our human nature in its common form.

Mere nature can never serve as a foundation, on which to bring up our children in the nurture and admonition of the Lord. We need surer and more solid ground; not a subjective presumption simply but an objective verity, that may be apprehended as such by faith; not an organic law in the sin-disabled nature of our children themselves, but the law of the spirit of life in Christ Jesus, organically joined to our nature, as its proper supernatural complement, in the Church.

The Church, we say, *has* a right to look upon her infant children comprehended in the privileges of the christian covenant; and christian parents accordingly are not only allowed but *bound*, to bring them up in the Lord, that is, in the consciousness of a saving relationship to the blessed Redeemer. On what ground? Such a duty supposes an objective basis, on which to rest, in some form. Mere opinion, hope, presumption, private ratiocination, fall short of what the case requires. What is the objective basis, I ask again, on which it becomes the privilege and duty of Christian parents to bring up their children, notwithstanding the fact of their natural depravity, as fit subjects for the kingdom of heaven? Shall we be told, that they have a title to be so considered and treated, on the ground simply of their natural *birth*? So some would seem to think, who at the same time profess to look upon this birth as a channel only for the transmission of corruption and sin. What do good men mean, when they tell us that the children of professing christians are christians likewise, members of the Church and heirs of all its grace, by their mere *natural birth*? If so, nature is after all the matrix of the new spiritual creation in Christ Jesus. Away with such a theory. That which is born of the flesh, *is flesh*;[10] we are all by *nature*, that is by the force of our natural birth, not the children of God; but "children of wrath."[11] Descent from godly parents cannot change this law. Our birth relation to pious parents may give us a right to be taken into the Church; but it can never of itself make us to be in the Church as our *born* privilege, authorizing our parents to bring us up as christians from the womb. The basis for such treatment, must come to us in some different form. It must come to us, out of the bosom of the Church herself! She makes us christians, in this sense, by the sacrament of holy Baptism, which she has always held to be of supernatural force for this very purpose; and on the ground of an actual relationship to the new life of the gospel thus constituted in a real objective way she says to each christian parent, Take this child, and nurse it, educate it *for me*, and for the Lord.

It is not possible to vindicate the idea of educational religion, on any other than this old church scheme. Faith *must* have a basis, in the case, beyond itself, on which to rest. Mere nature forms no such basis; the birth of nature leads only to despair. The basis then must be supernatural; and yet, in this character, objective and real. We have it, not in the world, but in the Church. Here then is room for the idea of organic, educational christianity, but not surely under any other form. Baptism places its infant subject in a saving relation to the new supernatural constitution which Christ has established in the Church; makes it possible for it to grow up, with natural development, into the form of a truly christian life, under the direct action of the resources which are comprised in the Church for this purpose; and it is faith in all this precisely, that is needed above all things to make christian education efficient and successful.

Some will have it that it is superstition to make so much account of baptism and the objective Church; but is it not something worse than superstition, to make mere natural birth the bond of relationship to the Christian life, and the basis on which to treat children as saints?

Refuse to admit the old church doctrine of baptismal grace, and I see no possible escape from the horns of a very simple dilemma. We must either renounce all faith, at the same time, in the whole idea of educational religion, which is to fall over at once into the arms of *Fanaticism*; or we must resolve christianity at last into the mere constitution of our common nature, and we so make it a thing of birth and blood descent, which is to sit down at the feet of *Rationalism*. True Church faith holds between both these extremes.

10. [John 3:6.]
11. [Eph 2:3.]

"Baptismal Grace": A Conversation between Nevin and "Inquirer" for the Weekly Messenger

[The Inquiry]

Professor Nevin having appeared in the *Messenger* as the advocate of what he denominates "*Baptismal grace*," we would beg leave, respectfully, to propose to him the following query, to which we trust he will cheerfully favor us with a clear and definite answer.

Does the Professor understand by "*baptismal grace*" the same as is commonly denoted by the phrase "*baptismal regeneration*"?—in other words, Does he believe that baptism, when rightly administered, is invariably and immediately accompanied with regeneration?

July 23d, 1847 INQUIRER

[Editor's Response]

The above question from a correspondent, we have no doubt, will receive a prompt and cheerful attention. We had intended ourselves to elicit the information sought for, though in a somewhat different form; not because we had any doubt as to the orthodoxy of the position of Dr. N.; but because we thought a fuller exposition of his view would be acceptable, and at the same time, prevent any false conception of its precise nature that might otherwise obtain currency with some. In presenting truths of the kind referred to, we conceive nothing so necessary as precision, in order to prevent misconceptions. We have an illustration of this truth in the article in the minister's department on the fourth page of our present number.[2] The article itself will be read with interest; but we fear that such language as the following, and that which is immediately connected with it: "The sacred ordinances, must be looked upon as something

---

1. [*Weekly Messenger of the German Reformed Church*, n.s., 12, no. 47 (August 4, 1847) 2475. "Inquirer's" question is followed immediately by an editorial comment.]

2. ["Samek." *Weekly Messenger of the German Reformed Church*, n.s., 12, no. 47 (August 4, 1847) 2476.]

more than merely external forms, which can be of no benefit to the soul, unless the exercise of our faith is directed beyond them to the heavenly throne; and engaged with Christ there at the same time," will be understood as teaching the *opus operatum* doctrine, that the participation of the sacraments necessarily confers grace upon the recipient, independent of the state of his mind at the time; though we are persuaded our correspondent never intended to teach such a sentiment.—*Ed. of W. Mess.*

Baptismal Grace[3]

"Does the Professor understand by 'baptismal grace' the same as is commonly denoted by the phrase 'baptismal regeneration'? In other words, does he believe that baptism, when rightly administered, is invariably and immediately accompanied with regeneration?"

This inquiry I find respectfully proposed, in the last number of the *Messenger*. A "clear and definite answer" requires a clear and definite question; and no doubt the one here presented is considered to be such, in the fullest degree, by the person from whom it comes. It is in fact however very far from such a character. The word "regeneration," and the phrase "baptismal regeneration," both need an interpreter, to make it precisely clear in what sense they are employed. I generally avoid them, when speaking of baptism, for this very reason; to secure *precision* if possible by the use of other language, and not with any wish assuredly to be obscure. The truth is too, I have already been much more *precise* in the case, than I am now required to be by the categorical question here stated.

Taking the question in what I know to be its general meaning in the mind of the person asking it, and in the sense which it will no doubt carry to the readers of the *Messenger* commonly, I have no difficulty at all in meeting it with a "clear and definite answer" in the negative. That any such change of the subject as is commonly understood in speaking of regeneration results necessarily from baptism, I do not of course believe. With the case of Simon Magus[4] full in view, to say nothing of the thousands

---

3. [Nevin, *Weekly Messenger of the German Reformed Church*, n.s., 12, no. 48 (August 11, 1847) 2478.]

4. [Acts 8:9–24. Simon was a magician in Samaria, who believed Philip's teaching and was baptized. He later offered Peter and John money so that he could receive the apostolic power to bestow the Holy Spirit (from this act we get the word *simony*, the purchase of religious office). Nevin apparently read the story to say that Simon, although baptized, had not been "regenerated." This reading is not self-evident. Simon submitted to Peter's harsh rebuke and begged him, "Pray for me to the Lord." Even if Simon was not "regenerate" at the moment he attempted to bribe Peter, he could have apostatized in the time after his baptism. Such a solution would have been consistent with Nevin's own theological framework, since he held to the possibility of actual apostasy from a state of genuine regeneration (see further below, art. 6). Furthermore, *Calvin* directly ascribed regeneration to baptism: In referring to the "similarity and difference between these two signs" of circumcision and baptism, he said, "The thing represented [in both] is the same, namely regeneration" (*Institutes*, ed. John T. McNeill, 2:1327). This was also implied in Calvin's defense of infant regeneration (ibid., 2:1339–41). Although his point was that "those infants who are to be saved . . . are previously regenerated by the Lord" (ibid., 2:1340), it certainly followed that infants should be baptized, since they could experience regeneration. Nevin

of cases in our own time, how could I entertain any so extravagant opinion? If this be what is meant by baptismal regeneration, as I suppose to be the case with the world generally in the use of the phrase at the present time, I have always carefully refrained from it, as feeling that it was particularly liable to be taken in such pernicious sense.

Still, I should be very sorry of course to place myself, by the repudiation of this phrase, in the same category or class with those, who in decrying the idea of baptismal regeneration, mean to decry in fact the idea of all objective grace in the holy sacrament. I do not like the word as a "shibboleth," one way or the other, simply because of its very uncertain and precarious sense.

In *baptismal grace*, I firmly believe. This faith does not require that I should be able to define clearly in what exactly the grace consists. Enough, that it lies in the very conception of a sacrament, and that it is clearly affirmed in the word of God. Whatever of force there may be in the constitution of the Church, objectively considered, for the purpose of our salvation, it is by baptism that we are come first regularly and fully within its range. Baptism is a divine *act*, as much so as the original outward call of Christ to the twelve disciples; which did not of itself convert them, as we see clearly from the case of Judas; though it certainly carried with it objectively a full real title to all that is comprehended in the Christian salvation, as this came to be actualized subsequently in all of them except Judas.

Baptismal Grace [Further Questions by "Inquirer"][5]

When we penned our inquiry on the above subject, we indulged the hope that we should receive both a definite and satisfactory answer. Our mind however, is far from being relieved, nor can we rid ourselves of the impression that the Professor, notwithstanding his repudiation of certain terms, maintains substantially the sentiment which those terms are designed to express. While he informs us that he "generally" avoids the word "regeneration," and the phrase "baptismal regeneration" when speaking of baptism; and also, that he does not believe "any such change of the subject is as commonly understood in speaking of regeneration results necessarily from baptism," he, at the same time, says, "I should be very sorry of course to place myself, by the repudiation of this phrase, in the same category or class with those, who in decrying the idea of baptismal regeneration, mean to decry in fact the idea of all objective grace in the holy sacrament. . . . In baptismal grace, [not italicized in Inquirer's quotation] I firmly believe."

---

had the scriptural, confessional, and ideological resources to make the argument for baptismal regeneration. The very next sentence in the text suggests the reason why he did not: "in the use of the phrase at the present time." The explanation for Nevin's reaction is to be found, not in the foundational sources of his tradition, but in the contemporary debates over the nature of Christian experience.]

5. [*Weekly Messenger of the German Reformed Church*, n.s., 12, no. 50 (August 25, 1847) 2486.]

As our object is to place the Professor's views in their true position, he will not deem it impertinent if we here propose to him a few additional queries.

1.) Is the grace, which he maintains is communicated by baptism, *saving* grace or is it not?

2.) If baptism confers *saving* grace, on what is the bestowment of that grace founded—on the faith of the parent in behalf of the baptized child, or on "the objective force" of the sacrament itself?

3.) If by "baptismal grace" be meant something short of saving grace, wherein does the Professor's views respecting the nature of baptism differ from the view entertained by those from whom he dissents?

All who hold to infant baptism admit that baptized children are commonly brought under influences peculiarly favorable for salvation, and that the promise of God authorizes the hope that, if they are properly educated, they will become partakers of the piety of the parents; but from the Professor's statements, it would seem that between baptism and salvation there is a far more intimate connection than this.... What then is the nature of that connection?

Holy Baptism [Response by Nevin][6]

Quest. "Is the grace, which he maintains is communicated by baptism, *saving* grace or is it not?"

Ans. If this means grace that actually saves the subject, *No*; if the sense be grace that is able through faith to save him, *Yes*.

Quest. "If baptism confers *saving* grace, on what is the bestowment of that grace founded—on the faith of the parent in behalf of the baptized child, or on "the objective force" of the sacrament itself?"

Ans. In the sense just stated, on the objective force of the sacrament itself; which when rightly administered is not the act of the minister nor of the parents as such, but as Calvin says, of the Lord Jesus Christ himself, as truly as though an angel were sent down to perform the service for him at the time.[7]

Quest. "If by *baptismal grace* be meant something short of saving grace, wherein does the Professor's views respecting the nature of baptism differ from the view entertained by those from whom he dissents?"

Ans. The answer is already given. I look upon baptism as a divine act, having force as such in its own nature for the purposes it contemplates, when not frustrated

---

6. [*Weekly Messenger of the German Reformed Church*, n.s., 12, no. 51 (September 1, 1847) 2490.]

7. [It is not clear which part of this statement was being attributed to Calvin. *Institutes*, ed. McNeill, 2:1314, says "For inasmuch as it is given for the arousing, nourishing, and confirming of our faith, it is to be received as from the hand of the Author himself." If Nevin was including "as though an angel..." phrase, the editor cannot find the reference.]

by unbelief. The view from which I dissent, makes it to be a mere human act, of no force whatever except as the dead token only of something else.

I have thus replied a second time to "*Inquirer*," though a good deal doubtful of the propriety of submitting publicly to such anonymous catechisation. In such a case, one needs to be well assured of the honesty and godly simplicity of the party with whom he is called to deal. "Inquirer" *may* be sincere; but that of course is not altogether certain. But again, such catechisation, to be for public edification, calls for a clear head as well as an honest heart; otherwise it only serves to create confusion. This business of asking questions, calls for some skill; for if the question itself be dark, it is not likely to generate much light out of itself; or at least the light would come to us with better effect in some other way. And then once more; a great deal depends on the standpoint of the questioner himself, in a case of this sort. Has he *any* standpoint at all; or is he a mere bundle of theological negations? And if he *has* a standpoint, where is it? It is but too plain, that "Inquirer," so far as he has any system, stands in the case before us wholly on rationalistic ground. Baptized children, he tells us, "are *commonly* brought under *influences* peculiarly *favorable* for salvation;" and beyond this, the sacrament is for him of no force. But this is plump, barefaced rationalism. Does not the Unitarian believe full as much? It can hardly be expected, that I should go on answering questions, when interrogated from the Unitarian or Socinian standpoint, under pretense of concern for our old German Reformed orthodoxy. The question whether there be such a thing at all as "*baptismal grace*," a mystical, sacramental force of *some* kind in the ordinance of holy baptism, it is not one I trust that we are called to discuss and settle *de novo* in the Church of the Heidelberg Catechism.

"Dr. Bushnell and Puritanism"[1]: An Argument for "Discourses on Christian Nurture," addressed to the Publishing Committee of the Massachusetts Sabbath School Society, by Horace Bushnell, Hartford, 1847. pp. 48.[2]

A new tract on the subject of educational religion, which the vast importance of the theme makes it proper to notice. Dr. Bushnell has found it necessary, it seems, to come to some explanation with the Puritanism of New England, on the question of his own orthodoxy; and the result is the respectable pamphlet, here submitted to our consideration.

I was not aware, when I began my review of his former tract, that it created dissatisfaction in any quarter. All the notices I had seen of it in the religious papers had been favorable; and as it bore upon its face at the same time the *imprimatur* of the Massachusetts Sabbath School Society, I took it for granted it must be in general good credit. This indeed surprised me; for it was plain that in accepting and endorsing such a publication, the reigning divinity of New England must contradict itself. But self-contradiction after all is not so uncommon in our theology at this time as to be an occasion for any very special wonder. Mr. Cooke's sermon on the mystical union,[3]

---

1. [*Weekly Messenger of the German Reformed Church*, n.s., 12, no. 51 (September 1, 1847) 2489–90.]

2. [Bushnell, *Argument for "Discourses on Christian Nurture"*; repr. in *Views of Christian Nurture*, 52–125. Citations will continue to be in the form, x/y, where x is the original 1847 edition and y is the 1848 reprint. Most of the polemical material, primarily at the beginning and end, was removed in *Views*. His daughter later described the first edition as "pungent" and "vividly characteristic of the writer at that period" (Cheney, *Life and Letters*, 182). Some of the excised material is quoted in *Life and Letters*, 180–81.]

3. [Rev. Parsons Cooke, "Parallel between the First and Second Adam," *New England Puritan*, 8, no. 26, Thursday, July 1, 1847. Boston: J. E. Woodbridge, 101–2. Nevin had noted and responded to this sermon six weeks earlier in "Our Union with Christ," 2465. He admired the "felicitous representation" of *the mystical presence* made by "one of the first preachers of Massachusetts," and hoped it would assist the readers in better understanding his own view. The sermon itself was reprinted in two parts in *Weekly Messenger*: "Parallel between the First and Second Adam," July 21, 1847, 2466, and July 28, 1847, 2469. Cooke thought that the best way of explaining the sense in which a Christians are "one with Christ" was a "union of life." First he applied "union of life" to the unity of Adam and every man: Adam, he pointed out, is really the name of the "race," rather than an individual. So Adam is the "race in its root." Inversely, "Christ . . . is the new race in its roots, or rather a new stock," upon which, in

we can all see, was in full opposition to modern Puritanism as a system; push it out to its necessary consequences, and it involves the idea of historical organic Christianity, a divine church, real sacraments, and all kindred points, quite against the abstract, unchurchly scheme of New England, as commonly presented to our view; and yet this same sermon was preached before the Massachusetts convention, and by their approving request is published in the *New England Puritan*, without a word of exception, as a fair exposition of New England orthodoxy. Here is contradiction with a vengeance. But it is all right. Puritanism includes a contradiction in its own nature, which cannot fail to work itself out, sooner or later, at different points in proportion as it is subject to the crucible of earnest theological thought. In such circumstances of course, the more confusion and inconsistency, the better. It betokens thought, and furnishes some hope of better things to come. Chaos is the mother of creation. The worst of all states, is that whose harmonious quiet is imaged by the grave, or the waters of the dead sea. This is not the state of New England in our day, and is not likely, I trust, to become so soon. The theology of that region is plainly not at peace with itself, even where it tries hard to carry such show. Hence the union of opposite tendencies, it is found so often to present. We come accustomed, in the midst of it, to theoretical and practical contradictions, and are pleased to meet them as signs for good.

But in the case before us, the opposite tendencies have in the end, it appears, refused to unite. Puritanism has not been able after all to get along comfortably with Dr. Bushnell's tract. And yet in rejecting it, the system again falls into self-contradiction, hardly less grievous than that which was involved in receiving it at first with favor.

The whole case, as a history of it comes into view in the second pamphlet, is somewhat curious. Dr. Bushnell's view, it seems, is no recent or sudden thing in his own mind. "At the time of my settlement in the ministry," he tells us in one place,

> the council came near rejecting me, because I could say nothing more positive concerning infant baptism. After two or three years of reflection, I came upon the discovery that all my views of Christian nurture were radically defective, and even false. And now what before was dark or even absurd, immediately became luminous and dignified—a rite the most beautiful and appropriate of all the ordinances of God.[4]

Subsequent study served only to confirm him, in the new direction thus taken; which was felt however to be somewhat divergent from the common creed. Finally he

---

the Johannine metaphor, Christians are grafted. "Christ took our nature, as the stock of an expanding life." He was "the root of a generic life," which Cooke described in familiar biblical language: the vine, the unity of marriage, the head and the members of the body, "living in the life of Christ," "stones on a living foundation," etc. He sensed that his listeners might find this theme "rather transcendental than scriptural," but admonished them "to recall the scriptural representations." Tragically, Nevin was not able to develop a conversation that might have developed with New England theologians and clergy, had he put aside some of his animus against the contemporaneous "Puritan" divinity.]

4. [Bushnell, *Argument for "Discourses,"* 24/85.]

was desired to submit his views of christian training to the ministerial Association, of which he is a member. This was done in the discourses, which have already been noticed. After discussion, they were approved, and recommended for publication. Then came a formal request, to have them published by the Massachusetts Sabbath School Society. The publishing committee of this body had the manuscript in their possession five or six months; it was much discussed; ultimately however it got before the world. At first, as we have seen, all seemed to work well. But soon there was a change. A charge was made upon the tract by Dr. Tyler, of the East Windsor Seminary, in the form of a *Letter* to the author, under the *unanimous* sanction of the North Association of Hartford county.[5] By the publication, it was represented to be full of "dangerous tendencies."[6] Some of the religious papers now took up the same key. A sort of theological panic followed in Massachusetts. To make the matter worse, the Unitarians professed to be greatly pleased with the tract, and offered to take it off the hands of the Sabbath School Society, for cheaper and wider circulation! In these circumstances, the Publishing Committee felt itself compelled to suspend the sale of the pamphlet; for a time at least; till the question might get decided in the popular mind, whether it be so terribly heterodox as has been feared or not. Such is the posture of affairs, in which this second tract of Dr. Bushnell makes its appearance before the world.

I have not seen Dr. Tyler's letter; and my knowledge of the opposition generally, which has been made to Dr. Bushnell's views in New England, is limited to a few notices in the *N. E. Puritan*,[7] and what he says himself in the present pamphlet. Of its character of course I have no right to speak. He treats it with very little respect; so far indeed as to decline all formal transaction with it, in the way of controversial argument. Of the East Windsor Seminary, in particular, he speaks in the most disparaging terms, as a "little institution, sworn every six months to suffer no progress,"[8] which to

---

5. [Tyler, *Dr. Tyler's Letter to Dr. Bushnell*. Each of the theologians in this debate lifted up one or two elements of a complex system, isolated it from the theological and spiritual matrix, and made it the focus of his reflection. Tyler had a federalist understanding of the fall, but now mediated federalism through Edwardsean conversionism; Bushnell believed that the infant was already part of the covenanted community, which in one sense was indeed the older view. Nevin thought Bushnell based the covenant on natural human generation and nurture; in contrast, Nevin thought that grace was "supernatural," in the sense that it came through the sacramental activity of the church—baptism, catechism, the Eucharist. For the permutations and peregrinations of Puritan theology, see Guelzo, *Edwards on the Will*, and Kuklick, *Churchmen and Philosophers*.]

6. [Bushnell, *Argument for "Discourses*," 4/54. Tyler himself said: "It is possible that you [Bushnell] have not been fully understood; and that your views, correctly interpreted, do not possess that dangerous tendency which they have been supposed to possess [by some purported "Christian public"]" (*Dr. Tyler's Letter to Dr. Bushnell*, 1).]

7. ["Letter to Dr. Bushnell," *New England Puritan*, 98; "Veritas," "Dr. Bushnell and His Reviewers," *New England Puritan*, 114; [Editors], "Dr. Bushnell and His Reviewers," *New England Puritan*, 118; "Honestas," "Dr. Bushnell and His Reviewers," *New England Puritan*, 118.]

8. [Bushnell, *Argument for "Discourses*," 28; these criticisms of Tyler's school (properly known as Theological Institute of Connecticut, now Hartford Theological Seminary) are deleted on p. 93 of *A View of Christian Nurture*. Tyler responded to these criticisms in "Dr. Bushnell and the Theological Institute of Connecticut," 129.]

make itself important must needs busy itself with a sort of general censorship over the theology of all new England. The charges brought against his tract are represented to be so vague and general, and for the most part[9] interwoven with misrepresentation, as to make it a perfectly vain business to think of taking them up in detail. So far as the whole New England attack is concerned, Dr. Bushnell contents himself, with an appeal of some length to historical testimonies, for the purpose of showing that his views of christian nurture are the same that were held by the early Church, and particularly by the church fathers of New England itself. This he does however, as he is careful to tell us, with true Puritan independence, "not because he does not feel himself at liberty, when truth seems to require it, to *defy all human authority*; but simply because it is pleasant to have the sanction of venerable names when we may, and especially when there seems to be many who are more fit subjects of authority than of reason."[10] While he endeavors to make good his own orthodoxy in this way, he brings a charge of defection from the truth against the general theology of New England, as it has stood since the days of the elder Edwards; and contends that his opponents, with all their zeal for the faith once delivered to the saints,[11] represent in fact after all only this modern defection, a sort of *new light* bastard Puritanism which has sprung up within the last century, and not the genuine old orthodoxy in which the Puritans took delight in the beginning.[12] This is something well entitled to our attention, and I hope to take some farther notice of it hereafter.

Towards the review of this tract lately published by myself in the *Messenger*, Dr. Bushnell is pleased to turn with a very different style of address; singling it out in fact, for special notice, as the only one that might be said to make room for any intelligent description of the subject at issue.[13] It was not to be expected of course, that the review would prove satisfactory to him at all points; but entering as it does with clear consent, into his great distinction between individual and organic life, it is taken to be of full

---

9. [There is a quotation mark before "the most part. . . ." However, since Nevin reordered the wording, the editor has deleted it. The source is Bushnell, *Argument for "Discourses,"* 29/94: "These misrepresentations are so interwoven with all their arguments against me, that I am discouraged from any attempt to answer them."]

10. [Ibid., 5/55, emphasis original.]

11. [Jude 1:3.]

12. [Bushnell, *Argument for "Discourses,"* 13–17/67–72. The editor is not aware that Nevin ever engaged Bushnell's explanation for the origin of "new light" Puritanism. Bushnell later admonished Nevin that the "defect of Puritanism . . . is not so much the defect of Puritanism, as of the new light form of it, introduced only a hundred years ago" (ibid., 26/89). While obviously not up to contemporary historiographical standards, Bushnell's summary displayed knowledge and insight, and one wishes that Nevin could have made use of it to bring some historical nuance into his criticism of "Puritanism."]

13. [Ibid., 69/89; 33–38/100–109. Bushnell also found the Episcopalians to have granted his argument "at least, qualified favor" (ibid., 25/88). Both Nevin and the Episcopalians showed understanding of the *organic/individual* distinction (ibid., 39/109). As we have *Argument for "Discourses on Christian Nurture"* in *Views of Christian Nurture*, Bushnell added a lengthy footnote that addressed the commentary in *Princeton Review* (*Views*, 86–87).]

force in his favor so far as the New England opposition is concerned; while he has sense and heart enough to honor objections also to his own system, that show themselves to be founded on some understanding of the points to which they relate. It is remarkable he says, that while the distinction between the *organic* and the *individual* seems to be so readily apprehended in the German Reformed Church, no evidence has appeared from any part of the Congregational press that it has entered as yet the mind of a single reader of his work![14] Remarkable enough, we may say, in one view; and yet not so remarkable either perhaps, if all things be rightly considered.

Dr. Bushnell shows a very commendable anxiety to roll off from himself the charge of *rationalism*, preferred against his tract in my review; and enters into a somewhat extended explanation of his views, for the purpose of relieving himself from the misconstruction to which he thinks he has been subjected at certain points, in what I have said on this subject. I cannot of course extract here all his defence, and a part of it would be hard to understand at all events, for those not acquainted with the theological relations of Connecticut; it is however nothing more than justice to the distinguished preacher, that he should have the full benefit of his own strong disclaimer of everything like rationalism, in the language he has himself employed for this purpose.

"It is most unfortunate," he says, "if I have left room for this truly serious objection. For so far from holding the possibility of restoration for men within the terms of mere nature, whether as regards the individual acting for himself, or the parent acting for his child, the incarnation of the Son of God himself is not, as I believe, more truly supernatural than any agency must be which regenerates a soul."[15] A passage is then quoted[16] from my review, in which Christianity is affirmed in the strongest terms to be a divine, supernatural constitution, incorporated with the course of nature, to which he gives his cordial assent. The object of his tract required that he should press especially what may be called the naturalistic side of the truth with which it was concerned; still, he says, he meant to interpose all the safeguards necessary to save himself from proper naturalism, and he supposed that he had done it. He adds: "I really think so now. The very first sentence of my tract is a declaration of supernaturalism. I find too that in as many as thirteen distinct passages, I have used language that has no proper signification at all, unless it carries the idea, either of a supernatural redemption, or of a want that requires it. I refer to four which ought to satisfy the most distrustful, pp. 21–2, 32–3, 35–6, 66–9."[17]

Dr. Bushnell concludes this reply by saying:

---

14. [The particular comment that Congregationalism had paid no notice to the *organic/individual* distinction is found on *Argument for "Discourses,"* 39/109.]

15. [Ibid., 34/101.]

16. [Ibid., 34/102.]

17. [Ibid., 36/105. The list of page numbers is identical to that found in *Argument for "Discourses,"* which would have pointed to the relevant pages in the first edition of *Discourses on Christian Nurture*. In *Views of Christian Nurture*, Bushnell updated the numbers to reflect the pagination of *that* edition: "18, 25, 26–27, 47–49."]

I have followed my reviewer into these objections, not for the purpose of self-vindication—he regards himself rather as favoring than as condemning, in general, the position I have I have taken, and I accept his objections as cordially as I do his approbation—but I have done it, that I may be able, in the handling of some view intelligently opposed to me, to develop more fully and distinctly my own doctrine.[18]

This is well; and it will be understood, I trust, that both in my original review and in this present farther discussion, *my* concern too is with the subject, rather than with the particular occasion by which in this case it happens to be brought into view. In differing from Dr. Bushnell, I do it always with sentiments of kindness and respect. I feel thankful to him for bringing forward the subject of this tract; not because I consider the view he takes of it absolutely sound and right; but because it is of the greatest consequence that the attention of the church should be drawn towards it in an earnest way, and his position seems well adapted to promote this object. It is always a satisfaction besides, to meet with a man who shows himself capable of thinking seriously, and at the same time effectively, on theological interests; even if his thinking be not altogether approved; it is still something vastly more wholesome than the sad want of thought, with which we are two commonly surrounded.

What we most of all need at this time, in our American Church, is an *earnest* theology. Huge contradiction and confusion reign throughout our religious life. Our theory of religion comprehends in itself the most discordant elements; is in fact a bundle of theories, that will not work together; and our practice is continually contradicting what we call our creed. And yet, for the most part, the evil is not perceived or laid to heart. It is quietly taken for granted that all is right, simply because there is not interest enough in the truth to make the want of it felt. As it regards all secular concerns, the material interests of politics and trade, we find the age sufficiently in earnest; actively thinking as well as actively working in its own way. But no sooner have we entered the sphere of theology, than all this show of real, stirring life is found to disappear. We have much that claims to be active religion, but we have no active theology; a very general impression, on the contrary, that theology has very little to do with religion, and that the less noise we make about it the better. Our theology is made up accordingly of dead abstractions, not concrete ideas that fill the soul with the sense of their own living warmth. Every sect among us has a somewhat different repository of such abstractions; its own museum of divinity carefully stored away under strong ecclesiastical lock and key; but these repositories all agree in this, that they are filled with the monumental *remains* of what was life once, rather than with the actual presence of what is life now. We rail against tradition, and yet tradition forms the very element in which we live, move and have our being.[19] Our hostility to tradition is itself

---

18. [*Argument for "Discourses,"* 38/108–9.]
19. [Acts 17:28.]

traditional; a thing we have, because it has come down to us, we know not how or why; and so in most other cases. Few think so far, as to feel the force of any difficulty that is actually involved in their own system. They go by their mechanical shibboleths (for the most part, *vox et praeterea nihil*[20]) and their traditional landmarks; without troubling themselves with the interior sense of things, one way or another; their *life* in fact altogether in another sphere. Nay, when it comes to actual thinking in any quarter, the chances are ten to one that it will be cried out against as dangerous and profane. We do not wish to be disturbed; and we feel that we have a right to get angry with any one, who presumes to unsettle in the least our cabinet of coldly cherished notions. We consider ourselves of course, in such a case, perfectly competent to step forward in defence of our traditions, though never so poorly armed for the task in the way of previous theological discipline. We are all ready to start up theologians at once, fully fit for service. Have we not a standing set of theological notions, pocketed away in one corner of our pericranium? Are they not clear? Do they not lie there, side by side, as peacefully as the slumbers of the grave? And shall they not be suffered now to repose in their place, and leave us at liberty to mind other things? In such a case, those who have given the least attention to what is broad and deep in divinity, are apt to feel themselves most able to settle all questions in the most summary manner. Who may not see, how much our theology is made to suffer in this way. While the profound feel it necessary too often to be reserved and silent, those who skim the surface are heard loudly determining, on all sides, the gravest questions, in their own dogmatic style. A man shall know no more of theology than what he has gathered by humdrum repetition some fifteen or twenty years ago, at the feet of an automaton book-bound preacher; his whole life spent since in the service of his profession as a trade; or even this exchanged at last, (no change in fact) for some openly secular pursuit; and yet of occasion, *he* too shall set himself up for a judge of orthodoxy, and read homilies to the Church on revivals of religion forsooth, and the duty of contending earnestly for the truth *as expounded by himself.*

In the midst of so much frivolousness, it is like cool water to a thirsty soul to come across anything that bears an opposite character. From my soul I honor an *earnest* man, who shows himself to be such in the sphere of religion. No other is entitled to respect. Right or wrong, such a man deserves our thanks; for his very errors look at least towards the truth. Of all shams, I know none worse than your sham orthodoxy; it turns God's truth into a cruel lie; it converts religion into a cloke of covetousness; like the dog in the manger, having no power to think itself, and too lazy to give up its snug traditional bed, it shows itself to be possessed of life, only by snarling and biting at all who presume to think in its stead, as though the stuff on which it sleeps were never designed to become *food*, and so flesh and blood, for any living creature.

Dr. Bushnell, in the close of his present tract remarks: "There is no instrument of power in this age, as we are just beginning to discover, that can be compared with

20. [Trans. "voice and nothing more."]

a *newspaper*. What now we want in New England, above everything else, is a great religious newspaper, edited with such a degree of ability, such firmness and breadth of understanding, as shall make it an instrument worthy of our churches and worthy of the age."[21] This is very true. The whole country needs here, what we have not at present, and cannot well have as things stand, a newspaper or review devoted to the cause of *catholic* christianity, and not simply to the interest of this or that sect or school. Our newspapers rule our theology, and alas, they are not fit commonly to exercise such rule. We have no truly independent theological review in the country. On all sides, our theology moves in the harness; not of science, but of denominational tradition; ignominiously bound to *isms* without end. When shall we have a free, catholic press?[22]

The readers of the *Messenger* need not be told, that in charging Dr. Bushnell's theory with rationalism, I did not of course intend to call in question his ecclesiastical honesty, as a professedly orthodox minister of New England. I have had no imagination at all of anything like a conscious scruple even in his mind, with regard to the supernatural character of the christian religion. His tract, as he himself remarks, carries in it full evidence to the contrary. But our idea of rationalism, in the German Church, is of much wider signification than this. As a *principle*, not carried out to its proper scientific consequences, it seems to us to enter largely into much of our divinity, where its presence is never suspected. It infects in particular the whole constitution of *Puritanism*, especially in its modern form. Dr. Bushnell has simply contributed to bring this fact into view, by pressing as far as he has done the claims of the interest to which his tract is devoted. If we consider him rationalistic then, it is only in the refined sense in which we believe that the New England theology generally has within itself a tendency to fall over to this form of error. There is such a thing as a rationalistic supernaturalism.[23]

21. [*Argument for "Discourses,"* 48, emphasis original. This text is not in *Views of Christian Nurture*. A fuller excerpt can be found in Cheney, *Life and Letters*, 181.]

22. [Here we may have the seed that later blossomed into the formation of the *Mercersburg Review*, as an organ for thought of Nevin, his colleagues, and his students. See Appel, *Life and Work*, 299, and Hart, *John Williamson Nevin*, 144; DeBie explained the need for such a theological organ, as an alternative to publishing lengthy scholarly essays in the church's *Weekly Messenger*, in his introduction to *Coena Mystica*, xl–xli.]

23. [Nevin gave a later (1870) interpretation of "rationalistic supernaturalism" in *My Own Life: The Earlier Years*, 106–16. He understood "rationalistic supernaturalism" as an affirmation of the supernatural character of Christianity through the use of human reason. In contrast, he thought for almost all of his adult life the only true evidence for supernaturalism was the supernatural power itself. One should not, indeed could not, "prove" supernatural truth by means of natural reality. So for Nevin, the truth was "the mystical presence" of Jesus Christ in the church, and through the church in the lives of believers. That truth had to be a self-evidencing reality, a supernatural power revealing its own reality. The emphasis on different aspects of Christian life would shift, and the accents would mutate; even so, in the judgment of the editor, Nevin's deepest insight never changed. For Nevin's version of this insight at the end of his life, see art. 7 below. Kuklick described one expression of "supernatural rationalism" in *Churchmen and Philosophers*, 82–83: "Proper understanding of the New Testament demanded the acceptance of miracles. Scriptural revelation rested on supernatural intervention. Miracles, the special acts of God related in the Bible, . . . demonstrated the peculiar aspects of the Christian faith. An

Dr. Bushnell and Puritanism

In speaking unfavorably of Puritanism at any time, I do not wish of course to be disrespectful; nor can I see that this is necessarily implied. The case calls for plain, intelligible speech. Puritanism is a well defined theory of religion in itself; materially different as I believe from the original form of the Protestant faith; possessed, as we all know, of many most admirable qualities; but characterized, at the same time, by serious defects, which it is highly important that we should try at least to understand. And why should we not then call it by its own name, and resist it also to the face in the things in which it may appear to be wrong? Puritanism itself should be the last to take umbrage at any such liberty. Is it not a protest against authority, in its very constitution? Does it not scorn all antiquity and tradition? And how can it require then that others should be bound by *its* authority, so far as not honestly to inquire at least if there be not after all a "more excellent way."[24] It will not pretend of course to make any such unreasonable demand; and it is not necessary that we should show any nervous delicacy, when we venture respectfully to bear testimony against its faults.

Dr. Bushnell is right, as at issue with Puritanism on the subject of organic, educational Christianity; and Puritanism is chargeable with immense self-contradiction, in refusing to admit thus far the soundness of his doctrine.

But Dr. Bushnell is wrong, I must still think, as at issue with catholic orthodoxy on the subject of the Church, though here of course on common ground with Puritanism itself. His standpoint at last would seem to be that of the New Haven divinity,[25] technically so called, which is throughout essentially rationalistic.

---

authoritative guide, the Bible documented the occurrence of miracles, testified to by irreproachable witnesses" (82). Kuklick was specifically referring to "liberals," so called because they rejected the traditional Puritan view of natural depravity, and thus were labeled "Arminians" in the New England context. The fusion of a natural theology informed by Newtonian science, and the belief in the Bible as a supernatural text, whose truth is verified through fulfilled prophecy and accounts of miracles in the Bible, continues to be generally held in evangelicalism.]

24. [1 Cor 12:31.]

25. [Bushnell is depicted as having rejected New Haven theology (the theology of Nathaniel Taylor), yet there were clear continuities. "The New Divinity became Bushnell's point of departure. He never lost the conviction of the overwhelming benevolence of God" (Cross, *Horace Bushnell*, 19). David L. Smith found continuity in Bushnell's acceptance of Taylor's commonsense realism, which taught that "principles of right and wrong were held to be immediately knowable"; Taylor and Bushnell also agreed on "notions of mankind's freedom, likeness to God, and moral ability" (introduction to *Horace Bushnell: Selected Writings*, 6, 8; on moral ability, also see Edwards, *Of Singular Genius*, 34–35).]

Article 2

"Noel on Baptism"

(By John W. Nevin)

Editor's Introduction

This volume's account of American Protestant piety has focused on the theological and spiritual origins of revivalism out of Puritanism. Contemporary with this development was another "evangelicalism" across the Atlantic, with similar traits, but a different etiology. English evangelicalism was Wesleyan, not Calvinist, in origin and therefore had a different tone.[1] The Westminster Confession had taught that true believers could "be certainly assured that they are in the state of grace, and may rejoice in the hope of the glory of God"; however, "this infallible assurance doth not so belong to the essence of faith, but that a true believer may wait long, and conflict with many difficulties, before he be partaker of it."[2] Early in the eighteenth century, English "Evangelicals" began to experience assurance as an *immediate felt* reality: a Howel Harris declared, "I *knew* that I was his child" and Charles Wesley exclaimed, "My God! I know, I feel thee mine."[3] Human experience soon showed that certain qualifications had to be made—it was not just based on feeling, but the "objective work of Christ," it could be temporarily withdrawn—but in general, Evangelicals believed that "assurance . . . is the normal experience of the believer from the time of his conversion onwards."[4]

This experience created a problem for the theological coherence of those who had remained in the Church of England. According to the Book of Common Prayer,

---

1. Short, "Baptist Wriothesley Noel," 51. See Bebbington, *Evangelicalism in Modern Britain*, 27–29, 34–42, on the connections and differences between English and American evangelicalism.

2. Westminster Confession of Faith, XVIII.1, XVIII.3. See Bebbington, *Evangelicalism in Modern Britain*, 43–44.

3. Qtd. in Bebbington, *Evangelicalism in Modern Britain*, 44.

4. Ibid., 45.

regeneration or the new birth happened in baptism. But every Evangelical understood regeneration as occurring in that moment of assurance. They used various strategies to mitigate the apparent contradiction: infant baptism signified hope for or confidence in future regeneration or ultimate salvation; others redefined regeneration as something "less decisive" than full conversion.[5] Unsurprisingly, efforts at adjustment did not always succeed. One Evangelical who experienced this "cognitive dissonance" was Baptist Wriothesley Noel. Noel was from an aristocratic family and was "brought up in an air of evangelical piety." He was called to an important Evangelical Anglican chapel in 1827.[6] Even as an established "churchman," he had argued for cooperation with Dissenters. He was an articulate spokesman on the issues of domestic and foreign missions and educational reform, and was the only Anglican leader to oppose the Corn Laws (tariffs on imported grain, which contributed to famine in Ireland). The episode that initiated Noel's removal from the establishment was the "Maynooth question." Maynooth College was a Roman Catholic school in Ireland for the education of priests. A bill had been proposed for the English government to increase its endowment. Although Noel's opposition was consistent with the position of the established church, his emergent rationale was not: no religion should be subsidized. He pointed out that supporting both Protestant ministers and Catholic priests in Ireland was the religious analogue of providing arms to two opposing armies. Furthermore, taxing Irish Catholics to support the Protestant establishment was asking Catholics to assist in the destruction of their own faith. Because he was ministering in an Evangelical chapel, he tried to persuade himself that he was not responsible for the errors of the establishment. However, he reversed that judgment by the end of 1848, and resigned his post in December 1848; he was rebaptized the following August. Noel's rebaptism appears to have been a later development; however, in his argument for voluntaryism, he had already complained about the pastoral consequences of infant baptism—the minister had to baptize all infants, regardless of the parents' spiritual state, he had to view baptized infants as Christians, and he had to submit them for confirmation, even if their lives failed to give evidence of regeneration. His position was already that of believer's baptism. Thus it seems probable that his repudiation of the establishment simply gave him the spiritual freedom to follow the path he was already on to its logical end.[7]

In the following essay, Nevin was responding to Noel's defense of adult baptism. Nevin was concerned with the seeming inability of paedobaptists to both maintain their practice and rigorously defend the theological grounds of their position (a problem that would again emerge in Gerhart's essay "The Efficacy of Baptism"). Nevin distinguished two questions: the *mode* of baptism and its *subjects*. He quickly granted,

---

5. Bebbington, *Evangelicalism in Modern Britain*, 9.
6. Short, "Baptist Wriothesley Noel," 52; Bebbington, "The Life of Baptist Noel," 390–91.
7. Bebbington, "The Life of Baptist Noel," 394–96, 398; Short, "Baptist Wriothesley Noel," 54–56, 58.

based on a review of authorities from the both Patristic and Reformation eras, that immersion was the original and primary mode of baptism. Western diversity illustrated, he thought, a superior sense of Christian freedom, over against both sectaries as well as the Eastern Orthodox Church. The core of this freedom was the correct understanding of a sacrament as "inward grace under an outward form." This allowed freedom in the form so long as the church adhered to the mystical reality of the ritual itself. As he typically did, he rejected two extremes: the rationalism of Quakerism, which rejected the symbol; and the rationalism of Baptist practice, which rejected the sacramental power of the sign. Baptists consequently practiced the symbol as an "outward rule" (we would say, "legalistically") because they failed to grasp the mystical unity of sacrament and symbol. Still, the freedom Nevin viewed as the great merit of Catholic and Protestant sacramentology was not to be abused by reducing the sign to a mere token, which would also express a lack of respect for the sacramental act.

The focus of Nevin's argument, however, was on baptism's proper subject: the question of infant baptism. His fundamental objection was theological, not historical: Baptist religion was nonsacramental. Nevin understood a sacrament to be a unity of a visible sign and an invisible grace, held together mystically so that grace was experienced as a living power through the practice of the sign. Baptist baptism was not a sign because it communicated nothing that was not already in the mind of the new Christian (repentance and faith). It was not grace because *the grace had already been experienced*, when the believer *felt* the justifying word of assurance. When Nevin said this piety was "subjective," his analysis was more insightful than he knew: it was in the mental state of the believer. In contrast, Nevin located churchly piety in the *objective* power of the church's sacramental life to accomplish what the sacraments promised. To be *objective*, it had to be embedded in a way of life, a living community that included the whole of human experience. Nevin thought this was the primary argument for infant baptism: the church had to embrace all of human experience, infancy as well as adulthood. The question could not be answered either by consulting Scripture as a rule book, or examining diverse practices in history. It was a question of principle: salvation, the supernatural transformation of human experience, the promise of the ultimate meaningfulness of life, was promised in the church; if that salvation was to be extended to infants, then the sacramental sign of that salvific promise also had to happen in the church. Defenders of adult baptism recognized the problem of infant salvation; but they could only solve it through ad hoc declarations that infants and young children were saved *somehow*, outside of the church, and separate from the redeeming activity of Jesus Christ.

Later in the essay Nevin provided documentation that infant baptism was widespread by the middle of the third century. The fathers' arguments presumed its acceptance: for example, Origen, Cyprian, and Augustine[8] argued *from* infant baptism *to* a

---

8. These three early Christian writers represent a trajectory of African Christianity. Origen (c. 185–c. 254) was an important early scriptural exegete and theologian from Alexandria, Egypt, who

doctrine that infants are born with sin (rather than trying to prove the practice *by* the doctrine). The fathers felt no need to justify the practice itself. He then asked: How do we best explain this later development?[9] He saw only two possible answers: either we assume a church that practiced adult baptism, and then made a revolutionary change (without historical or theological meaning), or we recognize that infant baptism slowly emerged out of the spiritual foundation and theological principles of apostolic faith and practice. Nevin thought human communities do not make arbitrary, unexplained leaps. The church's practice in the third century was connected to and grounded in its earlier life. Moreover, any such change would have occurred gradually. Infant baptism did not suddenly appear in the third century; it was the final result of a slow process of maturation, and once one perceived the internal logic of early Christian experience, one was bound to understand that the practice was an *organic* result of a *living* reality.

In conclusion, Nevin pointed out that "Puritans" (revivalist paedobaptists) cut off the limb upon which they thought they stood. Like the Baptists, they appealed to the Bible; Nevin retorted that one could not resolve the question of infant baptism by quoting proof texts. The Bible was rather to be read in the context of the ecclesial life, to which the Bible belonged and in which it was properly interpreted. Likewise, the church fathers were not "puppets," to be yanked around repeating stock phrases. It was not enough to know that infant baptism was accepted by the third century; one had to understand *why* it was accepted, what spiritual and theological developments had emerged that made this apparent change a meaningful and valid manifestation of the internal churchly life. The fathers (like the Bible) could only be properly understood in their spiritual and ecclesial context—and that context was sacramental. Divine grace, God's saving action in the world, was revealed in and through the earthly signs of water, bread, and wine, as those signs were enacted in the life of the church. As noted earlier, Nevin's critique was even more perceptive than he could fully articulate. Revivalists and evangelicals had substituted a fundamentally different system of salvation: a private, subjective experience of God's voice. Christians with this experience could appeal to scripture or tradition as proof texts, but this appeal was separated

---

eventually founded a school in Caesarea (*Dictionary of the Christian Church*, 1193–94). He "developed the notion of allegorical interpretation," a key idea in the discussion in art. 7 below (McGrath, *Christian Theology*, 11). Cyprian (d. 258), bishop of Carthage, is especially noted for his writings on how to reconcile Christians who had "lapsed" under the Decian persecutions (*De Lapsis*); disagreements then developed between African bishops and Stephen, bishop of Rome, over the rebaptism of schismatics, and Cyprian responded with *De Catholicae Ecclesiae Unitate* [trans., "The Unity of the Catholic Church"] (*Dictionary of the Christian Church*, 441). Cyprian would be central to Nevin's reflection on the significance and implications of Schaff's theory of historical development. Both Origen and Cyprian were victims of the Decian persecution. Augustine (354–430), bishop of Hippo, is generally considered the greatest theologian of Latin Christendom, if not in all of Christian history (ibid., 128–29).

9. The first sign of Nevin's concern with this problem was "Historical Development," 512–14. He then went on to work on it in detail in "Early Christianity" and "Cyprian"; these latter two texts are projected for vol. 9 of MTSS. The analysis of this trajectory in the general introduction suggests that ultimately it did not help him to resolve the problems posed by historical change.

from the spiritual life that those sources originally possessed. Practices or concepts were dissociated from the context in which they rested, and rendered individual "bullet points" maintained arbitrarily (e.g., evangelicals who asserted "original sin" while denying the practice of infant baptism, upon which the dogma apparently rested).

"Noel on Baptism"[1]: *Essay on Christian Baptism. By Baptist W. Noel, M. A. New York: Harper & Brothers; 1850. Pp. 308, 12mo.*[2]

It is generally admitted, we believe, that this work is of no special weight for the controversy in whose service it appears. It presents nothing new, and it repeats but little of the old in any better form than it carried before. The work of a truth is emphatically lean and superficial. Still the highly respectable source from which it proceeds, and the widely public character of the occasion[3] to which it owes its production, entitle it to something more than common consideration; and altogether it may be taken as a very fit and fair opportunity for bringing to trial, in a general way, the theological and religious merits of the popular system to whose defence and recommendation it is so zealously devoted.

[The Popular Nature of Baptist Theory]

We call the system *popular*, with due thought and consideration. Its friends, we know, are fond of harping occasionally on the opposite idea; as though it needed more than common fortitude and resolution to fall in with the Baptistic theory, in contradiction to the old catholic faith. Mr. Noel evidently looks upon himself as something of a martyr, in the way of sacrifice and self-renunciation, for following his convictions into the bosom of his new communion, as much so as for following them in the first place out of the bosom of the Establishment; and he is prone continually to resolve the backwardness of others to acknowledge what he holds to be the plain sense of the Scriptures, into the moral cowardice that shrinks from the thought of losing caste, or suffering damage in some outward view, for the sake of an unfashionable and unpopular cause. But it is only in one *view*, that the system of the Baptists is found to be thus unpopular. It goes against antiquity and the authority of the universal Church; and in these circumstances it is hard not to feel, that it involves some loss of privilege, and

---

1. [Nevin, *Mercersburg Review*, 231–65.]

2. [Noel, *Essay on Christian Baptism*.]

3. [Since the English edition was published in 1849, it had to have been written within several months of Noel's (re)baptism, in August of that year.]

some serious spiritual hazard, which men should not be willing lightly to incur. This however is only the same sort of prejudice which is found to hold, in christian lands, against other forms of religious profession which are regarded as still more broadly opposed to the ancient faith; Unitarianism for instance or Universalism; which at the same time are but seldom allowed to carry with them any presumption of truth and righteousness on such account. It requires generally still more nerve in this view, to become a convert to Unitarianism, than it does to espouse the cause of the Baptists. In neither case have we any right to infer from the difficulty any such contrariety to the natural mind of the world, as may be taken for the criterion of divine truth. On the contrary, it requires no very profound examination to see that the system held in both cases falls in strikingly with what may be termed the natural mind of the world, and in such view is exactly suited to gain popularity and credit. The Baptistic theory excludes mystery, and turns religion into a thing of measurable intelligence and common sense.[4] It falls in thus with the tendency of Protestantism to assert the rights of the individual subject in religion, over against the claims of objective authority; a tendency which *ought* to be asserted within right limits; while it is particularly liable also, for this very reason, to be carried to an extreme, destructive entirely of what belongs to the opposite interest. It is not to be denied, that such extreme subjectivity or individualism has come to form the reigning character of Protestant Christianity at the present time; and especially may this be said to be the case in our own country, the land of universal toleration and freedom, where the very idea of the Church is in danger of being swallowed up and lost in the distraction of sects as the only true and proper form of the christian life. With this reigning spirit, the Baptistic view of religion stands unquestionably in very close correspondence and affinity. However it may have been persecuted in the beginning, under the mild theocracy of New England, it has long since ceased to be the faith of suffering exiles and martyrs. It has grown into a large world of christian profession, covering the length and breadth of the entire land. This is held together by no bond of unity indeed in other respects; for it belongs to its very nature to be as much as possible unchurchly and inorganic, a mere multitude of men and women following the Bible severally to suit themselves. But taking them simply as *Baptists*, sticklers for immersion and excommunicators of infants from Christ, they form collectively the most numerous religious body in the United States. They have the art of making proselytes, beyond almost all other people. The sect spirit,[5] as it

4. [Several years later, Nevin would say that Christianity is a "mystery, a constitution above nature, objectively at hand under a real historical form in the world, to which men must submit by faith" ("Evangelical Radicalism," 512). Christianity transcended mundane human understanding. One could not master it or confine it within the limits of a theological system. Being a "constitution," it was an organized body (thus *organic*) that was objective (psychologically transcendental) and historical (temporally transcendental). A key argument against "Baptist" spirituality was that it imagined that its own idiosyncratic expression was universally valid, both in time and space. ("The Sect System," 497–98; repr. *Catholic and Reformed*, 143–44; *Antichrist*, 55–56.). The mystery of Christianity required apprehension by *faith*, in contrast to the self-mastering certainty of the "Baptistic theory."]

5. ["The Sect System," in *Catholic and Reformed*, 128–73; Nevin, *Antichrist*; both texts are excerpted

prevails in all parts of the land, has a wonderful propensity towards the Baptistic system; for it is constitutionally unsacramental and rationalistic, and is always inclined to resolve religion into the thinking and working of man, to the exclusion of its mystical power as it lies on the side of God. Hence new sects are apt to take Anabaptist ground; especially where they have their origin, not immediately in some doctrinal interest, but in zeal rather for religious experience.[6] It is but too plain thus that the Baptists have a strong popular feeling on their side, which needs only to be set free still farther from the force of mere outward authority, standing in tradition and custom, to bring the world generally to espouse their cause.

This favorable state of the public mind in regard to the theory of the Baptists is not to be measured simply by their actual discipleship, or the preparation there may be in different quarters to receive in form their particular system; it shows itself also to a large extent in the indifference and want of faith, with which the contrary system is too generally maintained. It is of small account to oppose a system, if the principle of it, that from which it draws its life and strength, be the meanwhile silently allowed and approved. Opposition, in such case, may be kept up as a sort of outside fashion; but it will carry with it no real earnestness or power. It is in truth no better than treason at last to the cause it pretends to uphold. Of such character necessarily are all argument and practice against the Baptists, which do not rest truly on the old idea of the Church and its sacraments, but start from the premises of the Baptists themselves with regard to the nature of religion, virtually surrendering in this way the whole interest in debate.[7] Very much of our existing fidelity to the old church practice, it is to be feared, labors under this grievous defect. It is a matter of outward form and ceremony, more than of true inward faith and conviction. It makes common cause with the general scheme of the Baptists in regard to religion and the Church, and is obedient only to its own tradition in refusing to carry out this scheme to the same consequences. In these circumstances, no great account is made of the variation in which the system stands from the proper church practice. So far as it may be considered wrong, it is still viewed with the utmost indulgence and forbearance; the difference is taken to regard a mere circumstance in religion, without reaching at all to its main substance; and the only cause for regret and complaint in regard to it is, that the Baptists themselves should be disposed to lay so much stress upon it, as they generally do, in the way of uncharitable

---

in *The Mercersburg Theology*, ed. James Hastings Nichols, 95–119, and forthcoming in vol. 5 of MTSS.]

6. [Nevin shared the virtually universal view that the Anabaptists were unregulated religious fanatics, an orientation that quite logically led to the murderous revolution of Munster. Another expression of Nevin's view of the Anabaptists can be found in *The Mystical Presence* (MTSS ed., 132); see also the editor's footnote.]

7. [Here Nevin began an argument that both he and Gerhart (see below, art. 5, "The Efficacy of Baptism") would use: those communities who continued to hold to the outward forms of "churchly" piety found it impossible to resist the encroachments of sectarian and Baptist practices, since they had already surrendered the faithful, reflective "principles," the spiritual life, that could give those forms vitality and meaning.]

exclusiveness towards others. Mr. Noel's transition to their ranks is taken indeed for a mark of some weakness and eccentricity; but it is still not allowed to qualify materially, in this view, the vast merit which all non-episcopal bodies are expected, as a matter of course, to see in his previous abandonment of the English Establishment. It is but too plain from the way in which the subject is frequently noticed, that for a large part of this interest among us, the acknowledgment of a churchly and sacramental religion is something altogether worse than the virtual renunciation of the sacraments as it holds among the Baptists. Noel the Baptist, to this system of thinking, is much more respectable and every way intelligible, than Noel the Episcopalian. The difference which has place in the first direction, is regarded as small and comparatively immaterial. The great matter is that such a man has been able to leap the far more broad and serious chasm that yawns on the other side. Baptists and Paedobaptists, of the unchurchly stamp, have here common and like cause for gratulation. It is felt to be at last substantially one and the same gospel to which the illustrious convert has been won in either connection, and both unite accordingly in wishing him God-speed on his chosen way. For those who consider it rightly, this is something very significant and instructive. It was not so always. The Baptistic system, in the beginning, was held to be at war with Protestantism no less than with the faith of the ancient Church. Its deviation from the old church theory was felt to be something far more than a mere circumstance. How does it happen then that it should now be met with such easy toleration, as a thing of mere outward fashion and form? For the reason simply, beyond all doubt, that the view taken of the Church has undergone a material change. The sense of sacramental grace has to a wide extent passed away; and along with this, of course, the doctrine of infant baptism is to the same extent necessarily shorn of its proper meaning and force. The Baptistic principle has come to prevail far and wide among those who are not Baptists; and in this way the opposition even which is made to their cause is found to be in truth too often but little better than a feint and a sham. The controversy is transferred to false and untenable ground, and so carries in itself the necessity of defeat from the beginning. It yields at the outset the main substance in dispute, and makes but a vain show of battle afterwards for its mere name and shadow. Here it is precisely that the Baptists of the present time have the greatest advantage. Their premises and principles are allowed extensively by the opposite side; and all that they need, in such circumstances, is to show that these principles and premises carry in them by necessary consequence the sense of their own system. Without faith in the Church, no consistent or effectual stand can ever be made against their pretensions.[8]

---

8. [For Nevin, to have "faith in the Church" was to *trust* that the spiritual life the church claimed to be present, *was* present. It was to be confident that, e.g., baptism brought about the forgiveness of sins it promised; that when the church proclaimed, "this is my body," Christ was truly, even if "mystically," present, etc. His antagonism against the "Baptists" was rooted in his belief that they denied the authority of the church, while asserting the authority of their own profession and practices. "Who art thou, upstart system! that thou shouldst set thyself in such proud style above the universal church of antiquity . . . charging it with wholesale superstition and folly, and requiring us to renounce its creed,

[The Mode of Baptism]

The Baptistic controversy, it is well known, falls mainly into two questions, the first regarding the *mode* of baptism and the second its proper *subjects*. The only valid mode, according to the Baptists, is by immersion. The only fit subjects, they tell us, are personal believers. Sprinkling they take to be of no force for the rite; and the application of it to infants they hold to be no better than a solemn farce.

It is truly unfortunate, in the case of the first of these questions, that the advocates of the present reigning practice have been led so commonly by polemical zeal to place themselves on extreme ground; furnishing thus in the end an advantage to their opponents, which they would not otherwise possess. When it is pretended to show immersion an abuse, and sprinkling the only legitimate mode of baptism, from the force of the original terms employed in the case, the general evidence of the New Testament, or the practice of the early Church, more is undertaken a great deal than can be accomplished, and more at the same time in all respects than the argument properly requires; by which means harm only is done to the truth, and the cause of the opposite party made to seem far stronger than it is in fact. It needs but ordinary scholarship, and the freedom of a mind unpledged to mere party interest, to see and acknowledge here a certain advantage on the side of the Baptists. The original sense of the word *baptize* is on the whole in their favor. It corresponds with the idea of immersion much more than with that of sprinkling. This idea moreover undoubtedly lies at the bottom of the New Testament practice; although it would seem to be equally clear, for a candid inquirer, that this practice was not actually confined, under all circumstances, to the mode of immersion, in the literal and full sense. The allusion in Rom. vi. 4, and Col. ii. 12, to the form of going under the water and rising out of it again, as being at least the primary and fundamental character of the rite, is too plain to be misunderstood by any unsophisticated mind; and it is only a melancholy exemplification of the power which theological prejudice has over the best men, when otherwise able and faithful commentators of the anti-Baptist order are found vainly endeavoring, in modern times, to torture the passages into another meaning. The practice of the early Church too, as far back as we have any notices on the subject out of the New Testament, must be allowed to lie prevailingly in favor of the same view.

---

the whole scheme of habit of its religious life, and to accept from *thy* hands, in place of it, another form of belief, another scheme of doctrine altogether, as infallibly true and right? Who gave thee this authority? Whence came such infallibility? . . . Reason, every man's reason for himself, the world's private judgment and common sense with such religious illumination as it may come to in its own sphere, is the court, the tribunal, by which the law in this case is to take the form of truth and life. Is that not rationalism almost without disguise?" ("Evangelical Radicalism," 511).]

[Form and Freedom in the Sacrament of Baptism]

The most that can be said with regard to it, which however is a great deal over against the exclusive doctrine of the Baptists, is that the form of immersion was not considered indispensable to the validity of the sacrament. This is sufficiently shown by what is termed the *clinical baptism* of the ancient Church, aside from all other evidence. Clinical baptism was employed in the case of the sick, who were confined to bed or otherwise unfit to endure the rite of immersion. It consisted of a partial application of water, in the way of substitute for this, by a more or less plentiful affusion or aspersion. Persons thus baptized, if they afterwards recovered, were not considered eligible to any sacred office, as their profession might seem to have been forced upon them by sickness and so to be of doubtful sincerity; but no deficiency was held to attach to their baptism itself, and it was never felt necessary or proper accordingly to baptize them over again in a more full way. On this point, the testimony of Cyprian[9] is well known and conclusive, showing at once the fact of such baptism by aspersion in the early Church, and the acknowledgment of its sufficiency, as resting on the view that the application of water, in the sacrament, is efficacious not according to surface and quantity, as in common washing, but according to the accompanying grace of the Holy Ghost. "*In sacramentis salutaribus, necessitate cogente, et Deo indulgentiam suam largiente, totum credentibus conferunt divina compendia.*"[10] It is not to be disguised at the same time, however, that this allowance and apology for the validity of clinical baptism goes directly to show the general prevalence of baptism by immersion; and also the general feeling that it was regarded as the regular and proper mode, from which only in cases of urgent necessity it was considered lawful to depart. Cyprian's plea for it is worded with great caution and reserve, and treats it throughout as something in broad exception to the reigning practice. In the Oriental Church this practice has been preserved without change down to the present day; and the completeness of baptism is made to depend absolutely on its being performed by immersion, and not by any less universal application of water. In the Western or Latin Church a more free conception of the sacrament has prevailed; and from the thirteenth century particularly we find the practice of affusion or plentiful sprinkling gradually supplanting more and more generally the earlier method. The change seems to have grown to a considerable extent from the preponderance which the baptism of infants gained over that of adults, as the nations became generally christian, and the main use of the ordinance was transferred thus from heathen converts to the offspring of parents already in the Church. It was natural to extend the allowance of the so-called clinical

9. [The "*clinici*" (from Gk., κλινη, "bed") were primarily persons who were baptized in anticipation of imminent death. See Cyprian's response to the problem, "Letter LXXV" (§§12–16), in *Ante-Nicene Fathers*, 5:400–402.]

10. [Trans. "In the sacraments of salvation, when necessity compels, and God bestows His mercy, the divine methods confer the whole benefit on believers" (Cyprian, "Letter LXXV" [§12], in *Ante-Nicene Fathers*, 5:401).]

baptism in favor especially of very young infants, who might be regarded as infirm by reason of their infancy itself, and so rightly entitled to the privilege; and this way of thinking, once introduced, appears to have worked in no great time a general revolution in the practice of the Church. The Reformation, in the sixteenth century, found the Roman Church generally (with the exception of the Church of Milan which still adhered to the old form) no longer in the exclusive use of immersion, but allowing also in place of it, when preferred, a partial application of water only, by affusion on the head or some other prominent part of the subject baptized. The symbolical sense of the application was held to be the main thing; and this was supposed to be as fully secured by its being poured upon the head, or shoulders, or breast, as though it were made to circumfuse in full the entire body. The force of the symbol was not measured by its outward quantity.

The Reformers were disposed to prefer the ancient custom; not from any superstitious regard to the mere letter of the institution; but out of respect for antiquity, and from the feeling also of a certain congruity between the letter or form here and its proper inward sense. They questioned not the sufficiency of baptism by aspersion, but held the use of immersion to be on the whole more suitable and significant. Luther says, in a sermon on Baptism (Walch x, 2593):[11]

> Though it be the custom, in many places no longer to dip the children whole in the font, but only to pour water on them from it with the hand, it were better still and fit, according to the sense of the word *baptism*, that the child, or any one else who is baptized, should be entirely sunk into the water and drawn out again.... This would suit the signification of the thing, and furnish a fully complete sign.[12]

Both of Luther's formularies for baptism, accordingly, that of 1523 and the revision of 1524,[13] include the rubric: "Then let him take the child, and *dip it in the font*"—with clear reference to immersion. Calvin allows also indirectly a certain priority of worth to this mode, with full assertion at the same time of the proper freedom of Christianity in favor of the other practice. "Whether the whole person be

---

11. ["D. Mart. Luthers Sermon von Sacrament der Taufe, 1518," *D. Martin Luthers* Sämtliche Werke, vol. 10, ed. Johann Georg Walch (Halle in Magdeburgischen: Johann Justinus Gebauer, 1744), 2593.]

12. [See English translation in *Word and Sacrament I*, vol. 35 of *Luther's Works: American Edition*, 29. After the ellipsis, Nevin conflated several sentences: "This usage is also demanded by the significance of baptism itself. For baptism, as we shall hear, signifies that the old man and the sinful birth of flesh and blood are to be wholly drowned by the grace of God. We should therefore do justice to its meaning and make baptism a true and complete sign of the thing it signifies."]

13. [1523: Richter, ed., *Die evangelischen Kirchenordnungen des sechszehnten Jahrhunderts* (1871), 9; Sehling, ed., *Die evangelischen Kirchenordnungen des XVI. Jahrhunderts*, 19; trans., "Luther's First Taufbüchlein," in J. D. C. Fisher, *Christian Initiation: The Reformation Period*, 16; rev. 1526 (not 1524): Sehling, 23; trans., "Luther's Second Taufbüchlein," in Fisher, *Christian Initiation*, 25.]

immersed," he says, Inst. iv. 15,19,[14] "and this be once or thrice, or the water be merely poured on by aspersion, is of little account, and ought to be considered free to the churches according to their different regions. Though the word baptize does itself signify to *immerse*, and it is known that the rite of immersion prevailed also in the early Church." Several of the earlier Protestant church services call for dipping. In the first English Reformed Liturgy, a. 1547, a *trine immersion* of the child is prescribed, cases of infirmity only excepted;[15] and it was not till the beginning of the 17th century that sprinkling gained the upper hand, for reasons of convenience and health. Gradually the usage of all the Protestant Churches settled down upon the same practice which had already begun to prevail in the Church of Rome; with the exception only of the Anabaptists; who however rested their view on a different theory altogether of the nature and force of the sacrament itself, and for this reason were not regarded as any part of the Church, either Catholic or Protestant.

The freedom exercised, in this case, by the Western Church generally, we hold to be in full harmony with the true idea of Christianity; as the want of it on the side of the Greek Church is an evidence of its having lost the proper life and spirit of its own original faith. It has been throughout the lively apprehension of the spiritual realness of the sacrament, as the presence actually and truly of an inward grace under an outward form, which has enabled the Church of the West, whether as Catholic or as Protestant, to make an adiaforon[16] of the mere circumstances of the symbol, while continuing to hold fast with becoming reverence and faith the substantial matter of the symbol itself. This is something far more than either a rationalistic rejection of the rite on the one hand, or a slavish adhesion to the outward letter of it on the other. These two extremes might seem to be sufficiently far apart, the one forming the exact contrary of the other. And yet it is not so in fact. They start from substantially the same false posture, in regard to the christian faith; and they come in the end to substantially the same result. Either may claim to be, and has often claimed to be in fact, not only Christianity, but this also under its highest and most perfect style. In one view thus we have the spiritualism of the Quaker; in another view the spiritualism of the Anabaptist. Their affinity is shown strikingly by their tendency to flow together at particular points, both in the earlier and later stages of their history. Both are constitutionally rationalistic, notwithstanding the high wrought temperature of their first life, or rather for this very reason one may say, and sooner or later this defect is found working itself into view with clear historical evidence and proof. Quakerism runs naturally into Hicksite infidelity, and Anabaptism just as naturally into lifeless mechanism and form, the corpse of religion deprived of its living soul. The common principle of both is the want of faith in the true and proper *mystery* of the sacraments. The Quaker places religion wholly in the sphere of thought, the naked spirit of the subject, and so will have nothing to do with

---

14. [Calvin, *Institutes*, ed. McNeill. 2:1320.]
15. ["Baptism in the Prayer Book of 1549" (not 1547), in Fisher, *Christian Initiation*, 94.]
16. [Trans. "thing indifferent."]

the letter and sign. The Baptist places it there too, but makes a merit at the same time of honoring the letter and sign in a purely outward way, in token of his mental respect for the authority by which it is prescribed. In both cases, the grace and the sign are completely sundered. The Baptist turns the sacrament into a powerless ceremony as truly as the Quaker. Only he chooses to exercise *his* spirituality and rationalism, by squaring his practice in the case to the outward rule which God has been pleased to prescribe as the test of his pious obedience. In such view, of course, all turns on the letter; and the more precisely circumstantial this can be made, the more satisfactory it is taken to be as a trial of christian character. The Baptist, in this way, becomes a Jew.[17]

A right appreciation here of the old church faith, as holding in a living way between these two abstractions, while it leads us to do justice to the free practice of the Western Church within proper limits, will prevent us at the same time from approving such freedom beyond these limits. It cannot be denied that there is a strong tendency with our later Protestantism, especially under the Puritan form, to run the liberty of sprinkling, as it may be called, into actual licentiousness, by reducing the quantity of water used in baptism to the narrowest practicable measure. The force of the symbol does not indeed turn on the amount of the water employed; but something is still due to the reality and the original sense of the service in this view; and it is very certain that a true sacramental feeling must always operate, where it prevails, to produce a due regard to the mystical idea of the holy ordinance as joined with the water, which will not allow it to be stripped of its proper outward honor in the divine transaction. The old Church, in allowing a partial use of water, still required always that it should be in its measure plentiful and free. So also the Protestant Church of earlier times, in sanctioning the change from immersion to affusion. It marks no improvement on this in our own day, that the application is so frequently reduced to a few drops; the minister simply dipping his fingers in the water perhaps, and flinging some particles of what adheres to them into the child's face, instead of taking up as the old formularies prescribe at least his hand full of the element, and so pouring the same on its head. We have witnessed the service with pain performed in this style, where it was some relief to be sure that only a solitary drop reached the face of the infant, so utterly careless did the officiating priest show himself to be of anything more than the mere ceremony of

---

17. [For Nevin, the "grace and the sign" had to go together, be "organically" linked. Without this linkage, either the sacrament was comprehended conceptually separate from the sign, and therefore one could dispense with the sign (which Nevin thought was the Quaker option); or it became enforced "heteronomously" (which Nevin ascribed to the Baptist). In the latter case, one enacted the sign because one was "legalistically" required to do so, not because the sign bore the grace. On heteronomy, see Nevin, "Faith, Freedom, and Reverence," repr. in *The Mercersburg Theology*, 286–306, esp. 293. "No man can fulfill his true moral destiny by a simply blind and passive obedience to law. His obedience, to be complete, must be intelligent and spontaneous. In other words, the law must enter into and become incorporated with his life" (305). The principle was identical in the sacraments: one was baptized not because one was (merely) "obligated" to be so, but because there was a new spiritual life inherent in the act. The original and longer version of this essay, "Human Freedom," is scheduled for publication in vol. 13 of MTSS.]

going through the outward motions of the solemn rite. Now we know it is easy to say, that all depends on the Spirit, and that a single drop of water may be just as efficacious in his hands as all the rivers of Damascus, and Jordan along with them; but it is just as easy to go a single step farther also, and to affirm that the mere motion of the hand in imitation of the act of sprinkling would carry with it all the virtue and force of baptism, even if no water whatever were employed in the case. When it comes to this, of course, all faith in the sacrament as such is gone; the only religious reality owned in it is the *thought* of a certain spiritual work of which it is taken to be the emblem and sign; and it is hard to see why this might not be just as complete with the sign wanting altogether, according to the view of the Quaker. This disposition to rest in the merest minimum of the outward symbol, is something very different from the old sacramental faith, and may be taken always as the sure mark of its comparative if not total absence and failure. Hence it is, that it lends likewise powerful help always to the Baptist cause; not simply as it serves, like all ultraism, to bring reproach on the interest it affects to represent, but as it actually involves also the very spirit itself by which this cause is actuated. It argues an unsacramental habit; indifference or insensibility to the mystical import of the symbol employed in the transaction; and where this prevails, the only proper alternative is, no water baptism at all or else slavish confinement to it, as a purely outward law, after the Baptist fashion.

In this case we have a double cause for regret. First, that the question of *mode* should be made to seem the main point at issue, and be so managed at the same time as to array the practice of sprinkling or affusion against immersion, as though the last must be shorn of all right in order to justify the other; in consequence of which we have a great deal of false argument on this side, which only rebounds at last in favor of the opposite interest. Secondly, that the defence of sprinkling is too often based on so low a view of the sacrament as amounts well nigh to indifferentism itself, and thus in reality betrays the interest in whose service it appears. Any vindication of sprinkling which proceeds on the assumption that baptism in any shape is a mere ceremony, and that *therefore* no stress should be laid on the mode, must be regarded as a virtual surrendry of all that is material in the controversy, from the start.

[Scriptural Authority in the Baptist Theory]

The great question in truth however, in this Baptistic controversy, is that which relates to the proper subjects of the ordinance, and which is concerned particularly with the right of *infants* to be comprehended by means of it in the communion of the Christian Church. It is here, still more strikingly than in the other case, that we learn the distinctive character of this unchurchly system, and are brought to face in full at the same time the monstrous consequences to which it leads. Mr. Noel's book is occupied mainly with the lawfulness of infant baptism. He finds it a superstitious corruption, contrary to the Bible, contrary to reason, and contrary to primitive Christianity; and only wonders that all sensible and sober men, in so plain a case, should not long since have come to look upon it in the same light.

Mr. Noel professes great reverence for the authority of the Scriptures. He has thrown himself, he tells us, entirely on their guidance; carefully avoiding indeed all communication with Baptist writers, that his judgment might be formed in this way solely by divine teaching. He claims accordingly to be an original witness in the case, fresh from the fountain of all truth in the Bible. "Not having read a single Baptist book or tract, I publish the following work as an independent testimony to the exclusive right of believers to Christian baptism" (*iv*).[18] The book itself too shows the use of the Scriptures almost on every page. It abounds with quotations and texts. In this respect however it is only a striking exemplification of the vanity and nonsense of the pretension, on which it is thus ostentatiously made to rest. Mr. Noel affects to come to the Bible like an empty vase theologically, leaving behind him all other education and tradition, in order to be filled purely from its gushing contents; and yet it comes only to this at last, that he divests himself of the old universal church faith, the substance of catholic thought as we have it embodied in the Creed, and brings along with him another different habit of his own, which after all is the result too of education, and in this respect as far removed at least from independence as the most sound church feeling. It is perfectly idle for him to pretend, that he has studied the Bible without prejudice or pre-occupation. His study has been throughout from a given theological standpoint, carrying in itself from the start the necessity of just such views and aspects as it is found then to offer to his eye. Another standpoint would clothe it with a very different sense; and it is sheer impudence, when *such* private judgment[19] undertakes to make its observations of universal value, as the very mind of the sacred volume itself, and requires all other judgment, however widely and long established, to fall respectfully into its wake. Allow the premises of the Baptist, grant him his theory of Christianity to begin with (as Puritanism is prone always to do, holding in truth too generally the same theory as its own), and it becomes a comparatively easy thing for him to establish his favorite conclusions and also to find them satisfactorily reflected from many passages of the Bible. The universal necessary first condition for the right understanding and right interpretation of the Scriptures, is sympathy with the general fact of Christianity, and a living comprehension in its true catholic mystery as it has stood from the beginning. Without this, the more independent and single the expounder may be, the more empty and jejune ordinarily will be the character also of his expositions. Mr. Noel, we are sorry to say, furnishes no exception to this rule. His piety has no power to redeem the impotency of his false position. The use of the Bible in his hands is superficial in the extreme. We have text upon text, and quotation on quotation; the *sound* of the Bible forever ringing in our ears, from one end of the

---

18. [Noel, *Essay on Christian Baptism*, iii–iv.]

19. [On "private judgment," see Nevin, "The Sect System," 494–500; in *Catholic and Reformed*, 140–46; and "Evangelical Radicalism," 511–12.]

book to the other; but it is the Bible for the most part turned into mere commonplace and outside talk, with almost no regard whatever to its interior substance and sense.

[The Spirituality of the Baptist Theory]

The book exemplifies again the vanity of the pretence, that the unsacramental system is more favorable to religious *spirituality* than the catholic. The Quakers and Baptists both claim to be more spiritual than the Church generally; and they try to make good this claim, by reducing religion as much as possible to the actings of individual mind and will, in the case of those who are its subjects. But spiritualism, in this form, is not true Christian spirituality, when all is done. On the contrary, it is just the reverse of this, and left to itself is sure to end in rationalistic misery and starvation. Without faith in catholic realities, there can be no true Christian spirituality. Mr. Noel's book affects to move in the highest region of experimental piety; and all the world knows him to be a truly pious man; but we find no quickening, elevating spirit whatever, in what he has here written. It is an irksome, insipid task, to follow him in his views of religion; so dreary and dry is the region through which they carry us; so cold and cheerless the results to which they bring us as their necessary end. The freshness and depth of a truly spiritual mind form no part of this plea for "believer's baptism." On the contrary, it is altogether mechanical and outward in its spirit. We feel ourselves surrounded, in reading it, with the atmosphere of rationalism. We seem to be feeding on husks, or vainly endeavoring to satisfy ourselves with the substance of the east wind.

The fundamental controversy in this case lies quite back of all Mr. Noel's argument. The question of the proper use of the sacraments, must depend in the first place on the true idea of their nature. The difference of the Baptists from the old catholic faith begins here; and unless it be properly met where it thus begins, it is of comparatively small account to make it the subject of contention at any other point. The controversy regards the existence of the sacraments themselves. The Baptists allow no sacrament at all *in the old church sense*. Mr. Noel's book proceeds throughout on the assumption, that baptism is no such sacrament, but a mere outward rite of divine appointment, carrying in it a different import altogether. Allow the old idea of a sacrament to retain its force, and his argument would be at an end. The great question then, and it is one of the very highest solemnity, resolves itself into this: Is baptism a sacrament, as the Church catholic has always believed, or is it only an outward law and sign?

A sacrament in the true church sense is not a mere outward rite, made obligatory by divine appointment. It carries in itself a peculiar constitution of its own. It consists, according to the old definition, of two parts, one outward and the other inward, a visible terrene sign and an invisible celestial grace; not related simply as corresponding facts, brought together by human thought; but the one actually bound to the other in the way of most real mystical or sacramental union, causing the last to be objectively at hand in one and the same transaction with the first. Dissolve this mystical bond, and at once the old conception of a sacrament is gone at the same time. You may still retain a rite or ceremony which you dignify with this venerable name; but you will not have what the Church, from the beginning, has understood herself to possess in the holy mysteries of baptism and the Lord's supper.

Now Mr. Noel acknowledges no such bond whatever, in the ordinance of baptism. It is for him purely an outward institution, the whole sense and value of which turn on its giving the believer an opportunity to show his obedience to the authority by which it has been appointed. It is very significant, that the Baptists generally are so prone to speak of the ordinance as a rite or Law; showing themselves to have no sense of its being anything more, in this view, than an outward rule imposed by Christ. The "law of baptism," as they are fond of styling it, sinks into a full parallel with the services of the Old Testament, and due regard for it is then made to stand, naturally enough, in an exact compliance with all that may be supposed to belong to the letter of it in such view. The idea of a living power in the ordinance itself, seems to have no place at all in their minds.

Mr. Noel appears never to dream of the possibility of any such objective grace in baptism. It is for him mainly an act of mere profession on the part of the believing subject. "A true faith must manifest itself, and baptism is one appointed mode of its manifestation" (45).[20] "Since faith is said to save us, because it is the instrument through which God saves us, so baptism is said to save us, because it is the necessary expression of true faith" (46). "Baptism is the profession of faith, the public confession of Christ, without which confession there is no true faith and no salvation" (97). "If baptism be simply a profession of repentance and faith, then the expression, 'Repent and be baptized for the remission of sins,' is equivalent to, 'Repent and believe for the remission of sins.' Remission of sins attends baptism simply because it attends faith" (101). Could language well make the thing more explicit? The religious force of baptism is purely and wholly subjective; it is nothing save as it serves to represent and manifest a certain state of mind in the believer; the idea of any *other* power belonging to it as a Divine act is wholly excluded, as being no better than visionary superstition. In this way it ceases to be a sacrament altogether; for a sacrament carrying in it no objective grace, is a contradiction in terms. To abjure the idea of baptismal grace, is to break with the old idea of baptism throughout, and to treat it as an idle dream.

A certain relation to grace, indeed, the system is still willing to allow. But this is taken to be wholly outward. Baptism signifies something spiritual; only however in the way of suggestion to the human mind. No inward, necessary, present bond is allowed to hold between the sign and the thing signified. The transaction outwardly considered enters not at all as an essential factor, into the constitution of the fact which is consummated by its means. It is merely appended to this as an accidental badge. So Mr. Noel takes it throughout. But this is not the form in which baptism, from the beginning, has claimed to be acknowledged as a sacrament. Most clearly in the New

20. [The numerals in the text that follows are page numbers in Noel, *Essay on Christian Baptism*.]

Testament, it is made to enter efficaciously, as a divine act, into the mystery of the new birth. Whatever of difficulty may attach to this conception, we have no right to thrust it violently aside for the purpose of accommodating a different theory. The letter of the Bible is too plain, and the sense of it too awfully solemn, to bear any such spiritualism as that. Baptism here is no mere sign, no simply outward adjunct or accident. It is the washing of regeneration; it saves us; it is for the remission of sins. The mere ceremony of course is not this *per se*; but it goes actually to complete the work of our salvation, as the mystical exhibition in real form of that divine grace, without which all our subjective exercises in the case must amount to nothing. Such is the doctrine of the New Testament; and so accordingly the whole ancient Church believed. We have this faith formally proclaimed in the Creed; for the article there affirming the *remission of sins*, as may be easily shown, refers to this as a fact accomplished in the Church by baptism. The objective presence of such supernatural grace in the mystical transaction, is the very thing which faith is required to embrace; as without it indeed there would be no room for its exercise. That the Church otherwise attributed such grace to the sacrament, universally and at all times, is too well known to admit any dispute. Mr. Noel then, and the Baptists as a body, are completely at issue here with primitive Christianity; and the difference is one of vast magnitude and moment. It regards not simply the mode of baptism and its proper subjects, but its essential nature and constitution. Whether agreement in other respects can or cannot be shown, is after all comparatively immaterial; the grand discord, and that which must forever mar all harmonies besides, lies here at the very bottom of the entire subject. What the primitive Church owned and saw in baptism, Mr. Noel neither owns nor sees in it at all. It is for him no sacrament whatever, but only a rule or sign dignified with such title.

[The Effects of Baptism in the Baptist Theory]

He has one chapter devoted to the "effects of baptism," which sets this in the clearest light. Christianity, he tells us, stands in the pardon of sins through Christ for such as trust in his grace, and a life of subsequent consecration to his service. It is meet, in this case, that the believer should openly profess his faith. The Church too, "the society of Christ's disciples," needs some public guaranty of right behavior, on the part of those who are admitted to its fellowship. "Both these objects are secured by the appointed rite of baptism" (264). It works well besides on the subject himself, on the congregation he joins, and on spectators generally. The subject of so public and solemn a rite, by proclaiming his faith to the world, is laid under bond to follow Christ truly, and by such decision gains strength for the duty. "A thousand checks to sin and a thousand aids to godliness are that day assumed; faith, hope, and love are likely to be confirmed" (266). The sight is edifying to the church; as it serves to revive and quicken old associations. Witnesses, on the outside of the church, may be affected by it also in the way of salutary reflection. The rite serves the purpose of a key moreover, in the hands of a church, to lock out the world from her communion (269, 270). These good effects however belong only to the ordinance as applied to actual believers. Infant baptism works very differently. It sets aside the other practice, with all its connections so admirably suited for *effect*. "Through the baptism of unconscious infants, the solemn, affecting, and salutary baptism of repentance, faith, and self-dedication to God, has nearly vanished from the churches" (272). And what benefit has been gained by the substitution? Mr. Noel can find none whatever. Under the Mosaic economy, circumcision admitted its subject to great privileges from which the uncircumcised were excluded. But Christianity owns no such exclusion. The child, baptized or unbaptized, occupies the same ground. Parents too derive no help from the rite. "Pious parents do not need this new inducement to educate their children well; ungodly parents cannot feel its force" (273). The churches themselves regard it with no interest; "except as far as superstition has invested it with imaginary spiritual power, it seems [to me] to have dwindled into a formality" [274]. Even in this view however it works mischievously, as fostering always the notion of a saving relation in some way to Christ, in the case of all its subjects. Still worse, it runs naturally into the figment of downright baptismal regeneration.

Our object in this sketch of Mr. Noel's theory of what belongs, and what does not belong, to the efficacy of Christian baptism, is not to make it the subject of formal trial; but simply to show, how completely it excludes every thought of anything like grace or power, mystically present in the ordinance of itself; how it nullifies, out and out, the idea of its objective force as Christ's act, and resolves it wholly into a thing for effect, in the way of pure subjectivity, on the side of men; how, in one word, it overthrows its character as a *sacrament* altogether, in the old church sense, and mocks us in place of this with a rationalistic shadow played off in its name.

Such a view of baptism is inseparably joined with a corresponding view of the Church. This is no longer the living revelation of Christ in the world, the mystical body of which he is the glorious Head, but takes rather the character of an abstraction, signifying merely the general faith and union of those who embrace the gospel. This involves again a corresponding view of Christ's person, and so in the end of the whole system of Christianity. All has a tendency to quit the form of concrete fact, and run into the form of abstract thought.

[Objectivity and Subjectivity in Baptism]

Where theology comes to be of this sort, we have a dry mechanical separation perpetually between the objective and subjective factors of the christian salvation,[21] which

---

21. [A major argument of this editor's dissertation ("Revelation in the Praxis of the Liturgical Community," Temple University, 1994) was that Nevin distinguished himself from Princeton when he "abandoned the common sense dichotomy of objective doctrine and subjective experience" and replaced it with "a unitary realm of religious 'facts'"—"facts of a churchly religious praxis, a praxis of

has the effect in the end of thrusting the first out of the process altogether. Redemption is made to be a plan or device, over which God presides precisely as the mind of man may be said to rule a machine; and Christ comes in simply in the way of outward instrumental help, to carry out the scheme. The objective side of the salvation is wholly beyond the world, in the Mind of God; the subjective side of it holds in certain exercises brought to pass in particular men, in view of God's grace and by the help of his Spirit; Christ serves only to make room, in some way, for the ready communication of one world in such style with the other. One of the worst results of this way of looking at things is the notion of a *limited atonement*; according to which Christ is taken to have come into the world and died, not for the race as a whole, but only for a part of it, the election of grace as it is sometimes styled, culled out from the general mass beforehand by divine decree. Where Christ is made to stand on the outside of our salvation, and this is felt to have its principle in God's purpose and will touching men in a direct way, it is not possible indeed to avoid this consequence; unless by swinging over to the other extreme of such an indefinite atonement, as either turns Christ's work into a Pelagian show or lands us in the error of Universalism.[22]

The only full refuge from these false abstractions is found in the right sense of Christ, as being himself the sum and substance of the salvation he has brought in the world, and in this view the organic comprehension from the start of its whole compass and extent. The new creation is complete in him as a boundless whole, bringing our human life in full into union with God, independently of its triumphs in particular believers. So it comes before us in the Creed. Here are no abstractions. The world is saved in Christ; and this salvation is, in its own nature, as wide as the world. It challenges our faith and homage, as a power of redemption really and truly present in the Church, and fully commensurate in such form, at the same time, with the entire tract of our general human misery and sin.

[The Argument for Infant Baptism: Christianity Is a Life]

Here it is now that we reach the grand argument for infant baptism. It lies not in the letter of the Scriptures, but in the life of Christianity itself, the true idea of the Church, the mystery of Christ as the Second Adam, in whom redemption and salvation are brought to pass for the race. Let it be felt that Christianity is a new order of life constituted by the Fact of the Incarnation, and that men are saved only by being comprehended in it in a real way; and it will be felt at the same time, that it must be, in this form, fully commensurate with the fact of humanity itself as a whole. The

---

sacramental and liturgical life" (75, 78). Princeton understood Christianity to be a combination of objective doctrine, derived inductively from the Bible, and subjective piety. This material was rewritten for "The Sources of Nevin's Piety," 4–14.]

22. [Nevin's mature critique of scholastic Calvinism was expressed in "Hodge on the Ephesians;" scheduled for inclusion in MTSS, volume 5.]

conception of a partial Christ, a Mediator representing in himself thus a part only of our general manhood and not the whole, strikes directly at the realness and truth of the whole mystery. What a gross imagination it would be, for instance, to limit and bound the capacity of this Mediatorial constitution, by any merely chronological or geographical line in the history of the race; allowing it to be of force for one certain tract of time, but not for another; restricting it to one country or continent with the exclusion of the whole world besides; making it a sufficient source of redemption for Caucasian blood, but not for that of the Negro or Malay! But can it be any more tolerable to right christian feeling, we ask, to limit and bound the force of this salvation by a line sundering in fancy and childhood from riper age, and to make it of real effect on one side of this line only and not on the other? Humanity is not merely our mature human life, but all the stages also through which this is reached. It includes infancy and childhood as a necessary part of its constitution; a large proportion of it exists always under this form; nearly one half of it perhaps is cut off by death before it comes to any higher state. Now the question is not simply: Can such infants be saved if they should happen to die? But this rather: Is there any real room for them, living or dying, in the concrete mystery of the new creation, in the communion of Christ's Mediatoral Life, in the bosom of the Holy Catholic Church?[23] Does the nature of the Second Adam take in one half of the necessary life of the race only, while it hopelessly excludes the other? Such a thought goes at once to undermine the whole fact of the Incarnation. Christ must be of the same length and breadth in all respects with humanity as a whole, in order to be at all a real and true Mediator. He must be commensurate with the universal process of humanity from infancy to old age, as well as with its mere numerical extent. This is implied in the manner of his incarnation itself. His manhood was a process, starting in the Virgin's womb; and in this character it took up into itself, as a power of redemption, the entire range of our existence. He sanctified infancy and childhood, says Irenaeus, by making them stages of his own life.[24] This expresses a

---

23. [This argument seems an important element of nineteenth-century paedobaptism: What was the spiritual destiny of children who die before they can make the voluntary commitment Baptists considered a prerequisite for baptism? It is therefore worth noting that Calvin rejected the major premise: "we must utterly reject the fiction of those who consign all the unbaptized to eternal death" (*Institutes*, ed. McNeill, 2:1349). To be sure, children, as "children of Adam," were "left in death," and had to be regenerated. Still, Calvin held that infant regeneration does occur, since those infants "who are to be saved . . . are previously regenerated," albeit in a manner "beyond our understanding" (*Institutes*, ed. McNeill, 2:1339–41). Note that Nevin tried to shift the argument from pastoral concerns (what happens to unbaptized children who die) to theological grounds (how can we exclude children from the "new creation" that participates in "Christ's Mediatorial Life"?).]

24. [*Adversus Haereses* 2.22.4, trans. in *The Ante-Nicene Fathers*, 1:391. Irenaeus (c. 140–c. 203) was bishop of Lyon and author of *Adversus Haereses* ("Against Heresies"), a refutation of the many Gnostics heresies. While Nevin used Irenaeus to buttress this theme, it is not clear that Irenaeus was its sole source. As early as 1838, while Nevin was still at Western Theological Seminary in Pittsburgh, he said: "The true 'everlasting gospel' is that which reveals the Son of God, the eternal Word, *subjectively* in the believer's own life; and incorporates as it were into his personal experience the entire history of the Savior " ("The Seal of the Spirit," 15). The editor has argued that "*subjectively*," which Nevin

just and sound feeling. It grows forth from the true doctrine of Christ's Person. It lies involved in the Creed. It filled the heart of the ancient Church; and it found its natural, we might say almost necessary expression, in Infant Baptism.

This is more than any merely outward rule. The Baptist is forever harping on the letter of the law; and insists that a case which is not provided for in express terms by this, must be taken to be without force or right. We hold however that there is monstrous falsehood, as well as miserable Jewish pedantry, in pretending to get Christianity like so much clock-work from the text of the Bible, in such purely outward and mechanical style. Christianity has a life and constitution of its own, in the bosom of which only, and by the power of which alone, the true sense of the Bible can be fairly understood; and in this view it is, that the practice of infant baptism by the universal Church from the beginning comes to its full significance and weight. We not only infer from it the authority of express precept and example going before, in the age of the Apostles; but we see in it also (and this is its main value) the very soul and spirit of Christianity itself, actualizing and expounding in a living way the sense of its own word. If it could be clearly made out that the household baptism of the New Testament included no infants; nay, if it were certain that the Church had no apostolical rule whatever in the case, but had gradually settled here into her own rule; we should hold this still to be of truly divine authority, and the baptism of infants of necessary christian obligation, as the only proper sense and meaning of the New Testament institution, interpreted thus to its full depth by the christian life itself, in this way too the analogy of the Jewish covenant, embracing as it did infants as well as adults, and the analogy we may add of our universal human society, organized everywhere after the same law, bring with them at last their true force. On this subject Mr. Noel is exceedingly superficial and flat. True, Christianity is not a secular institute; its sphere is the spiritual world; its privileges are for the soul mainly and not for the body. But still, is it not a perfectly *human* order; nay, the absolute end and perfection of humanity; and must it not, in this view, show itself proportional and true throughout to the actual organization of man's life in its universal character? Make it an unearthly system, playing into the world's economy without any regard to its natural structure as this holds in other spheres, and you do as much as you well can to turn it into magic. As such a human constitution in Christ then, the new creation, with all its spirituality, must of necessity take up into itself the entire compass and power of the old creation; not destroying its constituent elements and laws, but fulfilling their inmost sense rather and raising them to their highest power. In harmony with the principle that underlies the covenant of nature, as well as the Jewish covenant, binding the state of children to that of their parents even in the lowest and most outward temporal interests, Christianity

---

himself highlighted, shows that in 1838 he was still thinking within a Princetonian, dualistic framework: Christian experience was subjective and had to be grounded in objective doctrine, constructed inductively out of Scripture (Layman, "Revelation in the Praxis of the Liturgical Community," 63). For a background discussion of Mercersburg's affiliation with "Irenaean Second Adam" theology, see Evans, ed., *The Incarnate Word*, volume 4 of this series, xxvii–xxviii.]

too, the end of all other covenants, in order that it may be found to be such universal truth in fact and no lie, must show itself able and willing to embrace children as really as adults in its bosom, thus covering with its grace the whole extent of our nature as it lies defiled and defaced by sin. If infants were not comprehended in the law of sin, there might be some reason for holding them to be also shut out from the law of life in Christ Jesus. To make them participant of the curse, and yet incapable of having part really in Him by whom it is removed, would be absolutely monstrous. Every such view is in full contradiction to Rom. v. 12–21; where we are plainly taught, that the grace of the Second Adam is, in its own nature, more than commensurate with the ruin of the First. The economy of salvation must necessarily be so framed, as to make room at least for every necessary class and state of our general life. Like its antitype in the days of Noah, the ark of the Church must be able to save infants and children, as well as persons of higher age. So the Church felt in the beginning; and on this ground, with the fullest right and reason, proceeded to incorporate infants into her communion by the initiatory seal of holy baptism. Not to have done so would have been to belie the profoundest instincts of the christian life itself, and to jeopardize at the same time all firm and constant faith in the objective mystery of her own constitution.

[The Spiritual Place of Infants in the Baptist Theory]

Here we see the lean and abstract misery of the Baptist system. Christianity, according to its apprehension, has no power to take up infants (a large part of the world at any given time) in a direct and real way, into its constitution. It has to do immediately and properly only with believers, personally conscious subjects. Are infants then incapable of salvation; or do they need no salvation? The Baptist is not prepared to rest in either of these alternatives. Infants he holds to be naturally sinful and unregenerate.[25] Those that die in infancy moreover, he tells us, are saved.[26] How? By the fiat of the Almighty changing their bad nature, as he might bid stones to become children of Abraham. And so it is allowed, that he may in rare instances regenerate also infants that do not die.[27] In both cases the regeneration is *for Christ's sake*, so far as motive is concerned in the Divine Mind; but in neither case can it be said at all to fall within the actual scope of the christian salvation, strictly so called, as we find it going forward in the Church. This is for believers only, and has no power to reach children in any natural organic

---

25. [E.g., Noel, *Essay on Christian Baptism*, 128, 135, 168, 192.]

26. [The editor cannot verify that Noel discussed "those who die in infancy." However, see ibid., 170, 172, on infant salvation. The theological and pastoral problems of the future state of dead infants was clearly a serious issue in Nevin's milieu. See, e.g., William Harris, *Grounds of Hope for the Salvation of All Dying in Infancy* (London: R. Clay, 1821) and John Cumming, *Infant Salvation; or, All Saved That Die in Infancy* (Philadelphia: Lindsay and Blakiston, 1855). Gerhart, in "The Efficacy of Baptism" (art. 5, below), said that "one-fourth (or one-third) . . . on an average, die during the period of infancy and childhood."]

27. [Noel, *Essay on Christian Baptism*, 288.]

way. If saved at all, they are saved out of Christ, and beyond the Church, by a grace for which he may be considered in some sense the occasion, but of which he is in no sense either the medium or source. And so as a general thing infants have no part or lot in his kingdom, no right, or title, or power, to be incorporated into his family. That saving grace of which baptism is the sign and seal, cannot be made in any way to come near to their fallen estate, or to fold them lovingly in its merciful embrace. They have no power yet to think, to understand, to repent, to believe, to accomplish in full the subjective side of this salvation; and so there is no room to conceive of their being set in any real connection with it under its objective view. They are by their very nature inaccessible to all its provisions and powers; as much so as though they had no part in the life of humanity whatever. They are disqualified constitutionally for *christian* salvation.

We see no escape from this conclusion, on Baptist premises. If children may not be baptized, they cannot in any way be gathered into the bosom of the Church. Then it cannot be said that Christ has room for them at present in his arms. His grace may have regard to them prospectively; but where they are just now, by the fearful disabilities of childhood, it cannot reach them or touch them in the way of help. Their only hope is in the "uncovenanted mercies of God,"[28] and his power at pleasure to save *without Christ.*

Dreadful, terrible thought! It is truly wonderful, that it should ever be endured at all by the heart of any Christian parent. The old catholic faith, with its ideas of sacramental grace and educational sanctification, the powers of heaven underlying and supporting the process of piety in a real way, through the Church, from the hour of baptism onward to the hour of death, as compared with this, may well seem like the land of Beulah, full of green pastures and springs, in contrast with a wilderness of sand.

[The Unchurchly Character of the Baptist Theory]

Infant baptism belongs essentially to the theory of Christianity, as this stood in the beginning, and as we find it uttered in the Apostles' Creed. This is generally admitted by such learned men as Augusti, Neander, Gieseler,[29] &c.; who at the same time

---

28. [Again, a phrase that this editor cannot locate in Noel. But it was in wide usage in Anglo-American theology, as can be seen from Holifield, *Theology in America*, 247–48.]

29. [Nevin certainly intended "Augustus Neander" (1789–1850). See Neander's *Geschichte der Pflanzung und Leitung der christliche Kirche durch die Apostel*, Erste Band (Hamburg: Bei Friedrich Perthes, 1847), 282–83; translated by J. E. Ryland as *History of the Planting and Training of the Christian Church by the Apostles*, rev. from the 4th German ed. by E. G. Robinson (New York: Sheldon, 1865), 164–65; also Neander, *Allgemeine Geschichte der christlichen Religion und Kirche*, Erste Band (Hamburg: Bei Friedrich Perthes, 1842), 537; translated by Joseph Torrey as *General History of the Christian Religion and Church*, vol. 1, rev. ed., A. J. W. Morrison (London: Henry G. Bohn, York Street, Covent Garden, 1850), 432. Philip Schaff would restate this argument in "The Apostolical Origin of Infant Baptism," art. 3 in this volume.

are found sanctioning the opinion, that it did not come into actual practice probably before the third century; and to whose authority accordingly the Baptists are now in the habit of appealing triumphantly, as in some sense settling the historical argument on their side. They run away with what is thus granted to them as a bare fact, without the least regard to the form and inward reason of it; and at once construe into a plump innovation and abuse, what these authorities take to be intelligible only as the fair and legitimate outbirth of the christian life as it went before. Allow that infants were not generally baptized before the third century, and the cause of the Baptists is still by no means made out. The question returns, How came such baptism *then* into quiet general use? Was it in full antagonism to the genius of Christianity as it stood before; or did it spring spontaneously out of this, in the way of natural and necessary derivation? In the last view, the fact is intelligible, and offers no offence to historical criticism. So it is taken by the learned men, Neander and others, to whom we have just referred. This however suits not at all the object of the Baptists. They insist on the other view, as the only one that deserves to be considered correct. Here however they part from their authorities altogether, and set themselves at the same time in broad and open conflict with the truth of history. They assume that the Church started with a theory of Christianity identical with their own, and that the practice in question crept in consequently in opposition to this as a gross downright corruption. But with the Baptist theory to start from, such as we now find it, not only in regard to infant salvation, but in regard also to the whole constitution of the Sacraments and the Church, it is fairly inconceivable that in the course of a single century any such change as this could ever have come to pass. The Baptist theory is root and branch unchurchly and unsacramental, spiritualistic, rationalistic, and opposed to all thought of mystical objective efficiency in the means of grace outwardly considered. How then could it generate in so short a time the idea of infant baptism? This would be, in such a case, no growth or development in any sense whatever, but direct contradiction and revolution; as much so as though we should fancy the doctrine of transubstantiation springing from the dry loins of Quakerism itself. It is most amply clear however that this whole most unnatural and unphilosophical hypothesis of the Baptists, is an *assumption* purely and nothing besides. However infant baptism came in, it never had a theory of Christianity behind it like that which stares upon us from Mr. Noel's book. There is not a trace of it to be found in the primitive Church, unless among the Gnostics.[30] If anything in

---

Johann Karl Ludwig Gieseler (1792–1854) was also a German Protestant church historian. Nevin might have already had in hand the English translation of *A Compendium of Ecclesiastical History* (New York: Harper & Brothers, 1849). The evidence from Gieseler on this point, at least in English translation, was sketchy: "The baptism of children was not universal, and was even occasionally disapproved," followed by the quote from Tertullian's *de Baptismo* that both Nevin and Schaff address (vol. 1, 163): "The baptism of infants did not become universal until after the time of Augustine" (vol. 2, 46–47).]

30. [The Gnostics were a diverse group of Christian heretics who in various ways viewed embodied existence as undesirable, if not evil, and sought to transcend physicality through a variety of practices, ranging from the ascetic to the transgressively and deliberately licentious.]

the world be plain, it is that the entire genius and faith of the early Church, from the very age of the Apostles, lay in the direction of this practice, and fell towards it with natural gravitation, instead of looking or leaning in any other direction.

But, says Mr. Noel, the Church fell also into the practice of infant communion, and continued it for centuries; which however has since come to be acknowledged universally an abuse; and this must neutralize completely the force of the view now presented.[31] Not at all, we reply. It only goes to show it more certainly true and correct. With the Baptist theory to start from, so easy and general a lapse of the early christian world into this practice must be counted still more inexplicable than the rise of the other superstition; as it must go still farther also to strip ancient Christianity of its last title to rational sympathy and respect. Allow however in the mind of the Church from the beginning the presence of a different theory, including the sense of an organic power working objectively in the christian communion, and concentrating itself especially in the mystery of sacramental grace, and it is no longer difficult to comprehend how it was possible to extend the use not only of the first sacrament, but of the second also, to infants as well as adults; while the judgment is still approved as wise and right, by which in the end a distinction was made between the two cases, and infant communion disallowed while infant baptism was suffered to remain in force. The Baptistic theory could never have made any such distinction; just as little as it could have had power to originate either the one side of it or the other. Sympathy with the sacramental faith of the early Church, will enable us to apologize here for this excess in her practice; while at the same time we have no difficulty in seeing and allowing it to have been an excess; and are not for this reason tempted at all to resolve the just conception from which such excess grew, and by which only it is made intelligible, into a baseless figment of superstition; as little precisely, we may say, as we are tempted to part with the whole mystery of Christ's presence in the Lord's supper, because it has been carried by some to the manifest extreme of transubstantiation. After all, even infant communion, properly set aside as it has been by the christian world, is far nearer to the first life of Christianity, and less revolting we will add to the sensibilities of a sound church faith, than the error which will not suffer infants to come to Christ in the Church at all, but by refusing them the sacrament of holy baptism virtually places that whole age, by physical calamity, beyond the pale of his redemption.

[Infant Baptism in the Early Church]

We do not allow however, in the view of the matter now presented, that the practice of infant baptism came in only with the third century. The concession as made by Neander and others would not save the cause of the Baptists, if it were true; for it rests on an entirely different view of early Christianity from that which *their* use of it requires. But

---

31. [Noel, *Essay on Christian Baptism*, 253–58.]

the concession itself, we are well satisfied, goes altogether beyond the line of justice and truth. The most that can be allowed is, that infant baptism in the beginning was overshadowed, and thrown out of sight to a great extent, by the far more prevalent and prominent use of the sacrament for full grown converts; and that no strict rule prevailed, making it of binding authority and necessity as in later times. That it was in actual use however, under such secondary and free aspect at least, even from the age of the Apostles, seems to admit of no serious question. It went hand in hand with the doctrine of native depravity, and gathered force more and more in proportion as this grew into distinct statement, and carried along with it the sense of its necessary counterpart in the doctrine of a real objective remedy for this ruin in Christ.

As presented to our view in the third century, the practice of infant baptism, as all scholars know, is no new or rare thing, but a fact of general and seemingly long established force. Origen never thinks of vindicating it as something lately introduced, but on the contrary appeals to it as an acknowledged church usage, of apostolical derivation, in support of other truth. He does not argue from the doctrine of native depravity to the necessity of infant baptism; but from this last rather, as a sure and solid ground at hand in the universal sense of the Church, he draws proof for the certainty of that doctrine. "As baptism is given for the remission of sins" he says *hom.* viii. *in Levit.*, "the grace of it must seem to be superfluous when extended to infants also, *as it is by the usage of the Church*, if they have nothing in them that calls for remission."[32] Again in *Luc. evang. hom*, xiv: "Little children are baptized for the remission of sins. Of what sins? When have they sinned? Or how can any use of the laver apply to their case, unless in the sense of what we have just said, that no one is clean according to Job xiv. 4. And because by baptism the pollution of birth is removed, *little children also are baptized*. For except one be born of water and the spirit, he cannot enter into the kingdom of heaven."[33] Again, *on Rom.* v. 6: "*The Church received from the Apostles a tradition, to baptize little children also.* For they knew, as stewards of the divine mysteries, that there existed in all the true stain of sin, which needs to be washed away by water and the Spirit, whence even the body itself is styled a body of sin."[34] Such is the clear testimony of Origen. That of Cyprian, in the same age, is if possible still more explicit and overwhelming. He indeed sets before us a dispute in relation to infant baptism. But this did not turn at all on the lawfulness or fitness of the thing itself. That was granted on all sides. Nobody then dreamed, it would appear, of calling it in question. The only doubt was, whether it was necessary to observe the analogy of the Jewish rule, fixing circumcision to the eighth day. Must infants wait at least that long

---

32. [8.3.5, emphasis Nevin's; *Origen: Homilies on Leviticus 1–16*, trans. Gary Wayne Barkley (Washington, DC: Catholic University of American Press, 1990), 158.]

33. [14.5, emphasis Nevin's; *Origen: Homilies on Luke; and, Fragments on Luke*, trans. Joseph T. Lienhard, S.J. (Washington, DC: Catholic University of American Press, 1996), 58–59.]

34. [5.9.11, emphasis Nevin's; *Origen: Commentary on the Epistle to the Romans Books 1–5*, trans. Thomas P. Scheck (Washington, DC: Catholic University of American Press, 2001), 367.]

for the sacrament, or might they be baptized at any time after birth? What a question this for the theology of our modern Baptists! Cyprian, supported by the unanimous voice of a whole council at Carthage a. 256, most distinctly affirms the latter view. The grace of God, he says, should be considered open and free to all, as it is needed by all; and we are bound accordingly to bring all, if possible, within its saving scope. If even grievous sins in the case of adults form no bar to their gracious acceptance in this holy sacrament, "how much less should the infant be debarred, which being recently born has not yet sinned at all, save as being naturally born from Adam it has contracted in its first nativity the contagion of original death, and which is the better prepared more easily to receive the remission of sins, for the very reason that the sins to be remitted are not of itself but from abroad (*non propria sed aliena.*)"—*Epist. LIX ad Fidum.*[35]

Origen and Cyprian, it will be borne in mind, belong to the first half of the third century. Their testimony then makes it clear, not only that infant baptism was in use at that time, but also that it was no partial nor new thing brought in a short time before. They refer to it as of general, everywhere acknowledged authority, and treat it as part and parcel of the ecclesiastical tradition handed down from the age of the Apostles. Now in these circumstances, it could not possibly have taken its rise only in the latter part even of the second century. Such a state of things of itself implies, that no memory ran to the contrary of it in the Church, and so that it must have started historically with the rise of the Church itself; and it is a strange judgment certainly which Suicer[36] is quoted as uttering, when he says: "For the first two centuries none were baptized, save such as were instructed in the faith and imbued with the doctrine of Christ, because of those words, 'He that believeth and is baptized;' afterwards the opinion prevailed, that no one could be saved without baptism." With the practice of Origen's time before us, and the quiet faith that prevailed in regard to it, we need no very explicit testimony to assure us of what had place during the century before. It is enough, that no opposing voice is heard, that the positive presumption already secured is met with no contradiction under a different form. The Baptists affect to make light of the historical authorities quoted from the second century in favor of infant baptism; they are so few and of so little force. Mr. Noel cites them from the pages of the learned Bingham,[37] with two marks of admiration in every case (thus!!), in token

---

35. [Cyprian, "Epistle LVIII" (§5) in *Ante-Nicene Fathers*, 5:354: "How much rather ought we to shrink from hindering an infant, who, being lately born, has not sinned, except in that, being born after the flesh according to Adam, he has contracted the contagion of the ancient death at its earliest birth, who approaches the more easily on this very account to the reception of the forgiveness of sins—that to him are remitted, not his own sins, but the sins of another."]

36. [Qtd. by Noel, *Essay on Christian Baptism*, 245 note, emphasis original. Johann Kaspar Suicer (1620–1684), a Reformed theologian of Swiss birth, was author of *Thesaurus Ecclesiasticus e Patribus Graecis Ordine Alphabetico* (1682, 2nd ed., enlarged 1728); also contributor to the *Consensus Helveticus* (the pan-Swiss Protestant confession of 1675).]

37. [Joseph Bingham (1668–1723) was the English author of *Origines Ecclesiasticae; or, The Antiquities of the Christian Church* (10 vols., 1708–1722). He was a major source for Noel, and the conduit for his quotes from Suicer.]

of his profound surprise, to find so vast a superstructure made to rest on pillars so very slender and slim. But it should be remembered in the first place, that we have but little patristic literature to quote from in the second century, on any subject. And then it should be remembered again, in the second place, that the *onus probandi*[38] here, the burden of citing witnesses and authorities, lies on the Baptists themselves, and not on the advocates of infant baptism; who have the clear practice of the universal Church on their side at the going out of the second century, and most full right accordingly to take the same thing, for granted of the century throughout, unless cause to the contrary can be shown. The paucity and leanness of proof, in this view, fall wholly to the side on which Mr. Noel himself stands. All turns at last on a single passage from Tertullian; and this so little pertinent to the purpose it is employed to serve, that we might well bestow all Mr. Noel's marks of admiration upon it singly and alone. In the passage referred to, as is well known, (*de bapt. c.* 18,) Tertullian takes occasion, on a view of his own, to recommend a delay of baptism in certain cases and states.[39] Children in particular, he tells us, should wait till they are able to come on their own profession. Unmarried persons too he recommends to use a similar procrastination. And what now, we ask, follows from this strange oracle of the African Father? That infant baptism was a new thing in the Church, or of only narrow custom and use? Just the reverse. We *know* from the testimony of Origen and Cyprian, who join hands with him in time, that the fact was quite otherwise; and the same thing is implied most clearly in this passage itself. Tertullian offers no objection to infant baptism, as being an innovation, or a thing against common rule; which he would have done most certainly, if there had been room for objecting to it in this way. He tacitly allows its general ecclesiastical authority, and simply sets over against this his own private speculation, resting on the danger of post-baptismal sins. Strange theology too he makes of it, in order to carry his point. "*Quid festinat innocens aettis ad remissionem peccatorum?*"[40] The passage besides is as much against the baptism of the unmarried, as it is against the baptism of infants; and in this way, if it proves anything at all for the Baptists, it must be taken to prove vastly more than they want. Plainly, Tertullian stood here against the Church; and his voice passed off accordingly, almost without echo, in the progress of her subsequent history.

It is not necessary here to notice specifically the authorities back of Tertullian, that are brought forward by Bingham and others in favor of infant baptism. They are readily acknowledged to be somewhat vague and uncertain in their character; and

---

38. [Trans. "burden of proof."]

39. [Ernest Evans, ed. and trans., *Tertullian's Homily on Baptism* (London: S.P.C.K., 1964), 38, 40 (Latin); 39, 41 (trans.); see also the standard translation in *Ante-Nicene Fathers*, 3:678. Tertullian (c. 160–c. 225) was another North African church father. A tendency toward rigorism led him into the Montanist sect.]

40. [Trans. "Why should innocent fancy come with haste to the remission of sin?" (Evans, *Tertullian's Homily on Baptism*, 39). The text of Evans (p. 38) reads *aetas* in the place of *aettis*. Nevin implied that it is "strange" to assert that infants are "innocent."]

taken simply by themselves they would be by no means sufficient to establish its practice. But we have no right so to take them by themselves. They must be taken in connection with the light thrown back upon them by the known practice of the Church at the close of the century, as well as from the theory of sacramental grace answerable to this practice which we find in the Church from the beginning; and so taken, we have no hesitation to say, they are altogether relevant and full of force.[41]

It has been sometimes said that the practice of infant baptism gained credit and became general finally, through the influence particularly of Augustine's dogma of original sin. This however is altogether unhistorical. The necessity of it was not felt to lie in any relation to the special view of Augustine on this subject, but in the pressure of the universally acknowledged need of regeneration, as affirmed by our Saviour, John iii. 5; as we have had opportunity to see already in the quotation from Origen and Cyprian. Augustine himself moreover, like Origen argues not from his doctrine to the necessity of infant baptism, but just in the reverse order.[42] Infant baptism stands, in the controversy between him and his opponents, for a given sure and certain fact, of apostolical credit and force; and on the ground of this broad *datum* he plants one of the main pillars of his doctrine. The mystery must be taken, here to be fallacious he says, and not trustworthy, when infants are baptised for the remission of sins, if there be in them no sin to remit. Pelagius and his party felt themselves sorely embarrassed with this argument; but they never ventured to quarrel with the fact on which it was built. On the contrary, they allowed it also in its full length and breadth, showing plainly thus their sense of its impregnable settlement in the previous history of the church back to the time of the Apostles. For nothing certainly would have suited their cause better than to have been able to show the whole thing a superstitious corruption and abuse, brought in a few generations only before, *against* the universal practice of the primitive Church, and without mention till the time of Tertullian; as all this has now come to be clear and plain, in this age of telescopic vision, to the eyes of such men as Mr. Noel, looking back through a vista of more than fifteen centuries to the same period.

41. See the subject well presented in the work entitled: *Das Sakrament der Taufe nebst den anderen damit Zusammenhängenden Akten den Initiation*: By J. W. F. Höfling. Vol 1, 98–123 [Erlangen, 1846].

42. [A likely source for Nevin's claim is Augustine's *De peccatorum meritis et remissione*, trans., "A Treatise on the Merits and Forgiveness of Sins," in *Nicene and Post-Nicene Fathers*, vol. 5. See Book 1, esp. chs. 33–39. Augustine concluded: "Now seeing that they admit the necessity of baptizing infants—finding themselves unable to contravene the authority of the universal Church, which has been unquestionably handed down by the Lord and His apostles—they cannot avoid the further concession, that infants require the same benefits of the Mediator, in order that, being washed by the sacrament and charity of the faithful, and thereby incorporated into the body of Christ, which is the Church, they may be reconciled to God, and so live in Him, and be saved, and delivered, and redeemed, and enlightened. But from what, if not from death, and the vices, and guilt, and thralldom, and darkness of sin? And, inasmuch as they do not commit any sin in the tender age of infancy by their actual transgression, original sin only is left" (ch. 39).]

[The Incoherence of Paedobaptist Conversionism]

In this controversy with the Baptists, all depends on taking right ground. It regards not simply the difference of practice with which it is immediately concerned in an outward view, but falls over as we have seen on a difference back of this, and of far more inward and profound character, touching the nature of the Sacraments themselves and the true idea of the Christian Church. The true issue in the end is: Church or No-Church; sacrament or mere moral sign. The rejection of infant baptism turns on a full renunciation of the theory of Christianity, out of which the practice grew with inward necessity at the beginning. The modern Baptist is inwardly at war, in the whole posture of his faith, with the true sense of the Apostles' Creed. He has given up the whole idea of sacramental grace as an obsolete superstitious figment. What the ancient Church took to be the sense of a sacrament, and what in this view the Reformers also felt themselves bound to hold fast as a necessary part of Christianity, he most deliberately gives to the winds. A sacrament is for him another thing altogether. This it is, we say, that forms the real significance and the true deep solemnity of this controversy; and on this ground should it be made always to rest. It is of little account to contend with the Baptists, and the contest is likely always to have but small success in the end, if its true ultimate sense be not felt and asserted firmly in this way.

It is not to be concealed, however, that no small amount of the opposition which is made among Protestants to the system of the Baptists, at the present time, is not planted on the great ultimate issue here noticed at all; but on the contrary takes side in regard to it with the interest opposed, as though that primary issue were fully antiquated and no longer of any force whatever; in consequence of which all such defence of the truth (the outward shell of it only forsaken of its proper soul) is found to be more or less powerless and vain. It is a poor business to contend for infant baptism, if all the principles on which it rested in the beginning and that of right still lie at the ground of it, be in the first place rationalistically surrendered. Of such practical treason, secretly aiding and abetting the very enemy with which it outwardly makes show of battle, we have melancholy exemplifications on all sides. It is lifting itself into view continually among all our sects, as far as the Puritan principle has been able to gain onesided and separate supremacy at the cost of the Catholic. It fights the Baptists; but in doing so grants them all their principal premises, and so leaves nothing to fight about that deserves any true zeal. It eviscerates the sacraments of all objective force; denies their mystical character altogether; turns them into simple signs and ceremonies, that have no inward connection whatever with the spiritual realities they represent. What are we to think of a Presbyterian minister for instance, taking pains at the Lord's table, without the fear of Calvin or the Westminster Confession before his eyes, to guard his people against the danger of fancying any *mystery* at all in the transaction; or carefully reminding them, over the "laver of regeneration," that they must not dream for a moment of any grace, exhibited or conferred through the holy institution. And all this too, in token of his zeal for evangelical spirituality, poor man, as contrasted with the far off mummeries of Puseyism and Rome! When it has come to this, the defence of infant baptism is indeed reduced to bad plight; for its outworks are gone, and its main garrison is virtually delivered into the enemy's hands. It cannot be defended any longer as a sacrament, as the thing it was counted to be in the beginning; and so its defence cannot be made to rest on the grounds and reasons which originally brought it to pass. It is changed into a new sense. It has become a mere outward rule. It carries another relation altogether to the true and proper life of Christianity; and by such shifted position it is in fact shorn of its stays and props, whether in the form of testimony from the Bible or as offered in the voice and practice of the early Church.

Such unsacramental Paedobaptism labors, in truth, under a threefold fatal defect, in its war with the Baptists. *In the first place*, it puts a hammer in their hands to break its own head with, by yielding their false principle that the Bible *per se* must settle, in purely outward and mechanical style, this and all other points of christian faith and practice. That is not the way in which the Bible is to be used. It is not constructed on any such mechanical plan, and never offers itself so to our faith. Such slavery to the letter is Jewish, not Christian. By consenting to it, in the case before us, the unsacramental advocates of infant baptism kill their own cause at once. It is perfectly vain, to think of making out a clear plea for it from the letter of the Bible. It never came into practice that way at first, and there is no such foundation for it to rest upon now. Recourse is had accordingly to indirect and circuitous proof always, based more or less on analogy, inference, and presumption; and to crown all, the subsequent practice of the Church is lugged in as a sort of supplemental voucher. But here the Baptist falls in with a loud protest; and he has fair right to do so, on the *common* ground occupied by the parties. "The text, the text, and nothing but the text; no gloss, no hypothesis, no tradition; nothing less than a direct *Thus saith the Lord* can be entitled to confidence in so grave a case." Thus rims the everlasting watchword, and the mouth of the adversary is fairly stopped. He may talk on indeed; but his talk is to no purpose, unless it be simply to reveal the nakedness of his own self-contradictory posture.—*Secondly*, the advocacy in question is still farther at fault in the use it allows itself to make, supplementally, of Christian antiquity. The practice of infant baptism in the early Church grew forth, organically we might say, from a certain theory of Christianity itself, which stands out more or less clearly to view in all the doctrines and institutions of the Church at the time. It was no separate fact merely, resting on naked precept and tradition; it belonged to the life of the universal system in which it had place; its proper significance and force stood in its relations, in theological connections, its ecclesiastical surroundings. But now, in the case before us, no sort of regard is paid to this most obvious and simple thought. Puritanism as a general thing, if we may believe at least *some* of its witnesses, owns no agreement or sympathy with the mind of the early Church, as this meets us in the Apostles' Creed, considers its theory of Christianity superstitious, and repudiates especially out and out its imagination of grace in the Sacraments. And yet, in controversy with the Baptists, this same Puritanism appeals to the practice of the early Church in favor of infant baptism, and tries to eke out its *Bible* argument, otherwise most impotent and lame, by the convenient help here offered in the way of tradition! But this is unfair, and may be justly charged with practical equivocation. It is like the trick of arguing from the mere sound of a text in the Scriptures, without any regard to the sense required by its context. What right have those who refuse the ecclesiastical context of infant baptism, as it stood in the early Church, to go thither in quest of testimonies and authorities in favor of it, as it now happens to be in authority among themselves under a wholly different view? They pervert in such case what they are pleased to cite and quote, by sundering the fact in question from its necessary connections, and forcing it to stand in other connections altogether, that actually make it to carry a new sense. When Irenaeus, Tertullian, Origen, Cyprian, &c., are pressed into service as witnesses, by this unchurchly and unsacramental school, they are always of course turned more or less into the character of wire-worked puppets; and the shrewd Baptist may well be excused for his smile of sarcastic triumph, as he charges home on *such* adversaries the double inconsistency, first of calling in the aid of any tradition whatever, and then of wresting this tradition out of all its living articulations to make it fit for their own use.—And this brings into view finally the *third* defect belonging to the school. In thus refusing and disowning the connections out of which infant baptism sprang in the beginning, it shows itself insensible also to the true interior sense and reason of it in its own nature. Only in the character of a gracebearing sacrament, according to the view taken of it by the early Church, and only in connection with the idea of an objective salvation in Christ commensurate with the entire tract of our human life from infancy to old age, can baptism be vindicated rationally as the proper privilege of infants. Renounce this old theory of Christianity, and it is no longer possible to make any satisfactory stand here against the plausible reasonings of the Baptists. If baptism be a mere outward confession on the part of the subject, or if it be a sign simply of certain things which must be brought to pass by human thought and will, no good reason certainly can be assigned for employing it in the case of infants. Those accordingly who deny baptismal grace,[43] making the rite thus to be in reality no sacrament at all but only an outward law or rule of Divine appointment, show themselves unable always to meet the demands of this controversy, and in truth betray it, as we have before said, into the hands of the Baptists. As a mere sign, infant baptism has no authority in the Bible, no sanction in ancient church practice, and no apology in reason or common sense.

Where such low view of the sacrament has come to prevail, paedo-baptism falls necessarily into the character of a simple ecclesiastical tradition, and is looked upon as a sort of outward custom only, which it is not becoming to make the subject of any very earnest zeal one way or another. No special stress accordingly is laid upon it in a practical view; no special regard is had to it in the subsequent training of children.

43. [See Nevin, "Baptismal Grace," and "Holy Baptism," in art. 1.]

Pains are taken rather to make it of no effect for the purposes of Christianity. It is treated as a nullity. All faith in it as Christ's act, is carefully discouraged; and the first object oftentimes would seem to be to smother and crush in the baptized child all sense of privilege on the score of such adoption into God's family, and to substitute for it the sense of membership only and wholly in the family of Satan. We have heard a Presbyterian minister say publicly on this very subject: That he would consider it a calamity to have his children make any account of their baptism in this view. The sacrament to his mind palpably had no force whatever, except as the thing signified by it might be brought to pass subsequently, from a wholly different quarter and in a wholly different way; in order to which, the more it could itself be kept out of sight, in the meantime, the better. How is it possible, where practice thus gives the lie to all the mystery should mean, to show any proper zeal, or constancy, or ability, in its defence? Infant baptism, like the question of sprinkling, becomes a mere circumstance, lying on the outside of the "evangelical system," in which all spiritual christians, be they Baptist or Paedo-baptist, may still join happily with one and the same mind; provided only they have grace enough not to fall out by the way, over a matter of such subordinate worth. No wonder in these circumstances, that the cause of the Baptists, should eat like a cancer, and send its rationalistic roots forth far and wide into the life of the Church. No wonder that the *ceremony* of baptizing infants, even among those who are still nominally its friends, should seem to grow more loose and rickety always in actual practice; though we confess we were not prepared for some astounding results on this subject, which have been lately brought into view from an examination of the statistical reports published by the last O. S. Presbyterian Assembly.[44] The Episcopalians quote the fact in proof of a sad falling away from sound church feeling: while

---

44. ["O.S." = "Old School." The statistical reports Nevin mentioned are discussed at length in the Emanuel Gerhart essay, "The Efficacy of Baptism," art. 5 in this volume. In 1801, Presbyterians and Congregationalists had united their missionary efforts in the western territories through a "Plan of Union." This created "hundreds of 'presbygational churches,'" which were led by lay committees (instead of elders) not committed to Presbyterian doctrine and polity (Peter J. Wallace, "The Bond of Union," ch. 1, accessed March 15, 2015, at http://www.peterwallace.org/old/dissertation/1division.htm). In the meantime, the confessional side of the Presbyterian community had been reinforced by Scotch and Scotch Irish who had immigrated after the First Great Awakening. These confessionalists were concerned with the alleged inroads of "New Haven theology" (in the person of Nathaniel Taylor), which denied that Adam's original sin was imputed to all persons, and the corollary assertion that even though humans *would* sin, they had "the power to the contrary" (i.e., the power not to sin). According to Wallace, the labels "Old" and "New School" were first used in 1832. In 1837 "Old School partisans" were able to abrogate the Plan of Union, thereby excising the synods that had been planted as a result of the plan. At the following year's General Assembly, the synods were not recognized, and they withdrew with their supporters to form a new body. See *Dictionary of Christianity in America*, 815–16, 819–21, 842–43, 911; Ahlstrom, *Religious History of the American People*, 1:559–66; a detailed history can be found in ch. 1 of Wallace, "The Bond of Union." It should be noted that while Nevin (then still at Western, a Presbyterian school) supported the abolition of the Plan of Union, he, like Princeton, opposed the way in which the action was carried out (Nichols, *Romanticism in American Theology*, 32–34; DeBie, "Biographical Essay," in Nevin and Hodge, *Coena Mystica*, xxvii; Hart, *John Williamson Nevin*, 56–57).]

the Baptists echo it triumphantly, as a lively illustration of the variance which exists between the piety of the age and the force of this old tradition, as well as a pleasing evidence that it is destined soon to pass away entirely in the universal prevalence of their own truly rational faith. In any view it deserves attention.

[Conclusion]

Infant baptism taken as a mere abstract rite or usage, can never maintain its ground. As it grows from the church system, so it can never thrive or prosper truly save in the bosom of this system. It is properly but the initiative of all that is comprehended in a true church life, as a process of preparation for heaven. Take away the idea of this process, as something needed to carry forward and complete what is thus begun, and the true sense of the sacrament is gone. Infant baptism assumes the possibility of educational religion, under the special appliances of the Church, and it looks to it as its own necessary complement. The idea of *confirmation* is required to bring it to its true and full sense. Where faith remains at all in its character as a sacrament, it will be felt to carry in it a demand for such personal acknowledgment and response on the part of its subject, at the proper time, under the hand of the Church; which in such case will not be viewed as a new and independent transaction, however, but rather as the natural and suitable close of the baptismal act itself. Let the idea of confirmation, on the other hand, be strange to the mind of any part of the Church, and the continuity lost sight of thus that should hold of right between the beginning of infant baptism and its proper end, and it will be found that to the same extent the institution itself is shorn of its significance and turned into an empty form.

Mr. Noel advocates free communion, as it is called, in opposition to the more strict practice generally observed among his Baptist brethren. His liberality in this respect rests, consistently enough, on the low view he takes of the sacraments. They are both for him mere acts of profession appointed by Christ, which have their whole use in the opportunity they give for "fulfilling righteousness" or complying with a rule of duty. Christianity itself, standing in the work of the Spirit and a corresponding experience in the believer, has place before and beyond all such profession, when it is sincere, and is just as complete without it as with it. Baptism ought indeed to precede the use of the Lord's supper. But still a good profession may be made under this last form alone; and in the case of really pious persons, baptized in infancy, or rather according to this system not baptized at all, but afterwards self-devoted to Christ at the Lord's table, Mr. Noel thinks the rule in regard to the first sacrament (or *sign*) may safely be overlooked, in favor of Christian brotherhood and peace. And over against the strict theory as held by Baptists, this way of looking at the matter strikes us certainly as very reasonable and right. For what can well be a greater contradiction, than first to sunder the sacraments completely from the life and substance of Christianity, making them to be in truth no *sacraments* at all but only signs or statutes; and then to make the use of them under a given form notwithstanding the rule and measure of all full Christian communion, to the exclusion of a large proportion of the actually acknowledged piety of the world. To make at once so little of the sacraments, and yet again so much, is no better than letter-stiff pedantry of the most thoroughly Jewish type. We once heard a Baptist minister take great pains, on a communion occasion, to strip the service of every sort of mystical sense, setting it in full parallel finally with the Monument of Bunker Hill; and yet when all was done we were not allowed to come nigh it, although just before invited to participate in the services of the pulpit in front of which the monumental transaction took place. We felt it a real relief however to be thus excluded; for so utterly shorn of all true sacramental character did the altar appear in our eyes, that we could hardly have felt at liberty in our own mind to approach it as an altar at all. Strange and absurd exclusiveness, we felt at the time and still feel, which *includes* for its central mystery so poor a shadow!

We do not like the system of the Baptists. It overthrows the true idea of the Church. It makes the sacraments of no effect, and virtually destroys them altogether. It turns the whole gospel thus into a form different from that which it had in the beginning. The mystical side of Christianity is made to perish under its hands; while in every direction a cold calculating rationalism is offered to us in its stead. We do not wonder that it found so little favor in the eyes of early Protestantism; and the change which has come over much of our later Protestantism in regard to it, we hold to be an occasion for anxiety and alarm rather than for congratulation.

In all this article, it will be observed, we have carefully refrained from the question, What specifically is the power of baptism in the case of infants? This question is now moving the Church of England to its very foundations; and it is one undoubtedly of the most profound and far reaching interest, for the general theology and church life of the age. But we meddle not with it here, any farther than to assert the fact of grace objectively present in the sacrament under *some* form. Allowing this, there is room still for a difference of view in regard to its precise nature; just as there is room for a similar difference also in regard to the specific power of the Lord's supper. All such difference however comes of right *after* the question, whether there be any such mystic force at all in these solemnities *under any form*. It is with this first general question only, that we have been here concerned. The Baptists, and a large class besides whom we may style Crypto-baptists, as agreeing with them in principle while opposing them in form, most deliberately and distinctly empty the baptismal laver of all mystical sense, see in it only common water, and acknowledge in it no power or force whatever aside from the mental exercises of the baptized subject; which of course turns it into idle mummery as applied to infants. This sweeping and wholesale judgment it is, as it meets us in Mr. Noel's book, that we wish to protest with the true idea of the Church, with all Christian antiquity, and with the proper voice of the Reformation. We know that there are great difficulties attending the subject of baptismal grace. But let us not think to escape these, by throwing ourselves into the arms of Rationalism. Whether we can solve them satisfactorily or not, we are still bound, in the way of preliminary faith, to accept the mystery of such grace itself; since the only alternative to this, is to give up the doctrine of the holy sacraments altogether, in the old church sense, and so to bring in another gospel.

Article 3
"The Apostolical Origin of Infant Baptism"

(By Philip Schaff)

Editor's Introduction

Before Philip Schaff joined Nevin at Mercersburg, Nevin thought the source of churchly renewal lay in understanding and teaching the confessional heritage of the community of faith, and faithfully carrying out its "regular" or "ordinary life," which included revivalistic techniques. He understood this life to be the "organic" efflorescence of an already existent spiritual reality that was available to the believer in and through the church.[1] When Schaff arrived that same year, he came with a well-developed theory of historical development.[2] From Ferdinand Christian Bauer, he had learned that there was a "constant and progressive flow of thought" in the church;[3] then Ludwig von Gerlach passed on to him a "high church view of the church as the 'Body of Christ,'" in which "the church undergoes in the course of time development and growth yet remains always the same." Finally, from church historian Johann August Wilhelm Neander, Schaff realized that he could unite irenic scholarship and pietistic spirituality.[4]

Schaff presented his fully developed theory in *What Is Church History?* He claimed to be incorporating the "orthodox" and "rationalistic" "stand-points." Schaff agreed with orthodoxy that there was an "unchangeable," eternal element in Christianity; he

---

1. Nevin, *Anxious Bench*, in Yrigoyen and Bricker, ed., *Catholic and Reformed*, 117, 119–20. The major tasks—preaching, teaching and catechesis, visitation and discipline—are summarized on p. 101. See the general introduction for Nevin's evolution to this point, and the change introduced into his thinking by his interaction with Schaff.

2. Nichols has an older discussion in *Romanticism in American Theology*, 64ff., and largely followed David Schaff, *Life of Philip Schaff*, 17ff. The now-standard reading is that of Penzel, *German Education of Christian Scholar Philip Schaff*, 95ff.

3. Schaff, *Life of Philip Schaff*, 20; Nichols, *Romanticism*, 65–66.

4. Penzel, *German Education of Christian Scholar Philip Schaff*, 107, 113–14, 117.

identified this with "truth as objectively present in Christ and in the scriptures." This truth then was developed in the historical life of the church, which he described as "subjective Christianity." Therefore, Schaff agreed that churchly life was "moveable and flowing," which he took to be the truth of the rationalistic position. However, whereas the rationalists saw change as arbitrary, Schaff's theory held it to be "an ever-increasing stream" whose final path was "already prescribed" in God's providential plan.[5] Whatever Nevin's attraction to this theory,[6] he claimed to be simply wanting to present the data out of which any further theorization must flow. "Our concern," he wrote dismissively, "has been simply to give a true picture of facts."[7] Schaff was a master of the facts. He was already secure in *his* understanding of historical development, and was able to begin the historical scholarship that would secure him an honored place in American theology. In 1851, he published in German the first volume of *History of the Christian Church*. The following essay was deemed important enough to be excerpted and translated prior to the official translation of volume 1 in 1853. Schaff covered much of the same ground Nevin surveyed in the previous article. Just before beginning what was essentially an excursus on the patristic period, he summarized his argument for infant baptism from the apostolic era: the church offered salvation as a universal reality; baptism was the sign of covenantal membership analogous to circumcision; and infants were "organically" connected to their believing parents, and therefore should be baptized as a sign of the grace that flowed through their parents to them.

Schaff acknowledged that there was no evidence for infant baptism in the apostolic period, but he hoped to extract out of a negative argument from silence (the New Testament did not *prohibit* infant baptism), combined with a description of the "*spirit* of the Bible," an argument with "tolerable certainty" that it was practiced. Schaff stressed that the entire presentation was conditioned upon a "guarantee of a pious education." Infant baptism was a covenantal and social sign of the infant's participation in the spiritual matrix of a Christian home, family, and churchly life. The cosmic Christ embraced all of humanity, from infancy to maturity, saving all from sin and death—including infants, who were especially in that era subject to mortality. He took one of the Baptists' favorite proof-texts (the Great Commission, Matt 28:19) and turned it to his advantage: When Christians were commanded to go to all nations, were infants excluded from "nations"? He agreed that baptism was bound to proclamation and faith, but denied this implied that *conscious understanding and faith* were a prerequisite for baptism. What baptism "offered" was salvation. Reception of baptism

---

5. Schaff, *What Is Church History?*, 80–82; repr. in Yrigoyen and Bricker, eds., *Reformed and Catholic*, 96–98. *What Is Church History?* appears in vol. 3 of MTSS. See the general introduction for the nuances that distinguished Schaff's and Nevin's views of historical development and change.

6. For Nevin's summary of Schaff, see "Early Christianity," in *Catholic and Reformed*, 291ff., and summarized p. 294.

7. Nevin, "Cyprian," 562–63 ("Fourth and Last Article").

was a sign that one sought this salvation. He then used Acts 2:38 (Peter's Pentecost sermon) to show that repentance and the Spirit *followed* baptism, rather than being its prerequisites. The "*self conscious free* surrender" to the claims of the gospel could therefore occur at some later indeterminate point, nurtured by pious family life and catechetical instruction. Binding the felt experience to a process of spiritual nurture meant that the church as an organized body was essential to the process.

For Schaff, all humans sought God, desiring and reaching out to a "higher power." Children also both needed and could receive salvation, and infant baptism was the proper manner in which to nurture these movements in a child's soul. Furthermore, the child was biologically and psychologically connected to its parents, and the effects of grace in believing parents in some manner passed over to the child. Schaff didn't appear to have a developed theology of the "unitary covenant" (unlike Zwingli or Calvin); his interpretation of circumcision went no further than to say: Israelite infants belonged to the community by circumcision, so likewise Christian infants belonged to the church by baptism. Then he performed a swift intellectual inversion. If infants could anticipate adult faith, adults were to recapitulate childhood faith. He read Jesus' embrace of the children to say that *adults* could only be truly baptized, if they *became* spiritual children. Children were born into Christian homes where their spiritual longings could be nurtured and fulfilled. Infant baptism was the promise that they already belonged to the community, and that the church's sacramental life would, if entered into sincerely, bring about the salvation it promised.

Parallel to Nevin's biography, there is substantial evidence that this justification of infant baptism was grounded in Schaff's own spiritual journey. The offspring of an adulterous liaison, he was raised in a foster home and sent away to school. Klaus Penzel said his conversion was primarily the resolution of "an acute case of 'Swiss' homesickness." Schaff himself said much later that he had lacked "'childlike faith'" as a child, and presumably gained it in his adolescent conversion. The pietistic practice that then nurtured Schaff's devotion was founded on the "traditional means of the established church," in contrast to the new measures revivalism that Schaff would experience in the New World.[8] Similar to Nevin, Schaff apotheosized both what he missed as a child and how he resolved that lack in coming to faith during his adolescence.

---

8. Penzel, *German Education of Christian Scholar Philip Schaff*, 21–26.

"The Apostolical Origin of Infant Baptism"[1]: [From Schaf's Geschichte der Chr. Kirche][2]

As the apostolic church was a missionary church, the most of those baptized into it, were grown persons. Infant baptism has force and meaning, only in the fact of a parent church already existing, and the presumption of Christian education, which of course could not be expected of heathen or Jewish parents. Thus in our day, a missionary begins his work, with the instruction of adults, not with the baptism of children.

The question, however, presents itself whether in addition to the baptism of adults which, in the nature of the case, took place most frequently, there was not also in congregations already established the Christian baptism of infants, similar to circumcision, its type, which, the patriarch Abraham having first received as a seal of the righteousness of faith (Rom. iv: 11), forthwith performed upon his son Isaac, on the eighth day after his birth (Gen. xxi: 4); and which was made the sign of the covenant to all his posterity (Gen. xvii: 10. etc.). This question, we feel bound to answer affirmatively, although in doing so we have opposed to us, not only the Baptists, but also the authority of some distinguished Paedo-baptist divines; for instance, the venerable Dr. Neander, who denies that infant baptism was practised in the apostolical church.[3] It is true, there is no direct historical proof in support of it, to be met with in the letter of the N. T. nor in those passages in the Acts of the Apostles, in which the baptism of whole families is spoken of (Acts xvi: 15, 30–33; xviii: 8; comp. x: 44–48 and 1 Cor. i: 10) inasmuch as children are not expressly mentioned, and it is possible that the

---

1. [Philip Schaf, *Mercersburg Review* 4 (July 1852) 388–98. Schaff would later add an additional "f" to his last name.]

2. [*Geschichte der Christlichen Kirche, von ihrer Gründung bis auf die Gegenwart.* Vol. 1, *Die apostoliche Kirche* (Mercersburg, PA: Selbst-verlag des Verfassers, 1851), 490–500. Translated as *History of the Apostolic Church,* trans. Edward D. Yeomans (New York: Scribner, 1853), 571–81.]

3. A. H I. 278. &c. [Neander, *Geschichte der Pflanzung und Leitung der christliche Kirche durch die Apostel,* Erste Band (Hamburg: Bei Friedrich Perthes, 1847), 278; Translated as *History of the Planting and Training of the Christian Church by the Apostles,* trans. J. E. Ryland (New York, 1865), 162. This particular German edition is the only one that correctly matches the page numbers given in this essay. Schaff's own copy is still at the Philip Schaff Library of the Lancaster (PA) Theological Seminary.] Still, we must not overlook this important distinction, that according to Neander, infant baptism was developed from the pure spirit of Christianity, although it was not practised until towards the close of the second century, whilst the Baptists pronounce it to be an unscriptural and unchristian innovation.

families were composed exclusively of grown persons. Still less is there any passage to prove the contrary. We must have recourse accordingly to the spirit of the bible, which contains for more than is just expressed by its letter; and if it thence appears that infant baptism is necessarily included in the very draft and design of primitive Christianity, we will be able, in the total absence of proof to the contrary, to arrive at tolerable certainty that it was actually practised.

The strongest ground in favor of infant baptism, in connexion with and as a part of a well ordered Christian church, and with a sufficient guarantee of a pious education—for it is only upon this condition that we maintain it at all—lies in the universality of the very idea of Christ, which includes humanity itself. He is both able and willing to redeem all men, of every age and sex and description and condition of life. In the presence of the Saviour of the world, all these distinctions are lost in the general need and capacity of all men for salvation. A Saviour, who was only able and willing to save adults and not infants, would not be the Christ he is represented to be in the Gospel. There is no warrant whatever, in the word of God, for the exclusion of a part of our race, on account of their age, from the blessings of the kingdom of heaven, and our best feelings, and deepest and most inward religious consciousness revolt at a particularism, so gross as this.[4] In the significant parallel, Rom. v: 12, &c., the Apostle makes it very prominently to appear that the kingdom of righteousness and life, according to its divine intention and inward power, is altogether as comprehensive, indeed still more comprehensive and effectual, than the kingdom of sin and death, to which it is admitted children are subject, and that the gain and advantage secured to us by the second Adam far more than compensate for the loss and injury received from the first. It is for this reason, he repeats the expression, "much more," in the second member of the sentence (ver. 15–17). As is Jesus himself, so is his church exalted above every limitation of nationality and tongue and kindred and age. The similitude of the leaven, which leavens the whole lump (Matth. xiii: 33) is intended to represent the inward power of the kingdom of God to pervade all classes and conditions of human life,

---

4. And yet this is the inevitable consequence, and in fact the very principle assumed as a primary truth, by the Baptists. Dr. Alexander Carson their most learned apologist, asserts without reserve in his work (*Baptism in its mode and subjects* [5th Amer. ed., Philadelphia: American Baptist Publication Society, 1850], 173) that children cannot be saved by the Gospel, or by faith. "The Gospel has nothing to do with infants; nor have Gospel ordinances any respect to them. It is good news; but to infants it is no news at all. They know nothing of it. The salvation of the Gospel is as much confined to believers, as the baptism of the Gospel is. None can ever be saved by the Gospel who do not believe it. Consequently by the Gospel no infant can be saved." When therefore Baptists assume, as they generally do, that children are saved, without baptism or faith, or the Gospel, they upset the fundamental principle of Christianity that out of Christ there is no salvation, and that by faith in him only are we saved. "Infants who enter heaven," says Carson, "must be regenerated, but not by the Gospel. Infants must be sanctified for heaven, but not through the truth as revealed to man." (Is there then any other truth for this purpose, than that which is revealed? If there is it must be a contradiction, and such an outward anti-evangelical truth can never be saving.) "We know nothing," he adds, "of the means by which God receives infants; nor have we any business with it." Precious comfort to be sure for Christian parents, particularly, when standing by the graves of their children!

and when the Lord, after the solemn declaration that all power in heaven and earth was given him, commands his disciples, to make disciples (μαθητευειν) of *all nations*, by baptizing them in the triune name, and by teaching them his doctrine; there is no reason to think that it was to be limited to those who were of mature age. Or do none but adults belong to a nation, and not youth and children and infants?

In harmony and close connection with this, is the beautiful idea, so clearly expressed already by *Irenaeus*, the disciple of Polycarp, and the faithful bearer of tradition from within the sphere of the labors of St. John, namely, that Jesus Christ became a child to children, a youth, to those who were growing up, and a man to those of mature years, and in thus entering into the various states and stages of the development of man's, earthly life, he sanctified every age and period of life, his infancy, as well as his adult age.[5] According to the Baptist view, the childhood of Christ is robbed of its deeper significancy and most precious comforting efficacy.

But now, on the other hand, *Faith* is necessary as the indispensable condition of salvation, as the organ by which we embrace Christ and appropriate to ourselves his benefits; and here it is that we come into conflict with the main exegetico-dogmatic argument of the Baptists. Christian baptism, as they say, presupposes objectively the preaching of the gospel, subjectively, repentance and faith; infant children, however, can neither understand preaching, nor can they repent and believe; therefore they ought not to be baptised. As it regards this, the major proposition is correct enough, the minor, in this expanded form, is false, and with it the conclusion falls to the ground. The connexion of baptism with the preaching of the gospel, and with faith, is beyond dispute evident, in part from the words of the institution of the sacrament, Matth. xxviii: 19, and particularly Mark xvi: 16, "He that (*first*) believeth, and (then) is baptized, shall be saved," and in part from the examples given us in the Acts of the Apostles, according to which, the preaching of the missionary and the faith of

---

5. Irenaeus says, adv. Haeret. III, 22, [incorrect: *Adversus Haereses* 2.22.4] from a most inward consciousness of the full meaning of the incarnation, *omnes enim per semetipsum venit salvare, omnes, inquam, qui per eum renascuntur in Deum, infantes et parvulos et pueros et juvenes et seniores. Ideo per omnem venit aetatem et infantibus infans factus sanctificans infantes, in parvulis parvulus, sanctificans hanc ipsam habentes aetatem, simul et exemplum illis pietatis effectus et justitiae; et subjectionis, in juvenibus juvenis, exemplum juvenibus fiens, et sanctificans Domino.* [Trans. "For He came to save all through means of Himself—all, I say, who through Him are born again to God—infants, and children, and boys, and youths, and old men. He therefore passed through every age, becoming an infant for infants, thus sanctifying infants; a child for children, thus sanctifying those who are of this age, being at the same time made to them an example of piety, righteousness, and submission; a youth for youths, becoming an example to youths, and thus sanctifying them for the Lord" (*The Ante-Nicene Fathers*, 1:391).] That, by *renascuntur in Deum* ["born again to God"], Irenaeus refers to baptism, as the sacrament of regeneration, by which the infant is dedicated to God, Neander himself admits in his *Eccles. Hist.* vol. I [*Allgemeine Geschichte der christlichen Religion und Kirche* (1842 ed.)], 537, where amongst other things said concerning this expression of the Church father, he adds, "Thus, the practice of infant baptism is derived from the deepest conception of the very nature of Christianity, ruling our minds upon the subject" [See *General History of the Christian Religion and Church*, vol. 1, trans. Joseph Torrey (London, 1850), 432]. [On Irenaeus in Mercersburg Theology, see Evans, general introduction to Nevin, Schaff, and Gans, *Incarnate Word*, volume 4 of this series, xxvii–xxviii.]

the hearer, always precede and prepare for the baptismal act, Act. ii: 37, &c.; viii: 5, &c., 35–38; ix: 17; x: 42–48; xvi: 15, 33; xviii: 8; xix: 5. But here, we must not forget the limitation, overlooked by the Baptists, that in all these instances, the instruction given was very brief and summary, a mere announcement of the principal historical events of the gospel, and with it, but a low grade of faith, previous to their introduction into the church, and that their more perfect instruction in the apostolic doctrine, and their growth and improvement in faith took place after their regular connexion with the church. Primitive Christian baptism was neither compulsory, as for instance, the baptism of the Saxons by the command of Charlemagne,[6] nor yet a mere baptistic form, communicating nothing that was not possessed before, but simply sealing and confirming the already existing life of faith. The Apostles never demanded formal regeneration as a *condition* of baptism, but the earnest sincere longing of the soul after salvation in Christ, which was actually proposed and offered in baptism, and was sealed and afterwards developed and promoted by the other means of grace. "Repent," said Peter to the three thousand, who, on the day of Pentecost, after hearing with an earnest desire for salvation a single brief discourse, were baptized, "and be baptized every one of you, in the name of Jesus Christ, for the remission of sins, and ye shall receive the gift of the Holy Ghost."[7] Thus he places both these blessings, the negative and the positive, as the fruit and effect, not as the preliminary condition of baptism. This view is also confirmed by the frequently misunderstood passage, Matth. xxviii: 19, which should be rendered, according to the original: "Go ye therefore and make disciples of all nations, (by) baptizing them (βαπτίζοντες) in the name of the Father, the Son, and the Holy Ghost, and (by) teaching (διδάσκοντες) them to obey all that I have commanded you."[8] Here it is evident that "to make disciples" to Jesus (i.e. true Christians) is not one and the same thing as "to teach,"[9] but comprehends more than this, and indicates the object to be attained in the use of both the means to be employed, baptism, and the teaching which is to succeed it.[10] If it were possible

6. [Charlemagne's conquest of the Saxons took place in the 780s. It was the final phase of a long-running campaign to pacify the Saxons and bring them under Frankish hegemony. See Fletcher, *The Barbarian Conversion*, 213–16.]

7. [Acts 2:38.]

8. [The primary verb is "make disciples," (μαθητεύσατε: aorist); "baptizing" and "teaching" are participles. So "teaching" and "baptizing" are subordinate to "make disciples," in the manner indicated by Schaff.]

9. The Lutheran interpretation [Luther's translation: *Darum gehet hin und lehret alle Völker und taufet sie im Namen* . . . (Trans. "Go therefore and teach all peoples, and baptize in the name . . .")] here is inaccurate and misleading, in rendering μαθητευειν also, "to teach."

10. Dr. H. Martensen, the Danish divine, is accordingly perfectly correct in saying (Christ[ian] Baptism, and the Baptistic Question. Hamb. 1843, fol. 34), "The more general infant baptism becomes in the world, the more fully are the words of the Saviour accomplished, that *nations*, are made disciples, by baptism and teaching." [*Die christliche Taufe und die baptistische Frage* (Hamburg und Gotha: Im Verlage von Friedrich und Andreas Perthes, 1843), 24. Martensen's essay was translated and published in three parts in *Mercersburg Review* 4 (1852) 305–21, 475–85; vol. 5 (1853) 276–310. The above sentence is on 4:476.]

to become a confirmed Christian without baptism, and so also without a connexion with the church, the church would be altogether useless, at least not necessary, and to this the Baptistic theory also conducts, which always misapprehends the nature and pedagogical significance of the church, as an *institution* indispensable to salvation, and considers it simply in its ground as an *association* of saints. Besides to insist upon regeneration and conversion as a necessary preliminary condition to baptism renders this also impossible, or at least requires that it should be indefinitely postponed; inasmuch as God has not furnished us with the gift of infallibly searching the heart.

As it respects, however, the second proposition in the Baptistic argument, that is the inability of children to believe, from which is deduced their inadmissibility to baptism: we admit it fully, if by faith we are to understand, a *self conscious free* surrender of the heart to God. This can only take place after we have attained to consciousness—and for this we can fix upon no definite period—and thus infant baptism needs to be subjectively completed by means of catechetical instruction and confirmation, in which the believer having attained to spiritual maturity confirms his baptismal vows, and with full and free determination gives himself up to God. For this reason too, the baptism of the children of unbelievers, though they may be professing Christians, has really no significance, and is a profanation of this sacred rite, inasmuch as in such cases there is no sure warrant for the religious education and training demanded by the baptismal vow. The great error of that assertion, however, lies in this, that the conception of faith generally, and with it the efficiency of the Holy Ghost, is bound to a particular stage of the development of human consciousness, and is made dependent upon it. The true ground and condition of salvation lie generally, not in any thing subjective, as belonging to the creature, but in the depths of the divine compassion; and in faith itself we must be careful to mark different grades, from the first bud, to the ripe fruit. It commences already with our religious susceptibility and unconscious yearning towards God, and a childlike confidence in a higher power. It is not altogether a product of our own thinking or knowing, or feeling, or willing, but it is a work of grace and of the Divine Spirit, limited to no age, or stage of consciousness, but is like the wind which bloweth where it listeth, and when and whither it will.[11] Faith does not produce the blessings of salvation, it only receives them, and only in the receptive way, as the organ of appropriation, and not as productive, is it saving in its operation, inasmuch as otherwise, our salvation would flow forth from a creature source. This receptivity for the divine, is to be found however already in the child, and indeed purer, and less obscure than in later years. By virtue of its religious constitution and frame of mind it is accessible to the influences of grace, and may really be born again. To deny this, is to send all children without exception to hell. For they too have been conceived in sin (Ps. 51: 5) are flesh born of flesh (John iii: 6), and by nature the children of wrath (Eph. ii: 3 comp. Rom. iii: 22–24) and without being born again of

---

11. Comp. such passages as Rom. xii: 13; Gal. v: 5; 1 Cor. xii: 3–9; 2 Cor. iv: 13; Eph. ii: 8; Col. ii: 12; Phil. i: 29; Jn. iii: 8.

water and the Spirit, no one can ever, according to the unequivocal and express declaration of the Lord Jesus, enter into the kingdom of God (John iii: 5). "He that believeth not shall be damned" (Mark xvi: 16). When therefore Baptistic divines admit at least some children into heaven without regeneration and faith, they must to be consistent hold the Pelagian view of original sin and guilt or else open another way to salvation, of which the gospel knows nothing, and which stands in open contradiction to all this. There are however, in the scriptures, passages directly to the point, which place this susceptibility of the infant mind to Divine influences, beyond all doubt. If we even overlook the remarkable case of John the Baptist, who, "in his mother's womb, before he was born," was filled with the Holy Ghost (Luke i: 15–41), we nevertheless are assured from Matth. xviii: 2–5; xix: 14, 15; Mark x: 14, 15; Luke xviii: 16, 17, that the Saviour of the world himself took children into his arms, and blessed them, and spoke to them encouragingly of the kingdom of heaven; declared indeed peremptorily, that adults themselves must become children again, must partake of their simple, confiding, susceptible dispositions, in order to have part in the kingdom of heaven. Shall the Church then refuse baptism to those dear little ones, whom the Son of God embraced? Shall the Church reject as incapable and unworthy of her communion, the very persons, whom the Head of the church held forth as a pattern to all who wished to be his disciples? It is much more reasonable to infer from all this, strange as it may seem, that *every baptism, even that of grown persons, is in fact infant baptism*, inasmuch as Christ has declared the childlike spirit to be an indispensable condition of our entrance into his kingdom; and as baptism, moreover, as the sacrament of regeneration, demands of every one receiving it, penitentially to forsake their previous evil ways, and in faith to commence a *new* course of life consecrated to God.

The same objections, which are urged against the Christian baptism of infants, may with equal plausibility be made against the Jewish rite of circumcision on the eighth day. For this too was not an unmeaning ceremony, but a holy sign and seal of the covenant, by which the person circumcised assumed the obligations, and at the same time was admitted to the privileges and blessings of the covenant of the law (Gal. v: 3), which strictly taken could in like manner only be done, after he had attained to self-consciousness, and in the exercise of his own free will. If however, it be said that the circumcision of the Jewish children rested upon a divine command as is undeniably the case, Gen. xvii: 12, Levit. xii: 7, we can nevertheless, from this type derive a strong argument in favor of infant baptism, inasmuch as this has in a manner, certainly taken the place of the other, and for this reason is called the "circumcision of Christ" (Col. ii: 11, 12), with this great difference, it is true, that the ancient covenant, with all its arrangements was nothing more than a shadow of better things to come, whilst the new covenant of grace is the image and essential reality itself (Heb. x: 1, Col. ii: 17). If then the first, according to the promise of Jehovah (Gen. xvii: 7, &c.,) includes the whole posterity of Abraham, why this much more, far surpassing as it does the other in riches and fulness and depth. In this comprehensive sense, and in accordance with the analogy of the command of circumcision, must the Apostles as Jews have understood the injunction of the Saviour to baptize all nations, and if the children were to be excluded it would be somewhere mentioned. In fact, Peter at the feast of Pentecost in calling upon his hearers to be baptized, expressly declares this extension of the blessings of the gospel to children: "For the promise (the remission of sins and the gift of the Holy Ghost) is to you, and your children, and to all that are afar off, even as many as the Lord our God shall call."[12]

This important idea of an organic connexion between Christian parents and their children, and their being included in the same covenant duties and privileges meets us also in the writings of St. Paul. He regards the children as already belonging to the congregation, and enjoins upon them to obey their parents, "in the Lord," Eph. vi: 1, Col. iii: 20, which properly speaking, is only possible upon the presumption of their being engrafted into the body of Christ, and this is effected by baptism. In 1 Cor. vii: 14, he makes a very significant distinction, between heathen and Christian children, and speaks of the first as unclean (ακαθαρτα), the latter on the contrary as holy (αγαια) in virtue of their organic connexion with a believing father, or believing mother. As in a mixed marriage, of which he is speaking immediately before, the mightier divine power of the sanctified Christian wife prevails over the darkness of her heathen husband, so she also exerts a controlling influence upon their posterity. God is stronger than Satan. How much more must this be the case, when both parents are walking in the fear of God, and are thoroughly pervaded by the Spirit of faith! By all this, Paul does not pretend to deny the natural corruption of the children of Christians; but he teaches unequivocally that the blessings of the covenant pass over to them, and remove the curse, so that those, who in themselves were unclean, are by grace consecrated to God, and brought under holy influences. Here it is true the baptism of infants is not mentioned, but the idea of their baptism and the authority for it are necessarily implied.[13] For if the children, in virtue of their birth from believing

---

12. [Acts 2:39.]

13. This also Neander substantially admits when in speaking of the passage mentioned, he says Ap. H. I. fol. 282 "From the point of view here presented by Paul, though it does testify (?) against the existence then of infant baptism, we find still the fundamental *idea*, from which infant baptism afterwards must and did develop itself, and by which it was to be justified in the spirit of Paul: the acknowledgment of the preference that could be given to children born in a Christian communion, in allowing them by baptism to be consecrated to the kingdom of God, and thereby, from their first development, to spread abroad an immediate sanctifying influence." [*Geschichte der Pflanzung und Leitung* (1847), 282–3; translated in *History of the Planting and Training*, 164–65. Other German editions diverge significantly from this text, even though they keep the idea, essential for Schaff's argument, that the "idea" of infant baptism can be "justified in the spirit of Paul." The 1832 edition, followed by the editions after 1847, reads: *Hier finden wir nun auch die Idee, aus welcher die Kindertaufe sich nachher entwickeln mußte und entwickelt, und wodurch sie im Geistes des Paulus zu rechtfertigen wäre, wenn gleich es auch den bemerkten Gründen nicht wahrscheinlich ist, daß er unter den Verhältnissen seiner Würksamkeit deisen Gebrauch schon eingeführt haben sollte* (206). Trans. "So here we find the idea that was justified by the Pauline spirit, out of which infant baptism had to be and was produced, even if for the reasons stated, it is not probable that he would have introduced this usage under the conditions of

parents are already included in the covenant of grace, why should they be shut out from the sacrament, which impresses upon it the divine seal, and gives it, so to say, its proper validity? It is true that the passage, together with the claim and the right to baptism, is limited to the children of such parents, as are, or at least one of them, believing, inasmuch as it is only in connexion with a Christian family life, that this didaskein which, according to the command of Christ, is to follow baptism, and with it the maintenance and evolution of baptismal grace, can be expected to result in a substantial and confirmed life of faith.

If then the admissibility and propriety of infant baptism are grounded in the need which all have of salvation, in the very idea of primitive Christianity, in the extent and compass of the covenant of grace, in its analogy to circumcision, and in the organic, spiritual and bodily relation which believing parents sustain to their offspring; so may we suppose it extremely probable that its introduction would correspond with the first independent existence of a Christian congregation, and we have under such presumption every reason to believe that it was actually practised, when we read in the N. T. more than once, of the baptism of whole families, without any restriction whatever, (as we would have to expect, according to the Baptistic theory); such for instance, as the household of Lydia, and the Jailer of Philippi, and Stephanas of Corinth[14]; which are mentioned particularly as examples, though doubtless there were many similar cases, and it would be remarkable and contrary to daily experience, to take for granted that all these families were without children.

It is true that it has been attempted to set aside this exegetical result, by the testimony of a single witness, the well known polemic, *Tertullian*, who lived toward the close of the 2nd century, and from it to show that it had a proportionately later introduction. But this polemic himself most conclusively shows, that infant baptism did exist in his day, and with it the institution of sponsors. What is still more, Tertullian knew that the whole church *praxis* was against him, and he stood forth as a reformer in opposition to it. Had he referred to antiquity, and could he have spoken against infant baptism as an innovation, something new, he would doubtless have availed himself of this advantage. But he only calls in question, not its apostolic origin, not its admissibility, or propriety, but only its *expediency*. He considered it dangerous, inasmuch as according to his Montanistic view, an individual committing a mortal sin after baptism, must be shut out from church communion, and in all probability would be lost. Upon this ground, he advised that, not only infants, but also *grown* persons, who were not yet married, and had not taken upon themselves the vow of chastity, should put off their baptism, until they were fully secured against the temptation to

---

his activity" {reading *Wirksamkeit* for *Würksamkeit*}.]

14. [Acts 16:14–15, 16:29–34; 1 Cor 1:16.]

licentiousness.¹⁵ This whole controversy of Tertullian rests—which Neander, Gieseler,¹⁶ and others appear not to have noticed, or at least have not brought forward—upon mistaken impressions, in which the church did not participate, and has nothing more than the force of an *isolated private judgment* in opposition to the prevailing theory and practice, and proves clearly the very reverse of that which it has often been attempted to show. Just so much may we with tolerable safety infer from it, that infant baptism at that time, was not yet authoritatively established, but was left pretty much to the free will and judgement of Christian parents. Otherwise, Tertullian would scarcely have assailed it so vigorously. As, however, in this particular, the spirit of the age was against him, his opposition, which by the way, was also in contradiction to some of his own principles, produced not the slightest effect, and died away without an echo.

This was made perfectly evident in the following century. The African church itself, in a council at Carthage in the year 246, decreed that it was not necessary even to defer baptism to the eighth day, as was the case in circumcision, but that it might be performed (not must) on the second, or third day, after birth; and Cyprian who had the greatest veneration for his preceptor Tertullian maintained this view.¹⁷ So entirely at that time already was every trace of the controversy against infant baptism obliterated, that the only question concerning it at issue was, whether according to Jewish analogy, they must delay it for at least eight days! At the very same time, Origen of Alexandria, the most learned representative of the Greek church, who was himself baptized soon after his birth (an. 185), and at the death of Tertullian was 35 years old, speaks in the most unequivocal terms of infant baptism as an apostolic tradition, and a general church observance. If however from the silence of the church histori-

---

15. *Non minore de causa* he says *innupti quoque procrastinandi, in quibus temptatio praeparata est tam virginibus per maturitatem quam viduis per vagationem, donec aut nubant aut continentiae corroborentur.* [Trans. "With no less reason ought the unmarried also to be delayed until they either marry or are firmly established in continence: until then, temptation lies in wait for them, for virgins because they are ripe for it, and for widows because of their wandering about" (*Tertullian's Homily on Baptism* [§18], ed. Ernest Evans, 39; also translated in *The Ante-Nicene Fathers*, 3:678; the editor has corrected the text at one point, using the Evans text.)] Consequently, according to Tertullian, baptism would have to be confined to superannuated and married persons, and monks and nuns! And yet he maintains on the other hand, that we can only be saved through the water of baptism, *nec aliter quam in aqua permanendo salvi sumus* [Trans. "only while we abide in the water are we safe and sound" (*Tertullian's Homily on Baptism* [§1], 5).]. The wide difference between the standpoint of Tertullian and that of the Baptists, in the whole controversy, must be evident to any one possessed of any historical or critical skill. It is therefore perfectly absurd for the Baptists to refer as they do, with so much zeal to the African church father.

16. [Johann Karl Ludwig Gieseler (1792–1854), a German Protestant church historian, authored *Lehrbuch der Kirchengeschichte*. The English translation of vols. 1–2, *A Compendium of Ecclesiastical History*, was widely used in Great Britain, in part because of its selection of primary texts.]

17. [Cyprian, "Epistle LVIII: To Fidus, on the Baptism of Infants," *Ante-Nicene Fathers* 5:353–54. The date must be in error; the standard lists give no council of Carthage prior to 251. In any case, Cyprian was not bishop until 248/249, and "Epistle LVIII" presented the decision as one that he had participated in. According to Hefele, the council that responded to Fidus was "probably" the one in 252 (*History of the Christian Councils*, 96–97).]

ans previous to Tertullian in relation to infant baptism, we are to draw a conclusion against its practice, we should not forget, first that we have altogether very few written memorials of those times, and that there are many other points also in regard to which we are entirely in the dark; and then in the great missionary zeal of the age, and the rapid extension of the church, proselyte baptism would be most prominent, and in the nature of the case, would attract most attention. Still however there are not wanting, in the writings of Clement of Alexandria, Irenaeus and Justin Martyr,[18] indications that show more or less clearly the existence of infant baptism.[19] Especially is the passage, already cited from Irenaeus,[20] of the regeneration and sanctification of the period of childhood, by the childhood of Jesus, taken in connexion with his decided churchly habit of thought, and his close union of regeneration and baptism, a proof not only for the idea, but for the actual practice of infant baptism in his day. From this church Father, we may conclude back with great safety to his venerated preceptor Polycarp, and he was the disciple and personal friend of St. John, the favorite apostle of Jesus Christ.

Translated by B. C. W.
Baltimore, Md.

---

18. [Clement flourished c. 195–203; very little is known of his life. He is best known for his "trilogy" (in English): *Exhortation*, an argument for the superiority of Christianity over Greek philosophy and mythology; *Tutor*, which dealt extensively with the Christian moral discipline, and *Miscellanies*. He may have influenced Origen. Justin Martyr (c. 100–165) went through a number of philosophical schools before finding satisfaction in Christianity. Especially valuable are his descriptions of the early liturgy (including a baptismal service) and the practice of the Eucharist in *First Apology*. As his name indicates, he died a martyr.]

19. [Both the original German and the standard English translation break off at this point, adding the phrase "but which we here pass over, as we shall have to return to them in the history of the second period."]

20. [See above, footnote 5.]

ARTICLE 4

"Wilberforce on the Eucharist"

(By John W. Nevin)

Editor's Introduction

Eighteen hundred fifty-two was a watershed year for both John Nevin and Philip Schaff. In terms of productivity, they were moving in opposite directions. Volume 1 of Schaff's *Geschichte der Christlichen Kirche* was the beginning of many decades of historical scholarship. In contrast, while Nevin continued as an educator, preacher, and ecclesiastical leader, his theological contributions became episodic. He responded to fresh stimuli in the surrounding discussions with essays on his major interests: Christology, ecclesiology, and the sacraments.[1]

Among the theologians Nevin interacted with was Robert Isaac Wilberforce. Wilberforce was the second son of William Wilberforce, one of the leaders in the British abolition of the slave trade. He was drawn into the Tractarian movement, which attempted to uphold churchly ideals in debates with Roman Catholicism on one hand and Evangelicals and Dissenters on the other; their agenda was published in *Tracts for the Times*. Tractarianism, as well as its offshoot the "Oxford movement," was in part a response to the lessening of restrictions on Roman Catholics. Officeholders were no longer required to receive the sacraments in the Church of England. Concerned with the authority of the established church, the Tractarians attempted to show that the Church of England's episcopate was in an unbroken succession with the early church. In *The Doctrine of the Holy Eucharist*, Wilberforce was maintaining the thesis that the "real presence" of Christ in the Eucharist was the common presumption of the entire early Catholic Church, and thus was the proper understanding of the sacrament over

---

1. The only book Nevin wrote in this later period was *Vindication of the Revised Liturgy* (1867). The German Reformed Church had prepared a liturgy, which had been critiqued by a leader of the anti-Mercersburg party. An "Elders' Request" asked Nevin to explain its preparation. See Yrigoyen and Bricker, *Catholic and Reformed*, 314–15.

against the low-church parties.[2] Although Nevin found much in Wilberforce that confirmed his own perspective, he did have a problem with the underlying movement: "Anglican Episcopalianism" or "prelacy" focused, he thought, abstractly on the mere fact of an alleged Episcopal succession as grounding the authority of the church; it attempted to repristinate this early Catholic Church, bypassing the alleged corruptions of the later Roman Catholic Church. Nevin responded that what the history of the early church presented was not simply a menu of beliefs and practices from which one might select in accordance with one's own tastes. Both Puritans and Anglicans posited a fall from primal purity—for the former, after the apostolic era, for the latter, sometime after the fourth century. To the contrary, "there is no such chasm between this classic period and the time following"; indeed, against the Anglicans, any alleged "abuses of Romanism" were already present in the earlier period. The apparent similarities with the pristine era were merely a result of "outward artificial imitation"; what Anglicans (and all "primitivists") lacked was "presence of the same" *spiritual* "life."[3]

Although Nevin was not convinced that repristination of early Catholicism was the solution for the spiritual crisis of his era, he applauded Wilberforce's attention to the "mystery" that was present in its understanding of the Eucharist. He followed Wilberforce in reviewing the evidence for the "real presence" of Christ: John 6:25–59, and among the fathers, Ignatius and Justin Martyr[4] onward. Wilberforce argued that this position implied a prior consecration of the elements. The eucharistic elements were different from the water of baptism, insofar as water required no consecration in order to communicate the grace, whereas the eucharistic elements did require such consecration, and therefore required the presence of the priest.[5] His next move was therefore to respond to the Protestant arguments that he thought rejected the need for consecration. Nevin was naturally approving of Wilberforce's critique of "Zuinglius" (Ulrich Zwingli).[6] Zwingli's view of the Lord's Supper lacked a sense of "mystery" (of

---

2. On the spiritual background of English evangelicalism, see the introduction to article 2.

3. Nevin, "Early Christianity," in *Catholic and Reformed*, 204–5, 264; "Cyprian," 418–19 ("Third Article"). Both essays are slated to appear in vol. 9 of MTSS; the reader should consult the editorial material there. For Wilberforce's "primitivism," see *Doctrine of the Holy Eucharist*, 428. The standard texts on American primitivism are Bozeman, *To Live Ancient Lives*; Hughes and Allen, *Illusions of Innocence*, and Hughes, *American Quest of the Primitive Church*.

4. Ignatius, bishop of Antioch, wrote letters while on the way to Rome to undergo martyrdom (c. 105–110). He is especially known for his evidence for a single bishop in a city, and his description of the Eucharist as "the medicine of immortality." Justin Martyr (d. 165) has left us two valuable accounts of primitive Christian worship, including a clear statement of a "high" doctrine of the Eucharist, in his *First Apology*.

5. Wilberforce, *Doctrine of the Holy Eucharist*, 12ff. This particular claim as Nevin restated it seems problematic in light of the evidence that both oil and water were objects of sanctification for consecratory rituals (Bradshaw, *Search for the Origins of Christian Worship*, 136, 158). On the relative lateness of "application of sacerdotal language and imagery to Christian ministers," see ibid., 204, 201–3. This implies that the role of the priest as the consecrating officiant, and the very idea of sacerdotal consecration, only emerged gradually in eucharistic practice.

6. See the general introduction on Zwingli and the core of his sacramental doctrine.

spiritual meaning) and quickly degenerated into infidelity. Against Calvin, Wilberforce argued that any view that the sacrament was essential to receiving Christ's body was vitiated by his doctrine of election. If the person was truly saved because he or she was elected by God, prior to any participation in the sacrament, then the power was not in the sacrament itself. The sacrament was a sign that God promised to give Christ's body to the believer, but it was "limited" to the elect "by a secret article" of the decree of salvation.[7] A recipient of the elements could not be certain of receiving the grace they represented, unless he or she was vouchsafed supernatural knowledge of his or her election (the classical soteriological problem of Puritanism). Consequently, Wilberforce thought, the certainty of the "thing signified" (*res sacramenti*) was limited to divine "intention." God elected recipients of the sacramental realities, and ministered it to them through the power of the Holy Spirit. Thus Calvin's sacramentology became known as the "virtual presence," since the believer experienced the sacrament through a spiritual power (*virtus*).[8]

Having written *The Mystical Presence* seven years earlier, and having gone to considerable effort to present Calvin as an advocate of a "high" doctrine of the Eucharist, Nevin was not going to leave that interpretation unchallenged.[9] First he addressed Wilberforce's claim that Calvin substituted the Spirit for the body of Christ. He argued that Wilberforce confused *agency* with *virtus*. For Calvin, the Spirit was the agent who made the body of Christ present. But the *virtus* was the body of Christ. To say the elements became the body of Christ through agency of the Holy Spirit was synonymous with saying that the Eucharist was enacted in a supernatural (not natural) order. The elements were no longer merely bread and wine, but the body and blood of Christ—*though the Holy Spirit*. Nevin thought that was exactly what Wilberforce had been arguing all along. Another way of addressing this question was to inquire whether an unbeliever received the body of Christ in the sacrament. Did he or she receive the "thing signified" (*res sacramenti*) or a bare symbol (bread and wine)? Nevin was confident that Calvin would have affirmed the former: the unbelieving recipient truly received the body of Christ, but since he or she lacked faith, did not also experience its salvific efficacy. Nevin referred to Calvin's metaphor of rain falling on rocky ground. It was truly rain, yet it did the rocks no good. Consequently, Nevin argued, Calvin agreed with Wilberforce that the psychological "condition" of the sacrament's efficacy lies in the proper orientation of faith toward the elements; the only difference in Calvin's thought was that the "ability" to have this orientation was granted by divine election. Nevin didn't see how this stipulation should nullify the objective reality (independence of human subjectivity) of the body of Christ in the elements.

---

7. Wilberforce, *Doctrine of the Holy Eucharist*, 39.

8. Ibid., 141.

9. For Nevin's interpretation of Calvin's doctrine, see *The Mystical Presence and the Doctrine of the Reformed Church on the Lord's Supper* [MTSS edition], 58–65, 258–64.

In spite of this effort to defend Calvin against Wilberforce's claim, Nevin understood that a deeper conflict remained unresolved. Wilberforce was defending the "real presence" in the "elements" themselves (consecrated bread and wine), not merely in the "transaction" (the entire liturgical act of blessing and communing), and Nevin assented to his interpretation of the *facts*: the patristic doctrine was uniformly one of a real presence in the elements through the act of priestly consecration. Nevin knew that Calvin's doctrine could not be pushed that far. Since Calvin's virtualism fell short of the patristic doctrine of the real presence, was it not finally on the same theological level as generic Protestantism? Was it *theologically* coherent to say that Christ's body and blood was truly present in the eucharistic "transaction," but not in the elements? Nevin sidestepped the issue, and instead enacted a *tu quoque* ("you're another"): was it not equally true, he asked rhetorically, that Wilberforce's reading should force him to accept the teachings of the Roman Catholic Church? (As it turned out, Nevin was right. Wilberforce converted to Catholicism in the same year this essay was published.) In other words, Wilberforce's attempt at a *via media*[10] was unlikely to succeed. One had to either follow the church fathers to Rome, or embrace the radically antisacramentarian Protestantism of American evangelicalism.

Unless. Nevin still hoped that Calvin's "theory" could sustain and underwrite the sacramental mystery and Christian unity he considered essential to a vital churchly life, *in an authentically Protestant manner.* He acknowledged this theory was not the same as that of the church fathers yet hoped the differences could be explained through some understanding of change over time. The last four sentences of the essay were packed with hints of Nevin's struggle to sustain his evangelical Catholicism.[11] The only possible solution was a church that took seriously its rootage in an ancient churchly past and sought to renew the spiritual life revealed in that past, yet one that also recognized that life grew and therefore changed. He had thought that Schaff's "historical development" might be the solution, but at the end of "Cyprian" he snapped, "For development as such, in any shape, we care not a fig."[12] He was not to be tied down to a theoretical construct. What he *did* need was method or hermeneutic that could hold

---

10. "Middle way." It has of course become a standard claim of Anglicanism that it provides this middle way.

11. This struggle has entered Mercersburg historiography as a five-year period of "dizziness." The description and time frame originated with Good, *History of the Reformed Church in the U.S.*, 312 (quoting an unnamed adversary of Nevin). Regrettably for modern scholarship, Nichols used the word in the title of ch. 8 of *Romanticism in American Theology*. The present writer argued that Nevin's *theological uncertainty* began only with the conclusion of "Cyprian" (November 1852), and ended by November 1854, when he delivered the inauguration sermon for a new professor at Mercersburg (Layman, "Revelation in the Praxis," 131; cf. Hart, *John Williamson Nevin*, 165–68). There was a longer period when he was attempting to extricate himself from an extraordinary workload, and convalesce during a reoccurrence of his psychosomatic ailment, but that needs to be distinguished from the theological crisis (see Layman, "Revelation," 120–22; Hart, *John Williamson Nevin*, 141–44, 171–72).

12. Nevin, "Cyprian" ("Fourth and Last Article"), 562 note. Twenty years later, he dismissed "development" as a "treacherous amphibological term," and suggested it be replaced with "historical movement" (Nevin, "Reply to 'An Anglican Catholic,'" 421).

together a unitary spiritual life with growth and change and diversity over time. Thus, to "historical development," here he added "... and growth." That was perhaps the way out: a churchly (and therefore spiritual) life *that grew* through time.

"Wilberforce on the Eucharist"[1]

It speaks well, on the whole, for the Christian mind of England, that this important work[2] has met with so favorable a reception from it, as to have run already nearly, or by this time perhaps altogether, to the end of its second edition. The first seems to have been exhausted almost as soon as it came from the press. Considering the character of the book, this is something significant, and as we say furnishes just cause for satisfaction. Our satisfaction with it need not depend at all on the view we may take of the author's doctrine and argument. Whatever may be thought of this, all who care for theology and religion, which are still at last the greatest interests of the age, ought certainly to be pleased that the subject here discussed by Archdeacon Wilberforce, entering as it does into the inmost sanctuary of Christian science and life, should be found able to engage in this form so much prompt and active attention. There is a style of theology, we know, and a manner of religion, which would fain be done forever with all inquiry and discussion looking in any such direction; a theology and religion, for which the whole doctrine of the sacraments resolves itself into the simplest naturalism and every-day common sense, without any sort of mystery whatever, and in whose eyes accordingly every attempt to make more of them in any way is set down at once for solemn superstition and nonsense. But this system of thinking carries its sentence of condemnation on its own forehead. Wherever it prevails, Christianity is found to part continually more and more with its proper character, both as life and doctrine. Whether men choose to know it, and lay it to heart, or not, the view that is taken of the Holy Sacraments, as conditioning the view that is taken of the Holy Catholic Church, and, through this again the view that is taken of the whole mystery of the Incarnation; must ever be of radical and primary account in all true Christian theology. Especially must this be the case with the Sacrament of the Eucharist, which has been regarded from the beginning as the most solemn among all the services of the Church, the foundation of its entire worship, and the beating, living heart, we may say, of its universal life. Not to feel its central significance in such view, and not to take an active interest in the proper solution and settlement of the great questions which it

---

1. [J. W. N[evin], "Wilberforce on the Eucharist," *Mercersburg Quarterly Review* 6 (April 1854)161–87.]

2. *The Doctrine Of The Holy Eucharist.* By Robert Isaac Wilberforce, A.M., Archdeacon of the East Riding. London: 1853. Republished in this country by H. Hooker, Philadelphia.

involves as an article of piety and faith, is to stand convicted at once of being in a false position with regard to the grace of the Gospel generally. It is a position as different, as any that can well be imagined, from that of the ancient Church. It is completely at war also with the tone of thought which prevailed, on all sides, in the age of the Reformation. Its affinities are with heresy, rationalism, and unbelief. We have reason to welcome then any work, which, like this of Wilberforce, aims in a serious and earnest way, with powerful argument and comprehensive learning, to call the attention of the Protestant world to this momentous subject; and it is a gratification to know, that in the midst of the downward tendencies of the present time, a work on such subject and of such character should be received, as this has been at least in England, with so much interest and favor. We would be glad, if it could be brought to have still greater circulation in America. Not, as we have already intimated, for the sake of its own particular doctrine, so far as this may be considered peculiar in any view; but for the sake rather of its general object and purpose, the discussion namely of the true meaning of the Holy Eucharist, and the determination of what is to be considered the proper faith of Protestantism with regard to it, as measured by the faith and practice of the early Church.

The author tells us in his Introduction, that the present work is the sequel of his Treatise on the Doctrine of the Incarnation,[3] published a few years since. It was there asserted, that the "Sacraments are the extension of the Incarnation," and a chapter was devoted to the consideration of them in this view.[4] But the thought was felt to require more full discussion. Another work followed, accordingly, on the *Doctrine of Holy Baptism*;[5] and now we have, to complete the plan, this present volume on the *Doctrine of the Holy Eucharist*. The same general view of the nature of Christianity, of course, runs through all these three treatises. They go, in a certain respect, to make up a common whole, the view that is taken of the Sacraments being conditioned, as just stated, by the view that is taken of the mystery of the Incarnation. This is a relation, indeed, that must always hold in any theological system. As men think of the Sacraments, so will they be found in every case, on proper inquiry, to think also of the Incarnation. A Gnostic Eucharist or the contrary, implies a Gnostic Christ or the contrary.[6] It must not be supposed, however, in the case before us, that the author's

---

3. [*The Doctrine of the Incarnation of Our Lord Jesus Christ, in Its Relation to Mankind and the Church* (1848). Nevin responded in "Wilberforce on the Incarnation," repr. Nevin et al., *The Incarnate Word: Selected Writings on Christology*, MTSS 4:49–86. Nevin believed that Wilberforce correctly elevated Christianity's "true interior life" in the incarnate Christ, above the mere "formal system" of prelacy (ibid., 81, 82).]

4. [Wilberforce, *Doctrine of the Incarnation*, 410 (ch. 13).]

5. [Robert Isaac Wilberforce, *The Doctrine of Holy Baptism: With Remarks on the Rev. W. Goode's "Effects of Infant Baptism"* (London: John Murray, Albemarle Street; John and Charles Mozley, Paternoster Row, 1849).]

6. [Here "Gnostic" is shorthand for "purely spiritual," or "nonembodied." Gnostics viewed the physical universe as evil, to be transcended through mystical, elite knowledge.]

doctrine of the Incarnation and doctrine of the Eucharist are so bound together, as to make this last dependent absolutely on all the details which enter into the first. Some, we know, have taken exception to certain parts of the first work, as involving to their mind a questionable philosophy, which they have pretended to censure at times under the vague and convenient title of pantheism. We do not suppose it to be fairly open in truth to any such charge. But what we wish to say here is, that no philosophical difficulty which any may be pleased to attribute to it in this way, can be regarded as extending to the present work. So far as the author's view of the Eucharist is conditioned by his view of the Incarnation, it is not in any such way as to include the questionable conceptions which have been charged upon him by those of whom we now speak; on the contrary, these are carefully avoided, the consequences being so ordered here as to refuse rather than to require any sense of that sort for the premises exhibited in the other case. It is simply with the mystery of the Incarnation as a fact, in the form in which it comes before us in the New Testament and in the universal faith of the ancient Christian Church, that the relation is supposed to hold which imparts to the mystery of the Holy Supper, as a parallel fact, its true character and meaning. In the book before us, accordingly, the whole subject is treated as a matter of fact and authority merely, rather than as a matter of theory and speculation. On all points involved in the discussion, the appeal is in the first place to the Scriptures, and then in the next place to the judgment and practice of the Church in the first ages. Not as if this ancient tradition were taken to be an independent and separate authority, co-ordinate with the written word. "Scripture is referred to as the paramount authority, but when its meaning is disputed, the judgment of the early ages has been taken," we are told, "as being a safer exponent of its real purpose than mere logical arguments."[7]

"And surely there is no point," our author goes on to say,

> on which the judgment of primitive Christians is of more value than this. For it was a point on which their judgment was entirely unanimous. On many subjects the Church was early rent into parties; so that at times it was difficult to say what doctrine was predominant. But respecting the Holy Eucharist there existed no symptom of disagreement for eight centuries and a half. No doubt the received doctrine had been earlier disputed, but it was not by dissentients within the Church, but by external opponents. The Gnostics, who denied that the Holy Eucharist was the Flesh of our Lord, cut themselves off in the second century from the Church; and the Messalian heretics[8] who denied that this sacred food was either beneficial or injurious, were cut off from it by its public sentence in the fourth. These external assaults throw greater light upon the

---

7. [Wilberforce, *Doctrine of the Holy Eucharist*, 2–3.]

8. [Messalians were a fourth-century sect of Mesopotamian origin, which emphasized constant prayer to gain liberation from a demon to which one was bound as a result of original sin. They were mendicant ascetics, parallel to practices in many religious traditions; they held sacraments to be useless.]

unanimity which prevailed within. So that Paschasius[9] is the first author who has ever been alleged to have introduced any doctrine, which did not meet with universal approval; and the statements of earlier writers were admitted at the time to express the collective judgment of the whole community. Now those who look to the first Christians merely as witnesses, must allow that they were so far competent judges of the system which was delivered to them, that they could not all have been mistaken respecting its characteristic features. And those who take a higher view of the Church's judgment, and admit it to possess authority in controversies of faith, cannot dispute its decision upon a point on which there was no dissension. For the eight centuries and a half which precede Paschasius, are those also which precede Photius;[10] they are the period when the East and the West were yet undivided, and when the Church could appeal with the fullest confidence to the promise of a supernatural guidance.[11]

Pursuing this line of argument, the work devotes itself to the task of proving, "that Christ's presence in the Holy Eucharist is a real presence; that the blessings of the new life are truly bestowed in it through communion with the New Adam; that consecration is a real act, whereby the inward part or thing signified is joined to the outward and visible sign; and that the Eucharistic oblation is a real sacrifice."[12] These are considered to be practical points, on which it is possible to produce distinct evidence from Scripture and the primitive Church; whereas the mode or manner in which the general mystery is brought to pass, whether it be by transubstantiation or in some other way, is supposed not to have come under consideration during the first eight centuries; and for this reason it is not allowed to come here into any particular discussion.

The first point considered is the *consecration* of the elements.[13] The words of institution are found plainly to imply, that the bread and wine used in the Eucharist are made to receive a new quality or character, by God's blessing, by which they become distinguished from all other bread and wine, and acquire a fitness for the use here made of them which they would not otherwise have. The separation is not merely nominal, something that is of force only in the minds of those who take part in the service; it exists objectively in the elements themselves. They are not what they were

9. [Paschasius (Radbertus) was a Carolingian monk of the ninth century who composed the "first doctrinal monograph on the Eucharist." He defined the real presence as "the flesh born of Mary"; his critics considered this view as too realistic (*Dictionary of the Christian Church*, 1227).]

10. [Photius (c. 810–c. 895) was a court bureaucrat turned patriarch of Constantinople. A dispute over succession was appealed to the pope, but continuing disputes created the "Photian schism" between East and West. Wilberforce was simply using Photius as a marker for an undivided church: prior to Paschasius Radbertus, an approximate contemporary of Photius, the testimony of the church on the real presence in the Eucharist was (Wilberforce alleged) similarly universally held.]

11. [Wilberforce, *Doctrine of the Holy Eucharist*, 3–4.]

12. [Ibid., 6–7.]

13. [Ibid., ch. 1.]

before. It is not bread and wine in general that can serve the purposes of this Sacrament, as any water may serve the purposes of Baptism; the case requires bread and wine set previously in supernatural connection with that which they are employed to signify and represent. They are set apart and made meet for this use by their consecration; which therefore is a real act, that joins in a real way the thing signified with the sign. So the words of institution most naturally and obviously teach; and such, accordingly, was the interpretation they received from the first in the Christian Church. With regard to this point, all know, who have given the least attention to ecclesiastical history, that in the first ages, as far back as to the very time of the Apostles, there was but one opinion. The elements consecrated, the Fathers tell us from Ignatius and Justin Martyr onwards, were held to be no longer common bread and wine, but "the Flesh and blood of the Incarnate Jesus."[14] They must be consecrated, to become what the mystery of the Sacrament required; and when so consecrated they were made to possess in fact a new character that did not belong to them before, in virtue of which they might be considered and named the Body and Blood of Christ. Hence the vast importance which was always attached to the act of consecration; and along with this the belief also that it could not be effected, save by those to whom a specific commission had been transmitted, carrying along with it the power of a true priestly office. It is enough to refer here to the ancient Liturgies. They have but one voice on the subject; and every early writer utters himself, wherever he has occasion to do so, in the same general way.[15]

From this view of the consecration of the elements, as being an essential characteristic of the Eucharist, the consequence is supposed necessarily to follow that the inward blessing which results from it is bestowed through its outward form. The connection between the sign and the thing signified, in other words, is so real and objective, that the first carries along with it really and truly the presence of the second. The elements are not only a pledge, but the very vehicle itself of the grace or gift, to which, by previous consecration, they have become thus sacramentally bound. The relation of course is not physical, but moral; it holds not in the order of nature, but in the order

---

14. [Quoted in ibid., 10; see Justin Martyr, *The First Apology of Justin Martyr*, in *Ante-Nicene Fathers*, 1:185.]

15. [Nevin's effort to find a single eucharistic praxis in the early church is problematic in light of the evidence analyzed in detail in Spinks, *Do This in Remembrance of Me*, 30–93. Many early rituals lacked an institution narrative (32–33, citing Paul F. Bradshaw, *Eucharistic Origins* [London: SPCK, 2004], 1–23; see also p. 54), suggesting that words of consecration were not essential to the meaning of the rite. Justin Martyr understood the rite as a sacrifice, but understood it as being offered by *all* Christians as "the true priestly race" (p. 33, cf. p. 49 on Cyprian). Spinks claims that "there is no indication that a Eucharist meal was celebrated every Lord's Day" in Ignatius, also bringing into question the centrality of a ritual of consecration to Christian piety (p. 38). The Anaphora of Addai and Mari was primarily concerned with the remission of sins, and had an Epiklesis ("come down") that may represent a "quite distinct Christian form of invocation" (p. 58) (once more in contrast to a ritual of consecration). He concludes that the early eucharistic prayers examined in ch. 2 have "little in common" with each other (p. 66), and summarizes evidence of diversity in the next period on p. 92.]

of grace. Still it is none the less sure and certain on this account. In the economy of the Christian salvation, the Sacraments are made, by God's sovereign good pleasure and will, to be real, and not simply imaginary channels of the grace they represent; and in the case of the Holy Eucharist, the instrument of such consequence is not a sacramental act merely, as in the administration of Baptism, but the elements themselves solemnly prepared for the purpose beforehand by proper consecration. To prove the necessity of this view our author first takes up those modern systems by which it is denied, and tries to show that they necessarily run themselves into consequences that destroy faith altogether. These reduce themselves to the two theories of Zuinglius and Calvin.[16] With Zuinglius, all is made to depend on the mind of the receiver. Consecration adds nothing to the elements. The Lord's Supper sinks into a mere outward commemoration. There is no mystery in it whatever. This is such rationalism as runs at once towards open infidelity. So it was regarded by Calvin, who labored accordingly to give the institution a higher character for the Reformed Church. He insists much on the idea of our actual communication with Christ's Body, and maintains, that this interior benefit goes along with the participation of the sacramental elements in the case of true believers; while yet, according to our author, the inward and outward here are not allowed to come, to any true and real conjunction. The connection is regarded as holding only in the mind and intention of God; just as the bow in the clouds is a token of safety for the world, not because it has in itself any tendency to prevent a deluge, but because it expresses the intention of the Almighty to this effect. The efficiency of the institution is made to fall back thus on the secret counsel, by which God wills some of the human family to bliss and others to misery. To the former only are the elements really the seal of an inward gift; to the latter they are but the empty eating of bread and wine. The objection then against Calvin's theory of the Holy Eucharist, according to Archdeacon Wilberforce, is, "that it involves that dogma of reprobation, which is the opprobrium of his system;" from which it follows, that as the theory of Zuinglius is found to be inconsistent with the first principles of Christian piety, "so is Calvin's with any due respect for the declarations of Scripture and the character of God."[17] These theories being shown to be thus defective and false, the only view which remains is that which supposes the peculiar grace of the Eucharist to be comprehended, not merely in the disposition of the receiver, and not merely in the merciful purpose of God, but actually and truly in the consecrated elements themselves.

The work before us proceeds, accordingly, in the next place, to establish this construction of our Lord's words of institution by the testimony of the ancient Church. This divides itself into three parts. First, the evidence of the ancient Liturgies. These are numerous, reaching back to the first centuries, and representing, not the opinions of a few only, but the faith and worship of the Church in all parts of the world. They

---

16. [For the critique of Zwingli, see Wilberforce, *Doctrine of the Holy Eucharist*, 25–32 and passim; for Calvin, 32–40.]

17. [Ibid., 40.]

are, at the same time, with all their differences in secondary details, wonderfully harmonious in their general conception and sense, being all constructed on a common plan and embodying throughout one and the same reigning idea; a form of unity and universality, which can never be satisfactorily accounted for, except on the supposition of their being derived from a common usage, which extended back to the very earliest period of Christianity, and was regarded as carrying with it in some way the sanction of Apostolical authority.[18] Here the evidence for the point in hand is not simply full, but absolutely overwhelming. The ancient Liturgies turn throughout upon three main points, Consecration, Oblation, Communion; and "all these acts make that which is *done* to and through the elements the prominent consideration, and contemplate them as the medium through which the blessing is communicated."[19] This lies on the face of the service, in every case, from beginning to end. All goes on the assumption of a real transaction in the consecration of the elements of the most awfully solemn kind, by which they are taken to be afterwards, by the transforming power of the Holy Ghost, the mystery of Christ's actually present Humanity, his broken Body and his shed Blood, exhibited on the altar for the purpose of the Christian salvation. To this one thought these old Liturgies owe all their solemnity and sense. Without it they can neither be understood nor respected. This gone, all becomes mummery indeed and sounding bombast of the poorest and most tasteless kind. But secondly, we have in addition to this form of evidence, distinct statements, numerous and full, on the part of the ancient ecclesiastical writers, directly affirming that in the view of the early Church the elements were considered to be so changed by consecration, as to be themselves afterwards the outward form strictly and truly of the gift they represented, and the very medium of its communication. To this must be added, in the third place, the evidence comprehended in the known usages of the ancient Church with regard to the consecrated elements, plainly implying that they were regarded universally in this light. Such were the practice of sending the elements from one congregation to another as a sign of intercommunion, the practice of carrying them to those who were debarred from attending public worship, the custom of reserving them for subsequent use, the view which assumed that Christ communicated himself as a whole in every portion of the elements, the habit of receiving them fasting, with all the other demonstrations of profound reverence and respect which had regard to them immediately in the solemnity of the Eucharist. Altogether for the particular point here in consider-

---

18. [Paul Bradshaw believes there is good reason to deny a "single coherent line of liturgical evolution" from "the apostolic age to the fourth century"; rather, there was "considerable variety" over time and space, and perhaps even in a given locale (*Origins of Christian Worship*, ix, x). Similarly, Spinks has said that "the evidence for eucharistic practices and beliefs in the two centuries following the crystallization of the early Christian communities is sparse and is both geographically and community specific"; "it is impossible to extrapolate some common liturgical shape or some universal doctrinal understanding of the eucharistic rite" (*Do This in Remembrance of Me*, 51; see also p. 34 on early geographical diversity).]

19. [Wilberforce, *Doctrine of the Holy Eucharist*, 47–48; emphasis original.]

ation, and so far as the argument from antiquity is allowed to be of any force, the proof is complete. The Church in the first ages undoubtedly understood our Lord's words of institution, as we have them in the New Testament, to mean that the elements used in the Holy Eucharist, in virtue of what they are made to be by consecration, really include and convey the supernatural gift they are employed to express.

So much for the *subject*, in the words of institution, that to which in his own hands originally our Lord applied the term "This"—the bread and the wine, namely, not in their common and general character, but as made to be mystically, then and there, by his benediction, the outward, visible form of a higher invisible reality. And what now is it which is affirmed of this subject in the way *of predicate*? The answer is plain: "My Body—My Blood." Here we come, accordingly, to a new section of our author's argument, in which he endeavors to show that the gift bestowed in the Holy Eucharist is the presence of Christ through the medium of his humanity.[20] So much would seem to be implied at once by the words of institution; for what can be signified by the Body and Blood of Christ, if they express not his proper living Manhood, what he became, and what he still continues to be, in virtue of his Incarnation? The presence spoken of cannot be taken, of course, to exclude his Godhead; where his Humanity is, there must his Divinity be also in full reality; but it is emphatically by means of his Manhood, as such, in this case, that the presence of his whole person is represented as taking effect. When Rationalists tell us, that this is a hard saying, and not to be believed, because they see not how or why the Body of Christ should be communicated to men in this way, they do but repeat in fact the infidelity of those who formerly at Capernaum, when our Lord insisted upon the necessity of eating his body and drinking his blood, "went back and walked no more with him."[21] We have no right to say that the thing is impossible; for how little do we know of the nature of material substance, or of the qualities and properties it may be brought to assume in such an order of life as that to which it is advanced in the glorification of Christ? And just as little right have we to pretend that the thing is improbable; unless we choose to go the full length of such rationalistic scepticism, and call in question, for the same reason, the entire fact of the Incarnation. This mystery itself implies that the Humanity of Christ is the instrument and medium of our salvation. So too it is everywhere represented to be in the Scriptures. He is exhibited as the Second Adam—the Principle thus of a new human creation, in which it is made possible for men to be redeemed and saved from the universal ruin which has come upon the race through its comprehension in the First Adam. He himself plainly teaches, that this redemption is effected by an actual incorporation, in some way, with his Flesh and Blood, answerable to the participation we all have naturally in that Adamic life which is under the curse. Why then should it be said, that the idea of a real communication of Christ's Body and Blood in the Eucharist is incredible? It falls in exactly with the whole mys-

20. [Ibid., 89ff.]
21. [John 6:52–66.]

tery of the Gospel. It carries out the purpose for which the Word became Flesh. And when the appeal is made here again to the judgment of the ancient Church, it is found to be unanimous, as before, in favor of just this construction of what the Scriptures teach on the subject, to the exclusion of every other.

Next comes the question concerning the sense which is to be attached to the copula, by which subject and predicate are joined together in the words of institution, "This *is* my Body," and again, "This *is* my Blood." What is the relation, in other words, which is here affirmed to hold between the gift bestowed in the Eucharist and the elements, between the outward and inward sides of this august and mysterious Sacrament? Our author declares it to be that of sacramental identity, as distinguished from all mere representation. The outward and inward, the *sacramentum* and the *res sacramenti*,[22] as they are distinguished by St. Augustine, are by the act of consecration, united into a compound whole. This union is not physical. It has no parallel under any other form; and hence, as altogether peculiar in its kind, it requires a peculiar name. Still it is not on this account any the less real. "The two things are so united, that they must needs go together; and whoso receives the one, receives the other. So long as we remain in the region of the senses, and take account only of that which is visible to the outward world, the *sacramentum* is all which we know of; but judge of the matter by faith and revelation, and we are sure that the *res sacramenti* is present also."[23] Such being the principle then, of the Holy Eucharist, it follows "that the complete idea of this sacrament implies, not only the maintenance of the two portions of which this whole is composed, but the law of their combination" also;[24] and hence there is room for four errors with regard to it, which it is necessary to watch against and avoid. The true nature of the sacrament may be overthrown, by omitting either the outward or the inward part of it altogether, or by so confusing or so dividing them as to destroy the necessary form of their union. To suppose the Body of Christ present in the Eucharist under the same natural conditions which attached to it when it was upon earth, would be to set aside virtually the outward side of the mystery, and thus to fall in fact into the notion of the Capernaites, that he intended his Flesh to be distributed to men as natural food.[25] Just the contrary of this is the Zuinglian error, by which the *res sacramenti* or inward reality is made to be nothing, and the ordinance turned into a purely outward formality. The other two forms of error, the undue confusion of the two parts of the sacrament on the one side, and their undue separation on the other, are

---

22. [Wilberforce defined *res sacramenti* as "thing signified" (*Doctrine of the Holy Eucharist*, 21). So *sacramentum* is "signifier," or more simply "sign."]

23. [Wilberforce, *Doctrine of the Holy Eucharist*, 120.]

24. [Ibid., 120–21.]

25. [The story previously alluded to, in John 6:24–65, which takes place in Capernaum. It began with Jesus referring to the miracle of the five thousand (John 6:5–14). Jesus told them to seek eternal food. He then identified himself as "the bread of life." The Jews, missing the spiritual ("mystical") significance of Jesus' teaching, argued among themselves, "How can this man give us his flesh to eat?" (v. 52 NRSV).]

represented respectively, as Archdeacon Wilberforce supposes, by Luther and Calvin. Luther's principle of justification by sheer faith stood in the way of his acknowledging any real efficacy in the means of grace; and hence, while he persisted in asserting the old idea of the real presence of Christ's Body in the Lord's Supper, it became in his system something which carried with it no such force at all of its own for the purposes of man's sanctification, as had been ascribed to it before. This was to divest the reality of its true significance, and to deal with it as though it had been still an emblem only, confusing thus the functions of the outward sign and the inward grace. The theory of Calvin, on the other hand, is charged with so distinguishing the two, in accommodation to his doctrine of election, as to destroy their sacramental coherence, overthrowing in this way the purpose of the ordinance. In distinction from these four errors, the true relation in the case is, according to our author, such a sacramental identity as implies that the *sacramentum*, or outward sign, is the medium through which the *res sacramenti*, or inward reality, is communicated; which is the same thing as to affirm that the Real Presence of Christ is bestowed through the consecrated elements. Such a Presence the Lutheran scheme allows, as does also that Capernaitic view which invests it with a carnal or physical character; while the false and distorted forms in which they set the doctrine, are of themselves sufficient to set aside the systems without any farther refutation. The notion of Luther is so partial and self-contradictory, that it has found, Wilberforce thinks, few genuine supporters. It is over against the other two conceptions, then, of a merely *Symbolical* Presence, as taught by Zuinglius, and of a simply *Virtual* Presence, as here supposed to be taught by Calvin, that the work before us proceeds to establish the doctrine of a Real Presence as this has now been defined; proper pains being taken still farther to guard against mistake, by urging beforehand these two necessary qualifications: first, that the Presence in question is supernatural altogether, and not natural; and secondly, that it is sacramental only and in no respect sensible. It holds in an order of things above nature, and is not subject to the conditions of space and form. It cannot be reached by the senses, but only by the mind through the exercise of faith.

Is full justice done here, however, it may be asked, to the system of Calvin? It is admitted by our author himself, "that he did not suppose the Holy Eucharist to be merely an occasion on which God bestowed the general succors of grace, but that he asserted it to carry along with it a specific and peculiar blessing, namely, that relation to Christ which results from oneness with his glorified Humanity."[26] Again:

> It might be supposed that he entered into the relation between this sacrament and the reconstruction of mankind through Christ; and that he accepted St. Cyril's statements, that the Humanity of our Lord is the appointed medium through which spiritual blessings are conferred upon his brethren. A far deeper man than Zuinglius, he saw that the re-creation of mankind must be

---

26. [Wilberforce, *Doctrine of the Holy Eucharist*, 38.]

based upon that supernatural system of events which had its commencement in the Incarnation of the Second Adam; more clear-sighted than Luther, he discriminated accurately between the inward gift and the outward sign.[27]

As Eve and her posterity proceeded from Adam's side, he tells us after St. Augustine, so the Church and her children are derived from the side of the Man Christ; whose Flesh, accordingly, is the reservoir of all life for his people, of which all must participate in order that they may have part in the benefits of his redemption.[28] The Lord's Supper involves thus a real communication with Christ's Body. This is not at hand in any carnal or local way. It is exhibited in its virtue or essential power.[29] By this he did not mean a virtual exhibition, certainly, as distinguished from an actual, but one rather that comprehended in it the full force and living substance of Christ's proper Humanity, as it now reigns gloriously exalted at the right hand of God. Only the mode of the exhibition or presentation must be considered to transcend all the conditions of nature. It holds, not in the sphere of nature, but in the sphere of the Spirit. But it is not right to say then, as Wilberforce does, that "Calvin substituted the intervention of the Spirit, instead of the efficacy of our Lord's Body, as the true *res sacramenti*, by which a relation is brought about between God and man."[30] The Spirit with him is but the supernatural element as distinguished from the world of sense, in which the mystery of the sacramental participation takes place. Lifted into this reign of grace and power, the process is supposed to be at once beyond the objection drawn from distance. In the sphere of the Spirit, things at a distance from each other may be made to come really together—incomprehensibly, of course, for the natural understanding, but not therefore incredibly for faith. Whether this be said to be by the lifting up of the soul

---

27. [Ibid., 138.]

28. [There are two separate analogies here: Eve taken out of Adam's side (Gen 2:21–23), and blood flowing from Christ's side (John 19:34). Calvin used the second image, referring to Augustine: "our sacraments have flowed from Christ's side; for, when Baptism and the Lord's Supper lead us to Christ's side, that by faith we may draw from it, as from a fountain" (*Commentary on John*, vol. 2, trans. William Pringle, 241 (John 19:34); see also *Institutes*, ed. McNeill, 2:1298). Here the source was likely Augustine's *John's Gospel*, Tractate 102.2: "'One of the soldiers with a spear laid open His side, and forwith came thereout blood and water.' . . . thereby, in a sense, the gate of life might be thrown open, from whence have flowed forth the sacraments of the Church" (*Nicene and Post-Nicene Fathers* [hereafter, *NPNF*], 7:434; see also Tractate 15.8 [*NPNF*, 7:101]). The first analogy does not appear to have an origin in Calvin. Augustine developed the allegory of Adam and Eve in several of the *Expositions of the Psalms*. On Ps 40:9 he said, "When was Eve fashioned? While Adam slept. And when did the Church's sacraments flow forth from Christ's side? While he slept on the cross" (*Expositions of the Psalms, 33–50*, 235 [§10]). Using Ps 126:2 he elaborated: Adam's sleep was fulfilled when Christ "slept on the cross, for his side was struck with a lance and there flowed out the saving mysteries from which the Church was born. The Church is the bride of the Lord, made from his side, as Eve was made from Adam's" (*Expositions of the Psalms, 121–150*, 90 [§7]; see also on Ps 138 [ibid., 257 (§2)], and *Civitas Dei*, 22.17). It seems that Nevin was citing Calvin, but thinking of Augustine's interconnected metaphors.]

29. [The fundamental text of Calvin's "virtualism" is *Institutes*, ed. McNeill, 2:1370–71 and note 27.]

30. [Wilberforce, *Doctrine of the Holy Eucharist*, 141.]

to Christ, or by the coming down of his virtue to the soul, comes in the theory just to the same thing; for both forms of speech are figurative only, borrowed by necessity from the relations of nature to express a fact which is supernatural, and in regard to which no such local relations are considered to have place. Outward and inward meet here, in a way above all sense or understanding, by the wonder-working agency of the Holy Ghost. But this agency, as just said, is not itself the life-giving virtue of the sacrament. Calvin made the *res sacramenti* to be really and truly the Body of Christ, acting by its own objective force where the necessary conditions were at hand, and not simply through the mind of the worshipper. To say that the action is not truly that of Christ's Body because it is represented as taking effect by the intervention of the Spirit, is but to say, that it is not so because it is represented as having place in an order of things which is supernatural—the very thing which our author himself finds it necessary continually to assert. True, the inward part of the mystery, with Calvin, is not allowed to be inherent in any way in the elements, and so it cannot be said to be received along with them by the ungodly; but it was none the less certainly joined, for this reason, with the transaction. The *sacramentum* and the *res sacramenti*, in his system, come together truly in the service as a whole; so that while the believer takes part in the outward side of this, the inward side of it is considered as actually exhibited also for His use, by the power of the Holy Ghost—although out of that immediate transaction the symbols include in themselves no such supernatural relation. That the inward or visible reality, the virtue of Christ's Body, takes effect only on believers, according to the theory, cannot be said to contradict the idea of its objective presence in this mystical and supernatural view; for in any case, as our author himself admits, it is necessary to distinguish between the *res sacramenti* and the *virtus sacramenti*, "the effect which follows from Christ's Presence where there is a living relation between him and the soul;"[31] and this distinction being made, Calvin would have had no difficulty, if we understand him rightly, in granting the actual exhibition of the *res sacramenti* in the Eucharist, as he took it, in the case even of those who are without faith. He compares this very case in fact with the falling of rain upon stones and rocks, which does not cease to be rain because it is followed there with no such effect as when it descends upon genial soil;[32] and in another place says expressly, that however the want of faith may shut out the benefit for unworthy communicants, nothing still fails from the nature of the sacrament, because "the bread is always the true pledge of Christ's flesh and the wine of his blood and there remains always a true exhibition of each on the part of God (*vera utriusque exhibitio semper constat ex parte Dei*)."[33] The virtue of the sacrament, that by which it takes effect on the worshipper, his system confines to

31. [Ibid., 143.]

32. [Calvin, *Institutes*, ed. McNeill, 2:1411.]

33. [John Calvin, *Ultima admonition ad Westphalum*, in vol. 8, *Opera Omnia* (Amsterdam: John Jacob Schipper, 1667), 699; trans. "Last Admonition to Westphal," *Calvin's Tracts and Treatises*, 2:402. See the longer quote and context in *The Mystical Presence*, MTSS ed., 51–52 n. 27.]

the elect, and to these in a state of grace. But this is not just to "put the intention of Almighty God," as Archdeacon Wilberforce tells us, "in place of the *res sacramenti*, or actual gift."[34] It merely comes to this, that those who by their faith make room for its efficacious action in themselves do so by an ability, which they owe to God's election. The immediate condition of the benefit, subjectively considered, is still the same that Wilberforce himself makes it, namely, a right state of mind on the part of the communicant, whatever cause may be assigned for this back of the thing itself; and it is not easy to see certainly why this limitation should be taken to destroy the reality of the gift, objectively considered, in the one case, any more than it may be supposed to destroy it under the same view in the other.

We readily grant, however, at the same time, that Calvin's theory of election and reprobation does not fall in logically with the idea of sacramental grace, and that the two forms of thinking, therefore, cannot stand permanently in friendly connection. The Calvinistic theology carried in itself in this way a serious dualism, which could not fail to be followed in the course of time by the depression of one of these interests in favor of the other. In most sections of the Reformed Church, accordingly, the scheme of divinity which rests on the dogma of an Absolute decree as its principle, has gradually thrust aside Calvin's view of the Sacraments as being what Dr. Hodge calls "an uncongenial foreign element,"[35] that did not cohere with the true life of the system. The course of things, however, in the Reformed Church of Germany shows, that the elimination might be also the other way; since the doctrine of the Sacraments has so far prevailed with what passes for Calvinism there as to hold at bay continually the dogma of the Decrees.[36] We do not see that Calvin's theory of Christ's Presence in the Eucharist, has any necessary dependence on his theory of Predestination. It ought not, therefore, to be so joined with this, that both must be considered to stand or fall together.

Whether, under any circumstances, the theory can sustain itself, is another question. All we demur to here, is the judgment by which it is set down as affirming a simply Virtual Presence of Christ in the Eucharist, in the sense of this book of

---

34. [Wilberforce, *Doctrine of the Holy Eucharist*, 143.]

35. [Charles Hodge, "Doctrine of the Reformed Church on the Lord's Supper," *Biblical Repertory and Princeton Review* 20 (1848) 229. The text is located in the debate between Hodge and Nevin following the publication of Nevin's *The Mystical Presence* (MTSS ed., vol. 1), which was published (on Hodge's side) in *Princeton Review*, and then reprinted and critiqued by Nevin in the *Weekly Messenger of the German Reformed Church*. The full debate is superbly presented in vol. 2 of MTSS: Nevin and Hodge, *Coena Mystica*. The quoted phrase is found on p. 36; further see pp. xl–xliv for the context of the debate. Ironically, Wilberforce himself quoted it in its context: *Doctrine of the Holy Eucharist*, 252 n. 42, to argue that the principles of Calvin and the "Calvinistic confessions, make it nugatory to affirm that the Holy Eucharist rises above the level of other means of grace, and therefore that any peculiar relation to Our Lord's Humanity is conferred in this sacrament" (252). For more discussion of Hodge's attitude, see Gerrish, *Tradition and the Modern World*, 61ff.]

36. [Nevin discussed the alleged "dualism" between these two doctrines, and the orientation of the German Reformed Church in *The Mystical Presence and the Doctrine of the Reformed Church on the Lord Supper* [MTSS ed.], 301–2 and 311.]

Archdeacon Wilberforce—such a Presence as resolves itself at last into a mere Divine intention. As related to the *transaction*, the inward reality which Calvin maintained was, we think, much more than this; it comprehended Christ's very Body itself under an objective form. This our author will be ready to say, is such a view as cannot stand without the conception of such a relation of the *res sacramenti* to the elements, and not simply to the transaction, as must involve what he himself takes to be the necessary form of a Real Presence, in the sense of the ancient Church, as distinguished from such a Presence as is either Symbolical only or at least Virtual; and as Calvin, we know, did not allow any such relation, his theory must be considered as falling short of this distinction at last, and so sinking to the character which is here assigned to it, there being no middle ground in truth on which it is possible for any theory to stand. Here, however, the inquiry comes up, on the other side, whether there be any real middle ground between this view of Calvin and the doctrine in full of the Council of Trent.[37] Can the essential points of what was the original faith of the Christian world in regard to the mystery of the Holy Eucharist be so carried out in any other point (if this may not be considered satisfactory), that it shall not be found necessary to yield here in the end all that forms any fair matter of dispute with the Catholic Church? We fear not.

Be all this as it may, however, it cannot be said to affect the force of our author's argument, as he goes on in the work before us, to assert points which, according to his view, entered into the original faith of the Church on the subject in question, and endeavors to establish both from Scripture and from Christian Antiquity, the doctrine of a Real Presence of Christ's Body in the Holy Eucharist, as a mystery made to have place by priestly consecration in the elements themselves, in such sense that it may be said actually to exist and abide in these objectively as its proper outward form.

In the prosecution of this argument, special stress is laid upon the sixth chapter of St. John's Gospel,[38] which is held to be of classical authority for the proper explanation of other passages in the New Testament referring to this sacrament. Then, agreeably to the plan of discussion originally proposed in the work, an appeal is made to the testimony of the early Church, for the purpose of showing how the sense thus attributed to the Scriptures is confirmed by the judgment of the whole Christian world, in those first ages when the heritage of doctrine was still fresh and this judgment entitled to the greatest respect.[39]

And here, on the field of historical inquiry, the argument must be allowed, we think, to be unanswerably full and triumphant. Make of the matter what we may, it is shown most conclusively that the view taken of the Eucharist by the ancient Church was such, as clearly to exclude, in the first place, the conception of a merely Symbolical

---

37. [The Council of Trent (1545–1563) was the Roman Catholic Church's response to the Reformation, the decisive document of the Counter-Reformation, and the authoritative statement of the church's doctrines and practices in the modern period.]

38. [Wilberforce, *Doctrine of the Holy Eucharist*, 179ff.]

39. [Ibid., 196ff.]

or merely Virtual Presence, and then just as clearly to involve and positively affirm, in the second place, the fact of a Real Presence. The difficulty in such an argument, as Wilberforce remarks, is not to find testimonies, but to set them in any order that may be fairly answerable to the richness of the field from which they are taken. "The Holy Eucharist was so constantly present to the thoughts of the early Christians, that the references to it in their writings are almost innumerable."[40] These are often direct, but far more frequently indirect, and in the form of general and passing allusion. Much of the evidence can be fully felt only in its connections. In this way it comes up from different sides, and under different modifications, the variety adding force to the unity, and showing the subject to be woven into the very life of the religious system to which it belonged. To bring out this consent of antiquity, made luminous and strong by the very diversities under which it appears, the theology of the first seven centuries is exhibited as passing through five different forms or schools, in each of which a different relation to the mystery of the Eucharist prevailed, producing as many various ways of referring to it, while yet it is plain that through all these distinctions the fundamental idea with regard to it remained always the same. The Ante Nicene Period is distinguished for its unreasoning acquiescence simply in the fact of the Real Presence, as something about which all Christians are supposed as a matter of course to be agreed. Next, in the Period following the Council of Nice, we have the Eastern Scheme directing reflection, more than had been done before, to the change effected in the elements by consecration. Then the Anti Nestorian and Anti Eutychian Schools, guarding against wrong to either the outward part of the sacrament on one side, or to its inward part on the other. Finally, the Western School is found uniting the views of the other form, and giving to the doctrine thus a more scientific and comprehensive form.[41] All these schools agree in holding the fact of a real communication of Christ's

---

40. [Ibid., 227.]

41. [The "Ante Nicene Period" precedes the First Council of Nicaea (here called "Nice") of 325. The council was called by the Christian emperor Constantine soon after he captured the Eastern provinces and thus united the empire; he thought he needed to deal with Arianism (the denial of the full divinity of Christ) as a threat to the unity of the church. The label thus refers to the united ("Catholic") Christian church, prior to its legalization by Constantine. The representatives at the council were overwhelmingly Eastern, with the West sending less than a dozen bishops and priests. Although the council affirmed that Christ was "of one substance with the Father," it was only the beginning of a long discussion that continued for the rest of the patristic period. Initially there was the debate between two "schools" in the east of the empire: the theological orientations of Alexandria (in the Nile delta) and Antioch (in northwest Syria, where, according to Acts 11:26, "Christians" first received their name). Alexandria emphasized Christ's divinity, since its goal was deification (being taken up into the life of God), while the Antiochene school focused on Christ's humanity, since what humans needed was a moral "role-model," a divine-human being who showed us how to obey God (McGrath, *Christian Theology*, 287–91). Inevitably there were overcompensations on both sides. Nestorius (d. after 451) was accused of teaching that the "Incarnate Christ" was "two separate Persons," divine and human (*Dictionary of the Christian Church*, 1138–39). It followed then that in the Eucharist, the earthly bread and spiritual body of Christ were separate substances (Pelikan, *Emergence of the Catholic Tradition*, 238). Nevin would have thought that this wronged the "outward part of the sacrament" since it denied that the bread truly carried the body of Christ. Eutyches (d. 454) was an arch opponent of Nestorius,

Body and Blood, through the consecrated elements of the Eucharist. It comes up as a first principle in their theological reasoning. It entered into all their public worship. Every Liturgy involves it from beginning to end. It lies in the view that was taken of consecration. Two general criteria especially may be taken as perfectly conclusive on the subject. Religious reverence and worship were held to be due to the Presence in the elements; and the Body and Blood of Christ were supposed to be orally received through them, even by unworthy communicants. Where these ideas prevail, there can be no question but that the mystery of a Real Presence in the elements, and not merely in the transaction, is regarded as being the essential character of the sacrament. The reservation of the elements for subsequent use implies also the same thing.

But now along with this idea of Christ's Real Presence, as it prevailed in the mind of the ancient Church, goes by a sort of logical necessity another thought, namely, that the Holy Eucharist is to be considered a *sacrifice* as well as a sacrament; and one of the most important parts of the work before us, accordingly, (whatever we may think of the matter itself) is that in which the doctrine and belief of the first ages, in regard to this subject, are brought into view. We will not pretend here to follow the evidence. We only say that as to the *fact* there can be no doubt. The Church in the first ages held universally that the Christian ministry was a real priesthood;[42] that the so-called altar at which it served was an altar in truth and not simply in name; that a real offering was made upon it in the solemnity of the Eucharist; that this offering was nothing less than the body of Christ there present in the consecrated elements; that in this form the One Sacrifice of the Cross ("once for all"[43] or of perennial force) was exhibited continually before God for the sins of men; that the shadows of the Jewish Temple had thus their corresponding reality in the "pure offering" of the Christian Church (Mal. 1:11) and that the making of this sacrifice formed in truth the main work and carried with it the main worth and power of the sacred ministry, as it was emphatically the λειτουργια also, the true liturgy or service of the Church in all its solemn assemblies. Such is the simple historical fact. In what light it is to be regarded, or what use is to be made of it theologically, is of course another matter altogether.

---

and went to the other extreme of denying not only two persons, but two natures. Christ was of one nature; therefore it followed that his humanity was not "consubstantial with ours" (*Dictionary of the Christian Church*, 577). For Nevin, this would have wronged the "inward part" by denying that Christ's *person* was being communicated in the sacrament (see *Mystical Presence*, MTSS ed., 160–63). Finally, this theological feud in the "Eastern Scheme" was (at least temporarily) resolved by the intervention of Pope Leo, in his "Tome," which brought the Latin (Western) Christological doctrine to bear: "Jesus Christ is One Person, the Divine Word, in whom are two natures, the Divine and the human, permanently united, though unconfused and unmixed" (*Dictionary of the Christian Church*, 1631). This formulation was incorporated into the Council of Chalcedon (451). Frend gives a fine narrative of the "Road to Chalcedon" in *Rise of Christianity*, 752–73.]

42. [See Nevin's almost contemporaneous treatment of this issue in "The Christian Ministry," 68–93. This essay was first presented in November 1854, as the inauguration sermon for Dr. Bernard Wolff at Mercersburg Seminary. It is slated for publication in volume 5 of MTSS.]

43. [A theme that would become important for Nevin in his retirement years: "Once for All," *Mercersburg Review* 17 (January 1870) 100–24.]

With Archdeacon Wilberforce, however, the voice of antiquity is allowed to be conclusive in favor of the doctrine; and one object which he proposes to himself in his book, is the restoration of this aspect of the sacrament, and the revival of it as a daily service, in the Church of England. In following out this design, it is assumed that the English Episcopal Church is fairly and truly the continuation of the Catholic Church of the first ages, and that it carries in itself still all the provisions which are needed for giving effect to the sacramental theory here brought into view; whilst at the same time it is admitted that there has been a vast departure from it practically since the time of the Reformation. This departure, it is contended, however, is against the true genius of the Church, and must not be so laid to its charge as to be considered a part of its normal form and order. In this respect it is taken to be in a different condition from the Lutheran and Reformed Churches of the continent; which by casting off Episcopacy are supposed to have broken radically with the constitution of the Church as it stood before, and so to have lost altogether the power of correcting and restoring subsequently their own aberrations from the faith and practice of the first Christian ages. We have here, in other words, the well known Anglican or Tractarian theory of ecclesiastical legitimacy, of which so much was heard a few years since in connection with the University of Oxford, and on which much stress has been laid by some in this country also as a sufficient warrant for the pretensions of the Episcopal Church, over against all other Christian bodies both Catholic and Protestant.

We do not propose, in the present article, to enter at all into the merits of the main subject, considered as a question of actual theology for Protestantism as it now stands. That would be a task too large altogether for the limits to which we are here confined, even if we had the ability and the heart to undertake it; which we confess that we have not. We feel the difficulties of the subject, without having courage to attempt their solution. Let others, more competent for the service, put their hand to this work. We offer here no theory, we have no scheme to explain or defend.[44] All we aim at, is to urge attention to the subject, to press facts, to set home the problem which calls for an answer, and to make clear the necessary conditions of its solution. Let no one say, that this can be of no use. The interest which is here at stake is so very

---

44. [Nevin's attitude here, and even some of his phrasing, was identical to that expressed two years earlier, in the conclusion of his study on "Cyprian": "We are now done with Cyprian and his theology. Our object has been to describe simply, rather than to explain or defend.... We have had no theory to assert or uphold. We offer no speculation. Our concern has been simply to give a true picture of facts. The difficulty of the whole subject is of course clearly before our mind" ("Cyprian," 560, 563 ["Fourth and Last Article"]). Nevin refused to commit himself to any particular theory of historical development: he mentioned "methods of Newman, Rothe, Schaff, Thiersch ... [and] Neander" (562). He then thought that *some* theory of development might be necessary to account for the historical data—e.g., Cyprian's understanding of churchly authority, and its fundamental differences from nineteenth-century evangelical views—and to justify continued "faith in Protestantism" (562). Even so, "for development as such, in any shape, we care not a fig. We would prefer greatly indeed to have the riddle of church history satisfactorily solved, without recourse to any such help. Our trouble is altogether with *facts*" (562 note). "Cyprian" is slated to appear in vol. 9 of MTSS.]

important, that it is not possible to go too far in urging attention to it, independently of every particular theory or scheme that may be exhibited for its explanation. The facts of the case challenge our most solemn regard, in whatever light they may be viewed; and a properly awakened interest in them for their own sake, may be considered indeed the first necessary requisition for doing any sort of justice to the claims of the great theological question to which they belong. Indifferentism and obscurantism are the two things which need most of all to be overcome, in order that there may be any chance of having these claims rightly met. What is most worthy of sorrowful lamentation, is the habit of mind (exemplified on all sides), by which the subject is either held to be of no serious practical account, or else is passively taken to have its full and sufficient exposition in some vague hypothesis, at war both with history and logic, the unreality of which is not seen only because there is not honesty enough nor energy enough to subject it to any truly earnest examination. How much would be gained for our theology, and for our religious life too, if only this dream, this spell of the inward senses, could be effectually dissolved, and things were made to appear in their own true and proper light!

In such general view it is, as we have said before, that we consider it a privilege to call attention to this *Doctrine of the Holy Eucharist* by Archdeacon Wilberforce, without pretending either to endorse its conclusions (that we could not do fully indeed without bowing in form to the claims of the Episcopal Church), or to set up in the way of criticism any opposing or divergent view of our own. We have read the work with more than usual interest. It is eminently worthy of attention. The author occupies the highest rank as an English theologian. No one can dispute the learning of the treatise, nor its general ability. It breathes throughout also the most excellent spirit. The facts it presents are of universal significance and concern. Its theme is one, the importance of which it is not easy to exaggerate, as related especially to the circumstances and wants of the Christian world at the present time.

It is written indeed immediately for Anglicans or Episcopalians. But so far as the main subject is concerned, it has to do with what should be considered a vital and fundamental interest for all Protestant denominations. For Congregationalists, Presbyterians, Baptists, Methodists, and others, whether it be felt or not, there is no more momentous inquiry at this time than that which regards the *Doctrine of the Holy Eucharist*, looked at in the historical and theological relations which are here brought into view. We hazard nothing in saying, that the other subjects of discussion and debate with which these bodies are exercised, so far as there is any care for theology still left, are of far less consequence than this, involving as it does undoubtedly at last all the issues of the Church Question, back to its very source in the mystery of the Incarnation. Not to be alive and awake to the claims of theology in this view, is to be asleep with regard to them in every direction besides, mistaking dreams for realities and abstractions for living concrete facts. New England itself must yet come to see this, if Christianity be not doomed to run itself out there into a barren heath. If her theology is to be saved from starvation and inanition, it must pass beyond the questions which have heretofore engrossed its metaphysical digestion, the *loci communes*[45] of Andover and New-Haven,[46] and grapple earnestly with the questions which enter into what it is now too prone magisterially to waive aside under the title of the Church system, as something at war with evangelical religion and fit only for Puseyites and Catholics. We do not say that it must become either Catholic or Anglican. But it must learn to have some idea of the Church, some faith in the mystery of the Holy Sacraments, some sympathy with the mind of the universal Church with regard to them in the first ages, some sense of the necessity there is for a true historical reconciliation, in some way, between the Christianity of those first ages in this view and what is known as Protestant Christianity at the present time. The day for ignoring and despising these points, is fast coming to an end. The best men in New England are beginning to see and feel it. God grant that they may see and feel it more and more.

Whatever theory any may see fit to adopt in regard to the subject for themselves, there is a common obligation on all to understand and acknowledge at least, as a single fact of history, the view that was actually taken of the Eucharist by the ancient Church. It can never be right to mix up what is purely historical here with what is theological, in such a way as to confound the one with the other. In this work of Wilberforce, for instance, we have two general things, which, however closely they are joined in this argument, need notwithstanding to be kept continually distinct in the mind of the reader; his own scheme, namely, of Anglican divinity, and the historical premises from which he reasons in what he supposes to have been the faith and practice of the Church in the first ages. These premises are one consideration; the conclusions drawn from them are entirely another. To quarrel with the second, merely because we may happen to dislike the first, must be considered eminently absurd. Now it is of these historical premises or data, in the present case, we make the declaration, that they seem to us to be, as to all material points, faithfully represented in the book before us, and that this being so, they give it an interest and importance which all should feel to reach far beyond the range of its own immediate argument. This we may explode, if we please, as theological Puseyism or Popery; but there still are the facts of history, or what at least claim to be such, which refuse to be exploded in any like summary style. Calling nick-names and starting bugbears here, can answer no purpose. The facts remain just what they were before. No theory can set them aside. The universal Church in the first ages saw in the Holy Eucharist the Sacrament of Christ's Body and Blood;

---

45. [Trans. "common places."]

46. [Andover and New Haven (Yale Divinity School) attempted to defend different versions of New England Calvinism. In 1822, Yale became the home of Nathaniel Taylor, who rewrote the traditional federal interpretation of human depravity to make room for contemporaneous democratic ideals. Andover—founded in 1808 as a response to the Unitarian takeover of Harvard—was a center of "New Divinity" thought, which attempted to carry on Jonathan Edward's fusion of Calvinist dogma and conversionist piety. By 1850, it seemed apparent that New England Calvinism was a lifeless shell, masking meaningless debates over theological technicalities.]

they were supposed to be made present in the elements by priestly consecration; the service became in this way a sacrifice of thanksgiving and propitiation embodying in itself continually the full value of the offering made on Calvary for the sins of men; all was held to be an awful and sublime mystery, in which was comprehended day after day the objective force of the whole Christian worship, as the full counterpart or antitype in substance of all that had place as type and shadow in the sacrifices of the ancient law. What shall we say to this? To deny it successfully, as mere matter of history, is out of the question. To say that it does not concern us, is both stupid and profane. It does concern us deeply and seriously. We are bound to see and own the truth; to bring it home distinctly to our mind; to come to some right understanding with it, if possible, in our thinking and in our faith.

Shall we set the whole fact down for a delusion, an open falling away from the true sense and purpose of Christianity as we have this presented to us in the pages of the New Testament? See then how much this must involve. It is no mere circumstance that is here at stake. We have to do with something which goes to the very heart and core of the ancient faith. The whole theology of the early Church is conditioned by this view of the Eucharist. It forms the soul of its worship, the animating principle of its entire religious life. The doctrine is woven inseparably into the texture of its universal practice and belief. To pronounce it then absolutely false, is at once to turn all the Christianity of these first ages into a lie; for their error here, if it were such, is so vast and deep, as to leave no room for the least confidence in their system of thinking under any other view. It is only mockery and hypocrisy to talk of respecting and following the Church of these first days in anything else, if we make it radically wrong in that which formed, as the mystery of the Holy Eucharist did, the grand burden of its creed and worship. To be consistent, we must consign that whole Christianity to Satan, and disown in full the fellowship of the fathers, martyrs, and saints, who dreamed of being carried by it in their day to heaven. Are we prepared for that? Not surely, if we have not lost our spiritual senses. Faith, Hope, Charity, all cry out against such an act of ecclesiastical *felo-de-se*.[47] Infidelity and heresy only have a right to be thus desperately mad.

Can it be pretended then, that we have anywhere among our Protestant denominations, at the present time, this old theory and practice in regard to the Eucharist, still existing and in full force? For the most part, the answer is very easy. The fact of a very considerable difference between the ancient view and that which these denominations now generally hold, is too plain and palpable to allow a moment's mistake. They avow very distinctly themselves quite another way of looking at the subject, and have no wish to identify their doctrine with this Patristic scheme. Anglicanism, however, as represented in the able work which has called forth the present article, affects to occupy a different position, and to be truly one still, not in substance merely, but in actual form, with the Church of antiquity, in its doctrine of the Sacraments as well as

47. [Trans. "felon of himself"; i.e., suicide.]

at other points. Is the pretension properly sustained? We think not. This construction of Archdeacon Wilberforce, however well it may be put together, is not in reality the doctrine or practice of the Episcopal Church either in England or in this country. It will not be so accepted on either side of the Atlantic; for the satisfaction which a certain class may find in it as a merely private entertainment, is something very different from the mind and meaning of the denomination as such. The points of a real bodily presence above nature in the elements, of this as something abiding and not restricted to the immediate service of the communion itself, and of the power of a real sacrifice in the transaction for the sins of men, however they may find some slender hold to hang upon in the confused beginnings of the English system, and the shelter of some slight authority from the view of a few of its bishops and divines since (views generally in the *wilderness*) are yet too alien from the reigning make and genius of the Church altogether, to allow the supposition that they can ever be practically ingrafted into its life.[48] In this country, just now especially, the Episcopal communion is in such a state of general self-compromise with regard to all such points, that the grand Apostolic word, "We believe and therefore speak," is about the last thing concerning them that one expects to hear fall from its lips. If there is to be a real lineal connection here between Protestantism and the faith of the ancient Church, this fond dream of Anglicanism will not answer. It must be shown to hold in some wider view and under some different form.

In these circumstances it is, that the theory of Calvin, if it can be maintained, would seem to be after all most truly conformed to the wants and conditions of the problem which requires to be solved, aiming as it does to mediate between the difficulties of the case as it actually stands on both sides. On the one hand it seeks to avoid Zuinglianism, which by stultifying all antiquity stultifies and kills itself; while on the other it pretends to no such identification with the past, as leaves no room for Protestantism to stand upon in its distinction from the Roman Catholic Church. It asserts, accordingly, a real participation of Christ's Body and Blood in the Eucharist as a transaction; but denies their presence in the elements, and owns in the mystery no sacrifice. In these points it differs from the doctrine of the ancient Church. But must it not so differ, in order to be Protestant? The only question is, whether the difference be

---

48. [Nevin's judgment that Wilberforce's doctrine—both on the "real bodily presence" in the consecrated elements, and "the power of a real sacrifice in the transaction"—was out of keeping with the historic doctrine and practice of the Episcopal Church appears to be historically sound. In their book *The Mystery of the Eucharist in the Anglican Tradition*, H. R. McAdoo and Kenneth Stevenson are perhaps too eager to show basic continuity across the Anglican tradition (thus minimizing the distinctive emphases of some of the Tractarian thinkers), but their copious testimonies especially from earlier primary sources paint a fairly clear picture. See pp. 11–38 for sixteenth- to eighteenth-century Anglican views on the nature of the eucharistic presence as "not natural, corporeal, carnal, in itself local, but without any departure from heaven and supernatural" (this quotation from William Forbes, p. 36), and on the central importance of faithful reception. Pages 126–62 similarly demonstrate a consensus in favor of the Eucharist as merely a commemoration of Christ's once-for-all sacrifice, and a self-offering of penitent believers, in contrast to Wilberforce's sacrificial emphasis. (WBL)]

essential or simply accidental—the destruction of oneness and sameness absolutely, or such an outward diversity only as may resolve itself fairly into the laws of historical development and growth. And this is the question then for Protestantism as a whole interest; for as we have said before, there is no true middle position anywhere, as it seems to us, between the view of Calvin and the full dogma of the Catholic Church. If this Calvinistic doctrine, as we have it for instance in the Heidelberg Catechism, be not able to stand, it is not easy to see certainly how Protestantism itself can stand, as such, and keeping strictly to its own lines, unless as at open war with the whole faith that lives enshrined in the Liturgies of the Ancient Church. Mercersburg, Pa.

J. W. N.

Article 5
"The Efficacy of Baptism"

(By Emanuel V. Gerhart)

Editor's Introduction

By 1857, Emanuel Gerhart had made his peace with the current state of theological discussion in the German Reformed Church, for reasons explained in the general introduction. From the time he became president of Franklin and Marshall College in 1855, he was a central figure in the church's ecclesiastical discussions.[1] The problem that evoked the present essay was a discussion among Presbyterians on the churchly discipline of children. If children had been baptized as infants, were they in some manner Christian, and thus liable to spiritual oversight, or were they still "unregenerate"? The debate appears to have divided southern Presbyterian teachers from Princeton. The former, led by Dr. J. H. Thornwell of Columbia (Georgia) Seminary, said that baptism in no sense changed the spiritual state of a child. He or she had to be "regenerate," converted in order to be truly Christian. This could only take place in a person who had "recognized and accepted the obligations of the faith." As Nichols commented, this was "a virtually Baptist conception of church membership."[2] A Christian was someone who had had a "personal conversion experience." It is difficult to see what role infant baptism played in such a piety. It is no wonder that its practice had collapsed among the Reformed communities. The Princetonians (Charles Hodge and Lyman Atwater) also rejected any form of baptismal regeneration; but they still held baptized children were truly members of the church. Hodge solved the problem by holding that "the children of believers were federally holy and were baptized in recognition of the fact that they were *already* church members."[3] *Federal* holiness was

---

1. *Franklin and Marshall College Obituary Record*, 2:99–100.
2. Nichols, *Romanticism in American Theology*, 253.
3. Ibid., 255, emphasis original.

a holiness constructed out of the *covenant* among God, parents, and children. Infants were properly baptized because of the "covenant, promises, and averments" that "God will be their God; that he will so put the blessings of salvation with their reach or possession, that they cannot fail of them, without first spurning and disowning their birthright."[4] Thus, the church was incorporated into the covenantal promises that God made with the Israelites in the Old Testament.

The Presbyterian confessional documents held that baptism was a "sign and seal of the covenant of grace." The sign was the washing with water; the seal was the impartation of spiritual grace, "of [the baptized person's] ingrafting into Christ, of regeneration, of remission of sins, and of his giving up unto God, through Jesus Christ, to walk in newness of life."[5] After an opening critique of the "low view of the sacraments" found in contemporaneous divinity, Gerhart used those documents to argue that there was in baptism an "intrinsic efficacy" and that grace was "really conferred": as the Confession of Faith put it, "The efficacy of Baptism is not tied to that moment of time wherein it is administered; yet, notwithstanding, by the right use of this ordinance the grace promised is not only offered, but really exhibited and conferred by the Holy Ghost, to such (whether of age or infants) as that grace belongeth unto, according to the counsel of God's own will, in his appointed time."[6] Although the middle of that sentence clearly supported Gerhart, the beginning and end could be construed in different ways. Gerhart knew the confessions denied that the simple act of baptism conferred grace, and devoted some of his argument to analyzing that claim.[7] He explicitly affirmed that the sacramental transaction took place *through the Holy Spirit*, but nonetheless muted that motif in favor of the claim that baptism's efficacy was *intrinsic*.

A more serious contradiction between Gerhart and Princeton (Atwater and Hodge) arose out of the end of this paragraph of the confession. Gerhart accepted Westminster's doctrine of God's decree (ch. 3).[8] However, based on his preceding analysis of §6, the "grace" that "belongs" to the elect was manifested through the or-

---

4. "Children of the Church and Sealing Ordinances," 7.

5. Westminster Confession of Faith, XXVIII.1; available at http://www.creeds.net/reformed/BookOfConfessions.pdf and hereafter cited as WCF, chapter and paragraph. Chapter enumeration follows that of the United Presbyterian Church in the United States of America (right-hand column of the Book of Confessions.pdf), since that is the enumeration of the 1806 edition of *The Constitution of the Presbyterian Church in the United States of America*.

6. WCF, XXVIII.6.

7. He considered Q. 161 of the Larger Catechism, which said that "the sacraments become effectual means of salvation, *not by any power in themselves* . . . but only by the working of the Holy Ghost" (emphasis added). This appeared to contradict Gerhart's claim that baptism possessed "intrinsic efficacy." He resolved the problem by claiming that "sacraments" in Q. 161 referred not to its "full and proper sense" (in which a sacrament is both "sign and seal"), but to a defective sense that included only its "external element and external transaction." See below, 176–77.

8. For more on Gerhart's views on predestination, see his appreciative critique of Calvinism in Book 2, ch. 1 of his *Institutes* 1:97–118.

dinance of baptism. "The Sacrament of Baptism is, therefore, the ordinance in and through which the decree is operative effectually for the salvation of the elect."[9] God elected those who would be saved, but the grace of election was "really exhibited" and "really conferred" through the sacrament. He therefore could not comprehend Atwater's claim that baptism had no "intrinsic efficacy."[10] If union with Christ did not arise "intrinsic[ally]" out of baptism, then out of what did it arise? He quoted Atwater who said that "membership in the visible Church [was] founded on a *presumptive* membership in the invisible."[11] An infant was baptized because he or she was *presumed* to be a member of the invisible church. Since Gerhart thought the "invisible church" was the community of those who were united with Christ, he interpreted this to imply that union with Christ came through *natural* birth: the infant, having been born to one or both Christian parents, was to be baptized as a sign of his or her eventual incorporation into the community of those who were united with Christ. He found it astonishing that a Presbyterian would hold such a doctrine: it implied that an infant was incorporated into the body of Christ through natural birth. To the contrary, Charles Hodge claimed[12] in the very next number of *Biblical Repertory and Princeton Review* to be saying something else: he denied that the invisible church consisted of those united with Christ. He thought Gerhart's construction an "example of a learned man forgetting the lessons taught him by his mother." He was confident that Gerhart knew that "membership in the invisible Church 'consists *of the whole number of the elect*, that have been, are, or shall be gathered in one, under Christ the head thereof.'" Hodge understood "the elect" to be, not those who had been united with Christ, but all those, past, present, and future, who would be elected by God unto salvation. "Presumptive membership" was therefore not presumption of union with Christ, but presumption of *eventual* election. Children of Christian parents were *presumed* to be members of the elect (until such time as they gave evidence that they were not), and were therefore to receive the sign of covenantal membership.[13]

As in John Nevin's discussion with Horace Bushnell a decade earlier, a three-cornered debate was taking place. Evangelicals had the loudest voice: in order to be a Christian, one had to be converted (regenerated). Baptism followed as a sign of

---

9. See below, 175 (§6).

10. "Children of the Church and Sealing Ordinances," 21; see below, 185.

11. Ibid., 22; emphasis original.

12. Nevin thought Princeton would find it difficult to answer Gerhart's argument: Nichols, *Romanticism in American Theology*, 256–57, quoting an unpublished letter from Nevin to Schaff, January 28, 1858 (in the "Library of the German Reformed Church, Franklin and Marshall College"). This only goes to show how difficult it was for the German Reformed theologians and Princeton to understand each other's positions.

13. Hodge, "Church Membership of Infants," 375–76 note, emphasis original. Hodge was quoting WCF, XXV.1. In the body of the text, Hodge had said: "When, therefore, we assert the church membership of the infants of believing parents, we do not assert their regeneration . . . ; we only assert that they belong to the class of persons whom we are bound to regard and treat as members of Christ's Church" ("Church Membership," 351).

repentance and forgiveness of sins, which permitted one to be a member of the church. Infants could not experience conversion, and therefore could not be baptized. Hodge claimed that evangelicals (he called them "Baptists," like Nevin) confused "What is the church?" with "Whom are we bound to regard and treat as church members?" He agreed with evangelicals that only the regenerate were members of the body of Christ. Nevertheless, the church was bound to "recognize many as Christians who are not real Christians" even among adults; so much the more ought it to recognize the infant progeny of Christian parents. Hodge was assuming several underlying principles here: humans could not know the spiritual state of a person (i.e., whether he or she had been regenerated); however, membership was not based on "evidence of regeneration." Furthermore, if people who were not known to be regenerated were accepted as members, then one had to draw a distinction between the visible church (as it appeared to human eyes) and the invisible (as it was known to God). He thought these assumptions were integral to "the general faith of Christendom."[14]

To the contrary, those claims did *not* have the consent of the church universal. Just as Gerhart misunderstood what was *presumed* by Princeton, Princeton refused to recognize the German Reformed theologians' rejection of the visible/invisible distinction.[15] Heirs of the magisterial Protestants wanted to include the entire community within the ambit of the community's guidance. All participants were *presumed* to be Christian and potentially the subject of God's electing and converting grace, but no one could claim certain knowledge of this election: thus the truly regenerate were "invisible." However, increasingly Reformed Americans were opening themselves to the experientialism of the Anglo-American awakenings, and the certitude that the regenerate *could* be recognized. As demonstrated most clearly in the history of the Puritans, this introduced a spiritual instability in the Reformed ecclesial praxis: if one was already within the community of the elect, why did one need to gain further certainty of one's election? This explains the collapse of the practice of infant baptism among Presbyterians, Dutch Reformed, and Congregationalists: in practical terms,

---

14. Hodge, "Church Membership of Infants," 349–51. Hodge then proceeded to explain and apply the claims of "covenant theology": God's covenant with his people always included the children of those people.

15. The confusion was not entirely Gerhart's error. He was able to quote Atwater (who is presumed to be, although not stated as, the author of this essay): "The administration of the seal is founded on the *presumption* that the things sealed will also be bestowed and accepted" ("Children of the Church and Sealing Ordinances," 24; emphasis original). "The things sealed" were that the infant would become a child who would eventually "personally accept by faith the blessings thus stipulated and sealed to faith, personally take his place as a professed follower of Christ" (ibid.). In that case, the *presumption* was *not* only of invisible election, but of eventual *visible* participation in the blessings of union with Christ—which generated, Gerhart thought, the contradiction of claiming that such participation came through natural birth, instead of the "intrinsic" grace of baptism. Hodge's visible/invisible distinction had already been opposed by John Nevin in "Hodge on the Ephesians," *Mercersburg Review* 9 (1857) 46–83, 192–245. He argued that Ephesians specifically, and the Epistles generally, viewed all Christians as elect, who could notwithstanding fall short of final salvation (72ff.). Thus there was no spiritual distinction between the invisible regenerate and the visible members of the church.

the majority lived as if election was evidenced by conversion, and not through the churchly covenant. However, Mercersburg had rejected conversionism, and led by Nevin, had never found the scholastic predestinarianism of Hodge persuasive.[16] Nevin had brought to Mercersburg an emphasis on the imperative of a felt, experientially vital religion. But he found it in the ongoing sacramental praxis of the community, at once objective in the action of the church and vital in its living power to bring transformation. Apparently, by 1857 Gerhart had been persuaded by that vision, and integrated it into his own theological understanding.

---

16. See the general introduction, as well as Nevin, "Hodge on the Ephesians." For Nevin's view that Calvin's doctrines of election and the sacraments were incompatible, and the possible role of Hodge in leading Nevin to believe that, see DeBie, editor's introduction to Nevin, *The Mystical Presence*, MTSS edition, xxxix; Thompson and Bricker, editors' preface to *Mystical Presence* (1966), 13. An important question for Reformed dogmatic history: Was Hodge's predestinarianism a commonplace, or did he construct it, doubtless out of preexisting elements? If it was indeed fundamental to Presbyterian dogmatics, why had Nevin never embraced it during his thirty-seven years as an old-school Presbyterian?

"The Efficacy of Baptism"[1]: *The Children of the Church And Sealing Ordinances. Art. I. Princeton Review. January, 1857. Neglect of Infant Baptism. Art. IV. Princeton Review. January, 1857.*[2]

To find two articles on the subject of Baptism in one number of the *Princeton Review*, the leading organ of Presbyterian Theology in America, the one inquiring into the status, or real position of grace, held by baptized children in virtue of Baptism, and the other exposing the "great sin" that at least one-half, if not two-thirds, of the children of communicant Presbyterians remain unbaptized, is certainly significant. Considering the general silence and apparent comparative indifference to so important an aspect of the Sacrament of Baptism, the articles, as well as the works on which they are based, indicate to us the operation of some special cause. This line of discussion is not demanded by any unusual amount of opposition from those who hold theories in conflict with the Confession of Faith. There has been no formal attack made of late upon the Sacraments as administered in the Presbyterian Church. The Baptistic controversy has in a great measure subsided. It is not then from without, we think, that the discussion receives its impulse. The cause must be sought elsewhere.

The Presbyterian Quarterlies, and the Theological Seminaries, generally, if not uniformly, set their faces against high views of the Sacraments. The pulpits and the weekly periodicals take up and perpetuate the opposition; and the warfare is thus carried into every church and into all the families of the churches. The result of a long continued and general opposition is the prevalence of a new theory—a theory that does not involve simply an important modification of the old Reformed or Presbyterian doctrine concerning the Sacraments; but that rests upon a negation of them as possessing any intrinsic efficacy. The new theory is *negative*. It denies that, by means of the Sacraments themselves, the worthy recipient is made a partaker of the grace which the Sacraments represent. They are *signs*—outward forms or transactions setting forth the regeneration of the heart, the forgiveness of sins, and progressive sanctification, through the operation of the Holy Ghost. They are *seals* also. But the proper meaning

---

1. [E. V. Gerhart, "The Efficacy of Baptism," *Mercersburg Review* 10 (January 1858): 1–44.]
2. ["Children of the Church and Sealing Ordinances," 1–34; "Neglect of Infant Baptism," 73–101.]

of seal is denied of the term; or explained away to such an extent that sign and seal come to signify the same thing; at least it is difficult to say in what respect they differ essentially.[3] The Sacrament as a seal is not an effectual means of salvation, does not assure the recipient that he is a partaker of an inward saving grace as certainly and really as he receives the outward sign, but it confirms the promise of the forgiveness of sins through faith in Jesus Christ. The seal assures the recipient that he will be saved from sin and death through Christ, if he repent and believe. The same assurance is given by the word. In the one case it is written or spoken; in the other it is exhibited in a visible symbol. The benefits of Christ's work are applied by the operation of the Holy Ghost, who may be imparted in the Sacrament; yet the Sacrament and the Spirit have no necessary connection. The Spirit is given without reference to the Sacrament; with or without the Sacrament; before or after Baptism, or the Lord's Supper, is administered. The promise given in the word is good alike for all, for the unbaptized as well as for the baptized; the one having no less reason to look for the inward saving work of the Holy Ghost on the heart than the other; for the promise is fulfilled in answer to prayer through the preaching of the Gospel to the unbaptized in the same sense in which it is to the baptized. A sacrament viewed as a *seal* is to be regarded, accordingly, as a confirmation of the promise of salvation through repentance and faith—a promise to which a person may lay claim with equal advantage, with or without, before or after, the administration of the sealing ordinance.

To this effect Ridgley says:

> A seal, according to the most common acceptation of the word, imports a confirming sign. Yet we must take heed that we do not, in compliance with custom, contain more in our ideas of this word, than is agreeable to the analogy of faith: Therefore, let it be considered, that the principal method God hath taken for the confirming our faith in the benefits of Christ's redemption, is, his own truth and faithfulness, whereby the heirs of salvation *have strong consolation*, Heb. 4: 17, 18, or else the internal testimony of the Spirit of God in our hearts. The former is an objective means of confirmation, and the latter a subjective; and this the Apostle calls our *being established in Christ, and sealed, having the earnest of the Spirit in our hearts*. 2 Cor. 1: 21, 23. This is not the sense in which we are to understand the word as applied to the sacraments; since if we call them confirming seals, we intend nothing else hereby, but that God has to the promises that are given to us in his word, added these ordinances; not only to bring to mind this great doctrine, that Christ has redeemed His people by His blood; but to assure them, that they who believe in Him, shall be made partakers of this blessing; so that these ordinances are a pledge thereof

---

3. Ridgley acknowledges the difficulty without hesitation: "The Sacraments are also said to seal the blessings that they signify; and accordingly they are called, not only signs, but seals. It is a difficult matter to explain, and clearly to state the difference between these two words, or to show what is contained in a seal that is not in a sign." Ridgley's Body of Divinity. Vol IV B. 163 [Thomas Ridgley, *Body of Divinity*, vol. 4 (Philadelphia: William W. Woodward, 1815), 163].

to them, in which respect God has set his seal, whereby, in an objective way, he gives believers to understand, that Christ, and His benefits, are theirs. (Body of Divinity, Vol. IV, p. 165)[4]

According to Dr. Ridgley, the principal method by which God confirms our faith in the benefits of Christ's redemption has no connection with the Sacraments. The confirmation of faith is affected principally by the truth and faithfulness of God as set forth in the preaching of the Gospel, and by the internal work of the Spirit on the heart. The Sacraments are of far less account, and hold a lower place in the economy of redemption, than the preached word or the internal testimony of the Spirit. They are only outward pledges that God will accomplish what he promises in His word to those who repent and believe. But they are not the outward certification that Christ really conveys or makes over to the recipient in the act of Baptism or Communion the saving grace which the sign represents.

So we understand Dr. Ridgley. His view of the Sacraments is somewhat higher on the whole, we think, than that which at present obtains generally throughout the Presbyterian Church. Substantially, however, it is the same. The prevailing habit of thought repudiates the idea that the Sacraments are in themselves effectual means of salvation, or that they conduct us to the thing signified and efficaciously accomplish that which they represent.

The language of Dr. Dick expresses, we believe, the most prevalent opinion in the Presbyterian Church on the subject of the Sacraments. After quoting some of the strongest and most explicit passages on the intrinsic efficacy of Baptism, he says: "It is not to be inferred from these passages, that remission is inseparably connected with baptism any more than regeneration, so that every person to whom it is administered, is immediately delivered from a state of condemnation. The idea is unscriptural, and is adopted only by those who are grossly ignorant of the economy of grace, in which God reserves to himself a right to give or withhold spiritual blessings according to his pleasure. But we are plainly taught that it is a sign of remission, or that the application of the water to the body, is a symbol of the purification of the soul from guilt, by the atoning blood of Christ. It holds out in figure the means by which children are delivered from original sin, and adults from both original and actual. In the ark, "a few, that is, eight souls, were saved by water; the like figure whereunto," says Peter, "even baptism doth also now save us, not the putting away of the filth of the flesh, but the answer of a good conscience towards God, by the resurrection of Jesus Christ." (1 Peter 3: 21.) It is the symbol of salvation; and those to whom the blessing signified by it is imparted, shall as certainly escape the avenging wrath of God, as Noah and his family escaped the destruction of the flood." (Dick's Theology, Vol. II, Lect. 89, p. 338.)[5] Dr. Dick's view of Baptism does not rise beyond the conception of a symbol or

---

4. [Ridgley, *Body of Divinity*, 164–65.]
5. [John Dick, *Lectures on Theology*, vol. 2 (New York: M. W. Dodd, 1850), 388 (*not* "p. 338").]

figure; and scarcely to the true conception even of that. For Baptism, as we interpret him, does not symbolize or exhibit a certain present spiritual blessing, but a blessing that may, or may not, be imparted through the atoning blood of Christ according to the secret counsel of God. It becomes thus an empty symbol—a symbol with which no corresponding meaning or force is objectively connected.

The natural tendencies of such low views of Baptism upon ministers and laymen—for we propose to limit our discussion to this Sacrament—have been two-fold. Those who hold the Confession of Faith and the Larger and Shorter Catechisms in good faith, as the authoritative exponents of the Holy Scriptures, and make earnest with the doctrines and order of the Presbyterian Church, are more or less sensible of a conflict between the teachings of their Symbols and the prevailing habit of thought in regard to this Sacrament. Sympathizing with current views and yet venerating the Symbols as teaching the truth, their position is unsatisfactory and painful. Too much under the influence of the prevailing unsacramental theology to yield a hearty assent to the Confession of Faith, and too much under the moulding influence of the Confession and the Catechism to ignore their theory of the Sacraments and be borne along unresistingly on the tide of the age, they hold no definite views respecting the benefits of Baptism; they do not know whether to regard baptized children as truly the lambs of the fold or not; whether to deal with them as the children of God, or as the children of the Devil. Unwilling or unprepared to take either horn of the dilemma, they enquire seriously: What is the *status* of a baptized child? "We have met many evangelical clergymen," says Dr. Atwater, the author of the article on *Sealing Ordinances*,[6] "in precisely this state of mind, full believers in the divine institution of infant baptism, yet craving more light as to its precise import and efficacy, and urging us in our poor way to examine and discuss the subject. We have met with few who have reached a mode of apprehending the matter altogether satisfactory to themselves."[7]

We may remark by the way, that we are gratified to find so free and full an acknowledgment of what we can not but believe to be the true state of the case. Yet what a sad and humiliating acknowledgment it is! Ordained ministers of the Gospel who have pursued a complete course of classical and theological preparation, and have been approved as well qualified to fill the pastoral office, do not know in what light to look upon the baptized children of the Church; do not know whether they belong to the Devil or to the Lord, whether they are in a state of condemnation or in a state of grace, whether they are in the kingdom of light or in the kingdom of darkness. These little ones are entrusted to the special care, guidance and protection of the ambassador of Christ. He is set for the express purpose of training them and nourishing them unto eternal life. They are the hope of the Church. But if he does not know what they are, how shall he be able to treat them properly? How shall he perform the duties of

---

6. [The author is nowhere identified in the volume of *Princeton Review*, but the essay is universally ascribed to Lyman Hotchkiss Atwater.]

7. ["Children of the Church," 5.]

his office efficiently? He is a workman in the garden of the Lord. Are these little ones living plants or are they poisonous weeds? If he can not answer the question, how shall he go to work? Shall he cultivate them tenderly as possessing a life which is to be more fully unfolded, or shall he pluck them up by the roots because they are evil? The question lies at the very threshold of the pastoral office; and we ask, how can a man take the first step intelligently and consistently who does not know what a baptized child is? What shall the husbandman do—what qualifications does he possess for his work, if when he sees young plants growing in his field he does not know whether they are *vines* or *weeds*? To be ignorant on this point is certainly as great a reproach to a minister as to have no definite views respecting the doctrine of the Trinity, or the doctrine of justification by faith.

The other natural tendency of low views of Baptism is to produce a neglect of the Sacrament; and neglect soon prepares the way for a total rejection of it. There may be few comparatively among laymen or ministers who draw legitimate inferences in a formal way from the principle, that there is no intrinsic efficacy in the Sacrament of Baptism. This, however, does not neutralize the force of the theory and hinder its natural result; for a principle works out its own proper results in practical life, whether the logical conclusion be deduced consciously from the premises or not. Though the people generally may not reason it out logically, they will come to *feel* at least, that if there be no advantage derived to an infant from Baptism itself, it will suffer no real loss from the want of it. And they will, in consequence, not long continue to practice an empty form upon their children simply because they are taught to believe that God has commanded the observance of it. Baptists in principle, it requires but a short process of development until they become Baptists in practice. This effect will follow in the case of that class of Presbyterians who have not been thoroughly indoctrinated. The Confession of Faith, or the Catechism, has no strong hold upon them; and they cherish no strong attachment to it. Their religious character has been moulded by the theological tendencies of the age and by a corresponding style of preaching the Gospel, rather than by the patient and believing study of Presbyterian Symbols. They have, therefore, but a slight, if any, sense of conflict between the doctrines which they profess to hold and the current views with which they are imbued. There is no restraint. Baptism is but a lifeless and powerless ceremony; and they give it up. No one sounds the alarm for years; and the Church at length wakes up to find that one half of her children are unbaptized.

Here, then, we find the cause of the more than ordinary interest which we rejoice to see evinced in the Sacrament of Baptism. The article on "The Children of the Church and Sealing Ordinances" gives expression to the one tendency to which we have referred, as following naturally from low views of Baptism in the Presbyterian Church, and seeks to solve the problem which can not but arise in the minds of the more earnest and thoughtful. The article on the "Neglect of Infant Baptism" shows to what an alarming extent the other tendency has already been developed among the people, and institutes an inquiry into the causes of so widespread a practical apostacy from the old faith. Both articles are timely and proper; they discuss questions which it is in the highest degree consistent for a conscientious Presbyterian to ask, in an interesting manner and with ability; and they indicate the presence of a healthful under-tone of sentiment in regard to the Sacraments, in the midst of predominant unsacramental and even anti-sacramental tendencies.

It is consistent for an earnest Presbyterian to put these questions and endeavor to solve them, because the Confession of Faith and the Catechisms of the Church inculcate high views on the necessity and efficacy of both Sacraments, and especially of Baptism. This position we have thus far assumed. We shall now endeavor to make it good; and then in the light of it examine these Articles on Baptism.

In answer to the question: *What is a Sacrament?* The Larger Catechism answers as follows:

> A sacrament is an holy ordinance instituted by Christ in His Church, to signify, seal, and exhibit unto those that are within the covenant of grace, the benefits of His mediation: to strengthen and increase their faith and all other graces; to oblige them to obedience: to testify and cherish their love and communion one with another, and to distinguish them from those that are without. (Q. 162)

> The parts of a sacrament are two: the one, an outward and sensible sign used according to Christ's own appointment; the other, an inward and spiritual grace thereby signified. (Q. 163)

To complete this view we quote from the Confession of Faith, Chap. 27, Sec. 2. "There is in every sacrament a spiritual relation, or sacramental union, between the sign and the thing signified; whence it comes to pass that the names and effects of the one are attributed to the other."

Rightly understood, we are willing to accept this statement as a correct definition of a *Sacrament*. The statement involves several particulars: 1. A sacrament is an ordinance instituted by Christ; 2. It consists of two parts; the one, outward and sensible, the other inward and spiritual; 3. These two parts are united in the Sacrament. It is a union of the outward and the inward, of the sign and the thing signified.

These several particulars are comprehended in one expression: A Sacrament is a *sign* and *seal* of divine grace. The outward element is both the sign and the seal. As a *sign* it represents grace—a spiritual good. As a *seal* it gives the assurance of a real and present grace. The thing signified is bound objectively to the sign. The outward element becomes a seal in being a *true* sign. Did the outward element exist by itself; were the union of the thing signified with the sign not necessary and real, but arbitrary and possible only, then the outward element would be in no sense a seal; it would not signify something present and real, but something that might or might not be present, according to circumstances. But in not signifying a reality, the outward element would lose its character also as a sign; it would simply be itself—water, or bread and wine; as for any thing spiritual, in real connection with the sign, it would be unmeaning and untrustworthy. A sign which does not represent any unseen reality to be in certain connection with it, is properly no sign at all. Thus if we divest the outward element in a Sacrament of the character of a seal, it ceases also to possess the proper character of a sign. The two conceptions demand each other reciprocally.

What a Sacrament is as an Institution of Christ it is also in its use by those who worthily observe it; that is, the sacramental transaction signifies and seals divine grace to a proper subject of the Sacrament. The impartation of the outward element signifies the impartation of an inward grace. Under this view it is a sign. But the sacramental transaction is not an illusion of the senses. It is a real transaction. The infant is really washed with water, and the believer really eats bread and drinks wine at the table of the Lord. As a true sign, therefore, the application of the outward element represents a real communication of divine grace. As such it is a seal. The sacramental transaction assures the recipient that he participates in the inward grace as really as he participates in the outward element. It conveys and confirms what it signifies. The two, the sign and the thing signified, are united in the transaction as truly as in the institution. The sign completes itself in the seal. Were the present communication of the inward, to those for whom it is designed, not as real as the present communication of the outward, the transaction would be without any corresponding meaning. It would represent what does not take place. The outward would be certainly communicated, but the inward might as certainly be withheld. The outward would, in consequence, not be a true but a false or empty sign. If, therefore, the administration of a Sacrament be not a *sealing* transaction, if it do not make over and convey what it signifies, and the one as really as the other, it is not, strictly speaking, a sign. It is an outward ceremony, and no more—a ceremony of an unmeaning or delusive character.

It is in this sense that the Presbyterian Symbols hold a Sacrament to be both *a sign and a seal*. At least we see no evidence to believe that words are used without attaching to them their proper meaning, The Confession of Faith says: *There is in every Sacrament a spiritual relation or sacramental union between the sign and the thing signified.*[8] Here we have a most important truth. It is the *union* of the outward with the inward, of the sign with the thing signified, that constitutes a Sacrament; not either part taken by itself. The sign, the outward element, though used according to divine appointment, is not a Sacrament. An external washing with water performed in the name of the Trinity by a minister of the Gospel, if it include nothing more than what is thus accessible to the senses, is but a formal washing of the body with water; it is not Baptism. The breaking of bread, the pouring out of wine, and the distribution of bread and wine to a number of persons who eat and drink sitting or standing together around a table, if not really connected with an efficacious supernatural power, make but a lifeless ceremony; these things, existing by themselves, do not constitute the Lord's Supper. Nor, on the contrary, is the inward, the unseen and the supernatural, unconnected with

---

8. [WCF, XXVII.2]

an outward representative form, a Sacrament. The efficacious operation of the Holy Ghost, renewing the heart in the image of Jesus Christ, is not Baptism. The intimate communion of Christ with the believer, and the quickening of his inner life and of all his spiritual graces, do not make the Lord's Supper. The two parts of the ordinance must be united. What God has joined together objectively, we dare not rend asunder in idea. We may not separate the soul from the body, nor the body from the soul; for the body is not a man, nor is the soul a man; but the organic union of the soul and the body make a real human being. So we dare not separate an invisible supernatural grace from a visible, natural symbol; we dare not separate an inward efficacious operation of Jesus Christ by the Holy Ghost from an outward transaction, in our conception of a Sacrament; but we must hold both parts as essential constituents of one concrete reality. Without either the inward or the outward, that which is called a Sacrament is no longer such really.

The fundamental truth may be viewed under two false aspects. Each one gives rise to a fundamental error; and each error is grounded in a corresponding generic method of thought. One error arises from a false view of the *connection* of the sign with the thing signified in a Sacrament. Instead of viewing the outward form and the inward grace as in real union, they are identified; the outward is transmuted into the inward; the sign disappears and is swallowed up in the thing signified; and the thing signified, the supernatural part or side of the Sacrament, becomes the whole reality. Thus arises the theory of Transubstantiation as taught, in regard to the Lord's Supper, by the Roman Catholic Church—a theory which destroys the conception of a Sacrament, because it destroys the integrity of the outward sign. It allows no proper reality to the outward element. Bread and wine are not real bread and real wine; each ceases to possess its peculiar distinctive properties; though they appear to be what they were originally, they are, nevertheless, substantially the very body and the very blood of Christ. There is thus no longer a real sign, and therefore no real Sacrament.

Transubstantiation is grounded in the Eutychean method of thinking.[9] Eutycheanism denies that the unmixed peculiar attributes of humanity can be predicated of

---

9. [Beginning at this point Gerhart attempted to apply the ancient heresies Eutycheanism and Nestorianism to his analysis: for background see the discussion at art. 4, note 41. Eutyches (d. 454) held that Christ only had one nature (not two, divine and human), and thus denied that Christ shared our human nature. Nestorius (d. after 451) was accused of holding the other extreme: not only were there two natures in Christ, but two *persons*. (Chalcedon would attempt to reconcile the conflicting dogmatic concerns by declaring that Christ was *two natures in one person*.) Gerhart's argument comes across as less successful than Nevin's earlier effort. To connect transubstantiation and Eutycheanism is simplistic: the former has to do with the claim that there is a "substantial conversion" of bread and wine into the body and blood of Christ (see Pohle, "The Real Presence of Christ in the Eucharist," accessed March 12, 2015, http://www.newadvent.org/cathen/05573a.htm). Once so converted, the "body of Christ" is the person of Christ as defined by the relevant dogmatic formulae ("one person, two natures"). One can argue with whether the application of ancient Aristotelian categories to eucharistic doctrine was either wise or necessary, but given the role of the Roman magisterium in defining the response to Eutycheanism, implying that there is a fundamental contradiction between its rejection of Eutycheanism and its acceptance of transubstantiation needs a more dialectically sophisticated

the person of Christ; and holds that the human is, in some sense, transmuted or absorbed into the divine nature. This theory destroys the proper conception of the incarnation; for how can Christ be truly incarnate—how can it be true that the Word was made *flesh*—if Christ be not really and truly bone of our bone and flesh of our flesh? But what Eutycheanism is with regard to the person of Christ, that Transubstantiation is with regard to the Eucharist; both theories being fatal to the reality of the outward, visible, tangible side of a great mystery.[10]

The other error arises from a false view of the *difference* between the sign and the thing signified. Instead of distinguishing properly between the outward and the inward, between the natural form and the supernatural grace, it separates the two parts and holds them entirely asunder. It does violence to the necessary objective connection which exists between the thing signified and the sign; the outward transaction may be performed with or without the presence and power of the inward grace. The sign does indeed represent grace, but a grace that is mechanically associated with the sign, rather than a part of the very constitution of a Sacrament. The separation may be so wide as to be equivalent to a direct denial of any objective connection whatever between effectual grace and the sacramental transaction; and the Sacrament then resolves itself into an empty sign—a merely commemorative ordinance—a lifeless form—a dead ritual service.

This false view is grounded in the Nestorian method of thinking. Nestorianism admits the reality of the divine and the human natures of Christ; but reacting against the confusion of substance which Eutycheanism teaches, it separates the one from the other; and thus denies the organic union of the two in the person of Christ. The two natures are held together outwardly, and not inwardly; they exist side by side and merely cooperate together in the work of redemption; but they are not integral parts of one mysterious constitution pervaded by the power of one life-principle. What Nestorianism is in relation to the person of Christ, that this dualistic error is in relation to the Sacrament of Baptism and the Lord's Supper; both theories negate the internal and necessary connection between the natural and the supernatural, and thus divorce two distinct things which God has joined together in a mysterious unity.[11]

---

argument than this. In fairness to Gerhart, the attempt to attach the placard of ancient heresies onto one's theological adversary was a common strategy in his day. There were no mentions of Eutyches or Eutycheanism in *The Mystical Presence*, and only one brief mention of Nestorius (MTSS ed., 151); but then Hodge lodged the charge (there spelled "Eutychianism") against Nevin (Nevin and Hodge, *Coena Mystica*, 134); Nevin answered on 135ff., responding with a countercharge of Nestorianism, see esp. 137–39, 167.]

10. [Again, one can argue that a true sacrament requires an *essential* remainder of the physical sign, but this editor is not convinced that an analogy with Eutycheanism is the best way to make that argument.]

11. [The analogy between Nestorianism and the Eucharist as an "empty sign" has more merit than the previous analysis, since Nestorianism appears to have held that, even as humanity and divinity in Christ were two separate persons, in the Eucharist physical bread and the body of Christ were two separate substances (Pelikan, *Emergence of the Catholic Tradition*, 238). Even so, it is anachronistic to

Nestorianism possesses strong affinities for Unitarianism; and one system may in consequence easily pass over into the other. Nestorianism, divorcing the divine nature from the human, holds the human as existing separately from the divine. It is but a natural development of such a false separation, first, to subordinate the divine to the human, and then to suppress it altogether, when the human nature becomes the proper personality of Jesus Christ; and we have the Unitarian theory. So does the dualistic view of the Sacraments possess strong affinities for the Socinian theory.[12] Denying the internal and necessary connection between the thing signified and the sign, and thus divorcing the outward sacramental transaction from the inward supernatural grace which it exhibits, it is an easy transition to the denial of any real connection whatever of grace with forms or signs, and to the assumption that the visible part, or the sacramental transaction, is itself the whole Sacrament. Then we get the Socinian theory, namely, that there is no divine grace in the Sacraments; that Baptism possesses no intrinsic efficacy; and that the Lord's Supper is not a mystery, but only a most impressive memorial of the death and sufferings of Jesus Christ.

Such has been the actual process of development through which the prevailing Theology of America has passed. From a denial of grace being necessarily connected with, or really bound to, the sacramental transaction, it has passed on to the theory that the visible symbols and the orderly and reverential use of them, constitute the Sacrament. There is, therefore, no supernatural grace in the Sacrament itself. The inward is first divorced from the outward, the supernatural from the natural; then the outward is affirmed to be the whole Sacrament; and finally it is regarded as a self-evident proposition that the outward is not the inward, that the natural is not the supernatural, the visible not the invisible, that a mere external ceremony can possess no objective spiritual efficacy. Baptism can confer no grace. The Lord's Supper can communicate no spiritual nourishment to the believing communicant; for each is in itself but an empty though a solemn rite of Christian worship. The blessing derived from the rite is not communicated by the rite, but depends upon the state of heart and the spiritual exercises of the worshipper. A legitimate conclusion, we admit. But the course of such reasoning is like taking a rich kernel out of a shell; calling the hollow shell a nut; and regarding it as a grave error to attribute any nutritive properties to a nut.

This Socinian view of the Sacraments following naturally from the Nestorian method of thinking, is altogether consistent upon the Unitarian principle. To deny

---

project the memorialism that originated with Zwingli, and was developed in the Radical Reformation, back onto fifth-century dogmatic debates. Gerhart's case becomes historically stronger when in the next paragraph he connects memorialism to what can be generally presented as "religious rationalism."]

12. [Socinians were Reformation-era Unitarians, originating with an uncle (Lelio Francesco Maria Sozini [1525–1562]) and a nephew (Fausto Paolo Sozzini [1539–1604]). The latter led an already-existing Unitarian church in Poland, which was especially accepted by the upper classes. "Socinianism" is best understood here as being shorthand for "religious rationalism."]

the divine personality of Jesus Christ, and to deny the intrinsic efficacy of the Sacraments or sacramental grace, is logical. The one leads legitimately to the other. Both doctrines are integral parts of but one system. But there is no room for the rejection of sacramental grace on the Reformed or Presbyterian principle, that Christ is the second person of the Godhead. To hold the divine personality of Jesus Christ, to hold the real union of the supernatural with the natural, of the infinite with the finite, of the divine with the human, in the person of our Lord, and deny the union of the supernatural with the natural in the Sacraments, is a logical contradiction. The two views presuppose and rest in opposite methods of thinking—an opposition that sooner or later must make itself felt, and produce a corresponding effect. There is no resemblance or affinity whatever between consistent Unitarianism and consistent Presbyterianism. Differing radically on what constitutes the fundamental principle of the whole Christian system, they must by necessary consequence be mutually exclusive also on all subordinate points of doctrine. The Christian consciousness of the Presbyterian Church can not, therefore, in the nature of the case, continue for a very long period in this state of self-contradiction—holding, not confessionally, but actually, the Unitarian theory concerning the Sacraments and rejecting the Unitarian theory concerning the person of Christ. If there be freedom of thought and speech, there must be a reaction in one direction or the other: a tendency to lower views of the person of Christ, or a tendency to higher views of the Sacraments. The one legitimate tendency is at work, we are sorry to believe, throughout many portions of the Congregational Church of New England; the other, judging from various indications, we have reason to think, is awaking in some parts of the Presbyterian Church. At least we indulge the hope that the reaction, which without any doubt must come under one form or the other, will be in the right direction, and result in restoring the teachings of the Confession of Faith on the Sacraments to their proper place in the faith and consciousness of those who, notwithstanding their present defection on this point from the creed of their fathers, still continue to hold it reverently as the authoritative exponent of the Sacred Scriptures.

As we must understand the Confession of Faith and the Catechisms of the Presbyterian Church, they exclude both the errors to which we have now referred. They neither transmute the sign into the nature of the thing signified, nor divorce from the sign the thing signified, and then deny its existence. But they maintain the reality of the sign, the reality of the thing signified, and the union of these two distinct things in the Sacrament; so that the names and effects of the one may properly be attributed to the other. A Sacrament is *a sign and a seal*—using both words in their true and full sense.

In accordance with this general view of a Sacrament, the nature of Baptism is defined by the Confession of Faith as follows:

> Baptism is a sacrament of the New Testament, ordained by Jesus Christ, not only for the solemn admission of the party baptized into the visible Church, but also to be unto him a sign and seal of the covenant of grace, of his ingrafting

into Christ, of regeneration, of remission of sins, and of his giving up unto God, through Jesus Christ, to walk in newness of life: which sacrament is, by Christ's own appointment, to be continued in his Church until the end of the world. Chap. 23, 1.[13]

The outward element to be used in this sacrament is water wherewith the party is to be baptized in the name of the Father, and of the Son, and of the Holy Ghost, by a minister of the Gospel, lawfully called thereto. Sec. 2.

In order to apprehend clearly the full import of these statements we quote in connection with them the 163d Question of the Larger Catechism: "What are the parts of a sacrament? Answer. The parts of a sacrament are two; the one, an outward and sensible sign used according to Christ's own appointment; the other, an inward and spiritual grace thereby signified." Taking all these statements together we can determine the theory of Baptism as taught in the Symbols of the Presbyterian Church.

There are two parts in the Sacrament of Baptism; the one, an outward and sensible sign; the other, an inward and spiritual grace. The outward part is not Baptism; nor is the inward part Baptism; but that is Baptism which includes both; and the one as really and necessarily as the other. The outward and the inward are each an essential constituent of this Sacrament; and no transaction can, therefore, be affirmed to be Baptism in which a sensible sign and a spiritual grace are not united. To call the outward sign, separately considered, the Sacrament, is plainly a misnomer; it is as serious an error as to call the external human, divorced in thought from the living soul, a real human being.

What the "outward sign" and the "spiritual grace" consist in, we learn from the Confession[14] as just quoted. The outward element or sign is water applied to the person baptized, in the name of the Father, and of the Son, and of the Holy Ghost, by a minister of the Gospel lawfully called thereto. The thing signified, or the spiritual grace,

---

13. [The text is ch. 28 (XXVIII) not 23 (XXIII).]

14. The Larger Catechism defines Baptism in nearly the same words as the Confession. In answer to the question: What is Baptism? it says:

"Baptism is a Sacrament of the New Testament, wherein Christ hath ordained the washing with water in the name of the Father, and of the Son, and of the Holy Ghost, to be a sign and a seal of ingrafting into Himself, of remission of sins by His blood, and regeneration by His Spirit; of adoption and resurrection unto everlasting life: and whereby the parties baptized are solemnly admitted into the visible Church, and enter into an open and professed engagement to be wholly and only the Lord's." Q. 165.

This definition is fuller and more explicit even than that given by the Thirty Nine Articles: "Baptism is not only a sign of profession, and mark of difference, whereby Christian men are discerned from others which be not christened, but it is also a sign of Regeneration or New-Birth, whereby as by an instrument they that receive Baptism rightly are grafted into the Church; the promises of the forgiveness of sins, and of our adoption to be the sons of God by the Holy Ghost, are visibly signed and sealed; Faith is confirmed, and Grace increased by virtue of prayer unto God." Art. 27. It is in the office for the administration of Baptism, as contained in the Book of Common Prayer, that the doctrine of the Episcopal Church concerning the efficacy of the Sacrament is most clearly brought out. The language of the Book of Common Prayer, however, is no less unambiguous than that of the Symbols of the Presbyterian Church.

is an ingrafting into Christ, regeneration, and remission of sins. These two things, the application of the water, and the accompanying work of the Spirit whereby the person baptized is ingrafted into Christ, are joined together in the baptismal transaction; for "there is in every sacrament a spiritual relation, or sacramental union, between the sign and the thing signified."[15]

The Sacrament of Baptism has accordingly been ordained by Jesus Christ for a two-fold purpose: 1. For "the solemn admission of the party baptized into the visible Church." But this is not the whole design of the Sacrament. It comprehends a great deal more. It is ordained "not only" for such solemn admission into the *visible* Church; but 2. It is to be unto the person baptized "a sign and seal of the covenant of grace"; that is, Baptism is ordained also for the admission of the person baptized into the *invisible* Church. This is evident from the accompanying explanation. A sign and seal "of the covenant of grace" is a sign and seal of "ingrafting into Christ, of regeneration and of remission of sins."[16]

Here it is necessary to bear in mind the true import of the words *sign* and *seal*. Baptism is a *sign*. The outward application of water to the body represents or exhibits the inward work of the Holy Ghost upon the heart, by which the person is united to Christ, regenerated and pardoned. But the sign is not an empty, lifeless form. It does not represent something that is not done. It is a true sign. The thing signified is present, certain, and real. Hence the sign is also a *seal*. The baptismal transaction *assures* the person baptized, that the inward work of the Holy Ghost is as certain and real as the outward use of the sign. He is as certainly introduced into the covenant of grace, that is, he is as certainly ingrafted into Christ, regenerated by His Spirit, and forgiven through His blood, as he is externally washed with water. The thing signified is objectively connected and conferred with the sign, as truly and really, as the sign itself is used.

Nor is this an unusual meaning of the word *sign*; it is the very sense in which the word is employed in all the affairs of actual life. The joining of hands in the ceremony of marriage is a sign; a sign that the parties take each other in good faith as husband and wife. So far from being a mere form, it is regarded as the outward expression of what is actually done—the assurance of sincerity and truth. If a bridegroom do not as certainly and really give the affections of his heart to his bride, as he extends to her his right hand; and if the outward transaction be not an assurance of his full determination to live with her in the state of matrimony according to the law of God; the solemn act is condemned by all the good as a profane mockery of God and men. The sign of a merchant is the outward indication of his business; but the business is as real and certain as the sign. If not, if the business is not really conducted at the time and place indicated, the sign is pronounced to be a base imposition upon the community; or if not an imposition, it cannot be regarded as being intended as a sign. Those who deny

15. [WCF, XXVII.2.]
16. [WCF, XXVIII.1.]

that God has connected supernatural grace with the outward baptismal transaction, or that He as really confers the thing signified as the sign is administered, do not attribute as much validity or reality to the ordinances of Christ in His Church as they do to the conventional arrangements of dealers in merchandize.

That we have rightly interpreted the definition of Baptism given by the Confession of Faith, will appear from some of the succeeding Sections. "Although it be a great sin to contemn or neglect this ordinance, yet grace and salvation are not so inseparably annexed unto it, as that no person can be regenerated or saved without it, or that all that are baptized, are undoubtedly regenerated." (Chap. 28, Sec. 5.) Three points are to be noted in this Section. It teaches that salvation without Baptism is not an impossibility; and that a person may be baptized without being regenerated and saved. Baptism is an effectual means of salvation to such only "as that grace belongeth unto, according to the counsel of God's own will."[17] It is the elect, not the non-elect, who are ingrafted into Christ by the Holy Ghost in the administration of the ordinance. But this Section affirms also by implication—the principal point to which we call attention—that grace and salvation are *inseparably annexed* unto Baptism. This is in full accordance with the statement that there is a "sacramental union between the sign and the thing signified."[18] The connection of grace and salvation with the ordinance is inseparable—the plain though indirect affirmation of the Confession; but the connection is not inseparable in such a sense that salvation is in all cases impossible without Baptism, or that every baptized person will undoubtedly be saved.

The language of the sixth Section is stronger still, and more direct. "The efficacy of Baptism is not tied to that moment of time wherein it is administered; yet, notwithstanding, by the right use of this ordinance the grace promised is not only offered, but really exhibited and conferred by the Holy Ghost, to such (whether of age or infants) as that grace belongeth unto, according to the counsel of God's own will, in his appointed time."[19] We will endeavor to analyze this plain and forcible statement.

1. Baptism *possesses efficacy*. The efficacy is not predicated of the repentance and faith of the party baptized, nor of the nurture and admonition in which Christian parents bring up their children, nor yet of the independent operations of the Holy Ghost, but it is predicated of Baptism itself. The efficacy is objective, or *in* the Sacrament, in other words, it is an *intrinsic* efficacy. If not intrinsic, it is *extrinsic*; for we can not associate any efficacy with the ordinance that is neither the one nor the other. But an extrinsic efficacy of Baptism is no efficacy at all. It is a power that lies outside of the ordinance—a power that is exerted by something which is distinct and different from the ordinance; and must in consequence be predicated of that by which it is exerted, and not of Baptism. There is no room, therefore, to speak of *the efficacy of Baptism*, as

---

17. [WCF, XXVIII.6.]
18. [WCF, XXVII.2.]
19. [WCF, XXVIII.6.]

the Confession does, unless it be conceded that that efficacy is intrinsic—in the proper administration of the ordinance itself.

2. The efficacy of *Baptism is not tied to that moment of time wherein it is administered.* The efficacy of the ordinance is indeed operative at the moment of time when it is administered; but not at that time exclusively. As according to an opinion of some of the Church Fathers, perpetuated for centuries in the history of the Church, Baptism availed only or chiefly for the remission of sins that were past, and not for the remission of such as were committed after the administration of the Sacrament, the Confession teaches, in opposition to such unscriptural limitation, that, beginning at the time when administered, the efficacy of Baptism extends over the whole of life and terminates in the resurrection from the dead; for it is a seal "of adoption, and resurrection unto everlasting life." (Lar. Cat. Q. 165.)

3. By the right use of this ordinance the grace promised is *offered* to such as that grace belongeth unto. Baptism bears or brings grace to those who are baptized, as that which belongs to them and is designed for their salvation.

4. The grace promised is really exhibited. Grace is not only borne or brought to the party baptized, but its nature and design are manifested, or set forth, in Baptism. As the application of water takes away the filth of the body, so does the grace of God, or the blood and Spirit of Christ, which is the thing signified in Baptism, cleanse the soul from the pollution of sin.

5. The grace promised is also *really conferred* by the Holy Ghost. For the adverb evidently qualifies both verbs. Grace is *really* exhibited and *really* conferred. It is both represented and actually communicated. A most unequivocal and forcible form of expression. The statement rises from the less to the greater truth, until it reaches the highest point of the climax, and brings out the intrinsic efficacy of Baptism with accumulated force. The efficacy is such that the grace promised is offered; it is at hand in the right use of the ordinance; not only offered but also exhibited; the party baptized sees in the visible transaction the nature and design of the ordinance to cleanse from sin, clearly set forth. But the grace promised is not only offered and exhibited, but *really conferred* by the Holy Ghost; that is, the party baptized is made a partaker of the grace which is offered and exhibited. The grace promised is the thing signified; and the thing signified is an ingrafting into Christ, regeneration and remission of sins. As the grace promised is really conferred in Baptism, it follows that in the right use of this ordinance the party baptized is ingrafted into Christ, regenerated, and receives remission of sins, by the power of the Holy Ghost.

6. The grace promised is thus really conferred upon *such as that grace belongeth unto*. According to the doctrine of God's Decrees, (Chapter III) that grace belongs to those who are predestinated and fore-ordained to everlasting life.[20] The Sacrament of Baptism is, therefore, the ordinance in and through which the decree is operative effectually for the salvation of the elect. The elect are ingrafted into Christ, and made

---

20. [WCF, III.4, 5.]

partakers of all His benefits, in virtue of the grace which is conferred on them in the right use of Baptism.

Such is the evident meaning of the explicit language of the Confession of Faith concerning the nature and efficacy of the sacrament of Baptism. We have endeavored to interpret its language fairly and consistently; and must regard the result as a legitimate conclusion.

We are well aware of an objection that may be raised against this conclusion on the ground of the 161st Question of the Larger Catechism. The Question is: "*How do the sacraments become effectual means of grace?*" To which the Answer is given: "The sacraments become effectual means of salvation, not by any power in themselves, or any virtue derived from the piety or intention of him by whom they are administered; but only by the working of the Holy Ghost, and the blessing of Christ by whom they are instituted."[21] If, however, this answer is considered in connection with other portions of the Confession and the Catechism, it will appear that it can not sustain any objection which is valid.

One important point is admitted and taught, namely that the Sacraments are *effectual means* of salvation; and that they become such by the working of the Holy Ghost and the blessing of Christ. So far the 161st Answer is in agreement with the passages already cited on the efficacy of Baptism. But it teaches also that the Sacraments become effectual means of salvation *not by any power in themselves*. The other clause referring to the intention of him who administers the Sacrament does not affect the question at issue, and may, therefore, be dismissed. The precise import of the answer depends upon the meaning of the word Sacraments. It may be used either in its full and proper sense, or in a restricted and improper sense.

Under the first-view, the answer teaches that the Sacraments have *no power* in themselves—a position that is in direct conflict with what the Symbols inculcate in other places. They teach, as we have seen, that a Sacrament is a sign and a seal of grace; that in a Sacrament there is the *union* of two parts, of the thing signified with the sign, of the grace promised, which is an ingrafting into Christ by the Holy Ghost, with the outward representation of it; and that, therefore, in the right use of the ordinance the grace promised is *conferred* as really as the outward transaction takes place. In other words, the Symbols elsewhere strictly affirm concerning the efficacy of a Sacrament what the 161st Answer denies.

But it is not necessary to take the word in its full and proper sense. Nor have we any disposition to charge the work of the Westminster Assembly of divines, for whose learning and piety we cherish profound respect, with being self-contradictory, unless there be no other alternative. The other view, we think, is the correct one. The word *Sacraments* is used in a restricted and improper sense. It denotes, not the Sacrament as the Symbols so carefully and unequivocally define them, but merely the external

---

21. [The original text says Question "191," but the source is correctly identified in the next paragraph.]

element and the external transaction, separately considered, which a Sacrament, properly speaking, includes. The Answer separates the working of the Holy Ghost from the Sacrament, and then denies of the visible ceremony what it attributes to the Holy Ghost and the blessing of Christ; whilst elsewhere the Symbols regard the thing signified, or the working of the Holy Ghost, as a constituent part of a Sacrament, disallow indirectly the application of the name even to a transaction which does not comprehend invisible grace, and consequently predicate intrinsic efficacy, or objective force, of the Sacrament itself. It is not, therefore, against the intrinsic efficacy of the Sacraments, rightly considered, but against the *opus operatum* theory of the Roman Catholic Church that this Answer is directed, according to which theory the performance of the external work itself confers grace; and it corresponds to the 72nd Question[22] of the Heidelberg Catechism. There is one important difference, however. Whilst the Larger Catechism denies here that there is any efficacy in the *Sacrament* itself, and thus seems to contradict what in other places it explicitly teaches; the Heidelberg Catechism denies intrinsic efficacy of the *external baptism with water*, but not of the Sacrament itself.

Whatever, now, we may think of the propriety of separating the sign from the thing signified, and then applying to the sign the name which belongs to the union of both, a method which the Scriptural idea of a Sacrament does not warrant, one thing is certain, namely, that no argument can consistently be derived from the 161st Answer against the interpretation we have given to the teaching of the Symbols concerning the efficacy of Baptism. Or, should such an argument be insisted upon, it would involve the Symbols of the Presbyterian Church in a direct contradiction.

In order to establish the doctrine that grace is inseparably annexed to Baptism, and conferred upon the party baptized in the right use of the ordinance, the Confession and Catechism cite a number of passages bearing upon the subject, from the Sacred Scriptures. We will transfer several of them.

Rom. 4:11, And he received the sign of circumcision, a seal of the righteousness of the faith which he had, yet being uncircumcised; that righteousness might be imputed to them also. Compared with Col. 2:11, 12. In whom also ye are circumcised with the circumcision made without hands, in putting off the body of the sins of the flesh by the circumcision of Christ; buried with him in baptism, wherein also ye are risen with him, through the faith of the operation of God, who hath raised him from the dead.

Acts 2:38. Peter said unto them, Repent and be baptized every one of you in the name of Jesus Christ, for the remission of sins.

Acts 22:16. Arise, and be baptized, and wash away thy sins.

---

22. Q. 72. Is then the external baptism with water, the washing away of sin itself? Answer. Not at all; for the blood of Jesus Christ only, and the Holy Ghost, cleanses us from all sin.— *Heidelberg Catechism* [trans. J. H. Good and H. Harbaugh (Chambersburg, PA: M. Kieffer, 1849), 165–66].

John 3:5. Verily, verily, I say unto thee, Except a man be born of water, and of the Spirit, he can not enter into the kingdom of God

1 Cor. 12:13. For by one Spirit are we all baptized into one body, whether we be Jews or Gentiles, whether we be bond or free; and have been all made to drink into one Spirit.

Gal. 3:27. For as many of you as have been baptized into Christ, have put on Christ.

Rom. 6:3, 4. Know ye not, that so many of us as were baptized into Jesus Christ, were baptized into his death? Therefore we are buried with him by baptism into death; that like as Christ was raised up from the dead by the glory of the Father, even so we also should walk in newness of life.

Titus 3:5. Not by works of righteousness which we have done, but according to his mercy he saved us, by the washing of regeneration, and renewing of the Holy Ghost.

1 Peter 3:21. The like figure whereunto, even baptism doth also now save us, not the putting away of the filth of the flesh, but the answer of a good conscience toward God, by the resurrection of Jesus Christ.

We give these passages, taken from the Confession and the Catechism, without comment. They contain others of similar import; but these may suffice. A candid mind cannot but be struck with the pertinence of these quotations to the design of establishing the doctrine of the efficacy of Baptism; and with the correspondence between the explicit teaching of the Confession and the forcible language of the New Testament. It would be simply absurd to suppose that the Westminster Assembly could adopt such language, and quote such passages of Scripture, if after all they intended only to teach that Baptism is a figure of grace, but does not really confer or make over in the sacramental transaction what it represents; or that it is only a sign of the covenant, but does not introduce the party baptized into the covenant and make him a partaker of its spiritual benefits.

In accordance with the doctrine of baptismal grace taught by the Confession, the Directory for Worship assumes that baptized children are *Christians*, and prescribes the manner in which they are to be treated accordingly:

> Children, born within the pale of the visible Church, and dedicated to God in Baptism, are under the inspection and government of the Church; and are to be taught to read and repeat the Catechism, the Apostles' Creed, and the Lord's Prayer. They are to be taught to pray, to abhor sin, to fear God, and to obey the Lord Jesus Christ. And, when they come to years of discretion, if they be free from scandal, appear sober and steady, and to have sufficient knowledge to discern the Lord's body, they ought to be informed it is their duty and their privilege to come to the Lord's Supper. (Chap. 9, 1.)[23]

---

23. [*Constitution of the Presbyterian Church* (1806), 452–53.]

The Directory presumes that baptized children are in the covenant, or in a state of grace; and not in a state of nature—a state in which they were in virtue of their natural birth. They are, therefore, called *young Christians* (Chap. 9:2.);[24] and are to be taught to pray and obey the Lord Jesus Christ. It is presumed that, being taught to repeat the Catechism, the Apostles' Creed, and the Lord's Prayer, and brought up in the nurture and admonition of the Lord, they will grow up in grace and in the knowledge of our Lord Jesus Christ; so that when they come to years of discretion they will be pious and possess sufficient knowledge to discern the Lord's body. If there be nothing to contradict this presumption—if they be free from scandal, appear sober and steady, they are to be informed by the minister, or officers, or parents, that it is their duty and privilege to come to the Lord's Supper. As they were baptized into Christ for the mortifying of sin and quickening of grace; as the grace promised was not only offered, but really exhibited and conferred on them by the Holy Ghost in the ordinance; as they were buried with Christ *by Baptism* into death; and as they who have been baptized into Christ, have put on Christ; they are to be treated as those who are saved according to His mercy, by the washing of regeneration, and renewing of the Holy Ghost; they are to be taught to walk in newness of life, like as Christ was raised up from the dead by the glory of the Father; and they are to be carefully instructed, watched over and prayed for, that they may not fall short of, or walk contrary to, the grace of Baptism, but that they may grow up to assurance of pardon of sin, and of all other blessings sealed to them in this Sacrament. (Vid. Lar. Cat. Q. 168.)[25] When, therefore, baptized children have come to years of discretion, they are to be examined in order to ascertain whether they have improved the grace of Baptism, and if they have properly improved it, admitted to all the privileges of the Church.

Whether true or false, Scriptural or antiscriptural, such is evidently the confessional theory of the Presbyterian Church concerning the condition, character and treatment of baptized Children—a theory that gives no countenance whatever to the modern system of periodical excitements, a system which repudiates "the grace of baptism," looks upon the baptized and the unbaptized as alike out of grace and children of the Devil, and trusts to extraordinary operations of the Holy Ghost, that is, operations which are independent of, and unconnected with, the Sacraments, as the only hope of the Church.

In the seventeenth century, and especially during the Sessions of the Westminster Assembly (1688),[26] no one uninspired man exerted so decided and controlling an

---

24. [Ibid., 453.]

25. ["*What is the Lord's Supper?* The Lord's Supper is a sacrament of the New Testament, wherein, by giving and receiving bread and wine according the appointment of the Lord Jesus Christ, his death is shewed forth; and they that worthily communicate, feed upon his body and blood, to their spiritual nourishment and growth in grace; have their union and communion with him confirmed; testify and renew their thankfulness and engagement to God, and their mutual love and fellowship each with other, as members of the same mystical body."]

26. [The Westminster Assembly was a reforming synod of the English church created by the Long

influence upon the government, and upon the formation of the theological opinions of the Presbyterian Church of Scotland, as John Calvin. As this is a historical fact, no one will gainsay it. It will be in place, therefore, to refer to what he says on the efficacy of Baptism. If his views contradict our interpretation of the Confession, there will be room for the presumption that there may be a flaw in the reasoning; but if he hold the theory which we find in the Symbols, he is to be regarded as bearing witness to the truth of the position which we have taken.

Opposing the opinion that Baptism is administered only for the remission of past sins, Calvin says: "We ought to conclude that at whatever time we are baptized, we are washed and purified for the whole of life. Whenever we have fallen, therefore, we must recur to the remembrance of baptism, and arm ourselves with the consideration of it, that we may be always certified and assured of the remission of our sins." (Inst. B. 4, Ch. 15, 3.)[27]

Commenting upon Rom. 6: 3, 4, he says: "In this passage he (Paul) does not merely exhort us to an imitation of Christ, as if he had said, that we are admonished by baptism, that after the example of his resurrection we should rise to righteousness; but he goes considerably further, and teaches us, that by baptism Christ has made us partakers of his death, in order that we may be ingrafted into it. And as the scion derives substance and nourishment from the root on which it is ingrafted, so they, who receive baptism with the faith they ought to receive it, truly experience the efficacy of Christ's death in the mortification of the flesh, and also the energy of his resurrection in the vivification of the spirit." (B. 4, Ch. 15, 5.)[28]

The following passage is equally explicit:

> The last advantage which our faith receives from baptism, is the certain testimony it affords us, that we are not only ingrafted into the life and death of Christ, but are so united as to be partakers of all His benefits. For this reason he dedicated and sanctified baptism in His own body, that He might have it in common with us, as a most firm bond of the union and society which he has condescended to form with us; so that Paul proves from it that we are the children of God, because we have put on Christ in Baptism. (Ch. 15, 6.)[29]

Speaking of the relation of Baptism to original sin:

> And therefore even infants themselves bring their own condemnation into the world with them, who, though they have not yet produced the fruits of their iniquity, yet have the seed of it within them, even their whole nature, is

---

Parliament. The members included advocates of different church polities (Episcopal, Presbyterian, Independent), but held a common Calvinistic theology. It wrote the two Catechisms and the Westminster Confession Gerhart has been quoting. The date is in error, since the assembly ran from 1643 to 1649. It may be a misprint for 1648, the year Parliament approved the two Catechisms.]

27. [Calvin, *Institutes*, ed. McNeill, 2:1305.]

28. [Ibid., 1307.]

29. [Ibid., 1307–8.]

as it were, a seed of sin, and therefore cannot but be odious and abominable to God. By baptism, believers are certified that this condemnation is removed from them; since, as we said, the Lord promises us by this sign, that a full and entire remission is granted both of the guilt which is to be imputed to us, and of the punishment to be inflicted on account of that guilt; they also receive righteousness, such as the people of God may obtain in this life; is, only by imputation, because the Lord, in His mercy, accepts them as righteous and innocent. (Ch. 15, 10.)[30]

We make one quotation more:

Now as we have stated what was the design of our Lord in the institution of baptism, it is easy to judge in what manner we ought to use and receive it. For as it is given for the support, consolation, and confirmation of our faith, it requires to be received as from the hand of the Author Himself: we ought to consider it as beyond all doubt, that it is He who speaks to us by this sign; that it is He who purifies and cleanses us, and obliterates the remembrance of our sins; that it is He who makes us partakers of His death, who demolishes the kingdom of Satan, who weakens the power of our corrupt propensities, who even makes us one with Himself, that, being clothed with Him, we may be reckoned children of God; and that He as truly and certainly performs these things internally on our souls, as we see that our bodies are externally washed, immersed and inclosed in water. For this analogy or similitude is a most certain rule of sacraments; that in corporeal things we contemplate spiritual things, just as if they were placed before our eyes, as it has pleased God to represent them to us by such figures: not that such blessings are bound or enclosed in the sacrament,[31] or that it has the power to impart them to us; but only because it is a sign by which the Lord testifies His will, that He is determined to give us all these things: nor does it merely feed our eyes with a fair prospect of the symbols, but conducts us at the same time to the thing signified, and efficaciously accomplishes[32] that which it represents. (B. 4. Ch. 15, 14.)[33]

The language of the great Reformer is direct and clear. If it teach any thing, it is that in the right use of Baptism, we put on Christ and become children of God;

30. [Ibid., 1311.]

31. The word must certainly be employed here in a restricted sense; and the whole clause be directed against the Roman Catholic dogma, according to which a Sacrament is efficacious, *ex opere operato*. Otherwise Calvin would deny of baptism, in this passage, what he so positively and studiously affirms of it in other places, and even in this Section. [McNeill translates: "Not because such graces are bound and enclosed in the sacrament so as to be conferred upon us by its power, but only because the Lord by this token attests his will toward us, namely, that he is pleased to lavish all these things upon us."]

32. *Neque tantum nudo spectaculo pascit oculos: sed in rem presentem nos adducit, et quod figurat, efficaciter implet.* Lib. IV. Cap. XV., 14. [McNeill translates: "And he does not feed our eyes with a mere appearance only, but leads us to the present reality and effectively performs what it symbolizes."]

33. [Calvin, *Institutes*, ed. McNeill, 2:1314.]

that we truly experience the efficacy of Christ's death in the mortification of the flesh, and the energy of His resurrection in the vivification of the spirit; and that the ordinance conducts us to the thing signified and efficaciously accomplishes that which it represents. Bearing in mind the close relation which Calvin sustained to the origin and development of the Presbyterian Church, these unequivocal statements of his views concerning the efficacy of Baptism ought to be regarded as the strongest collateral evidence of the truth of the interpretation which we have given to the Confession of Faith.

We have now carefully analyzed the Symbols of the Presbyterian Church on the efficacy of Baptism. The legitimate conclusion which we have drawn from them is, that they teach, that as a sign Baptism represents grace, and a seal assures the party baptized of being introduced into a state of grace; that it not only offers, but also really exhibits and confers that grace on those, whether of age or infants, to whom it belongs; in other words, that, in the right use of the ordinance, *the party baptized is ingrafted into Christ, is regenerated, and receives remission of sins, by the working of the Holy Ghost.* This conclusion is confirmed by the numerous passages which the Symbols quote from the Word of God; by the rules, laid down in the Directory for Worship, for the training of baptized children and their admission to the Lord's Supper; and by the unequivocal teachings of Calvin, than whom no man exerted a more decided formative influence upon the theological opinions as originally held in the Presbyterian Church. Indeed it is difficult to see how the Confession could have employed more explicit language, and given more apt quotations from the Scriptures, than it has, in order to teach and establish the doctrine of efficacious baptismal grace.

In the light, now, of what must undoubtedly be regarded as the true Presbyterian theory concerning the nature and efficacy of Baptism, we proceed to examine the manner in which Dr. Atwater disposes of the Confession, the Catechism and the Directory, in his enquiry into the *status* of baptized children. The question which he proposes to answer is not: What is the *status* of children of believing parents in virtue of their natural birth? nor, What is the *status* or position of children in virtue of the operations of the Holy Ghost? The question is a very different one. From the introductory remarks we learn what has been the occasion of the article. Many "are wholly at a loss as to the precise *status* of baptized children, the manner and extent in which baptism either signifies, seals, or procures any advantage which they would not possess without it." (p. 4.)[34] Speaking of those who desire to escape both "lifeless rationalism "and "equally lifeless formalism," he says: "Believing that there is both precious truth signified, and blessing sealed by infant baptism, and that it is of God, they would not surrender it for worlds. Yet they can not define its nature and effects fully to their own satisfaction, although they possess some dim and struggling conceptions of them." (p. 4.) Hence they crave more light as to the "precise import and efficacy" of Baptism, and

---

34. ["Children of the Church and Sealing Ordinances," 4.]

urge the author "to examine and discuss the subject."[35] The subject, then, is, *the nature and effects, or the precise import and efficacy of baptism*. The real question, accordingly, which he proposes to answer is: What is the status of baptized children *in virtue of Baptism*? And the conclusion at which Dr. Atwater arrives, must be regarded, in order to accord to him either candor or consistency—and we have not the least disposition to do any thing else—as his answer to *this* question; and not as an answer to either one of the two other questions just stated. Indeed there is neither point nor propriety in the whole article unless we take the result of his discussion to be a statement of the precise import and efficacy of Baptism. We take pains to determine this point, not only because it is in place to do so, but because in the progress of discussion he fails, as we think, to hold one question steadily before his eye, sometimes seeming to discuss the position of children in virtue of Baptism, and at others their position in virtue of being born of believing parents.

In entering upon the discussion of the subject, Dr. Atwater says:

> The catholic doctrine on this subject, as shown in the creeds of Christendom, is, that the children of believers are members of the Church, and are to receive baptism as the badge of such membership, and seal of the duties and privileges pertaining to it. But great diversities of opinion and practice prevail in reference to the kind of membership involved, and the doctrinal and practical consequences which thence result. (p. 5.)

We must dissent from the respected author at the threshhold of the argument. The creeds of Christendom do not teach that the children of believers are, as such, members of the Church, nor that Baptism is a badge of membership previously existing. They teach the reverse. The covenant is certainly designed for the children of believers as really as for themselves; in this sense children of believers are included in it; but they are not members of the covenant, nor of the Church, in virtue of their natural birth. Natural birth gives them the *right* to membership, but leaves them outside of the Church as long as they remain unbaptized. The male children of the Jews were included in the promise, and therefore had a right to circumcision, but they were excluded from all the privileges and blessings of members of the Church so long as they were uncircumcised. The Reformed Symbols proceed upon the same theory. Baptism is ordained "*for the solemn admission* of the party baptized into the visible Church," says the Confession (Chap 28, 1), an authority which Dr. Atwater will not refuse to acknowledge. It is almost superfluous to add that, if by Baptism children are admitted into the Church, they are not, and can not be members so long as they are unbaptized. All that the Confession and the Catechisms say concerning the blessings conferred in the right use of the ordinance, involves the same principle. To the same effect the Heidelberg Catechism teaches that, by Baptism, as a sign of the covenant, infants must

---

35. [Ibid., 5.]

also be "admitted into the Christian Church, and be distinguished from the children of infidels." (Q. 74.)[36] To multiply authorities is unnecessary.

The creeds of Christendom[37] teach accordingly that, whilst children of believers are included in the design of the covenant, they are not members of the Church in virtue of their natural birth, but become members in virtue of Baptism. The error of Dr. Atwater consists in confounding the *extent* of the covenant and the *right* of children of believers, with actual membership in the Church—an error which is traceable through the greater part of the whole article, and even renders ambiguous the final conclusion at which he arrives. Yet he is not always consistent even with himself. Discussing the practice of baptizing the children of non-communicants, he speaks of "parents being *by baptism* in the Church." (p. 17). If in the Church, or members of it, *by* Baptism, they are assuredly not members of it *without* Baptism. Without Baptism children of believers are in the world. Still the prevailing idea of his article is the one with which the author starts out.

Having laid down this untenable position, Dr. Atwater passes on to consider several false views concerning the import of Baptism:

1. That "they are members only quasi, or in such a sense that the Church owes them no duties nor privileges, above the unbaptized." "Although they are born, in a sort, members, and as such have the seal of baptism, yet this is a token and pledge of nothing but of that Christian instruction and training, which all pious parents impart." (p. 6).

2. That baptized children "are members of the Church universal, but not of any particular organized Church." (p. 7).[38] The theory held by Dr. Dwight and some other New England divines. With the consideration of this theory he connects a succinct history of Baptism among the Congregational Churches of New England, particularly of the *Half-way Covenant*[39] practice.

---

36. [*Heidelberg Catechism* (1849), 169.]

37. No one certainly would say that the creeds of the Roman Catholic Church regard the unbaptized children of believing parents as members.

38. ["Children of the Church and Sealing Ordinances," 8 (the reference begins on p. 7, but the quoted words are on p. 8).]

39. [The Puritan practice of baptism was initially what all the Reformed confessions called for: the children of a Christian parent were "within" "the covenant of promise" and therefore should be baptized: The Larger Catechism, Q. 166. However, (as outlined in the general introduction) American Puritans quickly added a complication: they expected baptized persons to provide a "conversion narrative" before they were admitted to the Lord's Supper. (It was also a prerequisite to full participation in the secular polity.) This narrative would recount how God had used the "means of grace" (Bible reading, sermons, prayer) to lead the person to a felt sense of conversion. (See *Dictionary of Christianity in America*, 316, 317, for key ideas and sources. See Ahlstrom, *Religious History of the American People*, 1:194–95, for a brief introduction.) By 1650, there was a large cohort of young adults who, although baptized, were not able (or willing) to provide the required narrative. They had not experienced their "elect" status, were not in a felt "covenant" with God, and therefore could not pass that relationship on to their children. So there were a generation of children who were not being baptized and were therefore not under the authority of the church. The "Half-Way Covenant" adjusted the conditions of

The Efficacy of Baptism

These theories Dr. Atwater presents as false, and argues against them. Of course in doing so he implies that the truth lies in opposite propositions, to wit, that baptized children are not only *quasi*, but in some sense, real members; that Baptism is something more than a token and pledge of Christian instruction and training; and that children become members by Baptism of some particular organized Church. If the course of argument be relevant at all to the subject in hand, he must mean that the benefits which baptized children possess, denied by the theories rejected, but affirmed by implication and besides perpetrates a fallacy—a *mutatio elenchi*.[40] For he is professedly discussing the precise import or efficacy, not of natural birth, but of Baptism.

To determine the true position of baptized children, the author refers to the Symbols; for they express the faith of the Presbyterian Church "with great precision," and "exhibit the truth in the premises intact and inviolate."[41] He gives a number of extracts in full from the Confession, the Catechisms and the Directory, including those which we have quoted. Without attempting an analysis or exposition of these extracts, he proceeds immediately to say: "To preclude misconstruction in any quarter, we observe, at the outset, that these articles deny all intrinsic efficacy to the sacraments, as such." (p. 21).[42] Deny all *intrinsic* efficacy! According to these very articles a Sacrament is the union of the thing signified with the sign; Baptism signifies and seals an ingrafting into Christ, regeneration and remission of sins, that is, assures or certifies that the thing signified is real and certain; grace and salvation are inseparably annexed to the ordinance; by the right use of the ordinance the grace promised is not only offered, but really exhibited *and conferred* by the Holy Ghost to such, whether of age or infants, as that grace belongeth unto; and they are *baptized into* Christ for the mortifying of sin and quickening of grace.

Yet directly in the face of such explicit language, teaching the faith of the Church "with great precision," Dr. Atwater says that the Symbols *deny* all intrinsic efficacy to the Sacraments. We are utterly at a loss to comprehend how a gentleman of candor and a Christian scholar can make such an assertion. If the efficacy of the Sacrament of Baptism is not intrinsic, what then is it? Is not efficacy in the very nature of the case intrinsic? Does it not lie in the subject of which it is predicated? If not, if it lies

---

infant baptism by saying that children of baptized, but unconverted, members could also be baptized, and were eligible to have their own children baptized. Such "'half-way' members were expected to live moral lives," and "assumed the responsibilities of mutual watchfulness incumbent" upon people who had "own[ed] the church covenant before the assembled congregation" (*Dictionary of Christianity in America*, 506; Ahlstrom, *Religious History*, 1:208–10). Although the Half-Way Covenant solved the short-term problem—it kept children of the unconverted in the covenant—it could not create a felt sense of God's covenantal act in a person's life. The Half-Way Covenant created a vacuum that would not be filled until the First Great Awakening.]

40. [Trans., literally, "changing the refutation," i.e., as can be seen from the context, making an argument that appears to be leading to one conclusion, and then changing the conclusion one claims is being proved.]

41. ["Children of the Church and Sealing Ordinances," 17.]

42. [Ibid., 21.]

in something else, it is an evident impropriety to speak of *its* efficacy. If the efficacy of Baptism does not lie in baptism itself, where can it lie? In faith? But faith as such is not Baptism. In the Holy Ghost? But the working of the Holy Ghost as such is not Baptism. In prayer and instruction? But neither are these Christian duties Baptism. No matter where efficacy lies, if it does not lie in Baptism itself, it is wrong to affirm the efficacy of Baptism, for the ordinance has no efficacy. To affirm or admit the efficacy of Baptism, therefore, and yet mean nothing more than the efficacy of something which is not Baptism, is a direct contradiction of terms—a contradiction in which Dr. Atwater involves the Symbols, when he asserts that they deny all intrinsic efficacy to the Sacraments. With all the care they take to set forth explicitly, and define, the efficacy of this ordinance, they must be understood as referring to the efficacy of something else, of something which is not Baptism, and as teaching that Baptism itself has no efficacy at all!

But, with all due respect for his sincerity and intelligence, we must add that the author involves himself also in a logical contradiction. The whole discussion proceeds on the assumption of efficacy in Baptism, and aims at determining what its precise import, or that efficacy, is. Hence he argues against several theories, because they divest the Sacrament of all positive force. Hence, also, he quotes the Symbols as authority in the decision of the question, because they teach "with great precision," nay more, in so many words, that the grace promised is really conferred by the Holy Ghost in the right use of Baptism. But when he comes to define precisely what the efficacy taught by the Symbols is, he says: "These articles deny all intrinsic efficacy to the Sacraments." The "nature and effects" or "the precise import or efficacy" of Baptism, consists in this, that Baptism itself possesses no efficacy at all! "Sacramental signs and seals of themselves convey nothing." (p. 24.)[43]

Yet, paradoxical as it may be, what is to be taken as the final conclusion or result of the discussion, is inconsistent with his denial of intrinsic efficacy. He says: Those incapable of a credible

> profession, may be visibly members of the Church, by virtue of God's revealed covenant or promise to be their God. This is precisely the case with infants and the ground of their baptism. But in either case, membership in the visible Church is founded on a *presumptive* membership in the invisible, until its subjects, by acts incompatible therewith, prove the contrary, and thus, to the eye of man, forfeit their standing among God's people.[44]

Membership in the visible Church is founded on a presumptive membership in the invisible. The rest of the article is devoted mainly to an argument in support of this proposition. Under one view, Dr. Atwater's position involves a great and profound truth. The outward is grounded in the inward, the visible in the invisible, the natural

---

43. [Ibid., 24.]
44. [Ibid., 22; emphasis original.]

in the spiritual. The admission of an adult or infant into the Church implies real union with Christ, as the basis of all external relations.

But the precise import and bearing of the author's position depends upon the way or means by which, in his judgment, the membership of an infant in the invisible Church is constituted. The same questions meet us again. Does an infant become a member presumptively of the invisible Church, in virtue of *Baptism*? Or does it become such in virtue of *being born* of believing parents? According to the answer given to these questions, does his position acquire peculiar significance.

Membership in the invisible Church is union to Christ, or regeneration by the Holy Ghost. The word *presume* means to admit a thing to be, or to receive a thing as true, before it can be known as such from its phenomena or manifestations. To presume an infant to be a member of the invisible Church, is therefore to believe it to be ingrafted into Christ and regenerated, before it gives any ordinary evidences of the fact. If, now, the author means that the presumptive membership of an infant in the invisible Church is constituted by *Baptism*, his position harmonizes with the teachings of the Presbyterian Symbols. And that he wishes to be understood thus would be inferable from another carefully worded remark: "The administration of the seal is founded on the *presumption* that the things sealed will also be bestowed and accepted, till the contrary is shown. On no other ground can infant baptism have significance or propriety." (p. 24).[45] In the previous statement, however, the *presumption* pertains to what precedes or attends, and, in this, to what follows, membership by Baptism in the visible Church. But we will not dwell on the inconsistency. He holds, therefore, that in the right use of Baptism an infant is ingrafted into Christ and regenerated by the Holy Spirit. Interpreted philologically,[46] and with logical propriety, it can mean nothing less than this. His language teaches the doctrine of baptismal regeneration with all needful plainness. But in doing so, he directly contradicts his assertion that the Symbols deny all intrinsic efficacy to the Sacraments, and that sacramental signs and seals of themselves convey nothing.

If, on the other hand, Dr. Atwater means that the presumptive membership of an infant in the invisible Church, or its vital union to Jesus Christ is effected, by *natural birth*, his position is entirely different. 1. He contradicts the Standards of the Presbyterian Church; for, as we have already shown, Baptism is ordained, according to the

45. [Ibid., 24, emphasis original.]

46. We have read the author's exposition of the word *presumptive* given in the *Presbyterian*. Whilst his effort to explain away the legitimate meaning of the word in order to disclaim the doctrine of baptismal regeneration, does not in the least break the force or affect the import of the language used, it shows very plainly, however, that he does not believe, and did not intend to teach, what his language clearly conveys. [This reference appears to be a careless error by Gerhart, as the editor has been unable to locate any discussion of "presumptive membership," or any essay by Lyman Atwater, in the *Presbyterian Magazine* from 1852 through January 1858. Gerhart probably meant to refer simply to the *Biblical Repertory and Princeton Review*, i.e., to the essay under discussion throughout this article ("The Children of the Church and Sealing Ordinances"); see pp. 22–24 of that essay for examples of the language of "presumptive" membership.]

Confession, *for the solemn admission* of the party baptized *into the visible Church*. 2. He teaches a very novel doctrine. "Our standards assert," he says, "that the children of believers are members of the visible Church—not *quasi*, but absolutely." But "membership in the visible Church is founded on a *presumptive* membership in the invisible."[47] And presumptive membership in the invisible Church, is the belief of vital union to Jesus Christ by the Holy Ghost. On this principle of interpretation, it follows, then, that children of believers are ingrafted into Christ, or regenerated, by the Holy Ghost, in virtue of natural birth. A new doctrine for a *Presbyterian*! Natural generation is the channel of grace, and not the ordinances of the Church.

3. He gives no answer to the question proposed for discussion. The natural and effects, or the precise import and efficacy, of Baptism, consists in this, that children of believers are presumptively members of the invisible Church in virtue of natural birth! We do not suppose that Dr. Atwater himself would say that such a conclusion has any connection with the premises.

Yet there is no escape from these consequences. The position of the author must be interpreted, if interpreted with any consistency at all, on one principle or the other. The alternative can not be avoided by asserting that the presumptive membership of infants in the invisible Church, or their vital union to Christ, is constituted by the working of the Holy Ghost. For in either case the only efficient agent is the Holy Ghost, whether the relation be constituted by Baptism or by natural birth.

Nor can the alternative be avoided by replying that the vital union of infants to Christ has no connection with either Baptism or natural birth. Grace flows through neither as its channel; but the children of believers are ingrafted into Christ by the Holy Ghost, operating independently of either birth or Baptism. What, then, has Dr. Atwater's conclusion to do, not only with the theme of the article, but with the whole discussion? Does not the significance of the whole argument hinge on the position of children who are born of believers, or of children who have received the solemn rite of Baptism? These are the main points in the enquiry. But if the proposed solution of the question, has no respect either to the benefits of natural birth or to the efficacy of Baptism, the whole discussion ends literally in nothing. A long and patient argument is conducted with a view to a certain end; but when we reach the end, when we come to what is proposed as a final conclusion, we have a proposition that has no connection at all either with the premises or with the argument. Certainly nothing else can follow, if both principles for interpreting his main conclusion are disallowed.

The inconsistencies and contradictions of Dr. Atwater—we speak respectfully, for we would not regard the author in any other light than as an earnest Christian scholar—arise from a persevering endeavor to perform an impossibility. The Symbols of the Presbyterian Church take high ground, as we have seen, on the subject of Baptism, as high as that of any other Protestant Symbol, that of the Episcopal Church not excepted; whilst Dr. Atwater may be regarded as expressing his own views when he

---

47. ["Children of the Church and Sealing Ordinances," 21–22; emphasis original.]

says: "These articles deny all intrinsic efficacy to the Sacraments as such;" and, "Sacramental signs and seals of themselves convey nothing."[48] Under these circumstances, he undertakes to determine the *status* of baptized children; and in doing so seeks to establish a theory which will reconcile the Symbols with the denial of the intrinsic efficacy of Baptism. As this is impossible, he swings from one point to another, and involves himself in self-contradictory positions. Unwilling to hold the plain doctrine concerning Baptism taught by the Symbols, yet unwilling to renounce their teachings entirely, he labors in vain to reach a conclusion which will avoid both alternatives; for there is no real middle ground between the doctrine of Sacramental grace, and the Socinian theory which resolves the Sacrament into an empty, lifeless form.

Thus we come back to the point from which we started out. The high views of Baptism inculcated by the Presbyterian Symbols are rejected by Dr. Atwater himself, as well as by those from whom he seems to differ, and whom he seeks to enlighten. We can see no essential difference between them. Both he and they deny the *intrinsic* efficacy of the ordinance. Sacramental signs and seals in themselves are but an external ceremony. Baptism cannot convey or really confer any grace. Assigning to words their proper meaning, we may, therefore, resolve the author's theory into what he attributes to Evangelical Churches in general: "We are sure," he says, "it is no exaggeration, when we say, that in a considerable portion of our Evangelical Churches there is no recognition, no consciousness of any relation being held by baptized children, prior to conscious and professed conversion, other than that of outsiders to the Church, in common with the whole world lying in wickedness." (p. 6.) No views concerning the relation of baptized children to the Church, essentially different from these, can be held by those who deny all intrinsic efficacy to the Sacrament of Baptism.

Here we find the true cause of the extensive neglect of infant Baptism, over which the *Princeton Review* so justly laments. The estimate is based on a judicious comparison of the Statistical Tables extending from 1807 to 1856, and sustained by a patient collection of facts from various other sources. According to these Tables, there was a gradual increase of the ratio of infant baptisms to the number of communicant members, from 1807 to 1811; but since that time there has been a gradual decrease, the lowest ratio occurring in 1849. In 1811 there were at the rate of 198 baptisms for every 1000 members; in 1849 not more than 49. "In 1811 there were only 23,639 communicants, and yet there were 4,677 baptisms. And yet, in 1856, with *ten times* as many members, we have only *twice* as many baptisms of children." (p. 84.)[49] After making due allowance for the operation of special causes, and adopting the principle that there should be at least one baptism for every ten communicants, the author of the Article, comes to the conclusion, that "if there are in the Church more children than one for every ten members, it follows, that *more than half*[50] of the offspring of the Church

---

48. [Ibid., 21, 24.]
49. ["Neglect of Infant Baptism," 84, emphasis original.]
50. "We must conclude that whilst there were but 205,041 children reported as baptized, during the

are deprived of this ordinance." (p. 86.)[51] The announcement of this estimate, as was to be expected, startled the whole Church, and called forth a number of communications on the subject in the weekly periodicals, nearly all of which, however, take the ground that there must be some error in the calculation, although no one has been able to discover it. One objection was thought to be unanswerable. According to the *Census* the increase of population by birth, per year, is less than one to ten; how then can there be *one* child in the Church for every *ten* communicants, not to speak of one for every *six*? But it must be remembered that the Census pertains only to the *net* increase of population; whilst, in estimating the probable neglect of Baptism, the Church must take into account *all* the children of believing parents, one-fourth (or one-third) of whom, on an average, die during the period of infancy and childhood. Hence the Census Tables can furnish no basis of judgment as to the true ratio of baptisms. The Statistical Tables of the Presbyterian Church must furnish that basis; and according to these we can see no reason, painful as the fact may be, to doubt the correctness of the estimate.

Various causes are assigned for such great neglect of infant Baptism, namely, the extraordinary efforts of the various anti-pedobaptist bodies to disseminate their views within the past thirty-five years—the neglect of pastors to give full and proper instructions to their people—the improper administration of the ordinance—the Church's failure to recognize baptized children as members after Baptism—neglect of family worship—the time and circumstances attending the administration of baptism, being such often as wholly to destroy the moral effect of the ordinance itself—and the influence of the "new measure" system. No doubt each cause assigned has had its influence. But all of them derive their force from a cause that lies far deeper. The Presbyterian Church has been drifting away from its Standards. The actual faith in regard to Baptism contradicts the faith which she professes. Hence the great practical defection. As Baptism is held to be but an outward ceremony, as *it* can convey no grace, both ministers and people must become comparatively indifferent to it, and then neglect it.

Here, we repeat, is the true cause. The *practice* of the Presbyterian Church is founded on its original *faith*. The one is the legitimate consequence of the other. If, therefore, it renounce its *faith*, it must also, in the course of time, just as it has done, forsake its *practice*. If the doctrine of baptismal grace, so plainly taught in its Standards, be given up, infant Baptism will be given up too; for, reduced to an empty, inefficacious ceremony, the people will have no sufficient motive to perpetuate its observance. The effect is natural and necessary. And so long as the immense contradiction of its *actual* to its *professed* faith, in which the Presbyterian Church is at present involved

last twenty years, the reports should have amounted to 618,339, leaving not less than 413,298 unbaptized. Thus have more than two-thirds of the children of the Church been 'cut off' from the people of God by their parents' sinful neglect, and by the Church's silent acquiescence therein! Is this indeed true? Is the one-half of it true? Then, indeed, is there not 'great sin' resting on the Church."— *Princeton Review*, Jan. 1857, p. 86.

51. ["Neglect of Infant Baptism," 86, emphasis original.]

continues, the cause of the sinful neglect of infants must continue to operate also, and the effect will as naturally follow, despite all the efforts to the contrary. To restore its practice, the Church must return to its original faith. If the Church renounce her lifeless formalism; if she revive true spiritual views of the Sacraments, neither faithful ministers nor believing parents will any longer feel indifferent to the holy ordinance.

We are aware that our Presbyterian Brethren, for whom we cherish no other sentiment but that of affection and regard, pique themselves on their spiritual religion, and lament over and sometimes seem to pity, the spread of formalism, as they call it, in the German Reformed Church. But with what propriety? They observe a form as a form; they value and adhere to a mere outward ceremony, a ceremony which they believe possesses neither life nor power; and call this *spiritual* religion. Others observe a form, not as a lifeless form, but because it is a spiritual reality; they value a ceremony because there is in real union with it, a divine life and power; and our Brethren call this *formal* religion. Those, then, who believe in the form without the spirit; who observe a religious rite but deny its living power and efficacy, are spiritual Christians: but those who believe in the form with the spirit; who observe a religious rite, ordained by the great Head of the Church, as an effectual means of supernatural grace, are formalists! Novel logic! Do our Brethren reason thus on other points? Is a man a formalist who prays without ceasing, because he *believes* in the efficacy of prayer as a means of grace? Is a minister a formalist who preaches the Gospel in season and out of season, because he believes it to be the power of God, and the wisdom of God unto salvation? How, then, can he be a formalist who values and observes the holy Sacrament of Baptism, because it is a sign and seal of ingrafting into Christ? No; such reasoning, if it deserve the name, is simply ridiculous, our opponents themselves being the judges. Truth requires the judgment to be reversed. To have the form and deny the spirit, is lifeless formalism. To adhere to and practice a religious rite, which has neither life nor power, is dead ritualism. To administer infant Baptism as a mere outward ceremony, to maintain it and contend for it, as having in itself no efficacy, and conveying no grace, is to convert a spiritual institution into an unmeaning and delusive show.

Such a lifeless ceremony, such an unmeaning show, can not long command the approbation, the confidence and regard of pious, intelligent and reflecting men, whether ministers or laymen. Nor can any efforts to define the status of baptized children, to determine the positive spiritual good derived to an unconscious child from an inefficacious outward rite, either prove satisfactory to an earnest, enquiring mind, or avoid a process of reasoning that is self-contradictory and therefore self-destructive. Baptismal grace and infant Baptism go together; but infant Baptism and the denial of baptismal grace, cannot be conjoined logically in theory, nor perpetuated in practice.

E. V. G.

Article 6
"The Old Doctrine of Christian Baptism"

(By John W. Nevin)

Editor's Introduction

Nevin had spent seven years in retirement from the rigors of theological combat. Most of that time had been spent in Lancaster County, Pennsylvania, more than one hundred miles east of Schaff, who at that time was in Mercersburg. He had moved to the city of Lancaster in 1858, to be close to the life of Franklin and Marshall College. As we saw in the previous article, Emanuel V. Gerhart, Nevin's erstwhile student, sometime friend, and colleague-to-be[1] defended a Mercersburgian understanding of baptism as the sacrament that brought a person, adult or infant, within the range of the church's sacramental and cultic life, and thus made him a *Christian*. The Princetonians had responded with an ecclesiology that separated *Christian* from *church member*. The latter was *presumed* to be elect, and thus included within the life of the church, but the truly elect were known only to God. With this construction, the Princetonians were able to keep the evangelical understanding of regeneration/conversion together with the magisterial Protestant expression of a unified church-in-society.

The discussion of "The Efficacy of Baptism" by Gerhart provides circumstantial evidence that Hodge's construction was, in its specific formulation, of recent vintage. Nevin, born and bred Presbyterian, did not recognize it. In "Hodge on the Ephesians" (1857), he had presented the exegetical argument that Hodge had imposed his own theological template upon the biblical sources. In the present essay, Nevin extended that argument to support it with patristic resources, specifically St. John Chrysostom. Nevin would use Chrysostom to argue that baptism was truly the entrance into eternal life, even while many of the baptized fell short of their confession, and were at risk

---

1. Gerhart would briefly be vice president of Franklin and Marshall under Nevin's leadership in 1866; they also worked together on the later Liturgical Commission.

of not entering into the eternal salvation promised them by the gospel. In other words, Nevin thought (contrary to Hodge's argument)[2] that uncertainty about the spiritual state of "visible" members of the church did *not* imply that such members were only nominally regenerate, and was using Chrysostom as evidence that this was a valid interpretation of the Christian consensus. Any baptized person, infant or adult, was not *presumed* to be elect, but actually and visibly so, through his or her participation in the sacramental life of the church; the moral failures of the baptized person did not contradict or nullify this election.

St. John Chrysostom (d. 407) gained his appellation, which means "golden mouth," sometime after his death.[3] His birth date is uncertain: perhaps as early as 344; he was born to a noble family in Antioch and trained in pagan philosophy and rhetoric. After his conversion, he lived an ascetic life for six years, but his health was broken by two years of solitude. He returned to Antioch and was ordained deacon in 381 and priest in 386, after which he became renowned for his oratorical skills in the church at Antioch. When the previous patriarch of Constantinople died in 397, he was chosen to be his successor but had to be tricked to go to the capital, where he was consecrated bishop and patriarch in February of 398. His ascetical impulses came to the fore as he lived simply and used his patriarchal income to aid the poor and needy. This brought him into conflict with both the imperial court, especially the empress Eudoxia, as well bishops and monks who were used to leisure and luxury. A coalition of empress and bishops was led by Theophilus, patriarch of Alexandria, who had already perceived the growing authority of the bishop of Constantinople as threatening the power of his own church. Chrysostom refused to appear at a synod led by Theophilus in 403 and was deposed and exiled. He was quickly recalled but was deposed and exiled a second time after his enemies disrupted the Easter Vigil and baptism of the catechumens in 404. After an exile in Armenia, his enemies "deliberately killed" him by sending him to a farther exile on the eastern shore of the Black Sea. During the forced march, he died in 407.[4]

Chrysostom was a preacher, not a theologian, but his oratorical abilities were accompanied by solid exegetical skills, making him the "greatest of Christian expositors." He interpreted the text in its historical and literal sense, while directing his application to the "moral reformation of the nominally Christian society."[5] Chrysostom's asceticism would have appealed to Nevin's personal austerity and insistence on the supernatural character of religious experience and life;[6] Chrysostom viewed baptism

---

2. Hodge, "Church Membership of Infants," 349–51.

3. The following biographical summary is based upon Berthold Altaner, *Patrology*, 373–86; *Encyclopedia of Ancient Christianity*, 2:429–33; *Dictionary of the Christian Church*, 342–43.

4. *Dictionary of the Christian Church*, 342.

5. Ibid.

6. For Nevin's critique of "naturalism" and "humanitarianism," more fully stated the following year, see "Jesus and the Resurrection," 183; Nevin expressed his ascetical spirit in "All religion resolves itself in this way into self-renunciation and conquering of the world" ("The Spiritual World," 502).

as a "*new birth*" and believed that the Eucharist "continues the real presence of God among human beings."[7] Chrysostom's theme in the present text—the forsaking of the pleasures of earth for the higher realities of the "country above"—would have agreed with Nevin's native mysticism.

Nevin read Chrysostom as saying that baptism was an "actual regeneration" that brought the baptized into a new spiritual life.[8] The baptism of John was the completion of the typological signification of the preceding "Jewish system." Neither the Jewish purification rituals nor John's baptism had the power to actually bring about the forgiveness of sins—until John's baptism of Jesus. At that juncture, the old and new covenants met, and were fused. The kingdom of heaven only anticipated in John's baptism was realized in the descent of the Spirit upon Jesus. Thereafter, Christian baptism enacted for every believer what John's baptism revealed in Jesus. Although every baptism could not be a fresh Pentecost, yet in faith the church knew that the barrier between the "world of grace" and the "world of nature" had been overcome and the newly baptized had been made a son of God.

In Nevin's interpretation of Chrysostom, baptism was specifically the sacrament of initiation into the community of those who possessed this new relationship with God. Chrysostom's sermons were not directed at non-Christians, but at either the baptized or catechumens.[9] Consequently, when he warned his listeners to fear the consequences of unbelief and unfaithfulness, his censures embraced those who were already participating in the "family of God." Nevin pointed out that Chrysostom was well aware that his auditors were selfish, worldly, profane, and continuing to take pleasure in pagan culture. Yet they were nonetheless sons of God, and exhorted to live up to the calling to which baptism had summoned them. The "modern dilemma" of "baptismal regeneration"—how could baptism be thought to bring about real spiritual renewal if its recipients did not evidence the transformation that baptism was supposed to bring?—did not trouble Chrysostom at all. It remained a true sacrament, actually enacting what the earthly symbols promised: forgiveness of sins, regeneration, adoption into God's family, and the gift of the Holy Spirit.[10]

One could, with the evangelicals of Nevin's era, reject Chrysostom's homiletical world in favor of the spirituality of conversion. Baptism was only an external symbol,

---

7. *Encyclopedia of Ancient Christianity*, 2:432.

8. As we have seen in art. 1, Nevin had rejected this conclusion up to his conversation with Horace Bushnell, and his concurrent exchange with "Inquirer."

9. Catechumens were persons undergoing instruction for baptism, but not yet baptized (which usually took place at Easter or Pentecost). Sometime before the Eucharist (the exact point in the ritual varied), they were dismissed, since they were not permitted to see or participate in the "mystery" of the eucharistic sacrifice. On the catechumenate, see Jones et al., *The Study of Liturgy*, 95–99; the dismissal of the catechumens is explained on pp. 187–88. The practice in the early third century is described in Frend, *Rise of Christianity*, 407.

10. A modern discussion of the practice and meaning of baptism in this period can be found in Jones et al., *The Study of Liturgy*, 95–110. Chrysostom's view is summarized on p. 106.

which might follow or precede the reality it signified, but had no essential connection to the internal change. The progress of history had shown Chrysostom to be wrong. Nevin thought such a judgment too easy, in part because evangelicals were begging the question: Chrysostom was wrong because modern evangelicalism was right. Furthermore, it was not clear why baptism would remain essential to evangelical spirituality at all. If the fruits of baptism could be produced without the sacramental act, then how would "Baptists" manage to keep it as a vital practice of Christian nurture? Already among the paedobaptists, having refused the understanding of baptismal regeneration, infant baptism was becoming defunct as an "obsolete superstition." The old questions crowded around Nevin; however, after years of hard-won theological peace, he seemed to have no passion to reenter the lists. He simply placed the questions before the theological public. Yet there also the challenge fell flat and evangelicalism went on its merry way.

"The Old Doctrine of Christian Baptism"[1]

I. An Extract from the Twelfth Homily of St. John Chrysostom on the Gospel of St. Matthew.[2]

"And Jesus, when he was baptized, went up straightway out of the water; and lo, the heavens were opened unto him."[3] Why were the heavens opened? In order that thou mightest learn, that when thou also art baptized the same thing takes place, God calling thee to the country above and urging thee to forsake the fellowship of earth. That thou seest it not, is no reason why thou shouldst not believe it. For it is the general rule, that in the beginning of extraordinary spiritual dispensations such sensible visions and signs should appear, because men are so slow to perceive spiritual realities, and require to have their attention roused by things which strike the senses; in order that even without the same signs afterwards, the things once certified by them may be accepted as sure by faith. Thus upon the apostles, we are told, there came the sound of a mighty rushing wind[4] and the appearance of cloven tongues of fire; not for their sake, however, but on account of the Jews then present. Though there be then no visible signs, let us still receive what they have once served to reveal. For the dove also appeared at this time, that it might as a seal designate to those present, and to John, the Son of God. And not for this only, but to teach thee also that the Spirit descends upon thee in like manner at thy baptism. We have no longer need of the sensible vision, faith answering for all; for signs are "not for them that believe, but for them that believe not."[5]

But why in the form of a dove? It is a gentle and pure animal. And so the Holy Ghost, as a spirit of meekness, takes its appearance. There is regard in it besides to ancient history. For when the general flood was upon the earth, threatening to make full shipwreck of the human race this bird appeared, announcing the end of the storm,

---

1. [*Mercersburg Review* 12 (April 1860) 190–215.]

2. [*Homiliae in Matthaeum*, in *Patrologia Graeca*, 57:203–7; trans. *Nicene and Post-Nicene Fathers*, 10:77–79. The editor follows *NPNF* in providing alternative translations.]

3. [Matt 3:16.]

4. [Acts 2:2.]

5. [1 Cor 14:22.]

and with the olive branch[6] proclaimed the glad tidings of peace upon the earth; all which was a type of things to come.

As then indeed matters were in much worse state than now, and men deserving of far greater punishment. That thou mayest, not despair then, call to mind that history. For even in that desperate extremity there was a certain relief and restoration; then however through punishment, whereas it is now through grace and unspeakable gift. On which account also the dove appears, not bearing a branch of olive, but pointing out to us the deliverer from all evils, and holding forth to us heavenly hopes. A messenger, not to bring one man out from the ark, but to conduct the whole world to heaven, offering to the race at large instead of an olive branch the precious boon of adoption. Considering then the greatness of the gift, let not the dignity of the giver seem any less great in thine eyes from his appearing in such form. For I hear some say, that as much difference as there is between a man and a dove, so much there is also between Christ and the Spirit, since the one appeared in our nature and the other in the form of a dove. But what must we say now in answer to this? That the Son of God did indeed take upon him the nature of man; but that the Spirit did *not* assume the nature of the dove. Hence the evangelist also does not say, in the nature of a dove, but in the form of a dove; in which form, accordingly, the Spirit appeared only at that time, and not afterwards. But if this be taken to imply inferiority, the cherubim by parity of reasoning will be found to be likewise of higher dignity, in proportion as an eagle is superior to a dove; as being fashioned to such likeness; and the angels again must be counted higher also, since they have often appeared in human form. The truth, however, is widely different from all this. The reality of a dispensation[7] is one thing, the accommodation of a transient vision altogether another. Be not ungrateful, therefore, toward thy benefactor, and, think not poorly of him who has bestowed upon thee the fountain of blessedness. For where the dignity of sonship[8] is, there the removal of all evil is also, and the gift of all good.

[§4] The completion of the Jewish baptism thus is the beginning of ours; and what took place in the case of the passover, happens also in this case. For there one transaction is made to embrace both the old and the new, in such a way as to abolish the one and introduce the other; and here, having fulfilled the Jewish baptism, he at the same time opens the doors of the Church, as in one table there, so in one river here, filling out at once the shadow and adding to it the truth. For this baptism alone has the grace of the Spirit; that of John was destitute of this gift. Hence nothing of the sort occurred in the case of the others who came to his baptism, but only in the case of him who was to bestow this; showing it to be thus, not from the sanctity of the baptizer, but from the power of the person baptized. Then also, accordingly, the heavens were opened, and the Spirit descended. For from this time he leads us forth from the

---

6. [Gen 8:11.]
7. [*NPNF*, 10:77: "economy."]
8. [*NPNF*, 10:78: "adoption."]

old into the new order of life, both opening for us the celestial gates, and sending his Spirit from thence to call us to the country above; and not simply to call us, but to do this also with the most exalted honor. For he has not made us angels and archangels, but constituting us sons and beloved of God, he draws us thus toward that inheritance.

Considering then all these things, show a life worthy at once of him that calls thee, and of the heavenly citizenship, and of the honor thou hast received. Being crucified to the world, and having it crucified for thyself, cultivate the life of heaven with all diligence; neither suffer thyself to think, that because thy body has not yet passed into that higher world thou hast anything in common with this earth; for thou hast thy head seated above.[9] And for this reason, the Lord, having come here first attended with angels, when he had taken thee into union with himself afterwards returned on high, in order that thou mightst learn even before thy ascent thither, how it is possible for thee to occupy the earth as heaven. Let us continue then to hold fast the nobility which we have received from the beginning, and let us seek every day those royal abodes, holding all things here as a mere shadow and dream. For if only an earthly king, finding thee poor and begging, should suddenly make thee his son, thou wouldst not surely make account of thy hovel and its mean provision; although the difference in that case would not be so very great. Here then also make no account of things before; since thou hast been called to far greater things. For he that calls is the Lord of angels, and the benefits given exceed all utterance and thought. He doth not translate thee from earth to earth, as a king might do, but from earth to heaven, and from a mortal nature to immortality and glory unspeakable, which can only then fully appear when we come into its possession. Being about to partake of such blessings, then, dost thou make mention to me of riches, and cleave to the show of this world? And canst thou refuse to look upon all things visible as more mean than the beggar's rags? How then shalt thou appear worthy of that honor; and what defence shalt thou have to make or rather what punishment shalt thou not endure, having returned from such a gift to thy former vomit. For not now as a man simply shalt thou be punished, but as a son of God falling into sin, and the greatness of thy dignity will be for thee the passport to greater indignation. As we ourselves also do not inflict the same punishment on offending servants, as upon our children offending in the same way; especially if these have received large favors at our hands. If he who possessed paradise, was made to suffer so many dire evils, for one disobedience, after such high distinction, what indulgence shall *we* have—we who have possessed heaven and have been made fellow heirs with the Beloved—if after the dove we betake ourselves to the serpent?[10] We

---

9. [*NPNF*, 10:78: "And do not, because thy body is not translated unto heaven, suppose that thou hast anything to do with the earth; for thou hast thy Head abiding above."]

10. [*NPNF*, 10:78: "For if he who had paradise for his portion, for one disobedience underwent such dreadful things after his honor; we, who have received Heaven, and are become joint heirs with the Only Begotten, what excuse shall we have, for running to the serpent after the dove."]

shall not hear any more, "Dust thou art and unto dust shalt thou return,"[11] "Till the ground,"[12] and those other words of the former curse, but things much more grievous than these, outer darkness, eternal chains, the undying worm, the gnashing of teeth.[13] And with good reason. For he that is not made better by so great favor, should of right suffer the last and heaviest punishment.

Elias of old opened and shut heaven, so as to bring down and to hold back rain; but for thee heaven is opened not thus, but so as that thou mayest thyself ascend thither; and what is still greater, so as that thou canst not only thyself ascend, but if thou wilt mayest bring others there also, such liberty and power hath he given unto thee in all that is his own. Since then our home is there, let us there lay up all things and leave nothing here, that we may not suffer loss. For here, though thou mayest apply keys, and use bolted doors, and have thousands of servants to watch, and though thou shouldst surmount the arts of the dishonest and avoid the eyes of the envious, and though thou shouldst escape the moth and the decay that comes by time, which is impossible—still thou wilt not therefore escape death at last, and all these things shall be taken from thee in the twinkling of an eye; and not only taken away, but often so left as to pass into unfriendly hands. But pass all[14] into that higher home, and thou shall be master of all. No keys, no doors no bolts are needed there; such is the strength of that city; so inviolable is the region, and so completely beyond the reach of all corruption and evil.

How is it not then the extreme of folly, to heap up all where that which is laid away is sure to dissolve and perish while not even the smallest part is placed there, where what is stored is not only safe but certain to become more—and this too, when we are to spend there our whole future life! Hence it is, that the Greeks[15] also refuse to believe the things spoken by us; for they choose to make account of what we do, rather than of what we say; and when they see us building splendid houses, constructing gardens and baths, and buying fields, they will not believe that we are preparing for removal to another country. Since if that were the case, they say, we would see them converting all things here into money, and sending it there beforehand; and this they infer from what is usual in the present world. For we find always that those who have means employ them to purchase houses, and fields, and all other things, in those countries especially where they expect to remain. But we act differently; the earth, which we are to leave in a little while, is sought with the greatest diligence, not only money but blood itself being sacrificed for some acres of land and a few houses; whereas for the purchase of heaven we grudge to spend even our superfluous means, though we can have it at low price, and if we buy it are to hold it forever. For this reason the heaviest

---

11. [Gen 3:19.]
12. [Gen 4:12.]
13. [Matt 25:30.]
14. [*NPNF*, 10:79: "transfer them" (i.e., earthly goods).]
15. [*NPNF*, 10:79: "heathens" (see note).]

punishment awaits us if we pass into the other world naked and poor; and not for our own poverty simply, but for what we do also to make others poor, shall we meet severe retribution. For when the Greeks see those who have enjoyed such mysteries taken up with these things, they will much more cleave to the present world themselves. In this way we heap much fire on our own heads. For when we, who ought to teach them to despise all visible things, ourselves most of all encourage them in the love of these things, when may we hope to be saved, being held accountable for the destruction[16] of others? Dost thou not hear Christ saying, that he has sent us forth to be for salt[17] and as lights in this world, that we may exert a preserving power in the midst of its corruption,[18] and shine in the midst of its darkness. But if, instead of this, we help to draw men into darkness, and promote their corruption,[19] what hope can there be of our salvation? None whatever; but with wailing and gnashing of teeth, bound hand and foot, we shall go away into hell-fire, after having been thoroughly consumed by the care of riches here. Considering then all these things, let us break the bands of such present delusion, that we may not fall into those which shall consign us to unquenchable fire hereafter. For whosoever serveth riches, shall be subjected to bonds both in this world and eternally in the next; but he that is freed from this desire, shall find liberty both here and there. Which that we also may obtain, breaking the heavy yoke of avarice, let us wing our souls for heaven,[20] through the merciful kindness of our Lord Jesus Christ; to whom be glory and power through all ages. Amen.

II. Practical Reflections.

It is easy to see from this passage, that Christian Baptism was held by Chrysostom to be an actual regeneration, by the grace of God, to the power of a new and heavenly life. It was no sign simply of a spiritual fact, supposed to have place at some other time or in some other way; the token of an inward change already past, or the pledge of an inward change which was yet to come. It was not an act of profession merely, by which the catechumen became bound to the service of Christ, in the sense of what is called a church covenant among modern Congregationalists. The force of the sacrament was not subjective only, holding in the convictions and purposes, the views and feelings generally, of the human parties engaged in the transaction; it was at the same time most really and truly objective also, carrying with it the power of God's grace, and making what it signified to be actually at hand for its subjects, and available for their use thenceforward, as it had not been before.

16. [*NPNF*, 10:79: "perdition."]
17. [Matt 5:13.]
18. [*NPNF*, 10:79: "brace up those that are melting in luxury."]
19. [*NPNF*, 10:79: "make them more dissolute."]
20. [*NPNF*, 10:79: "make ourselves wings toward Heaven."]

All this is regarded as flowing necessarily from the relation, which the baptism of Christ himself sustained to the Jewish use of the ordinance, advanced to its highest meaning in the ministry of John. The whole Jewish system was typical and prefigurative of things to come; it was not itself the substance of what it exhibited in the way of grace, but only its shadow and promise; and this character it retained on to the very last. Even in the person of its last and greatest representative, the immediate forerunner of the Messiah, its mission was still that of preparation only, showing the kingdom of heaven to be indeed at hand, but at hand after all in a form wholly different from itself. Greater than all born before him in the old order of things, the Baptist was at the same time, we are told, less than the least in the new order which was now about to take its place. His baptism thus had no power answerable to the proper spiritual significance of all such washing; it ended in being nothing more than a sign and type; there was no efficacy in it to take away sin. Of this no one was more sensible than John himself. "I indeed baptize you with water," he says, "unto repentance"—engaging you to confession of sin, and to such change of mind as may fit you to receive the grace by which sin is to be pardoned and taken out of the way—"but he that cometh after me," whose way I am sent to prepare, in whom all my ministry is to find its full sense and end, "is mightier than I; whose shoes I am not worthy to bear: he shall baptize you with the Holy Ghost and with fire."[21] In other words, his baptism shall be in full effect what mine is in shadow only and outward form; it will be not the symbolical washing of water only, but along with this the power of inward purification also by the Holy Ghost, which is needed to make the symbol complete. This relation of the two different kinds of baptism, that of the Baptist and that for which it was to prepare the way, comes strikingly into view in the history of what took place, when Jesus came to be himself baptized of John in the river Jordan.

It became him thus "to fulfil all righteousness,"[22] to take up into his own person the last sense of the Old Testament, and so to complete it and bring it to an end, while at the same time he brought in the higher reality itself in the presence of which the preparatory shadow was to pass away. Such is the general relation of the New Testament to the Old; Christianity appears in one view as the true historical continuation of Judaism, its legitimate outbirth, in which the peculiar significance of it is carried forward finally to its last result, and yet in another view it is the introduction of an absolutely new creation, transcending the measure of that old economy altogether, and turning it into mere figure and show. The baptism of John became thus, in the case of Christ, something far more than it had been in its own nature previously as applied to others. The Baptist saw his work as it were taken out of his hands, and carried forward by the intervention of another ministry infinitely higher than his own. The coming down of the Holy Ghost was the inauguration of a new baptism, a new order of truth and grace, which served to proclaim at once the advent of him whose way he was sent

21. [Matt 3:11.]
22. [Matt 3:15.]

to prepare. "I knew him not," we hear him saying, "but he that sent me to baptize with water, the same said unto me, Upon whom thou shalt see the Spirit descending and remaining on him, the same is he which baptizeth with the Holy Ghost."[23] The new dispensation joins itself historically with the old, in the earthly ministry of John; but it is at once borne immeasurably above it, and beyond it, by another ministration, which comes not from earth at all, but directly and wholly from heaven. So much the transaction itself was clearly intended to signify and represent. "The heavens were *opened*," it is said—making way for a supernatural revelation which was not in the world before—"and he saw the Spirit of God descending like a dove, and lighting upon him"—entering into his person and abiding with him: "and lo, a voice from heaven saying, This is my beloved Son, in whom I am well pleased."[24]

The relation between the old and the new here, according to Chrysostom, is parallel with what had place at the institution of the Lord's Supper, the other Christian sacrament; when the celebration of the Jewish Passover was made the occasion of substituting for the type, the glorious reality which it foreshadowed from the beginning. As that transaction was made to embrace both the Jewish feast and the Christian, abolishing the one by completion, and introducing the other as a new and higher fact; so here also, "having fulfilled the Jewish baptism, he at the same time opens the doors of the Church, as in one table there, so in one river here, filling out at once the shadow and adding to it the truth."[25]

It is easy enough, however, to own this difference between the baptism of John and what was superadded to it in the case of Christ, without any faith after all in the divine power of the Christian sacrament in its ordinary form. It may be allowed, that our Saviour's baptism did indeed inaugurate the kingdom of heaven, showing that the way was now open for spiritual influences to descend upon men as they had not been known before; but this may be regarded at the same time as having place, mainly if not exclusively, under the form of a purely inward baptism, which is then taken to be the proper sense of the Christian sacrament as analogically set forth in the transaction of Jordan, while the outward rite of the sacrament is considered to be only the symbol of this grace, having no more necessary connection with the real presence of the grace itself, in the end, than the Old Testament baptism of John. But no such Gnostic apprehension as this was admitted in the mind of Chrysostom. He sees in the transaction of Jordan a revelation, not only of the power of the Holy Ghost, as it was to be exercised by Christ in a general spiritual way for the salvation of his people, but of this power as it was supposed to enter now into the constitution of all Christian baptism, making the sacrament to be as a whole something altogether different from what he depreciates in his own ministry as being a baptism of water only and nothing more. The Christian sacrament includes in itself really and truly, according to St. Chrysostom, what the

---

23. [John 1:33.]
24. [Matt 3:16–17.]
25. [Homily XII.4.]

other served only to prefigure as a weak outward sign; it carries with it the power of the Holy Ghost, answering in full to what took place at our Saviour's baptism, when the heavens were opened, and the Spirit came down in bodily shape upon his person.

The opening of the heavens on this grand occasion, he tells us, is to be regarded as a representation of what takes place in the sacrament of Christian baptism through all time. It matters not that the visibility of the fact is not repeated; that, like the sensible manifestations of the Day of Pentecost, was only to verify the commencement of the dispensation; for faith now, the mystery, once evidenced in this way, remains permanently sure, without the help of sense. In all Christian Baptism then, there is a real rending of the heavens—the canopy that separates the world of nature from the world of grace; way is made for the saving presence of the Spirit as it was not at hand before; an adoption takes place into the family of God—the constitution of a new filial relation, or sonship, which did not exist previously; and along with this goes the power of a divine vocation, a "voice from heaven," calling the favored subject of the ordinance to forsake the present world and seek the heavenly inheritance, and offering at the same time all the grace that is required to obey the call.

It will not do to say, that those high sounding representations are with Chrysostom mere rhetorical figures, employed to set forth the general privilege of those to whom the Gospel comes with its offers of mercy; the meaning of which must be reduced simply to this, that baptism certifies to men the great fact of the Christian salvation, and the possibility of their having part in it by repentance, faith, and new obedience—a possibility, however, which is in no sense conditioned by what takes place in this sacrament itself, but is to be considered equally open and nigh in fact to all who have the gospel preached to them, whether baptized or not. What is here affirmed, or rather we may say taken for granted, of the Christian sacrament, goes most manifestly very far beyond all that. The privileges and prerogatives of its subjects, while they are taken to be of the highest supernatural significance and most real objective force, are viewed at the same time as exclusively peculiar, the result strictly of that new position to which the baptized have come by means of the sacrament itself, and in no sort something common to them with the unbaptized world around. All men to whom the gospel is preached have the opportunity of being saved, and may be said to be placed thus within the range of the heavenly economy, by which it is made possible for sinners to become the children of God, and to enter into everlasting life; and this undoubtedly is a great distinction and privilege, which it must ever be a sin like that of Esau to undervalue or neglect. But here we have the idea of vastly more than this. Baptism is for its subjects not simply an expressive sign, picturing to the mind the sense of that general grace, which is offered to all, and which all are bound to receive; it is an actual election and vocation of God to gracious privileges, heavenly relations, special possibilities and powers of salvation, which are not at once comprehended in the general presence of Christianity. The subjects of it are brought into a new condition or state, broadly different from that of the general world around them. For others the presence of the Gospel is simply the opportunity of coming into the Christian fold in this way, and thus securing to themselves the rights and faculties of the kingdom of heaven; but for those who are in the fold by baptism these rights and faculties are already actually possessed; they have the power of being saved, not mediately only and through something else, as in the other case, but immediately in their position itself; a difference exactly like that of being in the ark, in the days of Noah, and of being only warned and called to take refuge in it from the impending flood.

It never could have entered into the mind of Chrysostom, to address the world at large in the language of Christian instruction and exhortation. His homilies are not for men in general, congregations composed promiscuously of baptized and unbaptized; they are properly speaking for the baptized alone; regard being had to others at best only as they had already become catechumens and candidates for baptism; while all besides were viewed as unbelievers, for whom the doctrines, promises, and precepts of Christianity could not be said to be of any practical account whatever. For all such it could have but one message still, as on the Day of Pentecost: "Repent, and be baptized every one of you in the name of Jesus Christ, for the remission of sins, and ye shall receive the gift of the Holy Ghost."[26] Without this first great act of submission to the heavenly constitution of the Church, they must be held to be spiritually incompetent for all the privileges and duties of Christianity beyond this; so that it could be only a sort of profane mockery to make such duties and privileges the matter of homiletic exhortation for them in any way. Full earnest is made thus with the distinction, between being in the Church and being out of the Church. The difference is taken to be not simply nominal, but in the most material sense actual and real.

Baptism, in the view of Chrysostom, is not merely a public profession of faith in Christ, but the act of putting on Christ and entering into the fellowship of his kingdom; a translation from the power of darkness into the marvellous light of the Gospel; a new birth, bringing with it the title and power of sonship in the family of God; which is such a dignity again as brings with it, we are told, "the removal of all evil and the gift of all good"[27]—the remission of sin, in other words, and whatever of grace is needed for securing everlasting life.

But with all the account which is thus made of the sacrament, as being the gate of paradise, the mystery of regeneration, and the very power of God unto salvation, we do not find the opinion entertained for a moment that it was sufficient of itself to insure the salvation of those who were its subjects. On the contrary, it is everywhere taken for granted, that it carried with it no such assurance whatever. Every homily of St. Chrysostom proceeds upon the assumption, that those who were baptized, and thus made the children of God and the heirs of eternal life, might notwithstanding

26. [Acts 2:38.]
27. [Homily XII.3.]

abuse this grace, allow themselves to continue still in the service of sin, and so come short of heaven at the last. It is painfully apparent indeed from his own discourses, that the great body of those to whom he himself preached, as the regenerated subjects of Christian baptism, were Christians in outward form and name only, whose walk and conversation, instead of adorning the doctrine of Christ, brought reproach upon it every day. He goes even so far as to say in one place, that too generally they were not to be distinguished from the unconverted world around them at all, except when they were seen to approach the sacramental altar. Hence in our present extract also, we find him turning what he conceives to be the unspeakable gift that goes along with Christian baptism, into an occasion for apprehension and alarm for those who enjoy it, in view of the possibility of its not being properly improved. As partakers of the heavenly adoption, they may still destroy themselves by sin; in which case, however, their perdition must be something worse than that of men who perish without having enjoyed the same high distinction. "What defence shalt thou have to make, or rather what punishment shalt thou not endure, having returned from such a gift to thy former vomit? For not now as a man simply shalt thou be punished, but as a son of God falling into sin, and the greatness of that dignity will be for thee the passport to greater indignation."[28] "If he who possessed paradise was made to suffer so many dire evils for one disobedience, after such high distinction, what indulgence shall *we* have—we who have possessed heaven, and have been made fellow heirs with the Beloved—if after the dove we betake ourselves to the serpent?"[29] The entire exhortation proceeds throughout on the supposition, not only that it was possible for those who were thus constituted the children of God to lose the benefit of their supernatural birthright, and to make shipwreck of their souls, but that there was in truth great danger always of such disaster, that it was sadly frequent and common, and that it needed all diligence to avoid it, so as to make the Christian calling and election finally sure.[30]

But still this view of the matter is not allowed in the least to discredit, or bring into doubt, the objective reality and significance of the grace conferred by baptism. This it is precisely that is taken to be the ground of special condemnation, in the case of those who have enjoyed that grace and yet yield themselves to the power of sin. What aggravates their guilt, is not just that they have had the gospel preached to them, that they have been placed under a general dispensation of mercy, that they have enjoyed the opportunity of embracing and using the means of salvation; nor yet, farther than this, that they have taken upon them the profession of Christianity, assumed its engagements, and joined in its solemn acts of worship; but that they have been made actually to possess the gift of righteousness, the power of salvation, that a price to purchase heaven has been fairly placed in their hands, and that notwithstanding all this they have forced their way down to everlasting death. This is the condemnation.

28. [Homily XII.4.]
29. [Ibid.]
30. [2 Pet 1:10; "shipwreck" is likely an allusion to 1 Tim 1:19.]

Having been constituted the children of God, by adoption in Christ, they have despised that glorious birthright, and allowed themselves to become again the children of the Devil. Having been washed from their sins, they have returned to wallowing in the mire. Having been called to holiness, and endowed with power from on high to follow after it to the end, they have turned aside to unrighteousness, and profaned the heavenly gift in the service of sin.

What is particularly remarkable, is the facility with which these contrary and seemingly inconsistent conceptions are thus constantly held together in the same system of thought, over against such an order of things as is known to have prevailed at the time in the outward Church. The notion of baptismal grace was apparently contradicted every day by the notorious fact, that the greater part of the baptized gave no evidence whatever of being in any better condition for the purposes of Christian piety, than multitudes around them who had never enjoyed the same heavenly privilege. How could that be a supernatural regeneration in any sense, a birth into God's family by the power of the Holy Ghost, which allowed its subjects to continue still the willing slaves of Satan and sin? Was not the lie given continually to Chrysostom's theory of sacramental saintship, by the crowd of professed believers, called in this way to be saints, whom he himself describes as patterns of selfishness and covetousness; examples of all worldliness; pleasure seekers, who could run from the church to the theatre, and there feast their eyes, and pollute their imagination, with licentious heathen spectacles and shows; brawlers, profane swearers, worshippers that carried the poison of asps under their tongues even in the sanctuary itself, blessing God and cursing man almost in the same breath, and filling the temple with noise and confusion in the very midst of the sacred services which were going forward at the altar? Such monstrous practice might indeed go along with a simply human profession. But did it not show, that the profession at last was human only, an act on the part of those who made it, and sealed it by the rite of baptism and nothing more? Did it not make void at once the idea of any properly objective force in the sacrament, and demonstrate in the most convincing manner that the established ecclesiastical style of speaking on this subject—with its terminology of regeneration, illumination, initiation, divine filiation, donation of the Spirit, remission of sins, and other such high sounding benefits—was in truth rhetorical only, and in no sense in strict agreement with the truth? Must not Chrysostom himself have known, in full view of the facts before him, that his way of dealing with such terms was more oratorical than logical; that he was discoursing of what ought to be in the case rather than of what existed in fact; that the outward symbols of the Christian salvation were made in his view, for the moment, to pass for the proper spiritual verities which it was their office only to represent? So it is natural to feel, in looking at the matter from the standpoint of what is considered to be spiritual Christianity at the present time. The case is found to involve a difficulty, at all events, which seems to demand some explanation; and we are apt to think, that such a man as Chrysostom must have felt himself constrained to take notice of it in some way. But, strange to say, it does not appear to give him any sort of embarrassment whatever. He moves along in his didactic and paraenetic course, as though no such obstruction crossed his path, or as though he at least had no eyes to note its presence. The modern dilemma in regard to baptismal regeneration, gore whom it may with its merciless horns, comes not at all apparently into his view. Both sides of the supposed difficulty are embraced in his thinking at once; and he passes back and forth from one to the other continually, without experiencing, as it would seem, the slightest sense of contradiction.

There is not the shadow of evidence anywhere, that the stress which he lays upon the heavenly side of Christian baptism was in his own mind a figure of speech only, substituting the sign for the thing signified, or allowing outward profession to pass for inward fact. Such a supposition would stultify his entire system of theological thought. In one view it might have been a relief to look at the matter in this light; as it would have served to show that the divine pretensions of Christianity were not to be tried or measured in any way by the unfruitful lives of bad nominal Christians, who as such must be considered hypocrites only, and not partakers at all of the proper supernatural power of the Gospel. But Chrysostom has no thought of saving the credit of the Church in this way. On the contrary, in full face of the acknowledged fact that thousands were all the time receiving the benefit in vain, he only insists the more upon the reality of the heavenly gift which was supposed to be conferred in baptism. That was not to be doubted or called in question, let it fare as it might with those who had received it. Let God be true, though all the world should be found false;[31] his faith was not to be made of no effect, however widely it might be met with unfaithfulness on the part of men. The objective presence of the grace which was lodged in the Christian sacraments, must not be measured by mere outward observation of any kind; it belonged to the sphere of faith, and was to be owned, therefore, independently of all experimental tests. To make it contingent on the purely subjective operations of the human mind, was necessarily to set aside the idea of its objective force altogether, and in the end to reduce Christianity to the character of a simply natural religion. If it might seem to be for the credit of the Gospel, to say that hypocrites and false professors had no part in its proper supernatural grace, and that *therefore* no argument could hold rightly against the reality and power of this grace, because it was found to have no salutary effect on their lives; it was undoubtedly for the true credit of the Gospel much more, that it should not itself be shorn of its own heavenly prerogative, as a system whose province it was, not merely to shadow forth, but to embody and exhibit in a real way, the blessings of salvation. This was an interest which lay much nearer to the faith of Chrysostom than the other. The Gospel, in his view, was the power of a new order of life always actually at hand in the Church. Christian Baptism was in full effect, what the Baptism of John had been only in figure and sign; it answered strictly to the contrast drawn by the Baptist himself, as being a baptism with the Holy Ghost

---

31. [Rom 3:4.]

and with fire in distinction from a baptism with water only. It opened the heavens; brought down the Spirit; wrought the remission of sins; regenerated its subjects, by a divine adoption, into the state and dignity of children of God. And yet this grace, transcending as it did the whole course of nature, might be abused, wasted, and utterly thrown away by men, just like the common blessings of nature itself. Chrysostom finds no more difficulty apparently, in supposing it possible for the subjects of such supernatural calling and election to miss the end of their heavenly qualification, than in conceiving it possible for those who are called and chosen, by real opportunity, to any simply worldly good, to come short of it in the same way; a failure, which does not show then that there was no qualification in their circumstances for securing the benefit, but only that there was no care to turn the qualification to right account. So we have the two conceptions continually moving, as we have said before, hand in hand together; without any sense of contradiction; without any thought of explanation.

It will be borne in mind, that we are not at present sitting in judgment, in any way, on this view of Christian Baptism. Our object is simply to exhibit it as the view that was held by St. Chrysostom, without any argument upon its theological merits.

The view, however, be its merits as they may, was in no sense peculiar to this eminently pious Church Father. It belonged to the universal orthodox Christian thinking of the age. And as we look farther, we find it in the thinking of previous ages also, back to the first Christian times. The ancient ecclesiastical Fathers are everywhere full of testimony on the subject. It is idle to quote particular authorities in the case; for the authorities are all one way. The universal Church in these first centuries held and taught, that Christian Baptism was not simply "unto repentance,"[32] like that of John, not merely a sign to represent the profession of Christianity, on the one side, and the power of its cleansing and renovating grace on the other; but that it was the very sacrament of this grace itself, the form of its first actual exhibition for the use of sinners, the power of God really and truly unto salvation, carrying with it the remission of sins, the gift of adoption, and the full possibility of eternal life. It was not pretended, that it secured the salvation of its subjects; they might prove unfaithful to their heavenly calling, and destroy themselves still by a life of sin; multitudes, it was too plain, were constantly falling into this condemnation; but no consideration of this sort was allowed to disparage the supernatural force of the sacrament itself. That remained an article of faith, under all circumstances, and in the face of all difficulties.

An article of faith, we say; which as such, accordingly, entered with a kind of inward necessity into the whole system of theological thought with which it was joined. In this view it is especially, that the old ecclesiastical doctrine challenges serious attention. If it appeared as a mere accidental opinion simply, sustaining only an outward relation to the general faith of the Church, it might be comparatively easy to dispose of

---

32. [Matt 3:11.]

it as being the result in some way of a wrong use of terms. But for any one who is willing to examine the matter for himself, it is impossible not to see that the very reverse of this is the truth. The idea of baptismal regeneration, as involving a real translation from the kingdom of Satan into the family of God, underlies the universal religious thinking of the ancient Church. The old Patristic doctrine of Christian Baptism is clearly enough revealed, in particular passages bearing directly on the point. But such separate and special testimonies form in truth by far the smallest and least weighty part of the evidence, that properly belongs to the case. This comes out fully, only in the way in which all Christian truth and life are made to include the tacit assumption of the doctrine, as being a sort of fundamental axiom in Christianity. We can hardly read for instance a single homily of Chrysostom, without feeling that his view of the Gospel, as a scheme of redemption and salvation, is conditioned throughout by the conception of supernatural privileges and powers conferred upon men through the sacrament of Baptism. His theology is constructed, in all its parts, in the most perfect harmony with this thought. It is everywhere sacramental and churchly, in the fullest sense of the terms. And the same thing is true manifestly of the theology and religious life of the first Christian ages generally.

Have we not this fact, indeed, plainly exhibited in the structure of the ancient Creeds?[33] They were in one view many; but the general tenor of them is always the same. They are in power and substance a single Creed; and this so constructed, as to be in itself a single whole, the organic evolution of one and the same grand fact from beginning to end. And here we find, conspicuous among its other articles, the doctrine of the Church and of "one Baptism for the remission of sins." What else is this than the sacramental theory of Chrysostom, and the old ecclesiastical writers generally? In no other view, indeed, could Christian Baptism be made an object of faith at all, in the sense of the Creed. For faith here, by its very conception, has to do with what is supernatural in Christianity, the objective presence and power of the new creation proceeding from Christ, in distinction from all subjective apprehension of it on the part of men. If Baptism then were not taken to be a mystery, hiding under its visible form, in the sphere of nature, the agency of God's Spirit working, at the same time, in a higher sphere, it could have no place properly in the Creed. The simple fact of its being there, as an article of faith, a primary constituent in the Christian salvation, is one of the clearest proofs we could well have of its being regarded all along in this light by the early Church.

That the view taken of Christian Baptism at the present time, in a very large part of the Protestant Church, is something broadly different from this, another theory of the

---

33. [The essays on the creed by Nevin and Schaff are scheduled for publication in vol. 8 of MTSS. See esp. Nevin's three essays on "The Apostles' Creed"; he saw fit to return to it twenty years later: "Origin and Structure of the Apostles' Creed" and "The Unity of the Apostles' Creed."]

sacrament in truth altogether, is too plain to admit of any question or to call for any proof. In the midst of much confusion in regard to what the ordinance positively does mean, there is a very general agreement in rejecting the meaning attributed to it by the Church of the first ages. The doctrine of St. Chrysostom on the subject is held to be unevangelical, and if he were alive to preach it now, would bring him into general discredit with all our evangelical sects. Whatever honor we may be bound to put upon the sacrament as a divine appointment, it must ever be a monstrous wrong, according to this reigning modern view, to make it of one order in any way with the operation of God's Spirit, by ascribing to it effects that are supernatural, and such as it is the province of the Holy Ghost alone to produce.

It is absurd, we are told, and something at war with the true idea of religion, to suppose that any external rite of this sort should take away sin, or carry with it the power of regeneration. The proper spirituality of the Gospel, it is taken for granted, must always suffer, where Christianity is made to be thus formal and sacramental. Religion after all is an inward, spiritual transaction, between God and the soul; which as such, may go along with the outward forms of worship, imparting to them energy and life; but which at the same time, is not bound to them, or conditioned by them, in any really necessary way.

Baptism thus as an outward ceremony is one thing, and what it is used to represent is another thing altogether, which is supposed to have place fully on the outside of the sacrament, and apart from all virtue in it whatever. Christian baptism is indeed more than the baptism of John; it regards as an accomplished fact, what this last anticipated only as something which was then still to come. It represents the grace of Christ as now actually at work in the world, through the Spirit, for the remission of sins and the conversion of souls. But in its relation to this grace, it is itself still only an outward washing with water, as much as was formerly the baptism of John. It has no saving efficacy in its own constitution; no power to remove the guilt of past sin, or to regenerate children of Satan into children of God. It signifies this; but only as a fact which must be spiritually experienced under another form. In the case of adults it should of right follow this experience, showing that it has already taken place—that the subjects of the ordinance, in other words, have already secured the spiritual reality of which it is the outward profession, are regenerated, justified, adopted into the household of faith, the citizenship of heaven, and in virtue of all this are entitled now to enter the visible Church in this way, and so to become Christians in name as they are already Christians in fact. In the case of infants, the change may be supposed to precede the ordinance occasionally, or in some instances possibly to accompany it, by an act of sovereign power on the part of God; but more commonly it is to be considered as being still a sort of covenant possibility only, which is hopefully expected to issue in actual conversion at some future time. In any case, however, there may be no inward change at all, answering either prospectively or retrospectively to the outward sign. So with adults, who often profess religion in this way without any sense of its proper power; and so also with infants, vast numbers of whom, after baptism, grow up, and pass through life, plainly impenitent and unconverted to the end. In all such instances, the relation between the sacrament and the grace signified by it, is clearly shown to be nominal only and nothing more; and the broad example, with which we are thus continually confronted in such form, is held sufficient to show that this is in truth the character of the relation universally, and that it must ever be idle, therefore, to speak of baptism as being itself, in any real sense, the vehicle of grace or the power of a new birth to righteousness and life.

We merely state this view here, in general terms; as we have tried to state before the doctrine of the ancient Church.[34] Our business is not now to discuss the actual merits of either theory. We wish only to place them in contrast, and to fix attention on the plain fact of their difference and contradiction. Such a difference, in a case whose bearings are so broad and profound, is justly entitled, we are very sure, to thoughtful consideration. It must ever argue a great want of seriousness, to regard it without interest or concern. It is not a matter, that we should be willing to have covered over with the mantle of historical ignorance. We are bound, in duty to ourselves, as well as in fidelity to the cause of religion, to bring the subject forward into the broad light of day, to converse with it fairly and openly in its own form, to see and acknowledge in regard to it what is the actual truth. When this is done honestly and candidly, we can hardly fail to perceive that the fact thus brought into view, is one which demands explanation; and it will be felt at the same-time, that what needs to be explained in the case is a question, not merely of theoretical curiosity, but of the greatest practical significance and account. Here are two widely different constructions of the religion of Jesus Christ. The sacramental system of the early Church, stands broadly opposed to the self-styled evangelical system of the present day, each protesting loudly against the other as an utter perversion of the true sense of the Gospel. Are they after all different versions only of the same faith? If so, how are their opposing modes of thought to be adjusted, so that we may have a right to be quiet and at rest in the modern theory, not ignoring the old, but looking it as a part of past history steadily in the face?

It will not do to say, there is no difficulty in the case; that the old view stands clearly condemned by the judgment of history itself; and that the truth is so plainly with the modern view, as to make it unnecessary for us to trouble ourselves with its justification. All *such* superiority to the claims of the problem is too easy, to deserve either confidence or respect. It demands a different solution. The conflict here is between forces, that are not simply imaginary but real. There are formidable difficulties

---

34. [In "Early Christianity," and "Cyprian." These essays are to be published in volume 9 of MTSS. Nevin's attitude here was also expressed in "Wilberforce on the Eucharist," art. 4 above; see esp. note 44. Nevin consistently denied drawing any constructive conclusions from his historical explorations.]

on both sides. If the ecclesiastical system seem dangerous in one direction, we may not close our eyes to the fact that the evangelical system has its dangers also in another.

Without going into any wider view at present, it is easy enough to see, for example, what questionable consequences thrust themselves upon us, as naturally flowing from the modern purely spiritualistic theory of Christian Baptism. If the sacrament be only the outward sign of a spiritual transaction, which is in its own nature complete under another form altogether—which has no inward connection with the sign whatever, and which indeed as related to the sign is purely ideal to such an extent that it may never become fact at all—it would seem certainly that no great stress should be laid upon the use of it in any way, and that it must always involve some jeopardy to the cause of true piety to suppose it dependent in the least upon any such form. Thus the Quakers, consistently enough, reject the outward sacrament altogether; it is for them a mere baptism of water; they will have only the baptism of the Spirit, which is a process that belongs by its very nature to the soul. This is an affectation of the highest order of spirituality; the dialectic counterpart and natural end of which, as we all know, is Socinian or Deistic Rationalism.[35] Another less extreme, but for this very reason also less consistent, undervaluation of the outward sacrament, is exhibited in the ecclesiastical practice of the Baptists; who refuse to baptize infants, on the ground that they have no power to repent and believe in Christ, so as to be the subjects of that inward spiritual conversion of which baptism is the profession and sign, and without which it can have no meaning. What conclusion, indeed, can well be more logical, if we are to believe that there is no objective power, no supernatural grace, in the sacrament itself, and that the whole virtue of it resolves itself at last into what goes forward in the minds of its subjects themselves under a purely subjective form? With such a theory of the institution, it is perfectly certain that the practice of infant baptism never could have prevailed as it did in the ancient Church. It belongs to the old order of thinking on the subject, as we have it in St. Chrysostom and the Christian fathers generally, which made baptism to be the sacrament of a real regeneration by the power of the Holy Ghost into the family of God. Why then should it not be given up, along with this, as an obsolete superstition? It is becoming but too plain, that the Paedobaptist part of the so-called Evangelical Christianity of the present day is not able to hold its ground steadily, at this point, against the Baptist wing of the same interest. The Baptistic sentiment grows and spreads in every direction. It infects more and more, the secret thinking even of those sects which still retain, in a traditional way, the old practice. The question of infant baptism is sunk in many quarters, as by general consent, into the category of *adiaphora*—things indifferent; as though it lay wholly on the outside of the proper sense and true actual substance of the Christian life. Some of our evangelical sects, it is easy to see, could at once part with the usage altogether, and not miss it in

---

35. [Socinianism was a Reformation-era expression of Unitarianism; Deism was a denial of the supernatural, revealed character of Christianity. So Nevin was arguing that if one rejected the sacramental as outward signs of a spiritual reality, then one ended up with a rationalistic view of spirituality.]

their scheme of practical religion. Hence, as a general thing, it appears to have fallen into very alarming neglect. Some of our more respectable denominations, or rather some thoughtful persons in these denominations, have in fact begun to take alarm from this cause, and are showing a disposition to lift the whole doctrine of Christian Baptism again, if possible, into a higher sphere, such as may correspond, in part at least, with the sacramental worth assigned to it in past ages. This, as far as it goes, is matter for congratulation. But it remains to be seen, how far any such reactionary feeling shall be able to stay and turn the tide, which still threatens to sweep all before it in the opposite direction. And who can say, what perils, not merely for the doctrine of Christian Baptism, but for the whole idea of the Christian Sacraments, for the very being of the Church, and in the end for the universal interest of Christianity itself, may not be involved in the full triumph of what claims to be the perfection of religion in such spiritualistic form!

What we mean by all this, is simply to show that the problem of settling the difference between the old doctrine of Christian Baptism and the view which has taken the place of it so widely in modern times—a difference which involves in the end two different schemes of Christianity—is not just to be disposed of satisfactorily by the simple assumption, that the difficulty of the question lies wholly on the one side, the doctrine namely of the ancient Church, and not at all on the other. There are real difficulties of the most embarrassing kind on both sides; and it must ever be an argument of the most superficial thinking, not to perceive them, or not to acknowledge their force.

Lancaster, PA. J.W.N.

ARTICLE 7
"The Bread of Life: A Communion Sermon"

(By John W. Nevin)

Editor's Introduction

James Hastings Nichols claimed that around Nevin's second retirement in 1876 (from the presidency of Franklin and Marshall College), he had "diverged sharply from . . . his Mercersburg period."[1] The standard interpretation of the alleged shift in Nevin's direction is that Richard Rothe motivated Nevin to read the theosophist Emanuel Swedenborg.[2] According to William Reily, Rothe's influence on Nevin was on the doctrine of the Bible's inspiration and authority.[3] Rothe did not understand inspiration as the miraculous protection of the truth of the biblical text. Rather, the supernatural element in Scripture was (firstly) the miraculous events it had witnessed and described, and (secondly) the internal witness of the Holy Spirit in making those events present and powerful in the Christian's life.[4] This witness was interpreted by Rothe in classical dogmatic terms as the *testimonium spiritus sancti internum*.[5] Rothe

1. Nichols, *Romanticism in American Theology*, 309. See the editor's response in Layman, "Revelation in the Praxis of the Liturgical Community," 155–83.

2. Appel, *Life and Work*, 170–71; DiPuccio, *Interior Sense of Scripture*, 85–93. Rothe (1799–1867) was a Lutheran theologian who finished his career at Heidelberg. *Theologische Ethik* was considered his magnum opus; but he was best known in England for *Stille Stunde* (*Still Hours*), a collection of theological aphorisms. Swedenborg (1688–1772) began his career as a scientist of "considerable inventiveness and mathematical ability." In 1743–1745, he began to experience the spiritual world directly. Subsequently, he attempted to bring together his scientific and visionary knowledge in a vast system based on a "'doctrine of correspondence' between the physical and spiritual world" (*Dictionary of the Christian Church*, 1563).

3. Reily, "John Williamson Nevin," pp. 326–27 (a review of Appel's biography).

4. Rothe, *Zur Dogmatik*, 68–69; Cf. Rothe, *Still Hours*, 217. See Barth, *Protestant Theology in the Nineteenth Century*, 602; Pannenberg, *Systematic Theology*, 1:224–26; Welch, *Protestant Thought in the Nineteenth Century*, 1:288–89.

5. Trans. "internal witness of the Holy Spirit."

rejected the prevalent view that the Bible communicated teachings or concrete content about the world, which then had to be supernaturally protected. Instead, the *testimonium* was the direct confirmation of revelation.[6] We can detect Rothe's influence when Nevin wrote (1870) that "All true faith in the Bible, then, is . . . faith . . . in the objective supernatural substance which goes along with the outward revelation, and . . . without its self-verifying presence for faith . . . the outward revelation itself would be no revelation at all."[7]

None of the standard interpretations give a clear explanation of the link between Rothe and Swedenborg. They both held to the immediacy of God's presence as a fact of consciousness: "God is to me more immediately certain than myself . . . I become first truly certain of myself by means of my certainty of God," Rothe said.[8] In Swedenborg, of course, this "certainty of God" was experienced in his mystical states. Rothe, like Swedenborg, has been interpreted as a "theosopher."[9] Nevin always needed a direct and immediate sense of God's presence—of spiritual life—and apparently found both Rothe and Swedenborg helpful in interpreting how that was possible and how that putative reality could be best understood. However, another element that might have brought Swedenborg to Nevin's attention was the loss of two sons (1867 and 1872).[10] We know exactly when Nevin began to read Swedenborg intensively, and the work he read: the Philip Schaff Library of Lancaster (Pennsylvania) Theological Seminary holds the thirteen-volume set of Swedenborg's *Arcana Coelestia*[11] from Nevin's library. His signature, "J. W. Nevin," is on the title page of the first volume, along with the date "Oct. 1874." *Arcana Coelestia* is a sprawling commentary, ostensibly of Genesis and

---

6. "*Das Demjenigen, der mit der heiligen Schrift auf die richtige Weise verkehrt, zu Theil werdende testimonium spiritus sancti internum dafür, daß sie Gottes eigenes Wort ist*" (Rothe, *Zur Dogmatik*, 140; trans. "To the one who associates with the holy Scripture in the right way, taking part in the *testimonium spiritus sancti internum*, it is God's very Word.").

7. Nevin, *My Own Life*, 114; see also p. 112. See further Nevin, "Christ and His Spirit," 363–64, 379–84.

8. Quoted in Schaff, *Germany: Its Universities, Theology, and Religion*, 364. In *Zur Dogmatik*, Rothe had put it as follows: "*Gott, indem er sich offenbart, offenbart sich selbst; Gott und lediglich Gott ist der Gegenstand, den die göttliche Offenbarung offenbart, Gott und sonst nichts*" (61; cf. *Still Hours*, 218; trans. "God is the one revealed; God reveals himself; God and only God is the object that the divine revelation reveals, God and nothing else.")

9. Thus both Schaff (*Germany: Its Universities*, 363) and a century later, Karl Barth (*Protestant Theology in the Nineteenth Century*, 597, 599).

10. Appel, *Life and Work*, 740; Nichols, *Romanticism in American Theology*, 204.

11. *Arcana coelestia: Quae in scriptura sacra seu verbo Domini, sunt, detecta: Hic primum quae in Genesi. Una cum mirabilibus, quae visa sunt in mundo spirituum et in coelo angelorum* (Tubingae: In Bibliopolio zu Guttenberg, 1833–; trans. "Heavenly Secrets, Contained in the Holy Scriptures or Word Of God Unfolded Beginning with the Book of Genesis Together with Wonderful Things Seen in the World of Spirits and in the Heaven of Angels.") The "redesigned standard edition" of the English translation is available at http://www.swedenborg.com/emanuel-swedenborg/writings/rse-downloads/. Further citations will be to this edition, using the paragraph numbering that is used in all editions, and runs continuously through the entire work, in the following form: *Arcana coelestia*, vol. x, §y.

Exodus,[12] but quickly putting out tendrils into the entire Christian canon, and reading every detail allegorically. Interspersed throughout are accounts of Swedenborg's experience of "eternal life," analogous to (and having many of the characteristics of) what are now called "near-death experiences."[13]

Nevin interpreted human experience as consisting of descending "orders" or "spheres": the spiritual, intellectual (rational), and the physical.[14] Therefore, all physical realities had their intellectual and spiritual counterparts, and were *real* because the spiritual reality descended and entered into their corporeal existence. Although modern, scientific humanity imagined that the empirical was paramount, in *truth* all natural reality was derived through the spiritual from God himself. Physical bread nourished the body, and rational bread nourished the intellect, *because* "celestial bread," through its sacramental sign in the Eucharist, nourished the spirit. Nevin then tied this celestial bread to other scriptural parables such as Melchizedek's offering of bread and wine to Abraham, which he blessed with "grand eucharistic words." Having shown how the Eucharist was anticipated in this pre-Mosaic history, Nevin brought the parallels up through the establishment of the Passover, with its "paschal lamb," the temple sacrifices and furniture (specifically mentioning the shewbread) and the double miracles of manna and water from the rock. All of these Old Testament stories were parables of solid food and drink as the true food for the spiritual life within a Christian.

Such spiritual food was *more* real, not less, because following Augustine, it was the word "added to the element" that made the sacrament. He conceded that perhaps, in an apparent apologia for past shortcomings in his long argument for the "mystical presence,"[15] in the past he had not sufficiently emphasized "the true and real preeminence of the Word above all sacraments." He was eager now to rectify that flaw. Through the word, "the being of God," in the twofold form of "the love and wisdom of the Lord," came into a person's life. Here Nevin restated an "ontology of revelation,"[16] consisting of two poles on four levels. The divine was revealed through "two ground

---

12. *Arcana coelestia: . . . hic quae in Exodo. . . .*, vol. 9– (Tubingae: In Bibliopolio zu Guttenberg, 1840–).

13. E.g., *Arcana coelestia*, vol. 1, §§168ff. and §§314ff. "I was reduced into a state of insensibility as to the bodily senses, thus almost into the state of dying persons, retaining however my interior life unimpaired, attended with the power of thinking, and with sufficient breathing for life, and finally with a tacit breathing, that I might perceive and remember what happens to those who have died and are being resuscitated" (ibid., §169).

14. Swedenborg's version of the hierarchy was celestial, spiritual (cf. German *Geist*, as "mind"), and physical.

15. Nevin, *The Mystical Presence*, MTTS ed.

16. First stated in 1877 in "Testimony of Jesus," 30–32. The "love"/"wisdom" dichotomy echoes Swedenborg: see e.g., *Arcana coelestia*, vol. 1, §§32, 107, 111, 590; vol. 4, §3021 [6]; even so, it has roots at least as far back as Nevin's 1848 essay, "Human Freedom": "The sphere of self-conscious spirit . . . involves two things, the light of intelligence and the power of choice. . . . Reason and will necessarily involve each other. . . . Self-consciousness is itself always self-action" (409; repr. in *Human Freedom, and A Plea for Philosophy*, 8, 9; projected for vol. 13 of MTSS). "Ontology of revelation" is this editor's description in his dissertation, "Revelation in the Praxis of the Liturgical Community," 170ff.

truths": the "glorified, actual Human Christ," and union with Christ that came about by "obeying the commandments of the Lord" as an act of "believing worship." These two "ground truths" were holistically united as the "obedience of faith." Descending from these truths were two "ground factors" of wisdom and love. Wisdom and love were revealed in the two tables of the law: love of God and love of neighbor; the two tables corresponded to, and were comprehended by, intelligence and will, which were "possibilities for" this "double reception."

Nevin still needed to address the issue of the state in which the Christian properly came to the eucharistic table. Three times he asked, "how shall we come?" before he was ready to give his answer. Neither "will-worship"—by which he seems to have had in mind evangelical memorialism, *willing* Jesus Christ to be present—nor "superstition"—imagining the symbols magically became body and blood—could make "the glorified life of the Lord" present to the believer. Rather, repentance and faith were the two sides of human reception of the mystery: repentance renounced all self-effort in making the mystery present, and faith looked to the Lord to reveal himself. Nevin was still trying to split the difference between evangelicalism and "Romanism" and hold to what we might call a radically catholic vision.

In an appendix, Nevin continued to develop the theme of Jesus Christ's glorification. The "the glorification of the humanity of our Lord into full oneness with his divinity" was the "one and universal sense" of both Testaments and the "soul of our doctrines." The Christian life was not vitalized by intellectual understanding of Christian truths, but by directly experiencing Jesus Christ in his glorified reality and being therefore "willing to do God's will." Thus here Nevin placed the will prior to the intellect, a posture he had held for all of his life. The Christian life was not primarily experienced by comprehending Christian truth. One had to live out the truth, having been apprehended by divine love. The glorification of Christ was sacramentally enacted in the regeneration of the individual believer.[17] After a lifetime of ambiguity, Nevin was clear that this was the entire process of a Christian's "spiritual new birth," not an instantaneous event at some precise point.

Nevin concluded with an argument for a spiritual, rather than naturalistic, interpretation of the Bible. His proof-text for the latter was the proceedings of an 1878 Prophetic Conference in New York.[18] Scripture was inspired, not because of some past and completed event through which its words were protected from error, but because the same Spirit that had brought its words into being was continuing to speak in and through it.

---

17. This position completes, and raises to a spiritual level Nevin's earlier argument that a person's "obedience [to the law], to be complete, must be intelligent and spontaneous. In other words, the law must enter into him and become incorporated with his life" ("Human Freedom," 417; repr. in *Human Freedom, and A Plea for Philosophy*, 22).

18. See General Introduction.

"The Bread of Life: A Communion Sermon"[1]: From the text: "Give us this day our daily bread."— Matt. vi. 11.

[Physical Food and Spiritual Food]

The life of man in the present world consists of different orders of existence. In broad view it may be distinguished into simple bodily life, natural life, and spiritual life; in other words, into the life of the body, the life of the natural mind, and the life of the rational mind or the spirit. These form totally distinct spheres; while they are joined together necessarily at the same time in the true wholeness of our human being. Such conjunction, it is easy to see, can be only in the way of inward organization; which implies superiority in one direction and subordination in another; and what the normal and only right order for this is, admits of no question. The life of the body appears first in time, and the life of the spirit last; but that is not the order of our actual substantive being. Here, as in general, the law prevails, the first last and the soul, the truly rational mind, irradiated by the light of heaven, flowing into it from a yet higher sphere. The whole life of man in this view is as a scale of ascending degrees, the bottom of which is his corporeal existence and the summit his spiritual existence; or say rather it is like a palace or temple, where the real meaning and worth of the exterior depend throughout on the significance of the interior—the spiritual forming here the inmost, the very *adytum*[2] or sanctuary of man's proper being, to which his merely natural mind stands related then as immediate vestibule, while his body surrounds all as outward court.

With this general distinction now in the unity of our proper human life corresponds in full, a like distinction in the idea of the nutriment or food by which the life needs to be supported and maintained. The law or necessity of such nutriment lies in the very conception of all so-called finite life; this can never be in animal, man, or angel, as any separate possession, but only as something continuously received from God; and the order of the universe shows this to be everywhere through divinely

---

1. Preached in Easton, October 27, 1878, during the late meeting of Synod in that place; reproduced and published now in this Quarterly Review by general request of the ministers and elders present on the occasion. [The *Reformed Quarterly Review* 26 (January 1879) 14–47.]

2. [Trans. "the innermost sanctuary of an ancient Greek temple."]

appointed *media* or means, in which the vivific presence of his word or spirit is embodied for this purpose. That is the fundamental sense of bread or food; as is signified indeed by the Old Testament declaration, "Man doth not live by bread only, but by every word that proceedeth out of the mouth of the Lord doth man live" (Deut. viii. 3); the pregnant scripture which was quoted with such grand effect by our Saviour in the wilderness, when the devil would have persuaded him to a magical inversion of the divine order of the world, by reaching through natural potency after what could be effectually gained only in the way of spiritual power descending from God (Matth. iv. 4).[3] That was the temptation; and here was the victory of the great captain of our salvation. An image of which we have in the life of every truly regenerated man. For whether we will lay it to heart or not, the question on which all regeneration turns for every one of us in the present world resolves itself just into this: shall we try to live by bread only, holding ourselves to the energies which go to make up for us here the conception of food for our material and merely natural existence; or will we allow the Lord of life and glory to enter into us as the principle of life above and *beyond* all this, so that the divine word proceeding out of his mouth (not dead, but living and life-giving), shall be in us the food of our true spiritual existence, "the bread which cometh down from heaven that a man may eat thereof and not die" (John vi. 50). Of one sense with which is the word going before in the same chapter "Labor not for the meat (or food) which perisheth, but for that food which endureth unto everlasting life, which the Son of man shall give unto you; for him hath God the Father sealed"; that is, the Divine in him hath made the human in him participant of all its own celestial life in order that the glorified humanity of the Lord might be thus the fountain head of life for all flesh to the end of time (John xvii. 1–5).

All this goes to show what we have here immediately in view, namely, not only that there are different sorts of food for the different spheres of life we have in us, but also that these different sorts of food are inwardly graduated and correlated one with another, in a way that answers exactly to what we have just seen to be the mysterious conjunction of the several lives they are appointed to feed and nourish. The body has its food of one kind; the natural understanding has its food of another kind; the rational spirit has its food again essentially different from both.[4] But the several foods, like the several lives, belong to one constitution and regard one end; and the order which binds them together, and determines their legitimate functions and use, is the

---

3. [Swedenborg, *Arcana coelestia*, vol. 1, §276: "By 'bread' is meant everything spiritual and celestial, which is the food of the angels, on the deprivation of which they would cease to live as certainly as men deprived as bread or food."]

4. [Cf. Swedenborg, *Arcana coelestia*, vol. 2, §1480: "But the various foods succeed one another in the following order: celestial food is all the good of love and charity from the Lord; spiritual food is all the truth of faith: on these foods the angels live; and from them comes forth the food, likewise celestial and spiritual, but of a lower angelic degree, on which angelic spirits live; from this again there comes a still lower celestial and spiritual food, which is that of reason and thence of memory—knowledge, on which good spirits live; and lastly comes corporeal food, which is proper to man while he lives in the body"; on the "influx from the Lord" needed to sustain all things, see further vol. 2, §2026 [2].]

same precisely that reigns in the organism of the several lives. The food of the body lowest or outmost; the food of the spirit highest or inmost. The outmost here again first in appearance, and the inmost last. But the inmost thus seemingly last, in true essentiality really first; and thus, of course, the veritable principle and true energizing power of all going before. This means necessarily, that whatever of potency there may be in material food to nourish the body, or in intellectual food (terrestrial science and knowledge of every sort) to nourish the natural mind, all such energy and force can be in these subordinate forms of nutrition only by direct derivation from the potency which belongs to food in its highest spiritual view—which, in its supreme sense, our Lord in the plainest terms declares to be himself. Man liveth by bread in any degree of his existence, only because of the word of God which is in it for this purpose. But who, with any thought, may not see that this of itself means that such word or law can be truly thus resident in a lower ordinance or appointment, only by the word in its highest view (the divine *logos*) reaching down to such lower range of existence with the full power of its own life?[5] In this view Jesus Christ is the beginning of the creation of God, and therefore also its end. He is before all things, and by him, or literally in him, all things consist (Col. i. 17).

[The Word as the Source of Spiritual Food]

That, therefore, which makes bread life-sustaining in its lowest form, and which causes it thus to *be* bread really and truly, is ever the benediction of the Lord, not resting upon it merely as an outward *power*, but entering into it from above in the most real and living way. So it is said of the Israelites, that in the use of the manna, which in itself was material though miraculous bread, "man did eat angels' food" (Ps. lxxviii. 25). Not that the angels actually do eat manna; but because the spiritual food by which the angels live, was bound by inward living correspondence to that lower terrestrial food; so that if there had been any spiritual sensibility on the part of the Jewish people (which as a general thing there was not), the use of this lower food would of itself have put them in real communication with the very bread of heaven which is here spoken of as angels' food. There is in this way, we may easily see, something sacramental in all natural bread.[6] It is universally the visible sign of an invisible grace. It is what it is

---

5. [Cf. Swedenborg, *Arcana coelestia*, vol. 1, §775: "From celestial and spiritual goods and their derivative truths, issue and descend natural goods and truths. For there is never any natural good and truth that does not spring from spiritual good, and this from the celestial, and also subsist from the same. If the spiritual should withdraw from the natural, the natural would be nothing. The origin of all things is in this wise: all things, both in general and in particular, are from the Lord; from him is the celestial; from him through the celestial comes forth the spiritual; through the spiritual the natural; through the natural the corporeal and the sensuous. And as they all come forth from the Lord in this way, so also do they subsist from him, for, as is well known, subsistence is a perpetual coming into existence."]

6. That our bodily food admits of easy comparison with what serves in a higher view to nourish the mind and soul, is universally acknowledged. But why it should be so is not so readily seen. With

as food not in virtue of its outward matter, but wholly and entirely in virtue only of the divine blessing which is in it mystically, the word proceeding out of the mouth of the Lord, which coming down from heaven lives in it perpetually and makes it to be bread indeed, having in it power to "strengthen man's heart." So much is signified at once in our Christian practice of asking the blessing of God on our daily meals. They are thus *sanctified*, raised from mere nature to the region of the spirit, by the word of God and prayer. The natural in no form or shape can be what it is required to be for even natural ends, except through conjunction with the spiritual; and the spiritual is nothing again except by direct living derivation from the divine. That is what all sanctification means. All blessing, whether in eternity or time, means that. It is the benediction of the Lord, proceeding from the fullness of life in the Lord himself, and descending from him, as the very power of his own life, through all the heavens, down to the uttermost part of the earth.

What has now been said may enable us to understand the petition, *Give us this day our daily bread*. It has been made a question, whether the prayer should be taken as referring altogether to mere natural food, or as meaning also something higher; and every such higher regard, in any case, has been commonly held to be a sort of secondary sense at best, derived from the other in the way of metaphor or ordinary figure of speech. But the relation of spiritual to natural is never any such mere metaphor or trope. The trope always inverts the true order of natural and spiritual, by making the natural to be first and the spiritual second; and is thus in truth nothing but a turning of the natural in one form into the natural in another form, which as such never reaches the sense of the real spiritual at all. The actual relation between the two orders of existence, nature and spirit, is always and at every point just the reverse of this; the spiritual first, inmost, primordially substantial and real; the natural secondary,

---

most persons, who ever think on the subject at all, it is taken to be something arbitrary, or the result at most of merely outside observation, fixing itself on certain points of resemblance in the comparison more fanciful than real. But it needs only small reflection to see that the case involves in it far more than this. Where minds of every order, young and old, rude and educated, savage and civilized, come together, as they do all the world over and through all ages of the world, in such a conception as this, so as not to be even aware generally of any comparison or metaphor whatever in speaking of the mind or soul as nourished by inward food—what can it possibly mean less than the living sense of a true interior communication between the two orders of existence thus correlated, which goes immensely deeper than the notion of any mere outward resemblance such as is implied by comparison or metaphor in the common view?

Indeed the more we look into the matter, the more we shall find that the force of all true comparison and figure of speech, resolves itself in the end into such under-sense of the world's life, as the only sufficient key for what comes into view on its surface. Thus every genuine comparison carries in itself a latent parable. This is eminently the case with all the tropical language of the Bible; as how indeed should it not be, if the mind of God, comprehensive of all truth in its universality and not merely in its particulars, be actually that which makes the inspiration of the Bible as we profess to believe it? But all genuine poetry, also, in its lower degree, addresses itself mainly to the interior inner sense of the world in the same way; and here is just the difference, between poets who have the true *poietic* or creative faculty, and poets who have no such faculty, but only in place of it the poor art of garnishing the outside of things with their own conceits and fancies.

outmost, phenomenally transient, and universally dependent on the spiritual every moment for any shadow of existence it may seem to have in its own right. The case being so, we may see what a madness it is with our natural science to make all of nature, as it commonly does, and nothing of spirit, or to dream of mastering the mystery of spirit by the outside dissection of nature in the study of God's universe. A task, desperate as the passing of a camel through a needle's eye! But must we not count it then a still greater insanity, to apply any such inversion of order to the interpretation of God's word, which by general confession is held to be the very presence of the divine itself under cover of human speech? Can the natural here be primary anywhere, and the spiritual only secondary and subordinate? Must not any imagination of that sort subvert effectually the very idea of sacred Scripture, the whole doctrine of inspiration?[7]

[The Meaning of "Give Us This Day Our Daily Bread"]

Apply this now to the point before us; and we may readily see what is the necessary sense of the prayer, Give us this day our daily bread. It does not exclude the thought of bodily food. The spiritual in a man never shuts out the natural in that mechanical way. On the contrary it needs and demands the natural; but then always only under the view of subordinate living coherence with the proper pre-eminence of the spiritual, whereby the natural shall be found to have in it the life of the spiritual as its own life. Nothing less than this, we have already seen to be the wide scriptural idea of bread or food. It is comprehensive of natural food, intellectual food, and spiritual celestial food—the bread of angels; but of these in the order of the several lives, which are thus

---

7. Inspiration means the mind or word of the living God. That can never be something dead. It lives and abides for ever. The living presence and power of the Lord are in it perpetually. It is so in nature. By the word of the Lord were the heavens made, and all the host of them by the breath of his mouth. Were they thus made in the beginning, and then left to exist afterwards of and from themselves? Nay verily; such a thought is the very madness of atheism. The word is still in them at every point as their living soul; so that all visible and material things are not only outward signs and tokens of things invisible and eternal, but the actual expression of such things, just as a man's bodily face is the express image of his soul. And what shall we say then of the mind of God in his word, as we have this not only once spoken but enduringly present in the Bible? Is that to be considered living or dead—a transient breath only of common human speech, or a divine "word forever settled in heaven"? On the answer of our inmost heart to that crucial question turns the whole worth of our profession of faith in the doctrine of inspiration. And if the outward side of nature be for its spiritual side what we have just seen, not a dead monumental remembrancer of this simply in any way, but its living, speaking mirror, as the body is of the soul, who believing in the Bible, will dare to say that the relation between outward and inward here can be any less vital and vivific? And in that case, from which side of the composite creation, body or soul, outward natural letter or inward living spirit, must the interpretation of God's Word proceed, if it is to be ever rational or truly sane? In the light of this solemn thought, we think of our modern vaunted science of biblical hermeneutics, and cannot help feeling with deep sadness, "*Thou art weighed in the balances, and art found wanting!*" [See article introduction for an explanation on the background of Nevin's hermeneutics; one should also consult DiPuccio, *Interior Sense*, 25–114.]

supported in man, that he may be a true image of God unto everlasting life. In this order, spiritual bread is prior and natural bread posterior; as the soul is first, and the body second in our common human constitution. So the angels of course see the case in the light of heaven; and so must it be regarded then everywhere by the Bible also, if this be indeed descended from the very light of heaven (which inspiration means), and be not a mere *ignis fatuus*[8] of earth dancing before the distempered vision of men in the name of such light.

And most of all, we may say, is it rationally unthinkable, that the Lord's Prayer, that wonderful synopsis of the kingdom of God, the New Creation in broad distinction from the old, should be guilty of any such anachronism, as would be implied by allowing the merely natural to appear in it anywhere, under any other view than as something wholly subservient to the true idea of this kingdom in its proper supernatural character and form.

No one can stand in the bosom of the Prayer itself, having in him any sense of the living inspiration which breathes in it still from the Incarnate Word by which it was first spoken, without feeling it to be from beginning to end, the living testimony of Jesus Christ, the very presence of the kingdom of heaven itself, moving in perpetual progress from its *alpha* in the Lord to its *omega* in the Lord. All starts in himself as the manifestation of the Father, in whom only God is knowable or approachable for men. The address, therefore, *Our Father who art in heaven*, can have properly no other object than his own glorified humanity.[9] Outside of that, God can be for men only an abstraction, an unreality, a mere mental figment, and so of course an idolatry. Hence it follows, *Hallowed be thy Name*. No earnest student of the Bible needs to be told what this name means. A thousand passages show it to have but one sense. It is God revealed or made known in Christ. Not through any outward revelation simply; for that would mean nothing. But through a real letting down of the Divine into the human in Christ, whereby this should become a living transcript and mirror of the Divine (as the old church fathers were fond of putting it), into which men gazing then by the vision of faith might be changed into the same image, from glory to glory, as by the Spirit of the Lord. All which is signified indeed in those words of our blessed Lord where he says: "I have glorified thee on the earth; I have finished the work which thou gavest me to do. And now, O Father, glorify thou me with thine own self, with the glory which I had with thee before the world was. I have manifested thy name unto the men which thou gavest me out of the world" (John xvii. 4–6). Here, as we can plainly see, the glorification of Christ's humanity is the manifesting or showing forth of the Father's name; which is declared to be, at the same time, the "finishing of the work"

---

8. [Lit., "foolish fire." Refers to flitting phosphorescent lights, especially over swamps or marshes, thus an "illusory thing."]

9. [Christ's "glorified humanity" is the first of two "ground truths" in Nevin's ontology of revelation (see article introduction). It corresponds to the lower levels of (1) faith, (2) the first table of the law as love of God, and (3) the "possibility of reception" of intelligence.]

for which Christ came into the world. And thus it is that the continuous glorification or hallowing of this name in heaven and on earth becomes of itself the highest conception we can form of the new creation, or universal reign of righteousness and salvation, of which Jesus Christ is at once both the origin and the end.

Hence accordingly the next petition, *Thy kingdom come*; and then immediately, in descending order, *Thy will be done in earth as it is in heaven.* The will of God thus done in heaven is itself the very substance of heaven, and so then of course the very substance of the same kingdom among men on the earth. And this can mean nothing less than life from the Lord in such doing of his will; since his will can have no substance that is not life in its inmost essence. In and by that life the angels live; it is for them evermore the very bread of heaven, not figuratively but most really and truly, as we have it symbolized in the manna with which the Israelites were fed of old in the wilderness.

And who now, with any sense of this in his mind, can help seeing that the petition next following in the Lord's Prayer, *Give us this day our daily bread*, must have for its object immediately and directly only the same celestial sense. It regards food, not in its ultimate mundane degree, but in its highest spiritual degree; from whence only any true vitalizing force can descend into what is mundane. The petition means: Give us continually the aliment by which the angels live, that we may do thy will as they do it, and thus have the kingdom of God brought into us more and more as righteousness, peace and joy in the Holy Ghost.[10] Let no one say that this is to resolve the idea of food into sheer abstraction. The will of God in the angels, as we have just seen, is no abstraction, no notion of their own simply in regard to divine truth and right; but positive living substance, of such sort that through the doing of the same it can be incorporated into their very inmost being, and so nourish them unto everlasting life. But we have a still higher example here than that of the angels, to lift us above the gross carnality of our common human thinking on this subject. Our blessed Lord himself, in the days of his flesh, found real substantial sustenance by appropriating to himself the divine will in the same way. "I have meat to eat," we hear him saying on one occasion, "that ye know not of. My meat is to do the will of him that sent me, and to finish his work" (John iv. 32–34). And so he tells us again: "I came down from heaven, not to do mine own will, but the will of the

---

10. [Nevin's reading is consistent with an important stream of patristic exegesis. The word for "daily" is ἐπιούσιον (*epiousion*), "superessential" or "supersubstantial," a word unique in all of Greek literature to the Matthean and Lukan versions of the Lord's Prayer. Origen thought it to be "that which nourishes the true humanity, the person created after the image of God." While Cyprian urged it to be "understood both spiritually and simply," he also emphasized that Christ as the "bread of life" is "not the bread of all" but the bread of "those who touch in body" the Eucharist. Asking for this bread *today* was a prayer that there would be no offense to keep Christians from receiving the eucharistic bread "daily." Jerome found a solution to the word's obscurity in its Aramaic equivalent *maar*: "it means 'for tomorrow,' so that the meaning is 'Give us this day our bread' for tomorrow, that is, the future." One could read this future as the eschatological banquet, since the Lord's Prayer itself is directed toward the arrival of the divine kingdom. See Manlio Simonetti, ed., *Ancient Christian Commentary on Scripture, New Testament* 1A: 135; The New American Bible, rev. ed., Matt 6:11 note (accessed at http://www.usccb.org/bible/mt/6:11).]

Father that sent me" (John vi. 38). This means no such miserable outside office work as our commentators too commonly make of it;[11] but a progressive growing of the human side of his life into the divine side, so that these became at last, in and by his glorification, fully of one constitution and measure; according to the clause in the Athanasian Creed, "As the reasonable soul and flesh is one man, so God and man is one Christ." Not two Christs, as in the Nestorian heresy.[12]

[Old Testament Types of the Sacramental Presence of Christ]

And this celestial food now, the bread of angels, the bread of life, which our Saviour calls his "flesh given for the life of the world," and of which he says, "he that cometh to me shall never hunger, and he that believeth on me shall never thirst";[13] this self-same

---

11. [The threefold offices of Christ—prophet, priest, and king—is a standard theme of Reformed dogmatics. See Calvin, *Institutes*, ed. McNeill, 2:15.1–6; Westminster Confession of Faith, VII.1. Nevin had registered his objection in "Sartorius on the Person and Work of Christ": "Christ executes all his offices in a comparatively outward way, parallel thus in kind with the Old Testament prophets, priests, and kings. . . . He reveals truth, buys righteousness, and exerts power, all in an external instrumental manner; instead of being in fact, as he always claims to be, in the very constitution of his own person, *the* way, *the* truth, *the* resurrection, and *the* life" (in *The Incarnate Word*, ed. Evans, 20).]

12. Among the various, we will not say absolutely false, but deplorably inadequate conceptions of the gospel, which narrow and lame the full sense of it with our different churches at this time, none is more melancholy perhaps than the general shade which is cast upon the significance of his glorification. If anything in the world is clear, it would seem to be this plain testimony of the Holy Scriptures, extending from Genesis to the Apocalypse, that our Lord's human life in the world, his glorious incarnation, was not a stationary wonder at any point, but a real progression (like all real human life), by which, through successive stages, he wrought out, by and of himself, the full union of the human with the divine in his own person; all this, only through measureless temptation, conflict, sorrow, and victory, ending in his passion on the cross; and thus only by his glorification "finished the work" which he had come into the world to do, and so made it possible for men to be saved in the sense of his own declaration: "Thou hast given him power over all flesh, that he should give eternal life to as many as thou hast given him; and this is life eternal, that they might know thee the only true God, and Jesus Christ whom thou hast sent." What does such language mean, if not that the whole Gospel is comprehended in the manifestation of God, brought to pass in the accomplished glorification of Christ's humanity as it could be in no other way? This was the supreme object of his incarnation. "To this end was I born" he says, "and for this cause came I into the world, that I might *bear witness to the truth*." [John 18:37] Whatever may be said of other doctrines then, they can have no real worth or force except by comprehension in what he himself makes to be the sum of all when he says, "Father, glorify thy Son that thy Son also may glorify thee." [John 17:1] This is the doctrine of all doctrines; the article, we may truly say, of a standing or falling church. But how little, alas, we hear of it in our evangelical pulpits and schools at this time. Our Christianity is weak for the want of it; and can have no strength against the "armies of the aliens" (infidel science and Roman superstition), so long as this want endures. That is the *revival* the church now needs; and it can come only from the Lord, as a new epiphany through his Word; as the prophet of old prays: "Oh that thou wouldest rend the heavens, that thou wouldest come down, that the mountains might flow down at thy presence, as when the melting fire burneth;—to make thy name known to thine adversaries, that the nations may tremble at thy presence!" [Isa 64:1–2.]

13. [John 6:35.]

food it is, we say, and no other, which is signified and sealed for our use in the holy sacrament of the Lord's supper under its simple symbols of bread and wine.

These symbols were not something new in the institution of the Lord's supper. They had been in use for the same general purpose long before; and it is only by considering this previous use, that we can at all rightly appreciate their full spiritual significance in the Christian sacrament. We find them brought prominently into view in the solemn religious service performed by Melchizedek, king of Salem, on the occasion of Abram's return from the slaughter of the kings as narrated in the 14th chapter of Genesis. This "priest of the most high God," it is written, representing in its decadence an older and far better dispensation of revealed religion than the Jewish, "brought forth bread and wine," and made them the medium of a holy spiritual intercommunication between the patriarch and the God whose minister he was; using for the solemnity such grand eucharistic words, as in their supreme sense can be understood most assuredly only of the great captain of our salvation, Jesus Christ. "He blessed him," we are told, "and said, Blessed be Abram of the most high God, possessor of heaven and earth: and blessed be the most high God, which hath delivered thine enemies into thy hand." And Abram, it is added, "gave him tithes of all."[14] Who, with any faith in God's Word, can help feeling, under the effulgent light especially of the 110th Psalm, and the use which is made of it in the 7th chapter of the Epistle to the Hebrews, how all this looks from that remote antiquity directly to the communion between the glorified Christ (possessor of all power in heaven and in earth, Matth. xxviii. 18), and his redeemed people to the end of time! And who then in the sense of that, can help feeling also the profound parable which lies in the elements of bread and wine, as they go here to make up together the idea of that divine food, by which alone through Christ communion of men with God in the way of life can be maintained? The parable does not start with Judaism. It belongs to the *origines sacrae*[15] of all heaven-descended religion, far back of that heavily beclouded dispensation. And that vast antiquity of itself shows the sign here as related to the thing signified, to be more than a mere arbitrary hieroglyphic. No *genuine* parable is ever that only. The significance of all parables rests in a real, and not simply imaginary or notional correspondence between the natural and the spiritual, as they are made to come together always in their constitution.

Coming down to the Jewish economy, we find ourselves confronted with the old idea of celestial food, under cover of material food, in all manner of ways. The Passover of course, in this view, is of central significance; out of which, as we know, springs immediately the institution of the Lord's supper, summing up finally the sense

---

14. [Gen 14:18–20.]

15. [Trans. "origins of the sacred." The allusion is probably to *Origines Sacrae*, a 1662 work by Edward Stillingfleet, and reissued in numerous editions. It argued that "sacred history," taken as a factual account, was trustworthy and superior to "pagan" history. Nevin was probably saying: the warrant for the truth of the Bible lies not in evidences supplied by human reason, but in the revelation of the glorified Lord through the Bible.]

of the entire Jewish worship, and thus bringing it to its full end in Christ. Here the flesh and blood of the paschal lamb occupy the foreground in the sacred picture; but it included, we know, both bread and wine also, the germs of the coming Christian sacrament. And the soul of the entire service, as it is also of this Christian sacrament, was the idea of living fellowship with God through spiritual food derived from himself for that purpose, and here symbolized by the material elements of the paschal feast.

And what other than this evangelical sense is it that looks out upon us from heaven, through the universal sacrificial system of the Old Testament. The altar of burnt offering and the altar of incense, the daily morning and evening sacrifice, the holocausts and endless other offerings, were they not all one vast scheme of pictorial worship, significant of incorporation with the life of God, the substance of heaven, by and through the bread of God which in the fulness of time was to come down from heaven in his Son Jesus Christ (John vi. 33, 51). And here again, it must not be forgotten, we have in addition to these offerings of flesh and blood, another class of offerings consisting of bread and wine, and going as it were hand in hand with them, to make their sense whole and complete. So ultimately, the system culminates in the table of the shew bread in the holy place, with its frankincense and wine, and its twelve loaves answering to the twelve tribes of Israel, which the priests in behalf of the tribes were to eat in the holy place every week as an offering "most holy unto the Lord."

It would carry us too far, to go here into any particular consideration of the manna, provided miraculously for the sustentation of the natural life of the Israelites in the wilderness. What it signified mystically is set forth so plainly in the New Testament, and with such emphasis especially by our Lord himself in the 6th chapter of St. John's Gospel, that there can be no room for question or doubt in regard to its meaning. And what is thus true of the manna, is no less true of its companion miracle, the water from the rock in Horeb.[16] Here we have the element of water in place of the element of wine; but the general mystical meaning is the same, though not without a particular difference which it is not necessary here to notice. "Baptized unto Moses in the cloud and in the sea," the Israelites, we are told, "did all eat the same spiritual meat, and did all drink the same spiritual drink, for they drank of that spiritual rock that followed them, and that rock was Christ" (1 Cor. x. 2–4.)

So universally throughout the Old Testament, we have this two-fold representation of meat and drink brought into view, to signify the aliment of the soul, the true spiritual bread of life, which is always represented, at the same time as being nothing less than a real communication of life to men from the Lord himself. Of which it may be sufficient to quote here that one classic example: "Ho, every one that thirsteth, come ye to the waters, and he that hath no money; come ye, buy and eat; yea, come, buy wine and milk without money and without price. Wherefore do ye spend money for that which is not bread? and your labor for that which satisfieth not? hearken

---

16. [Exod 17:6–7.]

diligently unto me, and eat ye that which is good, and let your soul delight itself in fatness" (Is. lv. 1, 2).

And to all this prefiguration and prophecy, the "testimony of Jesus,"[17] in the interior sense of the Old Testament, comes responsively then the open voice of the "faithful and true witness" himself in the New Testament: "I am the bread of life; he that cometh to me shall never hunger; and he that believeth on me shall never thirst." "As the living Father hath sent me, and I live by the Father, so he that eateth me, even he shall live by me." "If any man thirst let him come unto me, and drink." "Let him that is athirst come; and whosoever will, let him take the water of life freely" (John vi. 35, 57; vii. 37; Rev. xxii. 17).

In the Lord's supper, as already intimated, the Old Testament ritualism passes away as a scroll through the finished work of our Lord Jesus Christ. But not one jot or tittle of its interior sense, as he himself assures us, has been allowed to fail. All is fulfilled, and made of perennial force, in his kingdom; and thus it is, that in this simple institution, all the rays of heavenly light which we have found bearing on the great subject before us, from the earliest time, converge at last, as with a blaze of glory, in what is felt at once to be here their true focus. The universal sense of all meets us in the words: "As they were eating, Jesus took bread, and blessed it, and brake it, and gave it to the disciples, and said, Take, eat; this is my body. And he took the cup, and gave thanks, and gave it to them, saying, Drink ye all of it; for this is my blood of the new testament, which is shed for many for the remission of sins. But I say unto you, I will not drink henceforth of this fruit of the vine, until that day when I drink it new with you in my Father's kingdom" (Matth. xxvi. 26–29).

[The Sacrament and the Word of God]

The meaning of the holy sacrament, then, is sufficiently plain. It is intended to actualize, or make real, for the disciples of Christ, the idea of that spiritual nourishment or food (both as meat and drink), which according to the universal testimony of the Bible can be nothing less ever than real participation in the life of the Lord himself. The life, we say, is spiritual; not natural, and still less corporeal; and therefore not to be thought of for a moment as bound in any way in the material elements employed for its sacramental representation. But still not for this reason any less substantial, but only far more substantial, far more objectively real, than all natural or material existence. For it is the *word of God* divinely joined with the elements which makes the sacrament, according to the ancient Christian fathers; and this word, proceeding out of the mouth of the Lord, wherever it is found, hath that life in it by which only it is possible for men to live.[18]

---

17. [See Nevin, "Testimony of Jesus," 5–33.]

18. "*Accedit verbum ad elementum et fit sacramentum.*" [Trans. "The word is added to the element, and there results the Sacrament." (Augustine, *In Iohannis Evangelium tractatus*, 80, 3; trans. in *Nicene*

The Bread of Life: A Communion Sermon

The food, in one word, which is thus set before us on the Lord's table (whether we say *table* or altar here does not come to much), is the love and wisdom of the Lord, which together constitute the being of God, and which in the measure of his capacity for their conjunct reception constitute the being of man also, so that without them there can be no true human being for any man. Made in the image of God, men have in them two fundamental faculties or possibilities for such double reception, namely, will and intelligence; will for the admission of the divine love, which is essentially what good means, and intelligence for the admission of the divine wisdom, which is essentially what truth means. These are related as essence and form, inward and outward; the will as love always governing the understanding as truth; while in their union they form the only positive substance of every man; which is determined then wholly by what of life, in such double form, he is found to have in him from the Lord.[19] And thus it is that his mind and soul live only and always, not from himself, but from what thus flows into him from the Lord, in such spiritual force, just as really as his body is fed and nourished by food similarly received and appropriated in natural form. This also, as we know, only from the Lord, whose word perennially present in the food gives it such natural force. For in him, corporeally, naturally, and spiritually, in like degree and measure, we all live, move, and have our being.

We find it hard to conceive of our intellectual and spiritual life in this way; but only because the spiritual world has for us commonly no objective substantiality, answering at all to our sense of reality in the outward natural world. To speak of love and wisdom, of the good and true, as positive substances, having in them the very essence of life itself, in God first, and then from God in angels and in men, strikes

---

and Post-Nicene Fathers, 7:344.)] For the right understanding of the holy sacraments, no key is more useful than the patristic aphorism here quoted; only all depends in the case on our being able to enter into the patristic sense of the *word of God*, then, as distinguished from the far lower sense in which this is too commonly understood by our modern exegesis. The word of God in the general modern view is looked upon as only a human word, that is, as the divine let down into human thought and human speech, these having the power of the divine in them at best in the way only of outward fiat, breathed over them rather than into them as a real inspiration from heaven. Thought of in that way, the word of God joined to a sacrament can mean no more than its supposed divine appointment; which leaves the elements to their own nature; and then we have either fetischism or cold abstract intellectualism. But in the mind of the early Christians the word of God was immeasurably more than that. Its procession from the mouth of the Lord, was for them a continuous going forth of life from the Lord; and when it was thought of in this view as joined by the Lord himself to his holy sacraments, it was thought of as the living soul of these sacraments through all time. In our past controversies with regard to baptism and the Lord's supper we may not have done justice always to what must be considered in this way the true and real pre-eminence of the Word above all sacraments. In contending for the faith delivered to the saints in regard to the sacraments, we may have failed to intone properly what the presence of the Lord in his Word means, without which there is no room to conceive of his presence among men in any other form. Should this have been so, let us trust that it may be so no longer; while we unite mind and heart in seeking an understanding of divine inspiration better than that which now too commonly prevails, and join one and all, on bended knee, in the daily prayer, "Open thou mine eyes, O Lord, that I may behold wondrous things out of thy law." [Ps 119:18.]

19. [See article introduction for Nevin's "ontology of revelation."]

our mundane thought as absurd. True, the Bible is full of just such utterances; and our Christian creeds echo more or less distinctly the same mystical voice; and in our better moments we may seem to respond to it with some faint inward amen. But as a general thing, we do not believe a word of it. When our Saviour says, "The words that I speak unto you, they are spirit and they are life;"[20] that is, they have in them the very substance of eternal life; our impulse is at once to reply: "Oh, no; they cannot possibly be that; they are only abstractions, voices in the air, figures of speech, to be got rid of by the science of hermeneutics; this is an hard saying, who can hear it?"[21]

For all this, however, the foundation of God standeth sure, having this seal, The Lord knoweth them that are his.[22] Of all things real in the universe, the most absolutely real and substantial is the Word of God; which means the love of God dwelling in his will, and the wisdom or intelligence of God going forth from his love as truth, thought, speech, order, law; by which only, and in which, all things consist, and are what they are. And how is it to be imagined then for a moment, that angels or men should ever have in them any real being and life, except through comprehension in these ground factors of creation, the Divine love and the Divine wisdom, whose perfect union in the glorified Christ offers to our faith the full conception of the Christian redemption. That redemption holds supremely in the incarnate Word, thus glorified through the boundless sorrows of our Lord going before; and in this view it is the veritable spiritual food of which our Lord speaks, when he calls himself the bread of life; which he teaches us to pray for in the petition, Give us this day our daily bread; and which he offers to us continually in his holy sacrament, under the cover of bread and wine, through the affecting words: "*Take, eat, this is my body*; Drink ye; this is my blood of the new testament, which is shed for many for the remission of sins."

[How Do We Approach the Lord's Table?]

And how is it now that we are to approach the table of the Lord in his holy supper, so as to prove in ourselves what is that good, and acceptable, and perfect will of God, which is here brought near to us for such heavenly use? In other words, how are we to draw nigh to God through the outer court of the sacrament, in such sort that he shall

20. [John 6:63.]

21. ["This is an hard saying": John 6:60. Nevin dealt with "the science of hermeneutics" in "Sacred Hermeneutics." He reviewed the history of "modern" hermeneutics, arguing that it resulted in a false antinomy of rationalism, which reduced supernatural truth to natural human speech, and a rationalistic supernaturalism, "which affects to be the divine let down into the forms of ordinary natural thought and speech" (p. 11). The former he later called "realism" (the Bible was a religious text like any other); the latter he described as "verbalism," since the *words* of the Bible were supernaturally protected "from error" (Nevin, "Christ the Inspiration of His Own Word," 42; the latter view would develop into the evangelical doctrine of "biblical inerrancy"). But both sides of the apparent dichotomy made (Nevin thought) the mistake of thinking the Bible could be interpreted by the same hermeneutical rules that applied any other text ("Sacred Hermeneutics," 15; "Christ the Inspiration of His Own Word," 39).]

22. [2 Tim 2:19.]

draw nigh to us from its interior sanctuary (the holy of holies), inspiring into our souls from beyond the veil, and through the invisible presence of his holy angels, something of the very life of heaven itself, as the angels know it and find in it their eternal joy?

We answer, in the first place: Not by any activity from ourselves thrown into the sacrament, in the sense of that old Jewish question, "What shall we do that we might work the works of God?"[23] which means simply, How shall we handle God's power and agency instrumentally, like electricity or steam, for our own service and benefit? Alas, how much of our Christian creed and worship resolves itself at last into what we thus dream of putting into divine things from our own intelligence and will, instead of yielding ourselves to the actual power of divine things as they are in themselves. So the Israelites must operate the manna to suit themselves (Ex. xvi. 20, 27, 28). And so even Moses must sin along with the people at large, when he smote the rock in Kadesh, with that impetuous speech, Hear now, ye rebels, must *we* fetch you water out of this rock? That was the temptation of which God says: I proved thee at the waters of Meribah (Numb. xx. 7–13; Ps. lxxxi. 7).

But to the question, How shall we come before the Lord in this sacrament? we answer again in the second place: Not by virtue of any magical efficacy supposed to be lodged in the outward form of the sacrament itself. There can be no such power of the natural over the spiritual anywhere, that the natural may be said to rule the spiritual in its own right. The spiritual can never be thus imprisoned, or *banned*, in the bosom of the mere natural. That is the conception of a fetisch; and all worship turned to such an object is idolatry, and as the sin of witchcraft. The water in baptism can never be in this way the principle or efficient of regeneration; and just as little can the bread and wine in the Lord's supper be ever in themselves what they sacramentally represent, namely, the glorified life of the Lord, which he calls the bread of heaven, and also the living bread brought down from heaven in his own person, "that a man may eat thereof and not die."

How then, we repeat the question, are we to "come before the Lord and bow ourselves before the high God"[24] in this holy sacrament; so as to avoid both of the two errors now mentioned—the self-activity of mere will-worship on the one side, and the stock-passivity of mere blind superstition on the other side—and thus find in the sacrament what our Lord himself makes it to be, the communion of his own body and blood unto everlasting life?

The general answer is simple enough. We are to come by repentance and faith. But, alas, both these ideas are wonderfully mystified for most of us by our reigning worldliness and false theology. What is repentance? It is knowing, acknowledging, and inwardly feeling, that we are involved in spiritual evils or sins; in earnestly desiring to be delivered from them; and in seriously proposing to obtain such deliverance by ceasing to do evil and learning to do good, with our eyes turned steadily toward

23. [John 6:28.]
24. [Mic 6:6.]

the Lord, from whom only we can ever have truly any such expectation. And who may not see that such looking to the Lord is then just what is to be understood by faith, which is thus the indispensable accompaniment and complement of repentance? For in truth they go ever hand in hand together. There can be no true repentance without faith; and so neither can there be any true faith without repentance. And what both together mean in the case of the holy sacrament now before us, is sufficiently plain. It is nothing less, indeed, than the living reconciliation of those seemingly contradictory alternatives, which we have just seen to be in their dead abstraction alike fatal to the true idea of the sacrament from opposite sides. Repentance sinks into nothing the thought of all self-operation on our part in the Christian mystery; and faith owns the supernatural operation of the Lord in it as strictly all in all; while this is recognized at the same time, however, in its only rational view, as being not outwardly magical in any sense, but an actual coming down of the divine from its higher sphere into the real life-sphere of the human.[25]

It is not our theoretical doctrine of the holy sacrament, therefore, our notion of the manner of Christ's living presence in its outward symbols, that can in any case bring us into the actual experience of its quickening power. This may be more orthodox with some and with others less orthodox intellectually; but that difference need not affect at all the acceptable and effectual use of the sacrament; just because in the end, it is not doctrine intellectually considered, but the life of doctrine, as this reigns in the will, which can ever bring with it any real appropriation of the love of the Lord. And that love of the Lord thus flowing into the soul, is itself real conjunction with the divine life, which is love (1 John iv. 8), and therefore the inmost conception we can possibly have of the substantial spiritual food by which only men or angels can be nourished unto everlasting life. Our speculative orthodoxy can never bring us to that. On the contrary, there is the greatest danger always that it may lead us in the full contrary direction. It is on the pure in heart, and not on the strong in theological speculation, that the benediction is pronounced, They shall see God.[26] Unto babes in the kingdom of God things are revealed, which are hidden from the wise and prudent.[27] It was the children who welcomed the Lord into his temple, with their glad Hosanna to the Son of David; when the chief priests and scribes saw in the occasion only matter for sore offence, and drew upon themselves that withering castigation,

---

25. [Cf. Swedenborg, *Arcana coelestia*, vol. 2, §1594 [4]: "But mutual love, which alone is heavenly, consists in a man's not only saying of himself, but acknowledging and believing, that he is utterly unworthy, and that he is something vile and filthy, which the Lord from his infinite mercy continually withdraws and holds back from hell, into which the man continually strives, nay longs, to precipitate himself. . . . So far therefore as a man acknowledges and believes himself to be such as he really is, he recedes from the love of self and its yearnings, and abhors himself. So far as he does this, he receives heavenly love from the Lord, that is, mutual love, which consists in the desire to serve all."]

26. [Matt 5:8.]

27. [Lk 10:21.]

"Have ye never read, Out of the mouth of babes and sucklings thou hast perfected praise?" (Matt. xxi. 15, 16; Ps. viii. 2).

Let us take all this properly to heart. "Whosoever shall not receive the kingdom of God as a little child," it is said, "shall in nowise enter therein" (Luke xviii. 17). If that be true of Christian life and worship generally, it should be considered most especially true of central worship in the sacrament of the Lord's supper, the key-stone that binds all else together, the holy of holies, where we come most directly before the Lord enthroned on the mercy-seat, and between the wings of the cherubim. Here, if ever, the innocence, the simplicity, the self-oblivion, of little children, is the only attitude that can comport at all with the solemnity of the transaction with which we are engaged. For what does the transaction mean? Heaven open; the angels of God ascending and descending upon the Son of man in the sacrament of his own living presence. Himself the supreme sense of all, and the fullness of eternal life for his universal kingdom. His worshipping church on earth in the posture of purely and wholly passive reception, with only the sense of spiritual hunger and thirst, opening the soul for the food of angels thus proffered for its use without money and without price. Coming thus to the holy sacrament, with full apprehension of our own ignorance, weakness, misery, and sin, and looking with faith to the Lord of the sacrament, who fulfils the internal sense of it in heaven, we place ourselves in real communication with the heavenly side of the transaction. We partake of the elements as natural food, with faith directed toward what they represent, and correspond with, as spiritual food; and so far as we do that, in childlike trust and simplicity, we may be very sure that the Lord will not fail to actualize within our souls (in a way transcending all natural perception or thought), the mystery of his own words: "He that eateth me, even he shall live by me. Because I live, ye shall live also. I am the vine, ye are the branches: abide in me, and I in you; as the branch cannot bear fruit of itself, except it abide in the vine, no more can ye except ye abide in me."[28]

Even so, come, Lord Jesus.[29] Amen.

---

28. [John 6:57; John 14:19; John 15:5; John 15:4.]

29. [Rev 22:20. This is a translation of what was doubtless a primitive Christian prayer in Aramaic: *Marana tha* (see 1 Cor 16:22).]

Appendix

In the way of general note to the foregoing discourse, we add here some loosely connected observations on certain doctrinal topics, having relation, not so much to separate points in the discourse, as to the subject of it in its whole view.

[The Glorification of Christ's Humanity]

I. The glorification of our Lord's humanity has been spoken of as the cardinal truth of the gospel. It is so set forth in the Old Testament and in the New. We may safely say that neither the Jewish ritual, nor the Jewish history, nor the psalms, nor the prophecies, are at all intelligible without it; and it is thus emphatically what is to be understood by the language of our Lord, when he says: "Think not that I am come to destroy the law, or the prophets; I am not come to destroy, but to fulfil. For verily I say unto you, Till heaven and earth pass, one jot or one tittle shall in no wise pass from the law, till all be fulfilled" (Matt. v. 17, 18). So again: "O fools and slow of heart, to believe all that the prophets have spoken! Ought not Christ to have suffered these things, and to enter into his glory?—Then opened he their understanding, that they might understand the Scriptures, and said unto them, Thus it is written, and thus it behooved Christ to suffer and to rise from the dead the third day; and that repentance and remission of sins should be preached in his name among all nations, beginning at Jerusalem" (Luke xxiv. 25, 26, 45, 46, 47). This is plain, and it can have but one meaning; namely, that the Old Testament and the New Testament have inwardly one and the same sense, and that this one and universal sense comes to its whole completion in the glorification of the humanity of our Lord into full oneness with his divinity; by which his "coming out from the Father" became for both in this view a full "returning again to the Father,"[30] according to the mystery of his own prayer, "Now, O Father, glorify thou me with thine own self with the glory which I had with thee before the world was" (John xvi. 28; xvii. 5). Other things come in also of course for their verification in the light of the gospel thus thrown back upon the Old Testament, to the extent even of such apparently unmeaning outward incidentals, as "Out of Egypt have I called my son"—"He shall be called a Nazarene"[31]—and other particulars of like sort, on which

---

30. [Allusions to John 14:28; John 16:10.]
31. [Matt 2:15, 23.]

so much silly commentary has been wasted;[32] but all else is plainly part only of the general movement, by which the life of Christ in the world was steadily determined throughout to his coming glorification, as the one great scope and purpose of his manifestation in the flesh. So the mystery of godliness is made to run its course by St. Paul: "God manifest in the flesh, justified in the spirit, seen of angels, preached unto the gentiles, believed on in the world, received up into glory." (1 Tim. iii. 16).

II. The whole power of the Christian faith resolves itself, in that way, into the ability of seeing and owning the glorification of the Lord Jesus Christ; as he himself says after his resurrection in the soul-stirring words: "All power is given unto me in heaven and in earth. Go ye therefore and teach all nations; and, lo, I am with you alway, even unto the end of the world."[33] His kingdom starts there. All the realities and verities of his kingdom reveal themselves there, first of all, in himself, as head over all things to the Church; so that they cannot be seen and inwardly acknowledged at all as objects of faith, except in the light of what he has thus become as the alpha and omega of the new creation. It belongs to the very nature of Christian faith, accordingly, that it should draw its life directly from the living Christ himself, thus seen in his glory, according to what is said, "In thy light we shall see light;"[34] and again, "I am the light of the world; he that followeth me shall not walk in darkness, but shall have the light of life."[35] So that Peter's faith (Matt. xvi. 16,17) is signalized just for this, that it was an overpowering sense of the divine majesty of Christ, revealed in him from the presence of the Lord himself without any outside teaching or reflection. His faith might take in much of knowledge and doctrine afterwards which was not then in his mind; but only by virtue of this first central confession; which thus became necessarily the rock, whereon all else must be built, that should go to make up in him the full structure of the Christian life. And so it is with every true Christian still. The soul of all doctrines is found only in the power of believing in the everlasting, glorified Christ.

Only by virtue of this faith can we believe for example, the being of God, his triunity, the creation of the world by God, divine providence, the atonement, regeneration, the inspiration of holy scripture. We may indeed receive these and other of truths of revelation intellectually, and seem to ourselves to hold them on rational evidence. They may be in us scientifically, systematically, rationally, and even sentimentally. We may preach them, contend for them, and think that we do well to be angry with all who refuse to see them as we ourselves do. But with all this, if they be not seen in the celestial light of our Lord's glorification, they will not be seen by us really at all. They will not be in us as actual truths, but only as imperfect phantoms of truth; for

---

32. And which might almost seem, indeed, to be in the sacred text, for the very purpose of stultifying the false view of inspiration, which underlies all such merely naturalistic trifling with the Word of God.

33. [Matt 28:18b—19a, 20.]

34. [Ps 36:9.]

35. [John 8:12.]

the simple reason that they will have no life in them. That is the necessary character of all that belongs to the mere understanding, before this comes to be vitalized and energized by love and affection infused into it from the will, felt as a force determined toward action. It was to such mental *believers* that our Saviour said, "If ye continue in my word,[36] then are ye my disciples indeed; and ye shall know the truth, and the truth shall make you free" (John viii. 31, 32). So in another place: "My doctrine is not mine, but his that sent me. If any man will do his will"—literally, will to do his will—"he shall know of the doctrine, whether it be of God, or whether I speak of myself" (John vii. 16,17). It is not outward knowing then, nor yet outward willing merely, as it may be called—that is, willing from interest or motive other than God's will itself—which can ever make divine doctrine or truth real and living for any man; but only willing to do God's will, out of regard to this will itself, as made known by his spoken word. Short of this truth or doctrine in a man's understanding is not in him properly at all; it is not appropriated to him as any part of his life, but is in him at best only as food from without capable of such appropriation, but waiting for the law of life from within to convert it really to any such use. Only the will of the Lord as love, abiding always in his word, and meeting from within the otherwise only outward faith which a man may have in the truths of the word, can ever quicken this faith into true heavenly vitality, and at the same time glorify the word into the full light of its own divine inspiration.

[Love, the Will, and Regeneration]

III. It is an old controversy whether faith or charity should be regarded as first in religion;[37] and outside of religion, it has been similarly debated whether truth or good should be allowed such primacy in man's life. At bottom it is the question, which of the two ground factors of the human mind, the understanding or the will, is to be considered chief or central in its constitution. All sound psychology assigns this distinction to the will.[38] But it is wonderful how, nevertheless, the opposite view is all the time ready to assert itself practically, making the intellectual side of our life to be first and its voluntary or affectional side second, both in the secular view and in the

---

36. Literally, if ye *abide* in my word; the same term that is used John xv. 4, 5, 6, 7; where the sense is fixed by the analogy of the union between the vine and its branches; and where also it is plain that the *word or words* of Christ can only mean himself living in his own speech or spoken will. Why in John xv. 9, again, should our version substitute "continue" for "abide," as used in the context both before and after? When it is clear that the love of God there spoken of as the bond of his union with Christ and his people, is nothing less than the living active power of his will in his commandments or word. "If ye keep my commandments," it is said, "ye shall abide in my love, even as I have kept my Father's commandments and abide in his love." Altogether, the substitution of *continuing* for *abiding*, in the case of this whole mystery, is unfortunate; it has the effect of externalizing it, and thus hiding its true inward sense.

37. [See further Nevin, "Testimony of Jesus," esp. 31–32.]

38. [See Nevin, "The Spirit of Prophecy," 182. Nevin was always concerned with the foundations of ethical action. See his 1848 essay, "Human Freedom."]

APPENDIX

religious. Science and learning, in this way, are held to be all sufficient for the world's affairs; and education in our schools is made to resolve itself entirely into what is merely intellectual culture; under the notion that the knowledge of truth so taken into the mind, is all that the young need to make them good, and virtuous, and wise, and to qualify them for acting their part properly in their generation. The madness of this in the secular order beggars all description. But what less is it in the sphere of religion, when faith as bare intelligence is allowed to exalt itself in the same way, over charity or love as the source of good works in the will?[39] Justification by faith involves a great truth over against justification by works, considered as of man himself, and carrying in them the notion of self-merit. Such works are dead; just because they proceed from the love of self and the world,[40] which is directly antipodal to the love of the Lord, the only source of any life for the human spirit. But faith, as the mere intellectual apprehension of divine truth in no conjunction with this heavenly life—that is, *faith without works*, as St. James puts it—is also dead; and therefore of no worth. It is in reality no faith, and the divine truth it lays hold of in that way is in reality no truth. Only "faith which works by love" (Gal. v. 6), can be living faith, and then the life is not from the faith as such, but from the love of God which is in it through the will. "Now abideth faith, hope, charity, these three," it is said; "but the greatest of these is charity" (1 Cor. xiii. 13). It might seem as if faith must be the original principle of the Christian life, because it is here mentioned first, and actually appears first in the process of our regeneration. But the end, here as everywhere, is in fact the beginning. It is like the progressive development of leaf, flower, and fruit, in all plant life, where foliage and efflorescence are but stages, through which the life of the fruit works from the beginning to bring itself to pass.[41] So faith in the mere understanding first, by virtue of the divine force of the truth which is in it as the word of God, finds itself gradually lifted more and more into positive communion with the interior lightsphere of the word, as this proceeds from the Lord of life and glory himself; brightens thus into Christian hope; and through this comes to full fruitage finally, in that which has been all along the inward scope and power of the movement, "charity out of a pure heart and of a good conscience and of faith unfeigned" (1 Tim. i. 5).

---

39. [Immanuel Kant (1724–1804) made the standard philosophical argument that the only human act or condition unconditionally good was the "good will" (*Groundwork for the Metaphysics of Morals*, 9 [Ak 4:393]). A truly good will was one that did its duty, and duty was defined by the "categorical imperative," stated most succinctly as "One must *be able to will* that a maxim of our action should become a universal law" (ibid., 37, 41 [Ak 4:421, 424]). Nevin was clearly influenced by Kant (most obviously evidenced in "Human Freedom"), but the present text can be read as Nevin's reformulation of Kant: the ground of goodness was not duty presented as a universalizable obligation, but love, made present through regeneration.]

40. [Nevin had argued as early as 1835 that due to people's sensuality, they substituted spiritual life with external religious forms: "The Grand Heresy," 246–47; repr., *New Mercersburg Review*, 48–53.]

41. [Here at the end Nevin returned to a primarily biological metaphor for spiritual life and growth (instead of "historical development").]

IV. The glorification of Christ, making him to be head over all things to the Church, is not only the power of all righteousness and salvation in his kingdom, but becomes in that view necessarily the prototypal pattern also of all that enters into the constitution of this kingdom, both in the Church at large and in individual believers. "Behold, I make all things new," it is said. "I create new heavens and a new earth; and the former shall not be remembered, nor come into mind" (Rev. xxi. 5; Is. lxvi. 17). A new spiritual creation of course, that means; transcending the whole order of things going before, and proceeding, not as doctrine but as living reality, from him who is the alpha and omega of the whole, by virtue of the all power in heaven and in earth to which he has been advanced through his human glorification. The new order of life thus brought into the world is what is expressed comprehensively by the term regeneration, in the sense of our Saviour's discourse with Nicodemus. It is not just of one sense with our Lord's glorification; for there must ever be an infinite distance between what belongs to him, and what belongs to angels or men. But there is a real correspondence, nevertheless, between the work which he wrought in himself, that "being made perfect he might become the author of eternal salvation unto all that obey him" (Heb. v. 9), and the work by which then such as obey him are made to have part in this salvation. Their spiritual new birth, running all through their life, is an image and counterpart of his quickening or vivification in the spirit— in virtue of which he says, "I, if I be lifted up, will draw all men unto me."[42] Hence it is that the glorification of Christ becomes the necessary key, for the right understanding of man's regeneration; as this throws light back also again on the mystery of the glorification. So that it must ever be a very poor theology, as well as a very poor practical Christianity, which has not yet been awakened to any lively interest in the study of the two mysteries under this reciprocal view.

[Prophetic Literalism and Hermeneutical Naturalism]

V. And what shall we say then of that theology and Christianity, which can find no room for the glorified Christ in the Holy Scriptures, the inmost sense of which, we are told, he came into the world to fulfil? Must all things that enter into his kingdom undergo spiritual change; so that the very truths of heaven itself may be said to need regeneration in men before they can enter as living stones (and not as dead) into the structure of the New Jerusalem; and yet the Word of God itself, from which all these truths are derived be held to the cerements of its merely natural sense, as if the living should be sought forever among the dead, and the Lord were not himself the inspiration of his own Word in any real way whatever!

Those who remember our article on "Sacred Hermeneutics," published in the Mercersburg Review for January, 1878,[43] will understand the meaning of this general

42. [John 12:32.]
43. [Nevin, "Sacred Hermeneutics," 5–38.]

interrogation; though it is quite possible all may not be prepared to appreciate fully the significance of it in the present connection. The importance of this subject, however, is so great, that we offer no apology for bringing it here again under notice; especially as we feel deeply, whether others see it or not, that so long as the *eidolon*[44] of naturalism continues to reign in our doctrine of inspiration, and to sway its sceptre from thence over our biblical exegesis and theology, the spiritualities of religion, on which we have been insisting in our present article, are not likely to find much serious consideration.

Just at the present time a good opportunity is offered for fixing attention intelligently on the low view of the Scriptures to which we refer, by the proceedings of the late so-called *Prophetic Conference* in New York; which were all based, as we learn, on a carefully prepared digest of first principles, bearing directly on this very subject. The meeting was highly respectable; and the object which drew it together deserves to be spoken of only with commendation. We, too, believe in the second coming of Christ, and look for it as the great hope of Israel in the gathering tribulation of these last times.[45] Our business now, however, is not with the meeting or its doings; but only with its openly professed theory of biblical interpretation; for the popular trial of which, as we have said, it presents so favorable an occasion.

The Conference in its proceedings,[46] affirms and assumes three fundamental propositions, as being of what it holds to be axiomatic force for all its discussions. *First:* "The authority of Holy Scripture is the basis of all knowledge that Christ will in any" way "return to this earth"; *Secondly:* "The language of Holy Scripture is the source of all information concerning both the matter and manner of" his "return"; *Thirdly:* The ordinary "laws of language" are "the instruments by which we are to construe" for this purpose what God speaks in the Bible.[47] Allowing the first two of these propositions to pass now unchallenged, although we *feel* very distinctly that they also are not free from latent error—we join issue here openly and boldly with the third, and pronounce it wholly irreconcilable with the idea of any true celestial inspiration in the Word of God.

To show that this is no rash or inconsiderate charge, we quote from the document in question the following passage, in which the mere human character of the

44. [Trans. "image," "idol."]

45. [Christ's "second coming," the role of "Israel" (it is not clear whether Nevin meant this literally or figuratively of the church), an impending "tribulation," and the contemporary age as the "last [end] times" would have been and still are commonplaces of prophetic literalism. Taking his comment at face value, he only departed from this literalism in his rejection of its hermeneutical presuppositions.]

46. ["The Prophetic Conference: New York, October 30, 31, November 1, 1878: Christ's Second Coming," *New York Tribune*, Extra No. 46. This conference represented the "personal pre-Millennial Advent of Jesus Christ" (p. 2): Christ would appear for a second time, and his return would precede and usher in the millennium, his one-thousand-year reign on earth, as a political regime. His return was imminent. It could occur at any time, rather than being pushed off into a virtually infinite future. See Marsden, *Fundamentalism and American Culture*, 48–62, for the shifts leading to and varieties of belief in "biblical prophecy."]

47. ["Prophetic Conference," 7–8. The editor has added quotation marks where required.]

Bible is made to overshadow its divine character altogether; showing how easy it is for pietism to join hands with rationalism, as has often been remarked, even while ostensibly making war upon it.

Speaking of the last of the three postulates just mentioned, the paper says: "But for the mystical, spiritualizing school of expositors we should have no need to do more than state this proposition. It would seem to be involved in the popular character of our Bible. Not in cipher, hieroglyphic, or cabalistic signs; but in the language and dialect of living men, with which grammar, rhetoric, and logic can closely deal, has God made known his purposes to us. There is no esoteric sense between the lines and beneath the letter. Spiritual discernment is a knowledge by experience and does not imply a superior intellectualism. Even the symbolic books have their glossary in other and plainer Scriptures. Similes, metaphors, and parables, indeed, abound; but these are all subject to the rules of interpretation which control in secular literature. We affirm, then, the law of Bishop Newton, that a literal rendering is always to be given in the reading of Scripture, unless the context makes it absurd. To vindicate this law from all cavil and establish the proposition which it expresses, one need only appeal to the common sense of any casual stranger to scholastic theology. Is it honest to argue with infidels on the basis of the literal fulfilment of prophecies relating to our Lord's first coming, and allegorize the predictions connected with these, in chapter, verse, and often clause, because they refer to his second appearing? What reason have we for holding in opposition to the Jew, that it was foretold where Christ should be born, where he should begin to preach, how he should enter Jerusalem, what varied sufferings he should endure, that he should hang upon the tree, that not a bone of his body should be broken, that his garments should be parted and his vesture be transferred by lot, that with transgressors he should die, and yet with the rich make his grave—what possible basis have we for asserting the historical fulfilment of all these prophecies which the Jews symbolize, if we, in our turn, spiritualize the plain and closely joined predictions of the glorious Messiah, which they interpret literally? Surely as a key tied by a string close to a lock are the scriptural interpretations of fulfilled prophecy. With these at hand, it is not difficult for the serious student to open the secret things of God."[48]

According to this, the mind of God is in his Word no otherwise than as the mind of a man is in his ordinary speech. It is there at best only as a translation of the divine into what is thus purely and exclusively human. And let it be noted, it is not even the human renovated by divine grace which is supposed necessary to serve as an organ for this purpose. It is simply the general "dialect of living men with which grammar, rhetoric, and logic can closely deal." What becomes then, in all seriousness we ask, of

---

48. [Ibid., 8. It is easy to see from this terminology the linkage of premillennialism to "commonsense realism," the epistemology that held all phenomena were transparent to reason, and the Bible was simply another empirical reality, in this case a "text," to be inductively grasped, comprehended, and synthesized. See Marsden, *Fundamentalism and American Culture*, 55–62.]

Appendix

St. Paul's high talk about the impracticability of bringing down the "things of the Spirit of God" to the plane of the mere natural understanding of man?[49] What becomes of the old evangelical idea, that only regenerate men, in distinction from such as are unregenerate, can have any power at all to know, or to teach, God's truth as we have it revealed in the Scriptures? Are we done with all that? Has the modern theology turned it at last into full obsolescence?

Not so, we may be told; it remains still true, that only the spiritual mind can discern the things of the Spirit. But that is an office for the spiritual mind *outside* of the written Word. The word itself has in its bosom no such distinction. It is for all alike, purely human thought in purely human speech. But the spiritual mind sees into it from itself divine things, while the natural mind sees in it what alone in fact is there, namely, human and terrestrial things! This is called "spiritual discernment." And yet "there is no esoteric sense," we are told, "between the lines and beneath the letter."[50] Of course not; what the "spiritual discernment" thus foists into the sacred text is not *esoteric* in the smallest degree. It is all supremely exoteric. The sense is not in the text at all, except as it is put there by the serene self-complacency of the supposed spiritual man.

[Christ the Inspiration of His Own Word][51]

For those who think in this way there is, of course, no really spiritual or internal sense[52] whatever in the Bible itself, as distinguished from its outward, natural, and merely literal sense. To think of *more* there than the bare human words express, an actual *under-sense* from the mind of the Lord himself, involved in the words by a divine logic, far beyond the logic of all merely human speech, is something which this class of logicians can only stigmatize as mystical extravagance. And yet the Bible itself is full of this very idea; and some sense of it has been present in the mind of the Church through all ages. Here again, however, our literalists manage to keep themselves in some sort of countenance, by resolving the old notion of such an *inspired* under-sense into the character of a simply outward metathesis or transposition of the natural sense in one view over to the same sort of sense again in another view. "Similitudes," they

---

49. [1 Cor 2:14.]
50. ["Prophetic Conference," 8.]
51. [The title of Nevin's penultimate essay, in 1882.]
52. ["Internal sense" is a recurring phrase in Swedenborg's *Arcana coelestia*: "This then is the internal sense of the Word [*Hic nunc est sensus Verbi internus*], its veriest life, which does not at all appear from the sense of the letter. But so many are its arcana that volumes would not suffice for the unfolding of them. A very few only are here set forth. . . . It is thus that the angels perceive the Word. They know nothing at all of what is in the letter, not even the proximate meaning of a single word. . . . They have an idea only of the things signified by the words and the names" (vol. 1, §64; Latin accessed at http://heavenlydoctrines.org/Writings%20Latin/Arcana%20Coelestia.htm). He stated his concept in more detail in vol. 3, §§2310–2311.]

tell us, "metaphors, and parables, abound in the Bible; but these are all subject to the rules of interpretation which control in secular literature."[53] True enough, we reply; and just for that reason all such flashes of light from cloud to cloud in the sphere of mere nature fall utterly short of the true idea of an interior sense in the Bible. For if any such sense be there at all, being as it must be directly of God and not of man, it can be nothing less than real light from the spiritual world falling from within upon the word, in its natural form, and thus for the soul of the believer causing this to glow with new celestial meaning and power.

And why should it not be so, if the mind of God be really and truly in the Bible, as a present and not simply past inspiration? Even our common human speech has a great deal more in it always, than we can see or take note of when we speak. It is common to say, indeed, that our thought and word in speaking are exactly the same; and that is true as regards the thought coming immediately before the word and next back of it. But such immediately next thought, all that we can see by direct consciousness at the time, belongs only to our external natural mind which forms but a small part here of our full inward existence. Behind this again, or rather within it, is the sphere of our mind proper, our rational mind, opening still more interiorly right into the spiritual world itself; and there it is, that the real complex forces, which enter as innumerable fibres into the constitution of our outward conscious thought and speech, are all the time at work for this end—though we know it not. And thus it is, that the hidden unknown of our daily mental life, whether as thought or speech, is always immeasurably more than the open and known side of it which it turns to our common waking consciousness.[54] There is in this way in a man's words, especially in the words of a man who thinks earnestly, much more than he himself sees at the time; for back of his words is this interior ocean of things invisible, immaterial, and eternal—the region of the universal in distinction from the single and particular, the region of ends and causes in distinction from mere effects—which is continually pressing, as it were, to come to some utterance in his outward thought and speech; and there only, all the time, reigns accordingly the true internal life of the man, in distinction from his relatively superficial external life.

How grandly this comes out in the internal sense of the 139th Psalm, where the omniscient providence of the Lord is made to regard especially just these depths of the human spirit, so unfathomable for the human spirit itself. "Thou understandest my thought afar off," it is said; away back in the ten thousand rills, which are flowing toward it continually from the ends of the universe, before it has become actually mine. "For there is not a word in my tongue, but, lo, O Lord, thou knowest it altogether. Such knowledge is too wonderful for me. It is high, I cannot attain unto it. Whither shall I go from thy spirit? or whither shall I flee from thy presence?" "Thou hast possessed my reins; thou hast covered me in my mother's womb." The conception and birth of

---

53. ["Prophetic Conference," 8.]
54. [Nevin appears to have anticipated the modern psychological notion of the "subconscious."]

Appendix

the outward body simply, in this view, is a stupendous wonder; but how much more the bringing forth of the spirit, the soul, the true inward man in the outward man. "I will praise thee! for I am fearfully and wonderfully made! marvelous are thy works; and that my soul knoweth right well. My substance"—not my material protoplasm, O thou foolish scientist! but my spiritual substantial being from God—"was not hid from thee, when I was made in secret, and curiously wrought in the lowest parts of the earth;" that is, deep down in the swaddling-bands of nature, where all created spiritual being must begin. There "thine eyes did see my substance, yet being unperfect; and in thy book all my members (literally, all things of it) were written, which in continuance were fashioned, when as yet there was none of them!" Apply all this now to the Word of God, the mind, thought, speech of the living Lord, as we profess to have this in the Bible; there, not by transient inspiration merely, speaking it from heaven in the beginning, and then committing it to the custody of ordinary human speech and thought for all subsequent time; not by this only, but by constant and abiding inspiration, as it is in truth with the word of God in all his natural works; where, as we know, it is only through the ceaseless emission of this word, "running very swiftly" all the time, that even such inanimate things as snow, and hoar-frost, and ice, and winds, and waters, are all the time coming and going (Ps. cxlviii. 15–18): apply all this, we say, to the Bible in such view, and what patience then can we have with any theory for the interpretation of Holy Scripture, which sends us to Ernesti[55] as a master in Israel, or tells us coldly with Bishop Newton "that a literal rendering is always to be given in the reading of scripture unless the context makes it absurd!"[56] Who should not see that there must ever be *infinitely* more here, than thought or speech can ever compass in their natural human form. God's word, in heaven and from heaven, can never be thus bound on earth. There can be no such exhaustion, either of the glorified Christ himself, or of the Word which lives and abides forever in the indwelling presence of his glorification. On the contrary, it seems to us *exhausting*, even to the extent of spiritual deliquium only to think of such a thing.

---

55. [Johann August Ernesti (1707–1781) worked to "reconcile" theology and historical criticism, and held that Scripture was to be interpreted "by philological and grammatical" reasoning (*Dictionary of the Christian Church*, 559). For Nevin, this was unfathomable: the meaning of the Bible came from the same Spirit who inspired it, and not through unregenerate human reason. Thirty years earlier he was already convinced: "The supernaturalism of the school of *Ernesti* . . . was always external and abstract. . . . This was to . . . make common cause in a certain sense with the enemy, by consenting to meet him on his own ground, the arena of the mere finite understanding." "Ernesti, for instance, is entitled to no confidence whatever as a guide to the true sense of God's word as it is *spirit* and *life*" (*Mystical Presence*, MTSS ed., 130, 131 n.).]

56. ["Prophetic Conference," 8. "Bishop Newton" was almost certainly Bishop Thomas Newton (1704–1782), author of *Dissertations on the Prophecies*. The statement is probably a paraphrase of a commonplace: see, e.g., Edward Bickersteth, *A Practical Guide to the Prophecies*, 6th ed. (London, 1839), 114: "Every passage of God's word should be interpreted literally where the predictions can be literally fulfilled, unless there be a necessity from the subject or the context, to the contrary, or an absurdity by doing so." Newton was regularly cited by Bickersteth with little detail, as if he assumed all his readers would have known both the significance and pertinence of Newton's work.]

Not without some sense of such fainting in our own spirit, therefore, we leave the subject here for the present. And we will add also, not without some inward resonance of that mournful complaint of the ancient Jewish prophet, "Ah Lord! they say of me, Doth he not speak parables?"[57]

J. Williamson Nevin

---

[57]. [Ezek 20:49.]

Bibliography

Works Included in This Volume

Gerhart, Emanuel Vogel. "The Efficacy of Baptism." *Mercersburg Review* 10 (January 1858) 1–44.

"Inquirer." "Baptismal Grace." *Weekly Messenger of the German Reformed Church*, n.s., 12, no. 47 (August 4, 1847).

———. "Baptismal Grace." *Weekly Messenger of the German Reformed Church*, n.s. 12, no. 50 (August 25, 1847).

Nevin, John Williamson. "Baptismal Grace." *Weekly Messenger of the German Reformed Church*, n.s., 12, no. 48 (August 11, 1847).

———. "The Bread of Life: A Communion Sermon." *Reformed Quarterly Review* 26 (January 1879) 14–47.

———. "Dr. Bushnell and Puritanism." *Weekly Messenger of the German Reformed Church*, n.s., 12, no. 51 (September 1, 1847).

———. "Educational Religion." *Weekly Messenger of the German Reformed Church*, n.s., 12, no. 41 (June 23, 1847).

———. "Educational Religion: Review of Dr. Bushnell's Tract Continued [Part 2]." *Weekly Messenger of the German Reformed Church*, n.s., 12, no. 42 (June 30, 1847).

———. "Educational Religion: Review of Dr. Bushnell's Tract Continued [Part 3]" *Weekly Messenger of the German Reformed Church*, n.s., 12, no. 43 (July 7, 1847).

———. "Educational Religion, No. 4: Review of Dr. Bushnell's Tract, Concluded." *Weekly Messenger of the German Reformed Church*, n.s., 12, no. 44 (July 14, 1847).

———. "Holy Baptism." *Weekly Messenger of the German Reformed Church*, n.s., 12, no. 51 (September 1, 1847).

———. "Noel on Baptism." *Mercersburg Review* 2 (May 1850) 231–65.

———. "The Old Doctrine of Christian Baptism." *Mercersburg Review* 12 (April 1860) 190–215.

———. "Wilberforce on the Eucharist." *Mercersburg Quarterly Review* 6 (April 1854) 161–87.

Schaf, Philip. "The Apostolical Origin of Infant Baptism." *Mercersburg Review* 4 (July 1852) 388–98.

Works Consulted

Ahlstrom, Sydney E. *A Religious History of the American People*. Vol. 1. Garden City, NY: Image, 1975.

———, ed. *Theology in America*. Indianapolis: Bobbs-Merrill, 1967.

Albanese, Catherine L. *Americans: Religions and Religion*. 3rd ed. Belmont, CA: Wadsworth, 1999.

Altaner, Berthold. *Patrology*. Translated by Hilda C. Graef. New York: Herder and Herder, 1960.

The Ante-Nicene Fathers. Vol. 1, *The Apostolic Fathers—Justin Martyr—Irenaeus*. Edited by Alexander Roberts and James Donaldson; revised by A. Cleveland Cox. Edinburgh; repr., Buffalo, NY: Christian Literature Company, 1885.

The Ante-Nicene Fathers. Vol. 3, *Latin Christianity: Its Founder, Tertullian*. Edited by Alexander Roberts and James Donaldson; revised by A. Cleveland Cox. Edinburgh; repr., Buffalo, NY: Christian Literature Company, 1885.

The Ante-Nicene Fathers. Vol. 5, *Fathers of the Third Century: Hippolytus, Cyprian, Caius, Novatian, Appendix*. Edited by Alexander Roberts and James Donaldson; revised by A. Cleveland Cox. Edinburgh; repr., Buffalo, NY: Christian Literature Company, 1886.

Appel, Theodore. *Life and Work of John Williamson Nevin*. Philadelphia: Reformed Church Publication House, 1889.

Apple, Thos. G. "The Crown of Dr. Gerhart's Life." *Reformed Church Messenger* 65, no. 23 (June 10, 1897) 2.

Augustine. *Expositions of the Psalms, 33–50*. Translated by Maria Boulding, O.S.B. *The Works of Saint Augustine: A Translation for the 21st Century*. Part 3, vol. 16. Hyde Park, NY: New City, 2000.

———. *Expositions of the Psalms, 121–150*. Translated by Maria Boulding, O.S.B. *The Works of Saint Augustine: A Translation for the 21st Century*. Part 3, vol. 20. Hyde Park, NY: New City, 2004.

Baker, J. Wayne. *Heinrich Bullinger and the Covenant: The Other Reformed Tradition*. Athens: Ohio University Press, 1980.

Barth, Karl. *Protestant Theology in the Nineteenth Century: Its Background & History*. Valley Forge, PA: Judson, 1973.

Baxter, Richard. *Reliquiae Baxterianae; or, Mr. Richard Baxter's Narrative of the Most Memorable Passages of His Life and Times*. Edited by Matthew Sylvester. London, 1696.

Bebbington, David. *Evangelicalism in Modern Britain: A History from the 1730s to the 1980s*. Grand Rapids, MI: Baker Book House, 1989.

———. "The Life of Baptist Noel: Its Setting and Significance." *Baptist Quarterly* 24 (1972) 389–411.

Bickersteth, Edward. *A Practical Guide to the Prophecies*. 6th ed. London, 1839.

Bierma, Lyle, Charles Gunnoe, and Karin Maag. *Introduction to the Heidelberg Catechism*. Grand Rapids, MI: Baker Academic, 2005.

Billington, Ray Allen. *The Protestant Crusade, 1800–1860: A Study of the Origins of American Nativism*. Chicago: Quadrangle Paperbacks, 1964.

The Book of Common Prayer and Administration of the Sacraments and Other Rites and Ceremonies of the Church. According to the use of the Episcopal Church. New York: Seabury, 1979.

BIBLIOGRAPHY

Bozeman, Theodore Dwight. *To Live Ancient Lives: The Primitivist Dimension in Puritanism*. Chapel Hill: University of North Carolina Press for Institute of Early American History and Culture, 1988.

Bradshaw, Paul F. *The Search for the Origins of Christian Worship: Study and Methods for the Study of Early Liturgy*. 2nd ed. New York: Oxford University Press, 2002.

Brauer, Jerald C. "Conversion: From Puritanism to Revivalism." *Journal of Religion* 58, no. 3 (1978) 227–43.

Bromiley, G. W., trans. *Zwingli and Bullinger: Selected Translations with Introductions and Notes*. Philadelphia: Westminster, 1953.

Bushnell, Horace. *An Argument for "Discourses on Christian Nurture."* In *Views of Christian Nurture, and of Subjects Adjacent Thereto*, 52–125. Hartford, CT: Edwin Hunt, 1848.

———. *Views of Christian Nurture, and of Subjects Adjacent Thereto*. Hartford, CT: Edwin Hunt, 1848.

Butler, Jon. *Awash in a Sea of Faith: Christianizing the American People*. Cambridge, MA: Harvard University Press, 1990.

———. "Enthusiasm Described and Decried: The Great Awakening as Interpretative Fiction." *Journal of American History* 69 (September 1982–1983) 305–25.

Calvin, John. *Commentaries on the First Book of Moses Called Genesis*. Translated by John King. Vol. 1. Edinburgh: Calvin Translation Society, 1847.

———. *Commentary on the Gospel according to John*. Translated by William Pringle. Vol. 2. Edinburgh: Calvin Translation Society, 1847.

———. *Institutes of the Christian Religion*. Edited by John T. McNeill. Translated by Ford Lewis Battles. 2 vols. Philadelphia: Westminster, 1960.

———. "Last Admonition to Westphal." In *Calvin's Tracts and Treatises*, 2:346–494. Translated by Henry Beveridge. Grand Rapids, MI: Eerdmans, 1968.

Cheney, Mary A. Bushnell, ed. *Life and Letters of Horace Bushnell*. New York: Harper & Brothers, 1880.

The Constitution of the Presbyterian Church (U.S.A.): Part 1: Book of Confessions. Louisville, KY: Office of the General Assembly, 1999.

Coolidge, John S. *The Pauline Renaissance: Puritanism and the Bible*. Oxford: Clarendon, 1970.

Corwin, E. T., J. H. Dubbs, and J. T. Hamilton. *A History of the Reformed Church, Dutch; the Reformed Church, German; and the Moravian Church in the United States*. American Church History Series, vol. 3. New York: Christian Literature Company, 1895.

Cross, Barbara M. *Horace Bushnell: Minister to a Changing America*. Chicago: University of Chicago Press, 1958.

Cumming, John. *Infant Salvation; or, All Saved That Die in Infancy*. Philadelphia: Lindsay and Blakiston, 1855.

DeBie, Linden J. "Biographical Essay." In *Coena Mystica: Debating Reformed Eucharistic Theology*. By John Williamson Nevin and Charles Hodge. Edited by Linden J. DeBie. Mercersburg Theology Study Series, vol. 2. Eugene, OR: Wipf & Stock, 2013.

———. "First Signs of Contention: The Controversy over Nevin's Revival of the Heidelberg Catechism in the German Reformed Church." *New Mercersburg Review*, no. 34 (2004) 12–21.

———. "Germ, Genesis, and Contemporary Impact of Mercersburg Philosophy." *New Mercersburg Review*, no. 40 (2009) 5–51.

———. "German Idealism in Protestant Orthodoxy: The Mercersburg Movement, 1840–1860." PhD diss., McGill University, 1987.

———. Introduction to *Coena Mystica: Debating Reformed Eucharistic Theology*. By John Williamson Nevin and Charles Hodge. Edited by Linden J. DeBie. Mercersburg Theology Study Series, vol. 2. Eugene, OR: Wipf & Stock, 2013.

———. Introduction to *The Mystical Presence and the Doctrine of the Reformed Church on the Lord's Supper*. By John Williamson Nevin. Edited by Linden J. DeBie. Mercersburg Theology Study Series, vol. 1. Eugene, OR: Wipf & Stock, 2012.

———. *Speculative Theology and Common-Sense Religion: Mercersburg and the Conservative Roots of American Religion*. Eugene, OR: Wipf & Stock, 2008.

Diary of Joshua Hempstead of New London, Connecticut. New London, CT: n.p., 1901.

Dictionary of Christianity in America. Edited by Daniel G. Reid. Downers Grove, IL: InterVarsity, 1990.

Dictionary of the Christian Church. Edited by F. L. Cross and E. A. Livingstone. 3rd ed. Oxford: Oxford University Press, 1997.

DiPuccio, William. "Before Mercersburg: Nevin's Philosophy." *New Mercersburg Review*, no. 17 (1995) 15–24.

———. *The Interior Sense of Scripture: The Sacred Hermeneutics of John W. Nevin*. Macon, GA: Mercer University Press, 1998.

———. "Nevin's Idealistic Philosophy." In *Reformed Confessionalism in Nineteenth-Century America*, edited by Sam Hamstra Jr. and Arie J. Griffioen, 43–67. Lanham, MD: Scarecrow, 1995.

Dorrien, Gary. *The Making of American Liberal Theology: Imagining Progressive Religion, 1805–1900*. Louisville, KY: Westminster John Knox, 2001.

"Dr. Bushnell and His Reviewers." *New England Puritan* 8, no. 30 (July 29, 1847).

Dyer, John. "Dr. Horace Bushnell." *Penn Monthly* 7 (1876) 287–97.

Edwards, Robert L. *Of Singular Genius, of Singular Grace: A Biography of Horace Bushnell*. Cleveland: Pilgrim, 1992.

Encyclopedia of Ancient Christianity. Vol. 2. Downers Grove, IL: InterVarsity, 2014.

Encyclopedia of Philosophy. Volume 7. New York: Macmillan, 1967.

Evans, Ernest, ed. and trans. *Tertullian's Homily on Baptism: The Text, Edited with an Introduction, Translation, and Commentary*. London: S.P.C.K., 1964.

Evans, William B. General Introduction to *The Incarnate Word: Selected Writings on Christology*. By John Williamson Nevin, Philip Schaff, and Daniel Gans. Edited by William B. Evans. Mercersburg Theology Study Series, vol. 4. Eugene, OR: Wipf & Stock, 2014.

Finney, Charles G. *Lectures on Revivals of Religion*. New York: Leavitt, Lord, 1835.

———. *Lectures to Professing Christians*. New York: John S. Taylor, Brick Church Chapel, 1837.

Fisher, J. D. C. *Christian Initiation: The Reformation Period; Some Early Reformed Rites and Baptism and Confirmation and Other Contemporary Documents*. London: S.P.C.K., 1970.

Fletcher, Richard. *The Barbarian Conversion: From Paganism to Christianity*. Berkeley: University of California Press, 1997.

Foster, Frank Hugh. *A Genetic History of the New England Theology*. Chicago: University of Chicago Press, 1907.

Franklin and Marshall College Obituary Record, vol. 2. Lancaster, PA: Franklin and Marshall College Alumni Association, 1904.

Frend, W. H. C. *The Rise of Christianity*. Philadelphia: Fortress, 1984.
Gaustad, Edwin Scott. *The Great Awakening in New England*. New York: Harper & Brothers, 1957.
Gerhart, Emanuel Vogel. The Emanuel V. Gerhart Papers. Evangelical and Reformed Historical Society, Lancaster, PA.
———. *Institutes of the Christian Religion*. Volume 1. Introduction by Philip Schaff. New York: A. C. Armstrong & Son, 1891.
Gerrish, B. A. *Tradition and the Modern World: Reformed Theology in the Nineteenth Century*. Chicago: University of Chicago Press, 1978.
———. "The Word of God and the Words of Scripture: Luther and Calvin on Biblical Authority." In *The Old Protestantism and the New: Essays on the Reformation Heritage*, 51–68. Edinburgh: T. & T. Clark, 1982.
Gieseler, John C. L. *A Compendium of Ecclesiastical History*. Translated by Samuel Davidson. 2 vols. New York: Harper & Brothers, 1849.
Goen, C. C. *Revivalism and Separatism in New England, 1740–1800: Strict Congregationalists and Separate Baptists in the Great Awakening*. New Haven, CT: Yale University Press, 1962.
González, Justo L. *The Story of Christianity*. Vol. 2, *The Reformation to the Present Day*. New York: HarperCollins, 1985.
Good, James I. *History of the Reformed Church in the U.S. in the Nineteenth Century*. New York: Board of Publication of the Reformed Church in America, 1911.
Gorday, Peter, ed. *Ancient Christian Commentary on Scripture: New Testament*. Vol. 9, *Colossians, 1–2 Thessalonians, 1–2 Timothy, Titus, Philemon*. Downers Grove, IL: InterVarsity, 2000.
Guelzo, Allen C. *Edwards on the Will: A Century of American Theological Debate*. Middletown, CT: Wesleyan University Press, 1989.
Hall, David D. *Worlds of Wonder, Days of Judgment: Popular Religious Belief in Early New England*. Cambridge, MA: Harvard University Press, 1990.
Haller, William. *The Rise of Puritanism*. New York: Columbia University Press, 1938. Reprint ed., New York: Harper & Row, 1957.
Harris, William. *Grounds of Hope for the Salvation of All Dying in Infancy*. London: R. Clay, 1821.
Hart, D. G. *John Williamson Nevin: High Church Calvinist*. Phillipsburg, NJ: P&R, 2005.
Hatch, Nathan O. *The Democratization of American Christianity*. New Haven, CT: Yale University Press, 1989.
Hefele, Charles Joseph. *A History of the Christian Councils, From the Original Documents, to the Close of the Council of Nicaea, A. D. 325*. Translated by William R. Clark. Edinburgh: T. & T. Clark, 1871.
The Heidelberg Catechism. Translated by J. H. Good and H. Harbaugh. Chambersburg, PA: M. Kieffer, 1849.
Heimert, Alan, and Andrew Delbanco, eds. *The Puritans in America: A Narrative Anthology*. Cambridge, MA: Harvard University Press, 1985.
Hewitt, Glenn A. *Regeneration and Morality: A Study of Charles Finney, Charles Hodge, John W. Nevin, and Horace Bushnell*. Chicago Studies in the History of American Religion, vol. 7. Brooklyn: Carlson, 1991.
Hodge, Charles. "Bushnell on Christian Nurture." *Biblical Repertory and Princeton Review* 19 (1847) 502–39.

———. "The Church Membership of Infants." *Biblical Repertory and Princeton Review* 30 (1858) 347–89.

———. "Doctrine of the Reformed Church on the Lord's Supper." *Biblical Repertory and Princeton Review* 20 (1848) 227–78.

———. "The Neglect of Infant Baptism." *Biblical Repertory and Princeton Review* 29 (1857) 73–101.

Hoffecker, W. Andrew. *Piety and the Princeton Theologians: Archibald Alexander, Charles Hodge, and Benjamin Warfield*. Grand Rapids, MI: Baker Book House, 1981.

Holifield, E. Brooks. *Theology in America: Christian Thought from the Age of the Puritans to the Civil War*. New Haven, CT: Yale University Press, 2003.

"Honestas." "Dr. Bushnell and his Reviewers." *New England Puritan* 8, no. 30 (July 29, 1847).

Hughes, Richard T., ed. *The American Quest for the Primitive Church*. Urbana: University of Illinois Press, 1988.

Hughes, Richard T., and C. Leonard Allen. *Illusions of Innocence: Protestant Primitivism in America, 1630–1875*. Chicago: University of Chicago Press, 1988.

Jackson, Samuel Macauley, ed. *Ulrich Zwingli, 1484–1531: Selected Works*. Philadelphia: University of Pennsylvania Press, 1901. Reprint ed., 1972.

Jahn, John. *Biblical Antiquities*. Translated by Thomas Upham. Reprinted from the 3rd American ed. London: Thomas Ward, 1832.

Jones, Cheslyn, Geoffrey Wainwright, and Edward Yarnold, S.J., eds. *The Study of Liturgy*. New York: Oxford University Press, 1978.

Kant, Immanuel. *Groundwork for the Metaphysics of Morals*. Edited by Allen W. Wood. New Haven, CT: Yale University Press, 2002. eBook Collection, EBSCOhost. Accessed April 24, 2015.

Kidd, Thomas S. *The Great Awakening: The Roots of Evangelical Christianity in Colonial America*. New Haven, CT: Yale University, 2007.

Kuklick, Bruce. *Churchmen and Philosophers: From Jonathan Edwards to John Dewey*. New Haven, CT: Yale University Press, 1985.

Lambert, Frank. *Inventing the "Great Awakening."* Princeton, NJ: Princeton University Press, 1999.

Layman, David Wayne. "Nevin's Holistic Supernaturalism." In *Reformed Confessionalism in Nineteenth-Century America*, edited by Sam Hamstra Jr. and Arie J. Griffioen, 193–208. Lanham, MD: Scarecrow, 1995.

———. "Revelation in the Praxis of the Liturgical Community: A Jewish-Christian Dialogue, with Special Reference to the Work of John Williamson Nevin and Franz Rosenzweig." PhD diss., Temple University, 1994.

———. "'The Seal of the Spirit' (1838)." *New Mercersburg Review*, no. 17 (1995) 64–68.

———. "The Sources of Nevin's Piety." *New Mercersburg Review*, no. 17 (1995) 4–14.

"Letter to Dr. Bushnell." *New England Puritan* 8, no. 25 (June 24, 1847).

Lillback, Peter A. *The Binding of God: Calvin's Role in the Development of Covenant Theology*. Grand Rapids, MI: Baker Academic, 2001.

Loetscher, Lefferts A. *Facing the Enlightenment and Pietism: Archibald Alexander and the Founding of Princeton Theological Seminary*. Contributions to the Study of Religion, no. 8. Westport, CT: Greenwood Press for the Presbyterian Historical Society, 1983.

Long, Kimberly Bracken. *The Eucharistic Theology of the American Holy Fairs*. Louisville, KY: Westminster John Knox, 2011.

Lovejoy, David S. *Religious Enthusiasm in the New World: Heresy to Revolution.* Cambridge, MA: Harvard University Press, 1985.

Luther, Martin. "The Holy and Blessed Sacrament of Baptism." In *Word and Sacrament I*, pp. 29–43. Vol. 35 of *Luther's Works: American Edition.* Edited by E. Theodore Bachman. Philadelphia: Muhlenberg, 1960.

Marsden, George M. *The Evangelical Mind and the New School Presbyterian Experience.* New Haven, CT: Yale University Press, 1970.

———. *Fundamentalism and American Culture: The Shaping of Twentieth-Century Evangelicalism, 1870–1925.* Oxford: Oxford University Press, 1980.

Martensen, H. "The Doctrine of Christian Baptism and the Baptistic Question." Translated by H[enry]. H[arbaugh]. *Mercersburg Review* 4 (1852) 305–21, 475–85, [vol. 5] 276–310.

Maxwell, Jack Martin. *Worship and Reformed Theology: The Liturgical Lessons of Mercersburg.* Pittsburgh Theological Monograph Series, no. 10. Pittsburgh: Pickwick, 1976.

McAdoo, H. R., and Kenneth Stevenson. *The Mystery of the Eucharist in the Anglican Tradition.* Norwich, UK: Canterbury, 1995.

McCoy, Charles S., and J. Wayne Baker. *Fountainhead of Federalism: Heinrich Bullinger and the Covenantal Tradition.* Louisville, KY: Westminster John Knox, 1991.

McGiffert, Michael. "Covenant, Crown and Commons in Elizabethan Puritanism." *Journal of British Studies* 20 (1980) 32–52.

———. "Grace and Works: The Rise and Division of Covenant Divinity in Elizabethan Puritanism." *Harvard Theological Review* 75 (1982) 463–502.

McGrath, Alister E. *Christian Theology: An Introduction.* Oxford: Blackwell, 1994.

McLoughlin, William G. Introduction to *The American Evangelicals, 1800–1900: An Anthology.* New York: Harper Torchbooks, 1968.

Miller, Perry. *The New England Mind in the Seventeenth Century.* Cambridge, MA: Belknap Press of Harvard University Press, 1982.

Morgan, Edmund Sears. *Visible Saints: The History of a Puritan Idea.* New York: New York University Press, 1963.

Neander, Augustus. *General History of the Christian Religion and Church.* Vol. 1. Translated by Joseph Torrey. Rev. ed., A. J. W. Morrison. London: Henry G. Bohn, York Street, Covent Garden, 1850.

———. *History of the Planting and Training of the Christian Church by the Apostles.* Translated by J. E. Ryland. Revised and corrected according to the 4th German edition by E. G. Robinson. New York: Sheldon, 1865.Nevin, John Williamson. "The Anglican Crisis." *Mercersburg Review* 3 (1851) 359–98.

Nevin, John Williamson. *Antichrist; or, The Spirit of Sect and Schism.* New York: John S. Taylor, 1848. Reprinted in *The Anxious Bench, Antichrist, and the Sermon Catholic Unity.* Edited by Augustine Thompson. Eugene, OR: Wipf & Stock, n.d.

———. *The Anxious Bench.* Chambersburg, PA: Office of the "Weekly Messenger," 1843; 2nd ed., rev. and enl., 1844. Reprinted in *Catholic and Reformed: Selected Theological Writings of John Williamson Nevin*, edited by Charles Yrigoyen Jr. and George H. Bricker, 9–126. Pittsburgh Original Texts and Translations, no. 3. Pittsburgh: Pickwick, 1978.

———. "The Apostles' Creed." *Mercersburg Review* 1 (1849) 105–27, 201–21, 313–47.

———. "Catholic Unity." In *The Mercersburg Theology.* Edited by James Hastings Nichols. Oxford: Oxford University Press, 1966. Reprint, Eugene, OR: Wipf & Stock, 2007.

———. "Christ and His Spirit." *Mercersburg Review* 19 (1872) 353–93.

Bibliography

———. "Christ the Inspiration of His Own Word." *Reformed Quarterly Review* 29 (1882) 5–46.

———. "The Christian Ministry." *Mercersburg Quarterly Review* 7 (1855) 68–93.

———. *"The Claims of the Bible Urged upon the Attention of the Students of Theology": A Lecture, Delivered November 8, 1831, at the Opening of the Winter Session of the Western Theological Seminary of the Presbyterian Church.* Pittsburgh: D. & M. Maclean, 1831.

———. "Cyprian." *Mercersburg Review* 4 (1852) 259–77, 335–87, 417–52, 513–63.

———. "Early Christianity." *Mercersburg Review* 3 (1851) 461–90, 513–62, [vol. 4] 1–54. Reprinted in *Catholic and Reformed: Selected Theological Writings of John Williamson Nevin*, edited by Charles Yrigoyen Jr. and George H. Bricker, 177–310. Pittsburgh Original Texts and Translations, no. 3. Pittsburgh: Pickwick, 1978.

———. "Election Not Contrary to a Free Gospel." *Presbyterian Preacher* 1 & 2 (1832–1834) 209–24.

———. "Evangelical Radicalism." *Mercersburg Review* 4 (1852) 508–12.

———. "Faith, Freedom, and Reverence." *Mercersburg Review* 2 (1850) 97–116. Reprinted in *The Mercersburg Theology*, edited by James Hastings Nichols, 286–306. New York: Oxford University Press, 1966.

———. "The Grand Heresy." *Pittsburgh Friend* 2, no. 31 (February 5, 1835) 246–47. Reprinted in *New Mercersburg Review*, no. 17 (1995) 48–53.

———. "Historical Development." *Mercersburg Review* 1 (1849) 512–14.

———. *History and Genius of the Heidelberg Catechism.* Chambersburg, PA: Publishing House of the German Reformed Church, 1847.

———. "Hodge on the Ephesians." *Mercersburg Review* 9 (1857) 46–83, 192–245.

———. "Human Freedom." *American Review: A Whig Journal Devoted to Politics and Literature*, n.s., 1, no. 4 (1848) 406–18. Reprinted in *Human Freedom, and A Plea for Philosophy: Two Essays.* Mercersburg, PA: P. A. Rice, "Journal Office," 1850.

———. Introduction to *Christ's Warning to the Churches, to Beware of False Prophets, Who Come as Wolves in Sheep's Clothing: And the Marks by Which They Are Known*, by Joseph Lathrop. 11th ed. Pittsburgh: Luke Loomis, 1832.

———. "Jesus and the Resurrection." *Mercersburg Review* 15 (1861) 169–90.

———. *My Own Life: The Earlier Years.* Papers of the Eastern Chapter, Historical Society of the Evangelical and Reformed Church, no. 1. Lancaster, PA: Eastern Chapter, Historical Society of the Evangelical and Reformed Church, 1964.

———. *The Mystical Presence and the Doctrine of the Reformed Church on the Lord's Supper.* Edited by Linden J. DeBie. Mercersburg Theology Study Series, vol. 1. Eugene, OR: Wipf & Stock, 2012.

———. "Natural and Supernatural." *Mercersburg Review* 13 (1859) 176–210.

———. "Nature and Grace." *Mercersburg Review* 19 (1872) 485–509.

———. "Once for All." *Mercersburg Review* 17 (1870) 100–124.

———. "Origin and Structure of the Apostles' Creed." *Mercersburg Review* 16 (1869) 148–56.

———. "Our Union with Christ." *Weekly Messenger of the German Reformed Church*, n.s., 12, no. 45 (July 21, 1847).

———. "Religion a Life." *Pittsburgh Friend* 2, no. 25 (December 25, 1834) 198; no. 28 (January 15, 1835) 222–23; no. 29 (January 22, 1835) 230; no. 30 (January 29, 1835) 238–39. Reprinted in *New Mercersburg Review*, no. 17 (1995) 37–45.

———. "Reply to 'An Anglican Catholic.'" *Mercersburg Review* 21 (1874) 397–429.

———. "Sacred Hermeneutics." *Mercersburg Review* 25 (1878) 5–38.

———. "Sartorius on the Person and Work of Christ." In *The Incarnate Word: Selected Writings on Christology*, by John Williamson Nevin, Philip Schaff, and Daniel Gans, 4–28. Edited by William B. Evans. Mercersburg Theology Study Series, vol. 4. Eugene, OR: Wipf & Stock, 2014.

———. *"The Seal of the Spirit": A Sermon, the Substance of Which Was Preached in the Presbyterian Church at Uniontown, Pa. January 21, 1838*. Pittsburgh: William Allinder, 1838.

———. "The Sect System." *Mercersburg Review* 1 (1849) 482–507, 521–39. Reprinted in *Catholic and Reformed: Selected Theological Writings of John Williamson Nevin*, edited by Charles Yrigoyen Jr. and George H. Bricker, 128–73. Pittsburgh Original Texts and Translations, no. 3. Pittsburgh: Pickwick, 1978.

———. "The Spirit of Prophecy." *Mercersburg Review* 24 (1877) 181–212.

———. "The Spiritual World." *Mercersburg Review* 23 (1876) 501–27.

———. *A Summary of Biblical Antiquities: For the Use of Schools, Bible-Classes, and Families*. 2 vols. Philadelphia: American Sunday-School Union, 1829–1830; 2nd ed. [1 vol.], 1849.

———. "The Testimony of Jesus." *Mercersburg Review* 24 (1877) 5–33.

———. "The Unity of the Apostles' Creed." *Mercersburg Review* 16 (1869) 313–17.

———. "Wilberforce on the Incarnation." *Mercersburg Review* 2 (1850) 164–96.

Nevin, John Williamson, and Charles Hodge. *Coena Mystica: Debating Reformed Eucharistic Theology*. Edited by Linden J. DeBie. Mercersburg Theology Study Series, vol. 2. Eugene, OR: Wipf & Stock, 2013.

Nevin, John Williamson, Philip Schaff, and Daniel Gans. *The Incarnate Word: Selected Writings on Christology*. Edited by William B. Evans. Mercersburg Theology Study Series, vol. 4. Eugene, OR: Wipf & Stock, 2014.

Newton, Thomas. *Dissertations on the Prophecies*. 3rd ed. London, 1766.

Nicene and Post-Nicene Fathers. Vol. 5, *Saint Augustin: Anti-Pelagian Writings*. Edited by Philip Schaff. Edinburgh: T. & T. Clark, 1888.

Nicene and Post-Nicene Fathers. Vol. 7, *St. Augustin: Homilies on the Gospel of John. Homilies on the First Epistle of John. Soliloquies*. Edited by Philip Schaff. Translated by John Gibb and James Innes. Edinburgh: T. & T. Clark, 1888.

Nicene and Post-Nicene Fathers. Vol. 10, *St. Chrysostom: Homilies on the Gospel of Saint Matthew*. Edited by Philip Schaff. Edinburgh: T. & T. Clark, 1888.

Nichols, James Hastings, ed. *The Mercersburg Theology*. Oxford: Oxford University Press, 1966. Reprint, Eugene, OR: Wipf & Stock, 2007.

———. *Romanticism in American Theology: Nevin and Schaff at Mercersburg*. Chicago: University of Chicago Press, 1961. Reprint, Eugene, OR: Wipf & Stock, 2006.

Noll, Mark A. *A History of Christianity in the United States and Canada*. Grand Rapids, MI: Eerdmans, 1992.

———. *The Rise of Evangelicalism: The Age of Edwards, Whitefield, and the Wesleys*. Vol. 1 of *A History of Evangelicalism: People, Movements, and Ideas in the English-Speaking World*. Downers Grove, IL: InterVarsity, 2003.

Origen: Commentary on the Epistle to the Romans Books 1–5. Translated by Thomas P. Scheck. Washington, DC: Catholic University of American Press, 2001.

Origen: Homilies on Leviticus 1–16. Translated by Gary Wayne Barkley. Washington, DC: Catholic University of American Press, 1990.

Origen: Homilies on Luke; and, Fragments on Luke. Translated by Joseph T. Lienhard, S.J. Washington, DC: Catholic University of American Press, 1996.

BIBLIOGRAPHY

The Oxford Companion to Philosophy. New Edition. Edited by Ted Honderich. Oxford: Oxford University Press, 2005.

The Oxford Dictionary of the Christian Church. Edited by F. L. Cross and E. A. Livingstone. 2nd ed. Oxford: Oxford University Press, 1974, 1983.

Pannenberg, Wolfhart. *Systematic Theology.* Vol. 1. Translated by Geoffrey W. Bromiley. Grand Rapids, MI: Eerdmans, 1991.

Payne, John. "Schaff and Nevin, Colleagues at Mercersburg: The Church Question." *Church History* 61, no. 2 (1992) 169–90.

Pelikan, Jaroslav. *The Emergence of the Catholic Tradition (100–600).* Chicago: University of Chicago Press, 1971.

Penzel, Klaus. *The German Education of Christian Scholar Philip Schaff: The Formative Years, 1819–1844.* Toronto Studies in Theology, vol. 95. Lewiston, NY: Edwin Mellen, 2004.

Peters, Edward. Introduction to *Ulrich Zwingli, 1484–1531: Selected Works.* Edited by Samuel Macauley Jackson. Philadelphia: University of Pennsylvania Press, 1972.

Pitkin, Barbara. "John Calvin and the Interpretation of the Bible." In *A History of Biblical Interpretation,* vol. 2, *The Medieval through Reformation Periods,* edited by Alan J. Hauser and Duane F. Watson, 341–71. Grand Rapids, MI: Eerdmans, 2009.

Pohle, Joseph. "The Real Presence of Christ in the Eucharist." *The Catholic Encyclopedia.* Vol. 5. New York: Robert Appleton, 1909.

Rauch, Frederick A. *Psychology; or, A View of the Human Soul.* New York: M. W. Dodd, 1840. 4th ed., rev. and imp., 1846.

Reily, William M. "John Williamson Nevin, D.D., LL.D." *Magazine of Christian Literature* 2 (September 1890) 324–27.

Rothe, Richard. *Still Hours.* Translated by Jane T. Stoddart. London: Hodder and Stoughton, 1886.

———. *Zur Dogmatik.* Gotha: Verlag von Friedrich Andreas Berthes, 1863.

Schaff, David S. *The Life of Philip Schaff.* New York: Charles Scribner's Sons, 1897.

Schaff, Philip. "German Theology and the Church Question." *Mercersburg Review* 5 (1853) 124–44.

———. *Germany: Its Universities, Theology, and Religion.* Philadelphia: Lindsay and Blakiston, 1857.

———. *History of the Apostolic Church, with a General Introduction to Church History.* Translated by Edward D. Yeomans. New York: Scribner, 1853.

———. The Philip Schaff Papers. Evangelical and Reformed Historical Society, Lancaster, PA.

———. *The Principle of Protestantism as Related to the Present State of the Church.* Translated and introduction by John W. Nevin. Chambersburg, PA: "Publication Office" of the German Reformed Church, 1845.

———. *What Is Church History? A Vindication of the Idea of Historical Development.* Philadelphia: J. B. Lippincott, 1846. In *Reformed and Catholic: Selected Historical and Theological Writings of Philip Schaff,* edited by Charles Yrigoyen Jr. and George H. Bricker, 18–144. Pittsburgh Original Texts and Translations, no. 4. Pittsburgh: Pickwick, 1979.

Schmidt, Leigh Eric. *Holy Fairs: Scotland and the Making of American Revivalism.* Second edition with a new preface. Grand Rapids, MI: Eerdmans, 2001.

Short, Kenneth Richard. "Baptist Wriothesley Noel: Anglican—Evangelical—Baptist." *Baptist Quarterly* 20 (1963) 51–61.

BIBLIOGRAPHY

Simonetti, Manlio, ed. *Ancient Christian Commentary on Scripture: New Testament.* Vol. 1A, *Matthew 1–13.* Downers Grove, IL: InterVarsity, 2001.

Smith, David L., ed. *Horace Bushnell: Selected Writings on Language, Religion and American Culture.* AAR Studies in Religion, no. 33. Chico, CA: Scholars, 1984.

Spinks, Bryan D. *Do This in Remembrance of Me: The Eucharist from the Early Church to the Present Day.* SCM Studies in Worship and Liturgy. London: SCM Press, 2013.

Stark, Rodney. *The Triumph of Christianity: How the Jesus Movement Became the World's Largest Religion.* New York: HarperCollins, 2011.

Swedenborg, Emanuelis. *Arcana coelestia: Quae in scriptura sacra seu verbo Domini, sunt, detecta: Hic primum quae in Genesi. Una cum mirabilibus, quae visa sunt in mundo spirituum et in coelo angelorum.* 8 vols. Tubingae: In Bibliopolio zu Guttenberg, 1833–.

———. *Arcana coelestia: Quae in scriptura sacra seu verbo Domini, sunt, detecta: Hic quae in Exodo. Una cum mirabilibus, quae visa sunt in mundo spirituum et in coelo angelorum.* 5 vols. Tubingae: In Bibliopolio zu Guttenberg, 1840–.

———. *The Heavenly Arcana Contained in the Holy Scripture or Word of the Lord Unfolded, Beginning with the Book of Genesis.* Translated by John Clowes. Revised and edited by John Faulkner Potts. Standard edition. West Chester, PA: Swedenborg Foundation, 1999. Accessed 20 May 20, 2015. http://www.swedenborg.com/emanuel-swedenborg/writings/rse-downloads.

Thompson, Bard, and George H. Bricker. Editors' preface to *The Mystical Presence and Other Writings on the Eucharist.* Lancaster Series on the Mercersburg Theology, vol. 4. Philadelphia: United Church Press, 1966.

———. Editors' preface to *The Principle of Protestantism.* Lancaster Series on the Mercersburg Theology, vol. 1. Philadelphia: United Church Press, 1964.

Tyler, B. "Baptismal Regeneration." *New Englander* 2, no. 7 (1844) 397–414.

———. "Dr. Bushnell and the Theological Institute of Connecticut." *New England Puritan* 8, no. 33 (August 19, 1847).

———. *Dr. Tyler's Letter to Dr. Bushnell on Christian Nurture.* N.p., 1847.

"Veritas." "Dr. Bushnell and His Reviewers." *New England Puritan* 8, no. 29 (July 22, 1847).

von Rohr, John. *The Covenant of Grace in Puritan Thought.* American Academy of Religion Studies in Religion, no. 45. Atlanta: Scholars, 1986.

Wallace, Dewey. *Puritans and Predestination.* Chapel Hill: University of North Carolina Press, 1982.

Wallace, Peter J. "The Bond of Union." PhD diss., University of Notre Dame, 2004. http://www.peterwallace.org/old/dissertation/1division.htm.

Welch, Claude. *Protestant Theology in the Nineteenth Century. Volume 1, 1799–1870.* New Haven, CT: Yale University Press, 1972.

Westerkamp, Marilyn J. *Triumph of the Laity: Scots-Irish Piety and the Great Awakening, 1625–1760.* New York: Oxford University Press, 1988.

Whitefield, George. "An Answer to the Second Part of an Anonymous Pamphlet." In *The Works of the Reverend George Whitefield,* 4:150–69. London: Edwards and Charles Dilley, 1771.

———. "Law Gospelized." In *The Works of the Reverend George Whitefield,* 4:377–437. London: Edwards and Charles Dilley, 1771.

———. "Regeneration." In *Selected Sermons of George Whitefield,* edited by A. R. Buckland, 33–59. Philadelphia: Union, 1904.

———. "Remarks on a Pamphlet, Entitled, *The Enthusiasm of Methodists and Papists Compared*. . . ." In *The Works of the Reverend George Whitefield*, 4:229–49. London: Edwards and Charles Dilley, 1771.

Winthrop, John. "A Model of Christian Charity." In *The Puritans in America: A Narrative Anthology*, edited by Alan Heimert and Andrew Delbanco, 81–92. Cambridge, MA: Harvard University Press, 1985.

Yrigoyen, Charles, Jr. "Emanuel V. Gerhart: Apologist for the Mercersburg Theology." *Journal of Presbyterian History (1962–1985)* 57 (Winter 1979) 485–500.

———. "Emanuel V. Gerhart and the Mercersburg Theology." PhD diss., Temple University, 1973.

Yrigoyen, Charles, Jr., and George H. Bricker, eds.. *Catholic and Reformed: Selected Theological Writings of John Williamson Nevin*. Pittsburgh Original Texts and Translations, no. 3. Pittsburgh: Pickwick, 1978.

———. *Reformed and Catholic: Selected Historical and Theological Writings of Philip Schaff*. Pittsburgh Original Texts and Translations, no. 4. Pittsburgh: Pickwick, 1979.

Ziegler, Howard J. B. *Frederick Augustus Rauch: American Hegelian*. Lancaster, PA: Franklin and Marshall College, 1953.

Zwingli, Ulrich. "An Account of the Faith of Huldreich Zwingli Submitted to the Roman Emperor Charles." In *On Providence and Other Essays*, edited by William John Hinke, 35–61. Durham, NC: Labyrinth, 1983.

———. *Refutation of the Tricks of the Baptists by Huldreich Zwingli*. In *Ulrich Zwingli, 1484–1531: Selected Works*, edited by Samuel Macauley Jackson, 123–258. Translated by Henry Preble and George W. Gilmore. Philadelphia: University of Pennsylvania Press, 1901; reprint ed., 1972.

Works Cited in the Original

[where possible, the edition likely used by Nevin, Schaff, or Gerhart is provided; otherwise, either the original edition or a more modern edition is given]

Augustine. *Enarratio in Psalmum*. In *Patrologia Latina*, edited by J. P. Migne, vols. 36 and 37. Paris: Imprimerie Catholique, n.d.

Augustine of Hippo. *De peccatorum meritis et remissione*. In *Patrologia Latina*, edited by J. P. Migne, vol. 44. Paris: Imprimerie Catholique, 1845.

———. *In Iohannis Evangelium tractatus*. In *Patrologia Latina*, edited by J. P. Migne, vol. 35. Paris: Imprimerie Catholique, 1845.

Bushnell, Horace. *An Argument for "Discourses on Christian Nurture," Addressed to the Publishing Committee of the Massachusetts Sabbath School Society*. Hartford, CT: Edwin Hunt, 1847.

———. *Discourses on Christian Nurture*. Boston: Massachusetts Sabbath School Society, 1847.

Calvin, John. *Ultima admonition ad Westphalum*. In *Opera Omnia*, vol. 8, *Tractatus Theologici Omnes*. Edited by Theodore Beza. Amsterdam: John Jacob Schipper, 1667.

Carson, Alexander. *Baptism in Its Mode and Subjects*. 5th ed. Philadelphia: American Baptist Publication Society, 1850.

"The Children of the Church and Sealing Ordinances." *Biblical Repertory and Princeton Review* 29 (1857) 1–34.

BIBLIOGRAPHY

Chrysostom, S. P. N. Joannis. *Homiliae in Matthaeum*. In *Patrologia Graeca*, edited by J. P. Migne, vol. 57. Paris: Imprimerie Catholique, 1862.

The Constitution of the Presbyterian Church in the United States of America: Containing the Confession of Faith, the Catechisms, and the Directory for the Worship of God; Together with the Plan of Government and Discipline as Amended and Ratified by the General Assembly at Their Sessions in May, 1805. Philadelphia: Jane Aitken, 1806.

Cooke, Parsons. "Parallel between the First and Second Adam." *New England Puritan* 8, no. 26 (1847). Reprinted in *Weekly Messenger of the German Reformed Church*, n.s., 12, nos. 45–46 (July 21 and 28, 1847).

Cypriani, S. Thascii Caecilii. *Epistola S. Cypriani ad Magnum*. In *Patrologia Latina*, edited by J. P. Migne, vol. 3. Paris: Imprimerie Catholique, 1886.

Dick, John. *Lectures on Theology*. Vol. 2. New York: M. W. Dodd, 1850.

The Heidelberg Catechism; or, Short Instruction in Christian Doctrine. Translated by J. H. Good and H. Harbaugh. Chambersburg, PA: M. Kieffer, 1849.

Höfling, Joh. Wilhelm Friedrich. *Das Sakrament der Taufe nebst den anderen damit Zusammenhängenden Akten den Initiation*. Vol. 1. Erlangen: In der Palm'schen Verlagsbuchhandlung, 1846.

Irenaeus. *Adversus Haereses*. In *Patrologia Graeca*, edited by J. P. Migne, vol. 7. Paris: Imprimerie Catholique, 1857.

Justin, S. P. N. *First Apology of Justin Martyr*. In *Patrologia Graeca*, edited by J. P. Migne, vol. 1. Paris: Imprimerie Catholique, 1857.

Luther, Martin. "D. Mart. Luthers Sermon von Sacrament der Taufe, 1518." *D. Martin Luthers Sämtliche Werke*, vol. 10. Edited by Johann Georg Walch. Halle in Magdeburgischen: Johann Justinus Gebauer, 1744.

Martensen, H. *Die christliche Taufe und die baptistische Frage*. Hamburg: Im Verlage von Friedrich und Andreas Perthes, 1843.

Neander, August. *Allgemeine Geschichte der christlichen Religion und Kirche*. Erste Band. Hamburg: Bei Friedrich Perthes, 1842.

———. *Geschichte der Pflanzung und Leitung der christliche Kirche durch die Apostel*. Erste Band. Hamburg: Bei Friedrich Perthes, 1832.

———. *Geschichte der Pflanzung und Leitung der christliche Kirche durch die Apostel*. Erste Band. 4th ed. Hamburg: Bei Friedrich Perthes, 1847.

"Neglect of Infant Baptism." *Biblical Repertory and Princeton Review* 29 (1857) 73–101.

Noel, Baptist W. *Essay on Christian Baptism*. London: James Nisbet, 1849. Reprint, New York: Harper & Brothers, 1850.

Origen. *Commentariorum in Epistolam B. Pauli ad Romanos*. In *Patrologia Graeca*, edited by J. P. Migne, vol. 14. Paris: Imprimerie Catholique, n.d.

———. *Leviticum*. In *Patrologia Graeca*, edited by J. P. Migne, vol. 12. Paris: Imprimerie Catholique, n.d.

———. *Lucam Homiliae*. In *Patrologia Graeca*, edited by J. P. Migne, vol. 13. Paris: Imprimerie Catholique, n.d. "The Prophetic Conference: New York, October 30, 31, November 1, 1878: Christ's Second Coming." *New York Tribune*. Extra No. 46.

Richter, Aemilius Ludwig, ed. *Die evangelischen Kirchenordnungen des sechszehten Jahrhunderts. Unkunden und Regesten zur Geschichte des Rechtes und der Verfassung der evangelischen Kirche in Deutschland*. Vol. 1. Leipzig: Ernst Julius Günther, [1846 and] 1871.

Bibliography

Ridgley, Thomas. *Body of Divinity: Wherein the Doctrines of the Christian Religion Are Explained and Defended.* . . . Vol. 4. Philadelphia: William W. Woodward, 1815.

Schaf, Philip. *Geschichte der Christlichen Kirche, von ihrer Gründung bis auf die Gegenwart.* Vol. 1, *Die apostoliche Kirche.* Mercersburg, PA: Selbst-verlag des Verfassers, 1851.

Sehling, Emil, ed. *Die evangelischen Kirchenordnungen des XVI. Jahrhunderts.* Vol. 1. First Half. Leipzig: O. R. Reisland, 1902.

Tertullian, Q. Sept. Flor. *De Baptismo adversus Quintillam.* In *Patrologia Latina,* edited by J. P. Migne, vol. 1. Paris: Imprimerie Catholique, 1878–1879.

Wilberforce, Robert Isaac. *The Doctrine of Holy Baptism: With Remarks on the Rev. W. Goode's "Effects of Infant Baptism."* London: John Murray, Albemarle Street; John and Charles Mozley, Paternoster Row, 1849.

———. *The Doctrine Of The Holy Eucharist.* London: John and Charles Mozley, Paternoster Row, 1853.

———. *The Doctrine of the Incarnation of Our Lord Jesus Christ, in Its Relation to Mankind and the Church.* London: John Murray, Albemarle Street; John and Charles Mozley, Paternoster Row, 1848.

Subject and Author Index

Anabaptists, 85, 90 *see also* Swiss Brethren
ancient church, 24, 86, 100, 135
   and educational religion, 43
   baptism in, 209–213 *passim*
   liturgies and sacraments in, 96, 109,
      139–155 *passim*
   real presence in, 142, 177
   Also see Baptism, in early church
Andover Theological Seminary, 29, 152
Anglican, 19, 79, 132n10, 150–154 *passim*,
   154n48 *see also* Episcopalianism
Apostles' Creed *see* Creeds
apostolic Christianity, 23, 81 *see also* ancient
   church
assurance, 7, 9, 15, 78–80, 179
Athanasian Creed, 225
Atwater, Lyman, 59n4, 156–159 *passim*, 164,
   182–189
Augustine, 80, 81n8, 83n29, 108, 142, 144,
   216, 228n18

Baconianism *see* Commonsense (realism)
baptism, 1–5, 95–101, 156–161, 203–213
   passim
   as mere sprinkling, 87–88, 90–92, 112
   as sacrament, viii–ix, 2–4, 22, 37, 57, 59, 63,
      173–178, 200
   Bushnell's view of, 35–37, 42, 46, 48, 57–60
   circumcision type of, 4–5, 65n4, 117–118,
      124–126
   clinical baptism, 88
   efficacy of, 185–189
   in early church, 104–111 *passim*, 117–128
      passim, 193, 208, 212
   in Puritans, 8n48, 8n49
   Jesus's teaching of, ix, 122
   mode of, 87–92
   neglect of infant baptism, 1–2, 25–26, 165,
      189–190
   of adults, 79–81, 93

   of infants and children, vii–viii, 1, 25–28,
      35–48 *passim*, 58–63 *passim*, 79–82,
      97–128 *passim*, 182–185
   of Jesus, 194, 196, 201
   See also Calvin, John, view of baptism
baptismal grace, 2, 37, 63–68, 95, 111, 114,
   126, 178–182 *passim*, 191, 206
baptismal regeneration, viii, 2–3, 19–20,
   22n120, 59, 64–66, 156, 187, 194, 200,
   206–209 *passim*, *see also* regeneration
Baptists, vii, 1, 15, 28, 42–61 *passim*, 80–88
   passim, 93–94, 100–114 *passim*, 117,
   121–122, 127n15, 195, 212
Bauer, Ferdinand C., 116
Baxter, Richard, 40
believer's baptism, 79, 94 *see also* baptism, of
   adults
Bennet, Tyler, 19, 35, 71
Bible *see* Scripture
biblicism, 27–29
body of Christ *see* Christ, body of
Book of Common Prayer, 78, 172n14
Bradshaw, Paul F., 130n5, 138n15, 140n18
Bullinger, Heinrich, 5–6
Bushnell, Horace, vii, ix, 1–2, 17, 19, 24n129,
   25–26, 34–77
   See also Organic, Bushnell's concept of

Calvin, John, 28, 131–132, 143–147, 154–155,
   160n16
   View of baptism, 4–5, 65n4, 89, 99n23,
      180–182
Calvinism, 12n69, 27, 98n22, 146, 152n46,
   157n8
   and Arminianism, 26–7
camp meetings, 10–12
Cane Ridge, Kentucky, 10–12
catechumens, 193–194, 204
Chalcedon, Council of, 149n41, 168n9
Charlemagne, 122

Subject and Author Index

Christ, 6–7, 27, 117–126 *passim*, 140–145 *passim*, 148n41, 157–191 *passim*, 200–217 *passim* (*see also* mystery, incarnation as)
   Advent and second coming of, 29, 41n17
   as Mediator, 5, 99, 108n42
   as Second Adam, 16n92, 69n3, 98–99, 100n24, 101, 120–121, 141, 144
   baptism and ingrafting into, 173, 175, 178–182, 185, 191, 204
   body of, 108n42, 116, 125, 131, 141–145, 148n41, 149, 158–159, 168n9, 169n11
   church continuation of, 61–63, 98–99
   inspiration of his Word, 30, 230n21, 241
   life in, 37, 44, 53, 69n3, 235–236
   new creation in, 44, 62, 98–100, 201, 209, 223–225
   three-fold offices of, 225n11
   union with, 69n3, 158, 159n15, 187, 217, 236n36
Christianity
   as mystery, 84n4, 93, 99, 101, *see also* mystery
   new order of life, 98, 198, 207, 238
   See also church, as supernatural constitution
Chrysostom, John, 192–6, 200–212 *passim*
church, as supernatural constitution, 2, 37, 60, 62–63, 73, 84n4, 100
Church of England, viii, 25, 78, 114, 129, 150
Clement of Alexandria, 128
commonsense (realism), 28–29, 30n159, 37, 77n25, 87n8, 97n21, 240n48
Communion *see* Eucharist
Congregationalism, 1, 26, 34, 73, 112n44, 151, 159, 171, 184, 200
conversion, 3–22 *passim*, 34–42 *passim*, 53, 78–79, 118, 156–160 *passim*, 189, 193, 194, 210, 212
   and regeneration, 3, 9n51, 20–22, 79, 123, 192
   conversion narrative (relations), 7, 8n47, 14, 20, 184n39
   conversionism (as *praxis*), 1, 10–12, 20, 26, 44n2, 60n6, 71n5, 109, 152n46, 160
   also see Nevin, John, understanding of conversion of
Cooke, Parson, 69–70
covenant (*see also* federalism), vii, 4–9, 26–28, 62, 71n5, 117, 119, 124–127, 158, 159n14, 166, 171–186 *passim*, 194
   covenant of works, 6, 48n8
   Jewish covenant, 100, 194
   unitary covenant, 4–6, 118
creeds, 183–184, 230
   (Apostles) Creed, 62, 93–102 *passim*, 109–110, 178–179, 209

Cyprian, 80, 81n8, 88, 105–108, 111, 127, 138n15, 224n10
   Nevin's articles on, 24, 31, 33, 132, 150n44

Dabney, Robert Lewis, viii
Daub, Carl, 52
Davenport, James, 9
DeBie, Linden, 13, 14n83, 16n93, 19n103, 32n178, 76n22
Deism, 212n35
Decrees, Doctrine of *see* Election
Democratization of religion, *see* Hatch, Nathan O.
Dick, John, 163
DiPuccio, William, 30n161, 45n2, 222n7
Directory for Worship (Presbyterian), 178–179, 182, 185

East Windsor Seminary, 71
Eastern Orthodox Church, 80
Ebionism, 49
educational religion, 26, 43, 49–52 *passim*, 60–63
Edwardseanism, 19, 71n5, 72
election, 6–9, 21, 26–27, 98, 131, 143, 146, 158–160, 193, 203, 205, 208 (*see also* Nevin, John, election, early concept of)
Episcopalianism, 72n13, 86, 130 *see also* Anglican
Ernesti, Johann A., 243
eschatology
   and prophetic literalism, 30n159, 238–241
   postmillennial, 29
   premillennial, 27, 29–30, 41n17, 240n48
Eucharist, 10–11, 22, 30–31, 71n5, 128n18, 129–154 *passim*
   and the Word of God, 228–229
   Calvin's doctrine of, 31, 139, 146
   Christ in, 137, 141–142, 146
   consecration of, 132, 137–153 *passim*
   real Presence in, 129–154 *passim*, 168n9, 169, 194
   Zwingli's doctrine of, 4
Eutyches (Eutychianism), 148n41, 168n9, 169
evangelicalism, 10–11, 24, 41n17, 77n23, 132, 195, 217
   English, 78–79
   system of salvation of, 81–86 *passim*

fanaticism, vii–viii, 63
federalism (*see also* covenant), 4–6, 9, 26–27, 48, 71n5, 152n46, 156
Finney, Charles Grandison, 11–12, 18n102, 20–21, 35n4

Subject and Author Index

Franklin and Marshall College, 31–32, 156, 192, 214

Gerhart, Emanuel V., 1, 24–26, 30–33, 59n4, 79, 85n7 156–161, 168n9, 187n46, 192
Gerlach, Ludwig von, 116
Gieseler, Johann K. L., 102, 127
gnosticism, 49, 99n24, 103, 135–136, 202
Good, James I., 30, 52n4
Great Awakening, 3, 8–10, 112n44, 185n39

Half-Way Covenant, 8, 184
Harbaugh, Henry, 38n3
Hart, D. G., 12n73, 18n101, 19, 48n8
Hatch, Nathan O., 12n69, 27n149, 61n9
Hegelian theology, 52
Heidelberg Catechism, 3–4, 6n33, 22, 32–33, 155, 177, 183
 church of, 2–3, 68
Heidelberg College, 24, 31
hermeneutics, science of, 222n7, 230, 238 (see also Nevin, John, hermeneutics)
heteronomy, 91n17
Hewitt, Glenn A., 4n16, 19–21
historical development, 15, 23–24, 29, 31, 81n8, 81n9, 116–117, 132–13, 150n44, 155 (see also Nevin, John, concept of history)
Hodge, Charles, 24n129, 26–27, 47n5, 146, 156–160, 169n9, 192–193
Holy Spirit, 30, 35n8, 37, 65n4, 131, 157, 187, 214 (see also Testimonium spiritus sancti internum)

idealism, 13, 23n128, 24n129
incarnation see mystery, incarnation as
individualism, religious, 37n11, 38, 41, 44–46, 50, 57, 60, 84
infants see also baptism, of infants
 in Baptist theory, 80, 101–104
 included in salvation, 60, 99–101, 124
 mortality of, 99, 117
Irenaeus, 111, 121, 128
 concept of Second Adam of, 16n92, 99, 100n24

Jahn, John, 13n81
Jerome, 224n10
Jews (Jewish), 5, 16, 91–119 *passim*, 124–125, 183, 194–201 *passim*, 220–240 *passim*
John the Baptist, 124
Justin Martyr, 128, 130, 138

Kant, Immanuel, 52n4, 237n39

Lancaster Theological Seminary, xii, 31, 119n3, 215
Larger Catechism, The, 157n7, 164, 166, 172, 176–177, 184n39
Lathrop, Joseph, 13
Leo, Tome of, 149n41
Lord's Prayer, 178–179, 223–224
Lord's Supper see Eucharist
Luther, Martin, 20n108, 28, 89, 122n9, 143–144

Marshall College, 25, 30–31
Massachusetts Sabbath School Society, 36, 69, 71
McAdoo, H. R., 154n48
Mercersburg Seminary, 3, 12, 18–19, 52n4, 116, 132n11, 149n2
Mercersburg Theology, ix, 13, 16n91, 23–32 *passim*, 100n24, 121n5
Messalians, 136
Moody, Dwight L., 29
mystery
 of incarnation, 134–136, 141, 151
 of sacraments, 90, 109, 114–115, 134, 136, 139, 144, 153, 170
 See also Christianity, as mystery
mystical presence, 22, 30, 45n2, 69n3, 76n23
Mystical Presence, The, 13, 14n83, 16n93, 19n103, 22, 24n134, 32, 131, 145n33, 146n35, 169n9

naturalism, 73, 193n6, 238–239
Neander, Johann Augustus, 102–103, 119, 121n5, 125n13, 127, 150n44
Nestorius and Nestorianism, 148n41, 168n9, 169–170, 225
Nevin, John
 and Philip Schaff, see Schaff, Philip
 concept of history, 22–24, 81n9, 132–133, 237n41
 election, early concept of, 14–15, 18
 hermeneutics of, 30n161, 45n2, 222n7
 ontology of revelation of, 216, 223n9, 229
 organicism of, 2, 18–27 *passim*, 37, 47–48, 84n4, 116
 understanding of conversion of, 3, 13–22, 44n2
 supernaturalism of, 30, 44, 71n5, 193
New England Puritan, 69–71
New Haven Theology, 18n102, 77, 112n44, 152 see also Taylor, Nathaniel
Newton, Bishop Thomas, 240, 243
Nicea, Council of, 148
Nichols, James Hastings, 3n11, 13, 14n82, 16n93, 18n101, 26, 38n3, 132n11, 214

Subject and Author Index

Noel, Baptist Wriothesley, 78–114 *passim*

Olevian, Kaspar, 3n11
organic, vii, 125–126, 209 (*see also* Nevin, John, organicism of)
  Bushnell's concept of, 2, 37, 40–60 *passim*, 72–77 *passim*
Origen, 80, 105–108, 111, 127, 128n18, 224n10

paedobaptists, viii, 1, 26, 79, 81, 86, 109–113, 195 (*see also* baptism, of infants)
Paschasius (Radburtus), 137
Paul, St., 125
Pelagianism, 44n2, 46–47, 98, 124
Photius, 137
pietism, 240
Pittsburgh Theological Seminary *see* Western Theological Seminary
Polycarp, 121, 128
predestination, 7, 9, 14, 146, 157n8, 160, 175
Presbyterianism, vii–viii, 1, 26, 109, 112, 151, 156–191 *passim*
  John Nevin's, 12–13, 24n129, 192
  Old School, 18, 24n129, 112n44
  Scottish, 10–11 *see also* Sacramental fairs
presumptive membership, 27, 158, 186–188
  see also regeneration, presumptive
primitivism, 15, 130
Princeton (Theological Seminary), viii, 12, 44n2, 59n4, 97n21, 112n44, 156–160, 192
  see also Scripture, Princeton's view of
private judgment, 27, 55, 61n9, 87n8, 93, 127
Prophetic Conference of 1878, 29–30, 41n17, 217, 239, 241–243
Puritanism, vii, 6–21 *passim*, 35–49 *passim*, 60–81 *passim*, 91, 93, 109–111, 131
Puseyism, 110, 152

Quakers, 61, 94, 212

rationalism, viii, 2, 61–63, 68–94 *passim*, 114, 135, 139, 170n12, 182, 230n21, 240
rationalistic supernaturalism, 37, 76, 230n21, 243n55 (*see also* supernatural)
Rauch, Friedrich, 18, 23, 24n129, 31, 52n4
regeneration *see also* baptismal regeneration, 2–4, 19, 35n8, 36, 53–59 *passim*, 79, 99n23, 101, 108, 122–128 *passim*, 157–163 *passim*, 172–238 *passim*
  as conversion, 9n51, 20–22
  presumptive, 58–59 *see also* presumptive membership
Reily, William, 214
repristination, 24, 130 *see also* primitivism

revivalism, 10–15, 18–20, 27–29, 34–36, 44n2, 78, 118 *see also* evangelicalism
Ridgley, Thomas, 162–163
Rothe, Richard, 214–215

sacraments
  as sign and seal, viii, 102, 124, 157–173 *passim*, 185–191 *passim*
  opus operatum theory of, 65, 177
  See also mystery, of sacraments
sacramental fairs, 10–13, 24n129
salvation, 2–22 *passim*, 40n10, 60–68 *passim*, 79–80, 95–103 *passim*, 111–126 *passim*, 139–141, 157–185 *passim*, 193–209 *passim*, 219–238 *passim*
Schaff, Philip, 23–25, 30–33, 116–118, 119n3, 129, 192
Scottish piety *see* sacramental fairs
Scripture (*see also* biblicism, private judgment, *testimonium spiritus sancti internum*)
  Authority of, 27–28, 93, 136, 214, 239
  Inspiration, 214–215, 222
  Princeton's view of, 98n21, 100n24
  Sola Scriptura, 27
second Adam *see* Christ, as Second Adam
Second Great Awakening, 10
sectarian (Sect System), 27–28, 44n2, 57, 61n9, 85n7
Simon Magus, 65
Socinianism, 68, 170, 189, 212
Spinks, Bryan D., 138n15, 140n18
speculative theology (*see* idealism), Nevin's speculativeness, 30
Stevenson, Kenneth, 154n48
supernatural, *see also* rationalistic supernaturalism, vii–ix, 18–30 *passim*, 36–37, 44–50 *passim*, 60–63, 73–80 *passim*, 143–145, 167–174 *passim*, 193, 202–215 *passim*, 232 *see also* Nevin, John, view of supernaturalism
Swedenborg, Emanuel, 214–216, 219n3, 219n4, 220n5, 232n25, 241n52
Swiss Brethren, 4

Taylor, Nathaniel, 35–36, 77n25, 152n46 *see also* New Haven Theology
Tertullian, 103n29, 107–108, 111, 126–128
testimonium spiritus sancti internum, 214–215
Thornwell, J. H., vii, 156
Tractarianism, 129, 150, 154n48
Trent, Council of, 147n37
transsubstantiation, 103–104, 137, 168–169
Tyler-Taylor Controversy, 35 *see also* Tyler, Bennett

Subject and Author Index

Unitarian, 68, 71, 84, 170–171 *see also* Socinianism
Universalism, 84, 98
Ursinus, Zacharias, 3n11, 6n33

Waldensians, 23
Wesley, Charles, 8n51, 78
Wesley, John *see* Wesley, Charles
Western Theological Seminary, 12, 99n24
Westminster Assembly, 176, 178–179

Westminster Confession, 78, 109, 157, 176, 178, 225n11
Whitefield, George, 1, 8–9, 20–21
Wilberforce, Robert Isaac, 129–154 *passim*, 211n34
Winthrop, John, 6–7
Wolff, Bernard C., 30, 149n42

Yale, xii, 34–35, 152n46

Zwingli, Ulrich, 4–6, 118, 130, 139n16, 170n11

Scripture Index

Genesis

2:21–23	144n28
3:19	199n11
4:12	199n12
8:11	197n6
14	226
14:18–20	226n14
17:7	124
17:10	119
17:12	124
21:4	119

Exodus

16:20, 27, 28	231
17:6–7	227n16

Leviticus

12:7	124

Numbers

20:7–13	231

Judges

2:1–5	35n2

Job

14:4	105

Psalms

8:2	233
36:9	235n34
40:9	144n28
51:5	123
78:25	220
81:7	231
110	226
119:18	229n18
126:2	144n28
138	144n28
148:15–18	243

Isaiah

55:1–2	228
64:1–2	225n12
66:17	238

Jeremiah

31:34	41n17

Ezekiel

20:49	244n57

Micah

6:6	231n24

Malachi

1:11	149

Matthew

2:15	234n31
2:23	234n31
3:11	201n21, 208n32
3:15	201n22
3:16	196n3
3:16–17	202n24
4:4	219
5:8	232n26
5:13	200n17
5:17–18	234
6:11	218, 224n10
13:33	120

Scripture Index

16:16–17	235
18:2–5	124
19:14–15	124
21:15–16	233
25:30	199n13
26:26–29	228
28:18	226
28:18b–19a	235n33
28:20	235n33
28:19	117, 121, 122

Mark

5:9	61n8
10:14–15	124
16:16	121, 124

Luke

1:15–41	124
10:21	232n27
18:16–17	124
24:25–26	234
24:45–47	234

John

1:33	202n23
3:5	108, 124, 178
3:6	63n10, 123
3:8	123n11
4:32–34	224
6	227
6:5–14	142n25
6:24–65	142n25
6:28	231n23
6:33	227
6:35	225n13, 228
6:38	225
6:50	219
6:51	227
6:52	142n25
6:52–66	141n21
6:57	228, 233n28
6:60	230n21
6:63	230n20
7:16–17	236
7:37	228
8:12	235n35
8:31–32	236
12:32	238n42
14:19	233n28
14:28	234n30
15:4	233n28, 236n36
15:5	233n28, 236n36
15:6	236n36
15:7	236n36
15:9	236n36
16:10	234n30
16:28	234
17:1	225n12
17:1–5	219
17:4–6	223
17:5	234
18:37	225n12
19:34	144n28

Acts

2:2	196n4
2:37	122
2:38	118, 122n7, 177, 204n26
2:39	125n12
8:5	122
8:9–24	65n4
8:35–38	122
9:17	122
10:42–48	122
10:44–48	119
11:26	148n41
16:14–15	126n14
16:15	119, 122
16:29–34	126n14
16:30–33	119
16:33	122
17:28	74n19
18:8	119, 122
19:5	122
19:34	55n10
22:16	177

Romans

3:4	207n31
3:22–24	123
4:11	119, 177
5:12	48n7, 120
5:12–21	101
5:15–17	120
6:3–4	178, 180
6:4	87
12:13	123n11

1 Corinthians

1:10	119
1:16	126n14
2:14	241n49
7:14	125
10:2–4	227
12:3–9	123n11
12:13	178

Scripture Index

1 Corinthians *(cont.)*
12:31 — 77n24
13:13 — 237
14:22 — 196n5
16:22 — 233n29

2 Corinthians
4:13 — 123n11

Galatians
3:20 — 125
3:27 — 178
5:3 — 124
5:5 — 123n11
5:6 — 237

Ephesians
1:23 — 61n7
2:3 — 63n11, 123
2:8 — 123n11
6:1 — 125

Philippians
1:29 — 123n11

Colossians
1:17 — 220
2:11–12 — 124, 177
2:12 — 87, 123n11
2:17 — 124
3:20 — 125

1 Timothy
1:5 — 237
1:19 — 205n30
3:16 — 235

2 Timothy
2:19 — 230n22

Titus
3:5 — 3, 4n13, 178

Hebrews
5:9 — 238
7 — 226
10:1 — 124

1 Peter
3:21 — 178

2 Peter
1:10 — 205n30

1 John
4:8 — 232

Jude
1:3 — 72n11

Revelations
21:5 — 238
22:17 — 228
22:20 — 233n29

www.ingramcontent.com/pod-product-compliance
Lightning Source LLC
Chambersburg PA
CBHW081825230426